CAMBRIDGE
UNIVERSITY PRESS

CAMBRIDGE ENGLISH
Language Assessment
Part of the University of Cambridge

D0539385

Cambridge English

EMPOWER

ADVANCED
STUDENT'S BOOK

C1

Adrian Doff, Craig Thaine
Herbert Puchta, Jeff Stranks, Peter Lewis-Jones
with Mark Hancock and Wayne Rimmer

Contents

Lesson and objective	Grammar	Vocabulary	Pronunciation	Everyday English
Unit 6 Perspectives				
Getting started Talk about the impact of 3-D street art				
6A Describe photos and hobbies	Simple and continuous verbs	Adjectives: Describing images	Sentence stress	
6B Tell a descriptive narrative	Participle clauses	Emotions	Main stress and emphatic stress (adverbs and adjectives)	
6C Organise a presentation			Tone in comment phrases	Organising a presentation
6D Write a letter of application				
Review and extension More practice		WORDPOWER Idioms: Feelings		
Unit 7 Connections				
Getting started Talk about technologies in the classroom				
7A Speculate about inventions and technology	Speculation and deduction	Compound adjectives	Main stress: compound adjectives	
7B Emphasise opinions about the digital age	Cleft sentences	Nouns with suffixes: Society and relationships	Tone in cleft structures	
7C Apologise and admit fault			Sound and spelling: *ou* and *ough*	Apologising and admitting fault
7D Write a proposal				
Review and extension More practice		WORDPOWER *self-*		
Unit 8 Body and health				
Getting started Talk about physical activity in old age				
8A Describe sleeping habits and routines	Gerunds and infinitives	Sleep	Sentence stress	
8B Talk about lifestyles and life expectancy	Conditionals	Ageing and health	Pitch: extra information	
8C Negotiate			Intonation in implied questions	Negotiating
8D Write promotional material				
Review and extension More practice		WORDPOWER *and*		
Unit 9 Cities				
Getting started Talk about obstacles to urban development				
9A Talk about city life and urban space	Reflexive and reciprocal pronouns	Verbs with *re-*	Sound and spelling: *re-*	
9B Describe architecture and buildings	Ellipsis and substitution	Describing buildings	Word stress	
9C Deal with conflict			Sound and spelling: foreign words in English	Dealing with conflict
9D Write a discussion essay				
Review and extension More practice		WORDPOWER *build*		
Unit 10 Occasions				
Getting started Talk about an unusual wedding				
10A Give a presentation or a speech	Regret and criticism structures	Communication verbs	Word groups and main stress	
10B Talk about superstitions and rituals	Passive reporting verbs	Superstitions, customs and beliefs	Consonant groups	
10C Take turns in more formal conversations			Tone in question tags	Turn-taking
10D Write a film review				
Review and extension More practice		WORDPOWER *luck* and *chance*		
Communication Plus p.127	**Grammar Focus** p.138		**Vocabulary Focus** p.158	

4

CAN DO OBJECTIVES

- Talk about second language learning
- Describe languages and how they change
- Express yourself in an inexact way
- Write a web forum post

UNIT 1
Language

GETTING STARTED

a 💬 Look at the picture and answer the questions.

1 What do you think is happening? How successful do you think it will be? How do you think the woman and the ape feel?

2 What kind of things do you think the ape wants to communicate? What kind of things do you think the woman wants the ape to communicate?

3 What do you think the benefits of teaching animals language are for ... ?
- humans
- animals

4 In what ways do you think this ape's language-learning experience is similar/different to a human's?

b 💬 Discuss the questions.

1 In what other situations do humans and animals communicate with each other?

2 Which animals are known for their ability to communicate well with humans?

3 If you could converse with any animal, which one would it be? What would you like to ask it?

1A I learned French entirely by ear

Learn to talk about second language learning
G Adverbs and adverbial phrases
V Language learning; Noun forms

1 READING

a 💬 Do you agree with these statements about second language learning? Why / Why not?

1 It's helpful to get feedback from native speakers.
2 New words are more memorable if you like the thing they describe.
3 Communicating in another language makes you behave a bit differently.
4 Grammar is a waste of time – I don't even know it in my first language!
5 The biggest reward is being able to relate to people from another culture.
6 It's possible to learn a language without writing anything down.
7 When you've learned one second language, it's easier to learn another.

b Read about four language learning experiences. Who might agree with each of the statements in 1a?

c 💬 Read the texts again and discuss the questions.

1 Who do you think studies the most systematically?
2 Who do you think has/had the strongest motivation to learn? Why?
3 Whose language learning experience was the most challenging?
4 Which, if any, of the people do you relate to most?

THOMASINA MIERS
co-founder of *Wahaca*, a chain of Mexican restaurants in the UK

Native language: English
Second language: Spanish

Thomasina first travelled to Mexico after finishing school. It was the beginning of a love affair with the country's world famous cuisine and its language.

> *Basically, the learning of Spanish directed me to land in Mexico because I wanted to go and speak Spanish. I wanted to talk to everyone, I wanted to eat everything I could see, I wanted to just drink everything in. What I loved about the Spanish language is how guttural and earthy and unpretentious it was.*

The chef explains how she picked up the language dish by dish.

> *When you're travelling round the Yucatan coast you're tasting achiote and you're having habenero chillies and having cerviches with pulpo ... There's this whole resonating language going on that draws you in. The flavour and the language are linked because you know the taste and the memory and the words are all kind of caught up and bound into one, so there's this whole language of food and emotion.*

CAROLINE WYATT
Foreign correspondent

Native languages: English, German
Second languages: French, Russian

Caroline had a bilingual upbringing.

> *I struggled with the pronunciation of some words in English when I was very young, and I still can't say 'lunch' or 'shoulder' properly. Having another language from a very young age accustoms your mind to the idea that there are many different ways or words with which to express concepts and objects, and I suspect it must also shape the brain to make more connections between things.*

Her ability to speak German fluently got her a job as a journalist with the BBC in Berlin.

> *Speaking the language makes a huge difference to how people relate to you, and the experience that you have of that country. It enables you to relate to people in a different way, and understand vital nuances that are otherwise lost.*

She believes that using different languages changes her personality and mannerisms. She says she involuntarily uses her hands whilst talking in French, and in German becomes somewhat more direct.

ELLEN MACARTHUR
Round-the-world sailor

Native language: English
Second language: French

Ellen MacArthur's career forced her to brush up her schoolgirl French.

> *I had to repair a boat there [in France] and was working in a boatyard where nobody spoke English – you learn very fast when you absolutely need to in order to get a job done.*

> *You could say that my life depended on understanding the language. I was certainly able to be more competitive in the race as a result of speaking French – the experience was a great immersion.*

> *I'm now fluent, though having learnt the language almost entirely by ear while living in the country my written French is terrible.*

She reflects on her acquisition of French.

> *It opened up the warmth of a culture to me; a way into a world that I didn't at the time really understand, or even knew existed in my early teens.*

2 GRAMMAR
Adverbs and adverbial phrases

a Notice the highlighted adverbials in the texts. Add them to the lists below. The first one is done for you.

1 **Comment** (used to express the speaker's point of view): *clearly, apparently, actually,* basically
2 **Degree** (used to make the meaning stronger or weaker): *very, quite, ...*
3 **Manner** (used to say *how*): *slowly, on foot, ...*
4 **Time** *in the eighties, overnight, ...*
5 **Frequency** *never, ...*

b What position(s) can each adverbial take in these sentences? Which adverbials change meaning in different positions?

1 a in the end 1, 3   b eventually
   [1] I [2] managed to hold a conversation in Japanese [3].
2 a extremely   b often
   [1] I [2] found it [3] difficult.
3 a frequently   b all the time
   [1] I [2] made silly mistakes [3].
4 a slowly   b clearly
   [1] I [2] would like native speakers to speak to me [3].
5 a naturally   b well
   [1] I'm [2] quite envious of friends who can already speak the language [3].

CHRIS PACKHAM
TV presenter and naturalist

Native language: English

Second language: French

Having bought a house in the French countryside, Chris Packham had to work on his French.

I bought some wildlife books at a local bookshop and because I understood the context, I was able to read them cover to cover and <u>grasp some of what they were saying</u>. Then I said to my neighbours: 'Look, I'll speak to you in French and I want you to constantly correct me. I won't be offended.' And they were great, they did.

Despite the shaky start, his confidence has grown enormously.

If I'm away for a bit, which I often am, <u>I'll get rusty</u> ... The longest stint I've had there has been three months, and by the end of that I was thinking in French and putting sentences together in a French way, and it felt really good.

What's brilliant is that I can meet up with my neighbours now and have a laugh with them ... People have been extraordinarily welcoming.

c ▶ Now go to Grammar Focus 1A on p.138

d 💬 Use the adverbials in the box to describe an experience you have had of learning a new skill, without naming the skill. Can you guess what skill your partner is talking about?

in the beginning	obviously	extremely	eventually
properly	clearly	incorrectly	naturally	in the end

> Obviously, I was hopeless in the beginning.

> In order to do it properly, you have to concentrate on the ball.

> Playing a complete game involved a lot of walking and I was extremely tired afterwards.

3 VOCABULARY Language learning

a Look at the <u>underlined</u> parts of the texts. Match the words and phrases 1–4 with the definitions a–d.

1 ☐ pick up   3 ☐ grasp
2 ☐ brush up   4 ☐ rusty

a understand something, especially something difficult
b less able because you are out of practice
c learn something quite easily by being exposed to it
d improve your knowledge of something you've partly forgotten

b ▶ Now go to Vocabulary Focus 1A on p.158

c Read the questions about your English language learning background. Add two more to ask a partner.

1 When did you first start learning English?
2 How long was it before you could hold a conversation in English?
3 When did you first put your learning into practice?
4 Have you progressed as well as you expected?
5 Have you ever been immersed in an English-speaking culture? If so, what was it like? If not, is there a culture you would like to get to know?
6 How important is it to you to speak accurately? Why?
7 What level of competence would you like to attain eventually?
8 _____
9 _____

d 💬 Work in pairs. Ask and answer the questions in 3c.

4 LISTENING

a 💬 Discuss the questions.

1 Apart from English, what's an important second language in your country? Why is it important?
2 Do you speak this language? Is it widely spoken? Why / Why not?
3 In your experience, are native English speakers good at speaking second languages? Why / Why not?

b ▶1.7 Listen to language expert Susanna Zaraysky talking about second language learning amongst native English speakers. Tick (✓) the points she makes.

1 ☐ Native English speakers don't see second languages as being necessary.
2 ☐ Native English speakers lack opportunities to practise their second language skills.
3 ☐ Having to learn the grammar of a second language can be demotivating.
4 ☐ Being surrounded by different languages often helps people to learn a second language.

Susanna Zaraysky
First language:
Russian
Second languages:
English, French, Spanish, Italian, Portuguese, Serbo-Croatian, Ladino, Hebrew, Arabic, Hungarian

c ▶1.7 Listen again and answer the questions.

1 Why does Susanna think Brazilians are motivated to learn English?
2 How can media and music make it easier to learn a second language?
3 How did Susanna's childhood exposure to Spanish impact on her formal learning of it as an adult?
4 Susanna says 'your heart has to resonate with the language'. What does she mean by this? How does she suggest people do this?
5 What three reasons does she give for believing it's worth learning a second language?

d 💬 Discuss the questions.

1 Do you agree with Susanna about the importance of media and music for language learners? What are your earliest memories of English language media and music?
2 Are people in your country generally enthusiastic about language learning?

5 SPEAKING and VOCABULARY
Noun forms

a ▶1.8 What's the noun form of the words in brackets? Listen and check.

1 Is this _____ (reluctant) to learn foreign languages just a feature of Britain, or, do you think, all English-speaking peoples?
2 I agree with your previous speaker that there's a lack of _____ (necessary).
3 People don't see the necessity and, so, necessity breeds _____ (motivate).
4 English speakers have little to no _____ (expose) to the sounds of foreign languages.

b ▶ Now go to Vocabulary Focus 1A on p.158

c 💬 How can these factors have an impact on second language learning?

• the right mentality
• financial limitations
• distractions
• opportunities for interaction
• first language interference
• natural competence
• the prestige of knowing a second language

d Choose a person 1–3 and write five pieces of advice for them.

1 an English speaker who wants to learn your language
2 a friend who wants to pass a state English exam
3 a teenager who finds languages at school a turn-off

e 💬 Work in pairs. Compare your ideas in 5d and prioritise four suggestions which are useful for all language learners.

> The most universally useful suggestion here is to invest in a good dictionary.

> I couldn't agree more. I also think putting your learning into practice whenever you can is really important.

1B Language has been constantly evolving

Learn to describe languages and how they change
G The perfect aspect
V Describing changes

1 SPEAKING

a 💬 Look at these words. Do you know what each one means?

radio   **babysitter**   blog   selfie   in-joke   spacecraft   **brainwash**   sudoku

ecotourism   **Bollywood**

technophobe   **environmentalism**

b 💬 Each word in 1a was first used in a different decade, from the 1900s to the 2010s. When do you think each word first came into the English language, and why? Put them in order.

1900s radio
1910s …

c ▶️ 1.10 Listen and check your answers. What is the significance of photographs 1 and 2?

d 💬 Do you know any words that have come into the English language recently?

2 READING

a Read the introduction to an article about the way English has changed. Which <u>two</u> points does the writer make?

☐ English has become less complex over the years.
☐ Many changes to language take place gradually so we may not notice them.
☐ Modern technology has helped us to see how language is changing.

b Answer these questions.

1 What do you think the words in *italics* in paragraph 1 mean?
2 Can you think of an example of *the annoying inconsistencies between spelling and pronunciation in English*?

c ▶ Communication 1B Work in pairs. Student A: Go to p.127. Student B: Go to p.137.

d 💬 Look at each pair of sentences below. Do the sentences show a change you read about? Explain the change to your partner.

1 a Shall we meet at 6.00?
   b Do you want to meet at 6.00?
2 a I was fired from my job.
   b I got fired from my job.
3 a She started to cry.
   b She started crying.
4 a I ought to go soon.
   b I need to be going soon.

How quickly is the English language changing?

We all know language changes. People's favourite music was *far-out* in the 1960s, *rad* in the 1980s, *wicked* in the 1990s and *awesome* in 2010. You just need to watch a film from ten years ago to hear phrases that have come and gone.

However, there are far more subtle, ongoing language changes taking place at any given time. These changes may have a hugely significant impact but can go entirely unnoticed while they are in progress.
One lasting change to English that was barely perceptible at the time is known as The Great Vowel Shift. Over a period of 350 years (from 1350 to 1700), the long vowel sounds of English drifted so far that speakers at either end of the period could not have understood each other. However, nobody noticed for about 100 years after it had happened! The Great Vowel Shift was a major contributor to the annoying inconsistencies between spelling and pronunciation in English that have plagued users ever since.

These days no such important change would go unnoticed. Linguists can now analyse huge collections of text and transcribed speech and identify ongoing patterns of change that in the past would not have been visible for many years to come. Here are some of the less noticeable changes that are occurring in English right now:

3 VOCABULARY Describing changes

a Read the sentences about language change. Which words/phrases in bold tell the reader … ?

- a the speed of a change □□□
- b that a change is in progress □
- c how easy a change is to see □□□□
- d about something that is decreasing □□
- e how big or important a change is □□□
- f that a change is long-term or permanent □
- g about something that is increasing □□□

You will write some numbers more than once.

One ¹**lasting** change to English that was ²**barely perceptible** at the time is known as *The Great Vowel Shift*.

These changes may have a ³**hugely significant** impact but can go ⁴**entirely unnoticed** while they are in progress.

Here are some of the less ⁵**noticeable** changes that are occurring in English right now:

There was ⁶**a steady shift** toward more frequent use of the verb + *-ing* and these forms are still ⁷**on the increase**.

There are far more ⁸**subtle**, ⁹**ongoing** language changes taking place at any given time.

The use of continuous passive verb forms has also seen ¹⁰**a rapid rise**.

Modal verbs are ¹¹**gradually giving way to** other less formal expressions.

Stiff, formal words like *shall* and *ought* are ¹²**on the way out**.

Words which cover the same ground, such as *going to*, *have to*, *need to* and *want to* are ¹³**taking hold**.

The use of *get* passives has ¹⁴**grown substantially**.

b 💬 Write sentences about real changes. Then compare your ideas with other students.

1 something that is on the way out in your culture
2 a place that has changed substantially in recent years
3 a problem that is on the increase
4 a fashion that has taken hold recently amongst the younger generation
5 a subtle change to a popular product

4 LISTENING and GRAMMAR
The perfect aspect

a ▶1.11 Listen to four people commenting on the article in 2a and answer the questions.

1 What kind of language change does each speaker focus on?
2 What specific examples does each speaker give?

b 💬 Are the kinds of change the speakers mentioned happening in your first language?

c ▶1.12 Complete the sentences using the correct form of the verbs in brackets. Then listen and check.

- Language ¹_____ much faster since people started using the Internet. (change)
- In a few years' time, they ²_____ out of fashion and other new words ³_____ into the language. (go, come).
- I mean, people ⁴_____ using strict rules for punctuation. (stop)
- In about 50 years, most dialects of English ⁵_____. (die out)
- Older generations ⁶_____ about language changing. They ⁷_____ strongly about it. (always / complain, always / feel)
- People ⁸_____ photos of themselves before 2013, but they hadn't had a single word for it. (take)
- The word 'wireless' ⁹_____ a completely different meaning until computers came along – it meant 'radio'. (have)

d Answer the questions.

1 What time period do the examples c1–9 happen in?
a a period up to the present?
b a period up to a time in the past?
c a period in the future?

2 What do all perfect verb forms have in common? Choose the correct word to complete the rule.

All perfect verb forms describe actions, states and processes in the time period *before* / *after* a particular point in time.

e ▶1.12 **Pronunciation** Listen to the sentences in 4c again and notice the pronunciation of the words you added. What kind of words are stressed? What kind of words are usually unstressed?

f ▶ Now go to Grammar Focus 1B on p.139

g 💬 Talk about words in your own language. Think about:

- a word in common use now which hadn't been invented when you were a child
- a word that people have been using a lot this year
- a word that will have fallen out of use in 20 years' time
- a word that has changed its meaning.

5 READING and SPEAKING

a What is unusual about the remarks in pictures 1–3? What would you expect the people to be saying instead?

b 💬 Read the fact file and discuss the questions.

   1 What do you think each fact tells us about the speakers' culture or environment? Or the way they think about the world?
   2 Which language feature do you think is most unusual?

c **Language in context** *Expressing meaning*
Read the dictionary definitions and complete the example sentences with the correct form of a highlighted word from the fact file.

   1 to decide what the meaning of something is
   It's very hard to _____ the animal's behaviour.
   2 to notice or understand the difference between two things
   *It's very difficult to _____ **between** the twins.*
   3 to show the difference between things
   *The thing that _____ her **from** the others, is her taste in clothes.*
   4 to explain something more clearly by showing examples, pictures, etc.
   Why don't you include some stories to _____ your points?
   5 to show, point, or make clear in another way
   She shook her head to _____ that I shouldn't speak.
   6 to express a thought, feeling or idea so that it is understood by other people
   Her face _____ her feelings even if her words didn't.
   7 to represent an abstract quality or idea exactly
   We need a slogan which _____ the philosophy of our business.

d 💬 What facts about your own first language would you add to the fact file? Think of:

   • an area of meaning where there are many more, or many fewer, words than English
   • an idiom which can't be translated into English
   • grammar or vocabulary which might reflect the culture.

   Explain your list to a partner.

e 💬 Read the opinion below.

> Language is the main influence on how people view their world.

Do you agree? Why / Why not?

FACT FILE:
HOW LANGUAGES ARE SPECIAL

The **DANI OF NEW GUINEA** only distinguish colours from one another using two words, one for dark colours and the other light colours.

It is believed that the **INUIT IN NORTHERN CANADA** have about 50 different words for snow and about 40 ways to distinguish different kinds of ice from one another.

ALBANIAN has 27 different words for kinds of moustaches. *Posht*, for example, means a moustache which hangs down at the ends.

HAWAIIAN LANGUAGES have 108 words for sweet potato, and 47 for banana.

In the **NATIVE AMERICAN LANGUAGE HOPI**, the verbs do not differentiate between past and present. Instead, the forms of its verbs convey how the speaker came to know the information.

GUUGU YIMITHIRR, a language spoken in northeast Australia, does not have words for 'left' and 'right' as directions at all. Instead, they use north, south, east and west. When they want someone to take a turn in the road they'll say, for example, 'Turn a little bit west.'

In the language of **THE MARQUESAN ISLANDS**, directions are indicated with reference to geographical features – which can make them hard to interpret if you don't know exactly where you are. For example, a Marquesan might say that your bicycle is 'downstream of the house' or that you should 'Walk inland, then seaward' to get to your destination.

UNTRANSLATABLE

Most languages have unique words and idioms which are impossible to translate exactly. These words often embody the culture of the people who speak the language. Some examples that illustrate this:

ENGLISH: *cosy* = pleasantly warm and comfortable

GERMAN: *Fernweh* = a longing to be somewhere far away

JAPANESE: *Mono no aware* = a gentle sadness at the impermanence of things

DUTCH: *uitwaaien* = walking in windy weather for fun

GREEK: *parea* = a group of friends who meet to share ideas and experiences

KIVILA (PAPUA NEW GUINEA): *mokita* = the truth that everyone knows but nobody talks about

1 LISTENING

(a)

a 💬 Discuss the questions.

1 Have you or someone you know worked with a colleague for a long time? Who? How long?
2 What characterises a good working relationship?

b 💬 Answer the questions about picture a.

1 Where do you think Sara and Alex work?
2 What do you think their relationship is?
3 What do you think their conversation will be about? Why?

c ▶1.15 Watch or listen to Part 1 and check your answers in 1b. How and why does Alex think Sara can help him?

d Language in context *Irony and understatement*

1 Match Sara's and Alex's comments a–d with situations 1–4.

a ☐ Full of the joys of spring, I see!
b ☐ Don't sound so pleased to see me!
c ☐ It's not exactly good news.
d ☐ That'd be something of a surprise.

1 Sara is expecting the exact opposite to happen.
2 Alex notices that Sara's greeting is not enthusiastic.
3 Alex sees that Sara looks unhappy.
4 Sara has received a worrying message.

2 💬 Why do you think Sara and Alex don't say exactly what they mean? Do people do the same in your culture?

e ▶1.16 Watch or listen to Part 2. What is the relationship between … ?

- Nadia and Sara
- Sara and Oscar
- Alex and Emma

Nadia

Oscar

Emma

f ▶1.16 Answer the questions. Watch or listen to Part 2 again and check your answers.

1 What does Nadia want to talk about?
2 Why does she mention Oscar?
3 What does Nadia want from Emma?
4 What does Alex suggest is Nadia's reason for speaking to Sara?
5 What help does Sara ask Alex for?
6 What's Sara's impression of Emma?

g 💬 Discuss the questions about Parts 1 and 2.

1 What do you know about the company Sara and Alex work for? Do you think Sara and Alex do similar jobs?
2 How do you think Sara feels at the end of this episode?
3 What would be a suitable title for this episode of the story?

2 USEFUL LANGUAGE Expressing yourself in an inexact way

a In informal conversations, we often express things in an inexact way. Read sentences 1–4. Which character said each one? Match the expressions in **bold** with their uses a–d.

1 ☐ 'please' and 'thank you' and **stuff like that**
2 ☐ Max **whatsisname**
3 ☐ six authors, **give or take**
4 ☐ I'm out of here, or **words to that effect**

a used to give an inexact amount
b used to report someone's words in an inexact way
c used when you can't remember someone's name exactly
d used to refer to things of a similar type in an inexact way

b Which three expressions in **bold** below could you use in 1–4 in 2a? Rewrite three ideas in 2a, changing the word order if necessary.

1 There were **somewhere in the region of** 100 people.
2 She said **something along those lines**.
3 **Whatsername** was late, as usual.
4 I need **some bits and pieces** from the shop.
5 I said I'd give **thingy** a lift.

Which two expressions can't you use in 2a? Why not? Match them to their uses:

a ☐ used to refer to things of different kinds
b ☐ used when you can't remember a woman's name exactly

c Rewrite these sentences using expressions from 2a and b.

1 William Shakespeare, who wrote *A Midsummer Night's Dream*.
2 I went to the market and bought three items.
3 She told me to go away, saying, 'Please would you leave now?'
4 I know a little Polish – 'hello', 'goodbye', the numbers one to ten.
5 I've been to 15 countries.

d ▶1.17 Listen and compare your answers in 2c. Are they the same? Practise different ways of saying each sentence in 2b and c.

3 PRONUNCIATION
Sound and spelling: *ea, ee* and *ie*

a ▶1.18 Listen to the words in the box. What sound do the letters in bold make? Is this sound always spelt with two letters?

---
pl**ea**sed   m**ee**ting   d**e**cent   ser**ie**s
---

b ▶1.19 The spellings *ea, ee* and *ie* are not always pronounced with the vowel sound in 3a. Listen and put the words in this box in the correct column 2–6.

---
ch**ee**rful   b**ea**r   res**ea**rch   gr**ea**t   fr**ie**nd
---

1 /iː/	2 /e/	3 /eɪ/	4 /eə/	5 /ɪə/	6 /ɜː/
meet					

c ▶1.20 What sound do *ea, ee* and *ie* have in the words in this box? Add them to the sound groups in 3b. Listen and check. Practise saying the words.

---
learn   Greek   hear   heard   meaning
meant   increase   steadily   niece   pierce
idea   break   breakfast   early   pear   career

Which is the only short sound in 3b?

4 SPEAKING

a ▶1.21 Listen and answer the questions.

1 What experience does the speaker talk about?
2 The speaker says, *the full horror of the situation* dawned on her. What is she referring to?

b ▶1.21 Listen again and write down the expressions from 2a and b that you hear.

c Work alone. Plan to talk about an experience you have had, and make notes. Decide what exact details you will give, and what you will mention in an inexact way. Here are some ideas:

• A time when you got to know someone new on a long journey
• A time when you travelled somewhere new on the spur of the moment
• A time when you made an unplanned purchase

d 💬 Work with a partner. Take turns to talk about your experience. Use expressions from 2a and b to mention things in an inexact way.

Unit Progress Test

CHECK YOUR PROGRESS

You can now do the Unit Progress Test.

1D Skills for Writing
You're spot on there!

1 SPEAKING and LISTENING

a 💬 Look at these borrowed words from English used in other languages. Why do you think they are used?

(1) džús (Slovakian)

(2) outdoor (Portuguese, Brazil)

(3) lonche (Spanish, Mexico)

(4) janpa (Japanese)

(5) gol (Spanish)

(6) biznismyen (Russian)

(7) kampyutara (Hindi)

b 💬 Write down some examples of English words that are commonly used in your language. Then discuss the questions.

1 What are the main topic areas of borrowed English words in your language?
2 How do you / people in your country feel about adopted English words?

c 💬 You will hear a linguist, Maxwell Kingsley, talking about the dominance of English as a world language. What do you think he will say about … ?

1 around a billion people
2 an easy language
3 Latin
4 effect on the diversity of human languages
5 the only real disadvantage of the dominance of English
6 English as a truly global language

d ▶ 1.22 Listen and check. Make notes. Are there any points he makes which you find surprising?

2 READING

a Read the posts to a web forum. Which two people agree with each other?

b Which post … ?
• do you agree with most, and why?
• do you think makes the most interesting point?

3 WRITING SKILLS Expressing opinions

a Which elements (A–E) are used by each writer in the web forum?

A agreeing/disagreeing with a previous comment
B stating a new opinion on the topic
C describing cultural trends to support an opinion
D including personal experience to support an opinion
E making a summarising statement

b Write the highlighted phrases in the posts in the correct part of the table.

Disagreement	Agreement
That simply isn't true. That's easy to say, but … How can you possibly think that? That's a load of rubbish. 1 _____ 2 _____ 3 _____	That makes a lot of sense. You've hit the nail on the head. I would go along with that. 5 _____
Uncertainty	**Partial agreement / disagreement**
I've got mixed feelings about this. 4 _____	You've got a point, but … It's true that … but … On the other hand, I do feel … 6 _____

c Look again at the highlighted phrases for disagreement in the forum. Answer the questions.

1 What phrases do the writers use to soften the disagreement phrases?
2 Do you know any other words and phrases for softening your opinions?

d Look at all the expressions in the table. Which ones are informal? Use a dictionary to help you.

e ▶ Now go to Writing Focus 1D on p.169

Maxwell Kingsley makes the point that although English has become the dominant world language, this isn't a threat to other languages. Do you think he's right?

FLYING D

I'm in two minds about this.
I agree up to a point that there's benefit to be had from a shared global language – especially the opportunity to travel and speak to other people without constantly having to learn other languages. On the other hand, as people have said elsewhere, I do feel the dominance of English interferes with the uniqueness of many languages, for example, the way words are borrowed from English.

The world is made infinitely more fascinating by having a variety of cultures. Different histories, cuisines, habits, styles of communication … A huge part of this is our many unique languages and dialects.

Using the English language is by no means the only thing that's been undermining this uniqueness, but it clearly contributes to it.

———————————————— REPLY

NEULING

If you ask me, that's nonsense. I've lived in various countries and people speak their own languages 99% of the time.

Many do speak English as a second language for international communication, but as far as I can tell, that doesn't have much impact on their cultural identity. It's true that people are constantly bombarded with advertising words like 'style' or 'action', but these are just empty buzzwords so they don't matter that much.

Most non-native speakers see English as a simple tool, but they don't use it when they need to convey subtle details and differences.

———————————————— REPLY

ARIETE

Great comment, you're spot on there.
I speak English fluently but I use Finnish (and Swedish!) in everyday life, and, as far as I'm concerned, there's no way English is taking over my life. We all know it's a global language, but so what? Some language has to be. I get a lot out of being able to use English but I'm never going to stop using my own language. Why would I? I don't quite get what the fuss is about here.

———————————————— REPLY

PARSAUK

It seems to me all of you are missing the point here. Even if English does replace other languages, it's not the end of the world – just the opposite in fact. I think that having one international language is a great way to help unify the world and the human race in general. How can we expect cultures to keep peace between each other when they can't understand each other. Unique languages tend to isolate those communities which are most likely to be economically weak.

Our heritage is only history, and history will never and can never be more important than the present or the future.

———————————————— REPLY

f Compare Flying D's and Ariete's posts. Whose comments are more formal and abstract, and whose are more informal and personal? How can you tell? Think about …
- abstract nouns
- sentence length and structure
- personal examples
- questions and exclamation marks
- colloquial expressions
- first person

g What style of comment would you post on this forum: formal and abstract or informal and personal?

> **Writing Tip**
> In order to write good discussion forum comments:
> - Choose a style and keep to it. It can be informal and chatty or it can be more formal and serious, but it's better not to mix different styles together.
> - Before you respond to a comment, read it carefully to make sure your response is relevant.
> - Even if you strongly disagree with someone, try not to be impolite.

4 WRITING

a Read the opinions below and tick (✓) the ones you agree with.

1 ☐ **Countries need to protect their language from the influx of English words.**

2 ☐ **The effect of English on other languages has been more positive than negative.**

3 ☐ **'International English' used by non-native speakers is destroying the English language.**

4 ☐ **If you want to work for an international company, you should learn English.**

b Choose one of the opinions and start a discussion forum. Write a comment of about 5–6 sentences giving your point of view.

c Pass your post to another student. Read another student's post and add a comment. It can be a response, or a further comment on the topic.

d Repeat 4c until you have commented four times.

e Read the discussion forum which you started. Which comment do you think is most interesting?

UNIT 1
Review and extension

1 GRAMMAR

a Correct seven mistakes with adverbials.

1 Please slowly try to speak.
2 He will be probably late.
3 We do by hand our washing.
4 We will be living in June in London.
5 She made me so loudly laugh.
6 I in the end managed to get in touch.
7 You can compare easily the different brands.

b Choose the correct form.

1 I *have never visited / never visited* an English-speaking country in my life.
2 *I've been learning / I'm learning* English for ages.
3 I *had been crossing / was crossing* the road when the car hit me.
4 I *have wanted / wanted* to give up at the beginning but I kept studying.
5 She *has had / has* her hair cut. Doesn't it look nice?
6 I *will have been studying / will have studied* for five hours by the time you get home.

2 VOCABULARY

a Replace the words in *italics* with an expression in the box.

acquire   rusty   brush up   get to grips with
hold a conversation   immerse yourself in   struggle with

1 Sally really used to *have problems with* phrasal verbs.
2 The best way to learn is to *get to know fully* the culture.
3 Vladimir is amazing, he can *talk* with anyone in English.
4 How do young children *learn* their first language?
5 I'd better *improve* my French before the trip.
6 I can't *understand the complexities of* German grammar.
7 Mum's schoolgirl Spanish must be *worse than it was*.

b Complete the missing letters in each word.

1 Her popularity with teens has been on a r_____d rise.
2 Even a s_____e change in his hairstyle gets comments.
3 There has been a steady s_____t toward part-time work.
4 This will not result in a l_____g change.
5 Black jeans are on the w_____y out.
6 The o_____g changes are affecting productivity.
7 Perhaps the benefits will not be p_____e for a while.

3 WORDPOWER Idioms: Body parts

a ▶1.23 Complete the idioms with the words in the box. Listen and check.

shoulders   hands   tooth   nose   tongue   head   neck

1 Mark obviously **has a** _____ **for** business investment; he has never lost us any money yet.
2 I walked across to the photographers, shouting and yelling. I completely **lost my** _____.
3 Colleagues regard Mika as **a safe pair of** _____ who can be relied upon to step in when required.
4 It may happen, but I certainly wouldn't **stick my** _____ **out** and promise anything.
5 After five years training for this event, he's **head and** _____ **above** the competition.
6 I had to **bite my** _____ when my manager took credit for my work.
7 I will **fight** _____ **and nail** to prevent any scheme which threatens local livelihoods.

b Match idioms 1–7 in 3a with definitions a–g.

a ☐ take a risk
b ☐ try very hard to overcome opposition and get something you want
c ☐ be good at finding a specific thing
d ☐ stop yourself from saying something
e ☐ lose control of your behaviour
f ☐ someone other people trust to do a good job
g ☐ be a lot better than other competitors

c Complete the idioms from 3a in these questions.

1 In what situations do you think it's important to _____ out?
2 Who do you know who's got _____ for something?
3 Who's an actor you think is _____ above most others?
4 How do you react if someone you know loses _____ in front of you?
5 What's something you would fight _____ to prevent?
6 In what situations do you think people should _____ tongues?
7 Who do you know who's a _____ in an emergency?

d 💬 Discuss the questions in 3c.

↻ REVIEW YOUR PROGRESS

How well did you do in this unit? Write 3, 2, or 1 for each objective.
3 = very well   2 = well   1 = not so well

I CAN ...

talk about second language learning	☐
describe languages and how they change	☐
express myself in an inexact way	☐
write a web forum post	☐

CAN DO OBJECTIVES

- Describe extreme sensory experiences
- Talk about plans, intentions and arrangements
- Give advice
- Write a report

Going to extremes

GETTING STARTED

a 💬 Look at the picture and answer the questions.

1 Where is the man? Why do you think he's swimming here?
2 What are the possible risks of swimming here? What skills and attributes do you think a person swimming here needs?
3 What do you think this man does immediately after his swim?
4 Would you consider swimming in this location?

b 💬 Discuss the questions.

1 Imagine you're about to interview this man for the local newspaper. What questions would you ask him? Make a list.
2 What's the coldest/hottest experience you've ever had? Describe it to a partner.

Learn to describe extreme sensory experiences
G Comparison
V Multi-word verbs: Social interaction

1 SPEAKING

a ▶ 1.24 Listen to six sounds. Note down what you hear and ask and answer the questions.

1 How often do you hear these sounds? Where?
2 How does each sound make you feel?

b ▶ Communication 2A Now go to p.127

2 READING

a 💬 Look at the picture, read the caption and discuss the questions.

1 What do you think an anechoic chamber is?
2 Do you think you'd like to go to one? Why / Why not?

b Read about George Foy's visit to an anechoic chamber on p.21. Was it a positive experience overall?

c Read the text again and answer the questions.

1 Why did George begin his search?
2 What makes the anechoic chamber at Orfield so quiet?
3 Do most people enjoy being in the anechoic chamber? Why / Why not?
4 What physical and mental effects can the anechoic chamber cause in people?
5 Why was George concerned about going into the chamber?
6 What was George's first reaction to being in the anechoic chamber?
7 Did he enjoy all of his time in the chamber? Why / Why not?
8 What does George say people should do to deal with sensitivity to noise?

d Cover the text and try to remember why George mentioned these things.

1 the New York subway
2 a monastery and a mine
3 his blood
4 his scalp
5 beating the record
6 TV

e 💬 Do you think you could have lasted as long as George in the anechoic chamber? Why / Why not?

f **Language in context** *Sounds*

1 Match the definitions below with the highlighted words in the text.

a strange and mysterious and a bit frightening (adj.)
b so loud you can't hear anything (adj.)
c to make a sound by repeatedly hitting something hard (v.)
d to complain in a high, unpleasant voice (v.)
e the sound an empty stomach makes (v.)
f a long, loud, deep noise (n.)
g the sound of a heartbeat (n.)
h the sound made by using only the breath to speak (n.)
i units that measure loudness (n.)

The anechoic chamber, Orfield Laboratories, Minneapolis
The quieter the room, the more things you hear. You'll hear your heart beating, sometimes you can hear your lungs, hear your stomach gurgling loudly. In the anechoic chamber, you become the sound.

2 Underline the adjectives in the article that describe these nouns: *roar, whisper, thump.*

> 💬 **Learning Tip**
> When you make a note of a new word, it's a good idea to note down the collocation(s) as well. You can also look in dictionaries for other collocations to add to your notes.

3 Notice the words *noise* and *sound(s)* in *italics* in the article. What words in the text form collocations with these nouns? What part of speech are they? Use a dictionary to help you.

block out noise (v.) , a source of noise (n.)

I'VE BEEN TO THE
QUIETEST PLACE
ON EARTH by George Foy

My search started when I was in the New York subway. My children were whining, four trains came screaming into the station at once and I put my hands over my ears and cowered – the noise was deafening.

In cities, the ever-present dull roar of planes, cars, machinery and voices is a fact of life. There is no escape from it and I was beginning to be driven mad by it. I needed to find a place where I could recapture a sense of peace. The quieter this place was the more relaxing it would be.

I decided to go on a mission to discover whether absolute silence exists. I travelled to a monastery, and a mine 2 km underground – both very quiet but not the quietest place on earth. The one place I was most excited about visiting was the anechoic chamber at Orfield Laboratories in Minnesota.

This is a small room, insulated with layers of concrete and steel to block out exterior sources of *noise*, and internally lined with buffers that absorb all *sound*. Even the floor is a suspended mesh to stop any sound of footfalls. If a soft whisper is measured at 20 decibels, the anechoic chamber is one sixteenth of that. The anechoic chamber is considerably quieter than any other place on earth. Ironically, far from being peaceful, most people find its perfect quiet upsetting. Being deprived of the usual reassuring ambient *sounds* can create fear – it explains why sensory deprivation is a form of torture. Astronauts do part of their training in anechoic chambers at NASA, so they can learn to cope with the silence of space. The presence of sound means things are working; it's business as usual – when sound is absent, that signals malfunction. I had heard being in an anechoic chamber for longer than 15 minutes can cause extreme symptoms, from claustrophobia and nausea to panic attacks and aural hallucinations – you literally start hearing things. A violinist tried it and hammered on the door after a few seconds, demanding to be let out because he was so disturbed by the silence.

I booked a 45-minute session – no one had managed to stay in for that long before. I felt apprehensive for two reasons: would I go mad and tear off my clothes? Or would I simply be disappointed it wasn't as enjoyable as I'd hoped?

When the heavy door shut behind me, I was plunged into darkness (lights can make a noise). For the first few seconds, being in such a quiet place felt utterly peaceful, soothing for my jangled nerves. I strained to hear something and heard … nothing.

Then, after a minute or two, I became aware of my own breathing. The sound became more and more noticeable, so I held my breath. The dull thump of my heartbeat became apparent – nothing I could do about that. As the minutes ticked by, I started to hear the blood rushing in my veins. Your ears become more sensitive as the place gets quieter, and mine were going overtime. I frowned and heard my scalp moving over my skull, which was eerie, and a strange, metallic scraping *noise* I couldn't explain. Was I hallucinating? The feeling of peace was spoiled by a little disappointment – this place wasn't quiet at all. You'd have to be dead for absolute silence.

Then I stopped being obsessed with my body and began to enjoy it. I didn't feel afraid and came out only because my time was up; I would happily have stayed longer in there. Everyone was impressed that I'd beaten the record, but having spent so long searching for quiet, I was comfortable with the feeling of absolute stillness. Afterwards I felt wonderfully rested and calm. The experience was nowhere near as disturbing as I had been led to believe.

My desire for silence changed my life. I found that making space for moments of quiet in my day is the key to happiness – they give you a chance to think about what you want in life. How can you really focus on what's important if you're distracted by constant background *noise*? If you can occasionally become master of your own sound environment – from turning off the TV to moving to the country, as I did – you become infinitely more accepting of the noises of everyday life.

3 GRAMMAR Comparison

a Cover the text. Complete the sentences with the words in the box. Then check your answers in the text.

> considerably   the (x2)   and
> infinitely   nowhere near   more

1 The quieter the room, _____ more things you hear.
2 _____ quieter this place was the more relaxing it would be.
3 The anechoic chamber is _____ quieter than any other place on earth.
4 The sound [of my breathing] became more _____ more noticeable …
5 Your ears become _____ sensitive as the place gets quieter …
6 The experience was _____ as disturbing as I had been led to believe.
7 … you become _____ more accepting of the noises of everyday life.

b Answer the questions about the sentences in 3a.

1 Which sentences contain two comparative forms? Are the two qualities in these sentences independent of or dependent on each other?
2 Which sentence(s) describe something increasing progressively, over time?
3 Look at sentences 3 and 6. Which words in the box below are possible in each gap?

> nothing like   slightly   a good deal
> decidedly   not nearly   significantly

c ▶ Now go to Grammar Focus 2A on p.140

d 💬 Think of a place or an event that you had a strong physical or mental reaction to. Tell your partner.

1 Was this place different from your expectations? Why / Why not?
2 How did you feel? Did your feelings change the longer you stayed there?
3 Would you like to go back to this place? Why / Why not?

> The first time I had a sauna, it was considerably hotter than I'd expected it to be …

4 LISTENING

a 💬 Discuss the questions.

1 Have you ever stopped speaking for any reason? Why? How did you communicate?

2 What different reasons can you think of for stopping speaking?

b ▶1.30 Listen to the first part of Lena's story. Why did she decide to stop talking?

c ▶1.30 Listen to part one again. Summarise what Lena says about these things.

1 the dinner party   3 a spiritual vow of silence
2 her realisation   4 a public vow of silence

d 💬 What rules do you think Lena should make for herself for her vow of silence? What situations might be difficult?

e ▶1.31 Listen to part two. Does Lena mention any of your ideas from 4d?

f ▶1.31 Listen to part two again. What does Lena say about these people?

- herself • the person in the café • her friend
- the woman in the supermarket • her landlord

How did she feel at the end of her experiment?

g 💬 Discuss the questions.

1 What do you think of the experiment Lena did? Would you try an experiment like this? Why / Why not?

2 Are you surprised by the reactions of the woman in the supermarket and her landlord? Why / Why not?

5 VOCABULARY

Multi-word verbs: Social interaction

a ▶1.32 Complete the sentences below with the correct particles in the box. Listen and check.

down with to across out (x2)
in off back about

1 Talking is a way of **fitting** _____ – y'know, a way of showing that we belong to a social group.

2 How would I **come** _____ to other people?

3 … people go into some kind of retreat to **cut themselves** _____ from the outside world.

4 … when someone held a door open for me and a little 'thank you' **slipped** _____.

5 The most interesting thing was the way other people **related** _____ me.

6 She **bombarded me** _____ **questions**.

7 He always **goes on** _____ something when I go and see him …

8 He usually likes to **run** _____ some politician or other.

9 I often felt that my silence **brought** _____ **the best in people**.

10 I often wanted to, but I had to **hold myself** _____.

My vow of silence

b Write the multi-word verbs you completed in the sentences in 5a in the correct column of the table.

social interaction in general	spoken interaction
fit in	slip out

c ▶1.33 **Pronunciation** Listen to the phrase below. What sound joins onto the beginning of *across*? Why?

How would I come across to other people?

d ▶1.34 Listen to these phrases from 5a again. Where is there consonant–vowel linking? What sounds are used?

1 … cut themselves off from …
2 … and a little 'thank you' slipped out …
3 … goes on about something …
4 … my silence brought out the best …

Practise saying the phrases with consonant–vowel linking.

e 💬 Think of people you can describe using some of the multi-word verbs in 5a. Tell your partner.

Someone you know who …
- comes across well to new people
- relates to other people well
- often goes on about a problem they have
- brings out the best in you
- tends to cut themselves off from the outside world
- sometimes bombards people with questions
- likes to run down famous people

> 🖋 **Learning Tip**
> When you learn new multi-word verbs, thinking of personalised examples can help you remember the new vocabulary. You can record them in your vocabulary notebook.

6 SPEAKING

💬 Read the ideas about communication. What situations do you think the statements are referring to? How true do you think each statement is?

1 Communication isn't about what you say – it's about how you say it.

2 It's not the silence that's uneasy; it's your own thoughts that fill the silence.

3 Sometimes talking about a problem only makes it worse.

4 Good listeners make good leaders.

5 People who talk a lot often have the least of value to say.

2B I'll be jumping from 900 metres

Learn to talk about plans, intentions and arrangements
G Intentions and arrangements
V Verbs of movement

1 READING and SPEAKING

a 💬 Do you like speed and danger? Which of these activities would you enjoy?

- [ ] flying in a two-seater plane
- [ ] climbing a mountain
- [ ] going on a roller coaster
- [ ] driving at 130 kph on a motorway
- [ ] going on a small boat in a rough sea
- [ ] skiing

Order the activities from 1–6 (1 = least enjoy). Compare your order with other students.

b 💬 Work in groups of four. Read about one different sport each. Find answers to these questions where possible and report back to the group.

1 Where do you do it?
2 What do you wear?
3 What do you do exactly?
4 How dangerous is it?
5 How expensive is it?

c 💬 Have you tried or can you imagine doing any of these sports? Rate each sport by writing the initials *I*, *Z–L*, *Z*, *V* on the scales below. Then compare your answers with other students.

exhilarating ▬▬▬▬▬▬▬▬ no fun at all
absolutely terrifying ▬▬▬▬▬▬ not scary at all
worth every penny ▬▬▬▬▬ a waste of money

ITCHING FOR A GOOD THRILL?

TRY ONE OF THESE TO GET YOUR HEART PUMPING:

zip-lining

You don't need to be somewhere exotic to go zip-lining. Yes, it's most often associated with Costa Rica and Hawaii, but you can probably find it nearer home. No matter where you are, cables are strung between trees; participants wear a harness attached to a wheel that dangles from the line. In locales like Costa Rica, you'll be mingling with monkeys 80 feet above ground, with a bird's-eye view of the jungle. At a mountain resort, you'll go whizzing over ski slopes or a canopy of trees. The fastest zip lines reach speeds of up to 100 miles an hour. It usually costs between $100 and $300.

Indoor skydiving

Consider it a trial run before jumping out of a plane. At iFly facilities nationwide, you'll don a flight suit and helmet and go soaring inside a vertical wind tunnel. These are 14 feet in diameter and generate wind speeds of up to 160 miles per hour. Flights mimic the experience of free-fall skydiving without the parachute. If you're between ages 3 and 103, you can do it; cost typically ranges from $60 to $250.

Zorbing

Globe-riding. Orbing. Zorbing. This is the sport of climbing into a clear, plastic ball (typically 10 feet in diameter), and rolling downhill at high speed. It looks like a giant hamster ball. Zorbing first hit the extreme-sport scene in New Zealand, and now it's available anywhere in the world. Usually, riders are strapped against one of the ball's walls. Not in hydro-zorbing, though. In that case, the operator adds about 5 gallons of water, and passengers slip and splash as the ball rolls.

Volcano-boarding

Adrenaline junkies: head forth to Nicaragua. Prepare to zoom down a steep, 1,600-foot volcanic slope, on a plywood board reinforced with metal and Formica. One of the latest additions to the extreme-sport scene, it's only done on Cerro Negro, a charcoal-black active volcano that's erupted 23 times in the past 100 years. (The threat of another eruption always looms, though there hasn't been once since 1999.) Tourists pay $28 for the experience.

23

2 READING

a 💬 Why do you think people do extreme sports? Choose from these reasons. Read the article and check.

- ☐ to impress other people
- ☐ to feel more alive
- ☐ to feel they are in control
- ☐ to feel part of an exclusive group
- ☐ to test their limits
- ☐ to feel great afterwards

b Read the article again and answer the questions.

1 The article mentions volcano-boarding. What four other activities does it refer to?
2 What does the expression 'Type T' refer to?
3 How is biology relevant to Type Ts' behaviour?
4 What personality characteristics do Type Ts typically have?
5 Why do people feel happy after going on a roller coaster?

c **Language in context** Synonyms: *want, like, love*

1 Cover the text. Which expressions in the box were used instead of the words in *italics* in the sentences below? Check your answers in the text.

crave	be drawn to	be inclined	long for	thrive on

a Thrill-seekers *really want* that rush; they *love* it.
b These are people who *want* exciting, meaningful challenges.
c Dopamine and testosterone appear to affect how much someone *wants* to play it safe.
d Margaret J King studies why people *like* roller coasters.

2 How is each expression in the box different from the ones in *italics*? Which words have very similar meanings? Use a dictionary to help you.

d 💬 Do you think you have any Type T characteristics? Who do you know of who is definitely a Type T?

e ▶ 1.35 **Pronunciation** Listen to the comments and mark the word groups and main stress.

1 I like to make my own <u>decisions</u> ‖ and I never play by the <u>rules</u>.
2 I need a guide in new cities in case I get lost.
3 I do feel scared when I face danger but I know that I'll be OK.
4 I'm paid to innovate at work, so I spend half my time daydreaming!
5 I think people should dress neatly and look respectable, especially in public.

f Complete the rule with *first* or *last*. Practise saying the comments in 2e.

> The _____ word that carries meaning in each word group usually has the main stress.

g 💬 Which of the comments in 2e do you think a Type T person would agree with?

Why Some of Us Are Thrill-Seekers

Skydiving? Zip-lining? Volcano-boarding? Yes, say thrill-seekers, and there's a reason.

Every adrenaline junkie knows the feeling. Heart pounding. Hands trembling. Blood racing. And then all of a sudden—flying. Plunging through the air, 18,000 feet above the earth, clinging to a parachute that could by all means fail. Hurtling at 50 miles an hour down a 1,600-foot volcanic slope, on a volcano board popularised by young adventurers. Whooshing down whitewater rapids on a flimsy raft. Or being strapped into a zero-gravity roller coaster and preparing to whirl upside down, again and again. Thrill-seekers crave that rush; they thrive on it.

'It's the excitement,' says Frank Farley, a professor of educational psychology at Temple University in Philadelphia. 'It makes things interesting, keeps you going. When this life is over, you want to be able to look back and say, "I lived." As Helen Keller once said, "Life is a daring adventure, or it is nothing."

In the 1980s, Farley coined the term Type T personality to describe thrill-seekers, or those who crave variety, novelty, intensity, and risk. These are people who long for exciting, meaningful challenges. Some enjoy the physical sensations that come from being scared silly; others like the idea that they're pushing themselves to the extreme.

At least to some degree, Type Ts are born that way, Farley says. Though researchers don't yet have all the answers, it's clear that biology plays a role. Neurochemicals like dopamine and testosterone appear to affect how inclined someone is to play it safe or live on the wild side, as does the amount of white matter in the brain.

Other factors are psychological and rooted in personality. Thrill-seekers tend to be creative folks who like to make up their own minds. 'They're energetic and self-confident,' Farley says. 'And they feel in control of their fate. When they climb Mt Everest, they figure they're going to come back. If someone tells them not to do it, that sounds like a rule, so away they go.'

Margaret J King, director of Cultural Studies and Analysis, a Philadelphia-based think tank, studies human behaviour and, more specifically, why people are drawn to roller coasters. These days, riders are in for dangling seats that throw them upside down and backwards in gravity-defying loops and twists. 'You wouldn't think we would put ourselves in such a terrifying position,' King says. 'But terror gives us a chance to test ourselves, our own tolerance. We like the idea that we can get through it.' Boarding a roller coaster makes us feel like 'we're in imminent danger of dying,' she explains. 'All the signals in our body tell us we're headed in a bad direction. We can't get off. We can't stop the thing. And then when we do, there's a tremendous rush of adrenaline, of ecstasy and elation. That's why you see people bouncing off rides with their friends.'

3 VOCABULARY Verbs of movement

a Look at these sentences and answer questions 1 and 2.

a You'll go **soaring** inside a vertical wind tunnel.
b You'll go **whizzing** over ski slopes.
c This is the sport of **rolling** downhill at high speed.
d Prepare to **zoom** down a steep, 1,600-foot volcanic slope.
e **Plunging** through the air, 18,000 feet above the earth …
f **Hurtling** down a 1,600-foot volcanic slope …
g **Whooshing** down whitewater rapids on a flimsy raft …
h Preparing to **whirl** upside down, again and again …

1 Can each verb in **bold** above describe movement … ?
   • on land   • through water   • through the air
   Write *L / W / A* next to a–h. Use a dictionary to help you.

2 Which verbs suggest the sound that the action makes?

b ▶ Now go to Vocabulary Focus 2B on p.159

4 LISTENING

a ▶1.37 You are going to hear an interview with Ada, who is going base jumping.

1 Look at the picture. What do base jumpers do?
2 What do you think Ada might say about base jumping? Note down a few ideas.
   • before the jump *I've never done it before.*
   • after the jump *I was afraid the parachute wouldn't open.*

Listen and check your ideas.

b ▶1.37 Answer the questions. Listen and check.

1 What do these numbers in the interview refer to?
   a 10 minutes   b 300 jumps   c 900 metres
   d 25 seconds   e 20 seconds   f 30,000
2 What does Ada say about the risks of base jumping?

c 💬 Would you consider going base jumping?

5 GRAMMAR
Intentions and arrangements

a ▶1.38 Both future forms in each pair below are possible. Which sentence did the speakers use, and why? Listen and check.

1 a So Ada, you**'re about to go** base jumping.
  b So Ada, you**'re going to go** base jumping.
2 a I**'m due to jump** in about ten minutes.
  b I**'m planning to jump** in about ten minutes.
3 a I**'ll jump** from 900 metres.
  b I**'ll be jumping** from 900 metres.
4 a I**'m definitely going to do** it again.
  b I**'m definitely doing** it again.

b ▶1.39 Complete the sentences below with the words Ada used. Listen and check.

| intention   planning   aiming   thinking |

1 I**'m** also _____ **of trying** a tandem jump sometime.
2 There is a platform which sticks out over the cliff, and I**'m** _____ **to jump** off that one.
3 I**'m** _____ **to free fall** for exactly 25 seconds.
4 You come here **with the** _____ **of having** a great experience and … and that's what you do.

c ▶ Now go to Grammar Focus 2B on p.141

d Prepare to talk about your plans for next year. Are you planning to do / thinking of doing … ?
   • anything you've never done before
   • anything exciting or risky

Think how you could use expressions from 5a and b.

e 💬 Tell the other students about your plans. Is anybody planning to do something you'd like to do?

6 SPEAKING and WRITING

a 💬 Look at the photo. Where do you think it is? Why might someone want to live there?

b ▶ Communication 2B
Now go to p.135

Learn to give advice
- **S** Advise a friend on a tricky situation
- **P** Emphatic stress

Emma

Max Redwood

Alex

1 LISTENING

a 💬 Discuss the questions.

1 In your country, at what age do people usually … ?
   - leave home
   - rent or buy their first property
2 What are the pros and cons of living with … ?
   - relatives
   - people you don't know
   - friends your own age
3 What factors are important in making the decision to leave home?

b 💬 Look at pictures a–c. What do you think the connection between them is?

c ▶1.44 Watch or listen to Part 1 and check your answers in 1b.

d ▶1.44 Watch or listen to Part 1 again. Answer the questions.

1 What is Emma's problem? Why exactly is Max annoying her?
2 What has she done about it so far?
3 What is Alex's advice to Emma?
4 How do Emma and Alex feel about Max and his book?

e ▶1.45 **Language in context** *Being tactful or frank*

1 Match the halves of the expressions from Part 1. Listen and check.

   1 ☐ It's like **walking**
   2 ☐ I keep **dropping**
   3 ☐ Why don't you just **tell**
   4 ☐ **Don't beat around**
   5 ☐ There's a lot to be said for **being**

   a **the bush**.
   b **him straight**, then?
   c **hints**, but he doesn't seem to notice.
   d **upfront about things**.
   e **on eggshells** half the time.

2 Look at the expressions in 1. Which describe being tactful? Which describe being frank?

f 💬 Discuss the questions.

1 Do you think Emma is right to drop hints to her brother, or should she stop beating around the bush and tell him straight?
2 Have you ever had the experience of guests who outstayed their welcome? What happened?

2 PRONUNCIATION Emphatic stress

a ▶1.46 Listen to the sentences below. <u>Underline</u> the main stress in the word groups in **bold**. Which word in a word group normally has the main stress? Check the rule on p.24.

1 **Max is due back soon.**
2 **He's getting on my nerves.**
3 Isn't it about time **you asked him to leave**?
4 **Did you say his name is Max**?

b ▶1.47 Sometimes main stress does not follow the rule on p.24. Listen and <u>underline</u> the main stress in the word groups in **bold**.

1 **He's not still sleeping on the sofa**, is he?
2 **He is the guy** who wrote *Solar Wind*.
3 **You mean it is him**?
4 **Your brother is the Max Redwood**!

c Look at 2b again and answer these questions.

1 Why don't the phrases in 2b follow the rule on p.24?
2 What does Alex mean when he says '*the* Max Redwood'?

d Emphasising different words in a word group changes the meaning. Match sentences 1–5 with their meanings a–e. Practise saying the sentences with the correct main stress.

   1 ☐ Alex has read Max's <u>book</u>.
   2 ☐ Alex has read <u>Max's</u> book.
   3 ☐ Alex has <u>read</u> Max's book.
   4 ☐ Alex <u>has</u> read Max's book.
   5 ☐ <u>Alex</u> has read Max's book.

The speaker is telling us:
a what Alex has done with Max's book
b whose book Alex has read
c who has read Max's book
d that Alex has read Max's book, not his letter, email or blog
e that we are wrong to believe Alex hasn't read Max's book

e 💬 Look at this sentence with the main stress in three different places. Work in pairs. Create a short conversation for each sentence. Then practise your conversation.

<u>I'll</u> give you a ring later.   I'll give <u>you</u> a ring later.   I'll give you a ring <u>later</u>.

3 LISTENING

a 💬 Look at picture d. Who do you think says these sentences, Emma or Max?

1 I can't think about any of that right now.
2 There's nothing else to say about *Solar Wind*!
3 Don't get so wound up about it.
4 It's only an interview.
5 I'll just go far far away, take a vow of silence, live on a desert island somewhere …

b ▶ 1.48 Watch or listen to Part 2 and check your answers in 3a.

c ▶ 1.48 Watch or listen to Part 2 again. Answer the questions.

1 Why does Emma think it wouldn't be a problem for Max to move out now?
2 What advantages does Emma mention for Max if he buys his own place?
3 How does Emma suggest Max prepare for the radio interview?
4 How does Max feel about Emma listening to his interview?
5 Why does Max suggest he'll take a vow of silence?

d 💬 Discuss the questions.

1 How would you feel about doing a live radio interview?
2 What are the worst things that could happen?

---

4 USEFUL LANGUAGE Giving advice

a Answer the questions.

1 Is the farmer's advice in picture e appropriate for the situation? Why / Why not?
2 What would you expect the farmer to say if a train was coming?
3 In what other situations might you use the advice in picture e?

It might be a good idea to move.

b ▶ 1.49 Match 1–7 with a–g to make sentences from Parts 1 and 2. Listen and check.

1 ☐ **Isn't it about**
2 ☐ **There's a lot to be said**
3 ☐ **Have you thought about the possibility**
4 ☐ **It might be in**
5 ☐ **You might want to**
6 ☐ **Don't** get so
7 ☐ **You might as**

a **well**!
b **time you** asked him to leave?
c have a think about what you could say tonight.
d **of** finding your own place to live?
e **for** being upfront about things.
f wound up about it.
g **your interests to** invest some of it in property.

c Which two expressions in **bold** in 4b sound more polite and formal?

d Complete the advice with the expressions in 4b.

1 You _____ to read up about the company before your interview.
2 Have you _____ working overseas?
3 There's _____ having your own car.
4 You _____ well sell it and get a better one.
5 It might be in _____ keep on good terms with the director.

e 💬 Look at the pairs of sentences from two conversations. Which conversation is more formal? What do you think the context for each is?

Conversation 1
a Isn't it about time you were upfront about it?
b Don't beat around the bush!

Conversation 2
a It might be in your interests to contact a solicitor.
b Have you thought about the possibility of changing the terms?

f 💬 Work in pairs. Use your ideas in 4e to have two conversations.

---

5 SPEAKING

▶ **Communication 2C** Work in pairs. Student A: Go to p.127. Student B: Go to p.137.

Unit Progress Test

CHECK YOUR PROGRESS

You can now do the Unit Progress Test.

paintballing · pony trekking · bungee jumping · tree-top adventuring · karting · whitewater rafting

1 LISTENING and SPEAKING

a 💬 You have to choose a sports activity for a student social programme. Which of the activities in the photos would you choose? Think about:

- appeal of the activity
- skills required
- student safety
- cost
- chances to socialise.

b ▶ 1.50 Listen to four students talking about the sports activities on a social programme at a university in Australia. Make notes on their feedback.

Luba, Russia

Mehmet, Turkey

Paolo, Italy

Changying, China

	Positives	Negatives
bungee jumping		
whitewater rafting		
other feedback		

c 💬 Think about the students' feedback in 1b. Choose any two sports activities for next year. Explain your choices.

2 READING

a Read the report by a member of the social programme committee and compare the content with your notes in 1b.

1 Which aspects of the students' feedback are included?
2 What negative feedback is not included?

b Are the recommendations similar to your ideas in 1c?

SOCIAL PROGRAMME
REVIEW AND RECOMMENDATIONS OF THE COMMITTEE

1 _____

The purpose of this report is to review options for sports activities that would be suitable as part of a social programme for foreign exchange students. Last year we had two activities for exchange students: whitewater rafting and a bungee jump, both of which received mixed reviews. This report is based on feedback on these activities.

2 _____

Even though many students liked the extreme nature of last year's activities, some felt they were too challenging. Many young tourists who come to Australia are keen to do these activities. However, not all our students necessarily have the same ambition. Whitewater rafting was not possible for students who were not confident swimmers. On the other hand, the bungee jump did not require any particular skill or expertise. Nevertheless, the idea of jumping from a bridge was seen by several as being risky.

3 WRITING SKILLS
Reports; Linking: contrast and concession

a Add these headings to the correct paragraphs of the report.
- Safety concerns
- Recommendations
- Cost and budget
- Introduction
- Level of challenge

b What phrases are used in the report to give … ?
1 the reason for writing the report
2 recommendations

Are these phrases formal or informal?

c Which word in *italics* in each phrase below is not possible?
1 The *purpose* / *aim* / *agenda* / *objective* of this report is …
2 I would *establish* / *recommend* / *suggest* / *propose* that …
3 My *recommendation(s)* / *conclusion(s)* / *suggestion(s)* / *resolution(s)* is/are …

d Look at the highlighted linkers in the report and decide which word(s) in **bold** in these sentences they could replace.
1 **Unlike** whitewater rafting, bungee jumping is relatively safe.
2 Go-karting is cheaper than skydiving. **Despite this**, skydiving is still more popular with students.
3 You could go pony trekking. **Alternatively**, you could go bungee jumping.
4 **In spite of** the cost, many people go sky diving regularly.
5 **Although** it is very expensive, many people go skydiving regularly.

---

3 _____

Safety issues were raised with both activities. One whitewater raft overturned and a student suffered concussion when he hit his head on a rock. Likewise, another student sprained her ankle in the bungee jump.

4 _____

Both activities were quite expensive so, despite the generous budget, we were obliged to ask students to make a contribution, which many were not happy about. The cost of providing transport to the venues for the activities drove the costs up further.

5 _____

For the students who are due to arrive this year, we would recommend that we choose slightly cheaper options and that we offer one extreme sports activity as well as something that is, by comparison, considerably less challenging. In contrast to whitewater rafting, tree-top adventuring is a relatively inexpensive extreme sport with an excellent safety record. Alternatively, less adventurous students could try paintballing, which is a low-cost and fun option that does not require any skill. Use of the local paintballing venue would cut transport costs, and we would suggest using the savings as a way of subsidising these activities for students.

---

e Match 1–6 with a–f. Underline the linkers of contrast and concession in the complete sentences. Include any prepositions that form part of the linker.
1 ☐ For all that extreme sports are generally seen as fun and exciting,
2 ☐ Despite the fact that many students said they were keen to try a bungee jump
3 ☐ Some students had no objection to paying a small amount towards the cost of the activity.
4 ☐ When compared to contact sports like rugby and ice hockey,
5 ☐ Regardless of savings we make on transport,
6 ☐ While many students indicated that they have to live on a tight budget,

a On the contrary, they had assumed they would have to make some kind of contribution.
b there has been some negative feedback on last year's activities.
c several said that the activities were affordable.
d we cannot afford to subsidise very expensive activities.
e extreme sports begin to look very safe.
f many failed to book when this activity was advertised.

f ▶ Now go to Writing Focus 2D on p.170

4 WRITING

a 💬 You are on a committee that has to organise a three-day tourist itinerary for a group of foreign students. Imagine problems previous groups might have had. Think about:
- range of sites visited
- transport
- refreshments
- time to visit sites
- availability of guides
- costs.

b Plan a report that discusses these problems and suggests solutions.

> **Writing Tip**
> You probably discussed a lot of ideas in 4a. However, it may not be possible to mention them all in detail in the report. In a report of this nature, you should address three or four key issues, so you may have to prioritise some points over others. It is preferable to mention problems that you can suggest a solution to.

c Write a report of between 250 and 300 words on the tourist itinerary.

d Read another student's report. Do you both mention the same problems and solutions?

UNIT 2
Review and extension

1 GRAMMAR

a Complete the sentences with one word.

1 The sound quality wasn't as high __as__ I expected.
2 3D films are a great _____ more expensive to make.
3 This is by _____ the tastiest meal I've had in months!
4 The higher you go, _____ further you can see.
5 I was getting more and _____ worried by the sounds.
6 Real coffee tastes nothing _____ the stuff from a jar.
7 They didn't make anywhere _____ as much mess as I thought they would.
8 The first place was really noisy and the second was just _____ bad.

b Choose the best option.

1 My brothers *are going to / are thinking of* attempt to climb K2.
2 The race *will begin / begins* in five minutes, so get ready.
3 How are you *getting / going to get* there on time?
4 What *will you be / are you* wearing when I see you?
5 The police are *to / thinking to* speak to those involved.
6 The plane is *due to / about to* arrive at 7.00 tomorrow morning.

2 VOCABULARY

a Match sentence halves 1–5 with endings a–e.

1 ☐ Unfortunately, she can come
2 ☐ I wish you wouldn't go
3 ☐ Living in a small village I felt cut
4 ☐ Don't worry about fitting
5 ☐ A crisis brings

a on about the neighbours all the time.
b out the best and worst in people.
c in, your new colleagues are very friendly.
d across as a bit arrogant.
e off and isolated.

b Answer the questions with one word.

1 Would you *stroll* in a park or a train station? park
2 What could *hurtle* past you – a feather or a cat?
3 If something *whirls*, does it travel in a straight line?
4 What could *whoosh* past you – a truck or a tortoise?
5 Who might *stagger* – someone ill or someone angry?
6 What might *crawl* – a small child or a plane?
7 What could *roll* better – stones or boxes?
8 What surface can you *slide* on – ice or sand?

3 WORDPOWER Idioms: Movement

a ▶151 Replace the words in *italics* in each sentence with the correct form of a verb in the box. Listen and check.

plunge   whizz   soar   drift   whirl   crawl

1 a After a clever marketing campaign, the company's profits are *going up*.
  b Temperatures *went down suddenly* to a record low of –35° last night.
2 a I sat looking out of the window, letting my thoughts *go where they wanted*.
  b My mind was *full of thoughts going round in my head* and I simply couldn't decide what to do next.
3 a I'm enjoying my job so much that time seems to be just *going really quickly* past.
  b I hate long-haul flights. Time always seems to *go very slowly* past.

b Match the expressions in **bold** with their definitions.

1 Don't be so scared of going back to university. I'm sure it'll be great. Come on, **take the plunge**.
2 Climbing down the rock surface, I **felt a rush** of adrenaline!
3 If I was offered a job in Japan, I would **jump at the chance**.
4 **I'm on a roll** with my academic work, otherwise I'd be really nervous about my next exam.
5 I know you don't like technology, but I'm sure you'll love this phone if you **give it a whirl**.

☐ get a sudden strong feeling
☐ accept something eagerly
☐ do something you are afraid of
☐ try something for the first time
☐ having a series of successes

c Choose two words or expressions from 3a or 3b and write two sentences but leave a gap for the word/expression. Read out your sentence. Can other students guess what goes in the gap?

↻ REVIEW YOUR PROGRESS

How well did you do in this unit? Write 3, 2, or 1 for each objective.
3 = very well   2 = well   1 = not so well

I CAN ...

describe extreme sensory experiences	☐
talk about plans, intentions and arrangements	☐
give advice	☐
write a report	☐

CAN DO OBJECTIVES

- Emphasise positive and negative experiences
- Describe journeys and landscapes
- Paraphrase and summarise
- Write a travel review

UNIT 3
Travel and adventure

GETTING STARTED

a 🗨 Look at the picture and answer the questions.

1 What's just happened? Where do you think the bus was going? What factors might have led to the situation?

2 Who do you think the people pushing the bus are? How do you think they feel?

3 What's the man on the right doing? Why?

4 What do you think will happen next?

b 🗨 Work in pairs. Use your answers in a to retell the events of the day this photo was taken.

c 🗨 Would you enjoy the type of trip these people are on? Why / Why not?

1 READING and SPEAKING

a 💬 Which of these volunteer jobs looks most interesting to you? Why?

1 working at a children's home in Belize
2 coaching sport to schoolchildren in Ghana
3 rescuing and caring for endangered bears in Cambodia
4 conserving coral reefs in the Caribbean

b 💬 Have you ever done any of the activities in 1a? Where? When? Why? Would you be prepared to use your holiday time to help? Why / Why not?

c Read the two reviews of volunteer experiences. Answer the questions.

1 What are the similarities and differences in the two experiences?
2 What specific negatives does each review mention?

THINKING OF VOLUNTEERING ABROAD?

Here are two inspiring stories from volunteers who joined on-going projects organised by PoD (Personal Overseas Development), an ethical, non-profit volunteer organisation.

Ghana

DEBBIE *Looking after children, Ghana*

There are a few village life truths that everyone forgets to mention. You will sweat profusely, you will get bitten by a million different insects, you will miss home comforts and no doubt feel frustrated by a fair few things. However, despite all this, you will forget all these worries in a heartbeat. No sooner had I woken up each morning than I would see a smiling face and hear a child's giggle that would melt my heart. Whether you are going to Ghana to build a school or to build a child's future your heart will break when it's time to leave because the people become your world. Never have I had such a rewarding and truly enlightening experience. Without a doubt, it will be the same for you.

The day starts with breakfast at 7 am. I worked in the kindergarten so it was up to class for 8:30 where I worked till lunchtime. Afternoons could be anything from extra classes, arts and crafts, sports coaching or even digging on the building site. Evenings were for chilling around the fire or having yam parties with the neighbours or playing silly games with the other volunteers. Normally we were all so tired from the long day that we were all fast asleep by 9 pm.

It's difficult to adjust to the intense heat and it really does sap a lot of your energy. It's also difficult when you want to do as much as possible to help but find yourself restricted by your own physical shortcomings.

The most rewarding part for me was the relationships that I built; there is no better feeling in the world than having a child run to you in the morning with pure happiness on their faces at seeing you.

LINDA AND MALCOLM
Working at a children's home, Belize

My husband and I spent two weeks at the children's home in Belize and we both thoroughly enjoyed every minute of it. The experience of living with these warm, friendly people was something we will always remember and we would certainly like to return in a couple of years. We were not really prepared for the intensity of the heat even though we had holidayed in the Caribbean previously.

The children were a joy and such characters, and we created some very special bonds. There was a lot of maintenance work to do and Malcolm, who was able to carry out more manual work, was at an advantage. We also did a lot of gardening and helping in the kitchen (my favourite). Time off was when you wanted it and with Belize being such a beautiful place with plenty of history and places to explore, you really need to make the most of it and see all you can.

Volunteering was something I have always wanted to do. We made some lovely friends and worked out of our comfort zone quite often, which for me made the experience even more special. At no time did we regret the decision to go there.

We loved being with the children, giving them little treats and helping make their environment better. We made them a special meal of burgers and chips, and the enjoyment on their faces made it so worthwhile. Little do children back home realise how the food they take for granted is a genuine treat for children here.

d 🗩 Which review would you find more helpful if you were a prospective volunteer? Why?

e Language in context *Unusual experiences*

1 Match 1–8 with a–h to make an expression used in the reviews. Check new expressions in a dictionary.

1 ☐ miss home	a	your energy
2 ☐ melt your	b	special bonds
3 ☐ have a rewarding	c	comforts
4 ☐ sap a lot of	d	life skills
5 ☐ create some very	e	heart
6 ☐ make the	f	and enlightening experience
7 ☐ take for	g	granted
8 ☐ acquire	h	most of it

2 Complete these expressions with the correct preposition. Check your answers in the reviews.

1 _____ a heartbeat
2 _____ of your comfort zone
3 a feeling _____ self-worth and satisfaction

2 GRAMMAR Inversion

a Notice the phrases in **bold** in the sentences below. Why did the writers use these phrases?

☐ for emphasis   ☐ to soften

1 **No sooner had I woken up** each morning than I would see a smiling face and hear a child's giggle that would melt my heart.
2 **Never have I had such** a rewarding and truly enlightening experience.
3 **At no time did we regret** the decision to go there.
4 **Little do children back home realise** how the food they take for granted is a genuine treat for children here.

Belize

One of the great things about volunteering is that you are acquiring life skills and experiences you will get nowhere else. A volunteer does not do the work just to help others, but for themselves too, to get a feeling of self-worth and self-satisfaction, to learn and experience the way other people live and how other cultures work, and to be part of this.

b Look at the phrases in **bold** in 2a and complete the rule.

For emphasis, the writers use a [1]*positive / negative* adverbial and [2]*statement / question* word order: adverbial + auxiliary verb + subject + verb

c Rewrite the sentences in 2a without an inverted word order.

d ▶ Now go to Grammar Focus 3A on p.142

3 SPEAKING and WRITING

a ⏵**1.53** Listen to the examples. Who or what do you think each person is talking about?

1 **Not only are they the nicest people in the world**, they're the best cooks, too.
2 **Only when we got to the beach** did it all become worthwhile.
3 **Not until the end of the holiday** did we realise how attached we had become to them.
4 **Never before** have I seen such enthusiasm and excitement.
5 **Not in a million years** would I have imagined building something from scratch.

b ⏵**1.53 Pronunciation** Listen to the examples in 3a again. Does the tone of the phrases in **bold** … ?

• rise then fall ⤴   • fall then rise ⤵

c 🗩 Tell a partner about the highlights of a travel experience. Use inversion after some of the adverbials in the box. Make sure you use the correct tone.

rarely …   no sooner …   at no time …
not in a million years …   only after …
only when …   not until …

• first impressions of the journey/place
• new experiences you had and your reaction
• a moment when you realised something
• something unique about the experience

I was staying with a host family. No sooner had I arrived than everybody rushed to meet me.

I went to India in January. Not in a million years did I think vegetarian food could taste so good.

d Write a paragraph for a blog about your experience. Use two sentences with inversion.

only by chance …   little …   hardly …
seldom …   never before …

Little did I know how eventful this holiday was going to be.

Never before had I experienced such heavy rain.

4 LISTENING

a 🗩 Imagine you and your friends wanted to start a volunteer project to build a school in a developing country. What problems could there be?

b ▶1.54 Listen to Daniela Papi talking about her experience in Cambodia. Does she mention any of your ideas in 4a?

c ▶1.54 Listen again. Summarise what Daniela says about these topics.

1 her initial plans for volunteer work in Cambodia
2 problems with this plan
3 her six years in Cambodia
4 her beliefs after ten years' volunteer work
5 the problems with good intentions and praise

Daniela Papi

d 🗩 What specific criticisms do you think Daniela will go on to make in her speech? What questions would you like to ask her about this kind of work?

5 VOCABULARY Wealth and poverty

a Do the words and phrases in **bold** below relate to wealth or poverty? Make two lists. Which word/phrase applies to people with any level of income?

1 Many farmers *are facing real economic* **hardship** after the drought killed all their crops.
2 There's no money to help **impoverished** *communities* build basic facilities like schools and medical centres.
3 In **affluent** *suburbs* like this one, house prices are extremely high.
4 There's a direct relationship between a good education system and the *economic* **prosperity** of a country.
5 Even though I got a pay rise last year, I still *find it difficult to* **make ends meet**.
6 My grandparents used to be *relatively* **well off**, but they lost all their money in bad investments.
7 He lives with his parents and pays no bills, so he has a lot of **disposable income**.
8 In the most **deprived** *areas* of the city, unemployment stands at around 50% and social problems are rife.
9 We can't go on using our credit cards all the time. We have to *learn to* **live within our means**.
10 They lost everything they had in the flood and were *left* **destitute**.

b Answer these questions about the words and phrases in **bold** in 5a.

1 Which noun has the opposite meaning of *hardship*?
2 Compare the adjectives *impoverished, deprived* and *destitute*. Which one is more severe than the other two?
3 Compare *affluent* and *well-off*. Which one are we more likely to use when we speak?
4 Compare *make ends meet* and *live within our means*. Which expression suggests more of a struggle?
5 Which of these noun phrases has a similar meaning to *disposable income*?
a living expenses   b spending money

c ▶1.55 **Pronunciation** Listen to the sentences in 5a and underline the stressed syllables in the words and phrases in **bold**.

d 🗩 Look at the phrases in *italics* in 5a. Think of an example of each from your own knowledge/ experience. Compare your ideas with a partner.

> People here faced economic hardship during the recession.

6 SPEAKING

a Think of someone you know well. Choose a suitable volunteer project for them, or think of another.

1 saving cheetahs from extinction in South Africa
2 conserving the Amazon rainforest in Peru
3 helping build schools in Ghana
4 coaching sport to schoolchildren in Nepal

b What could you say to the volunteer about ... ?

• practical preparation *learn local customs*
• psychological preparation
• positive impact of volunteers
• negative impact of volunteers
• likely personal development and life skills

c 🗩 Tell a partner about the person you chose in 6a and what you would say to them about volunteering.

3B I was expecting it to be tough

Learn to describe journeys and landscapes
G Future in the past; Narrative tenses
V Landscape features

1 READING and GRAMMAR
Future in the past

a 💬 Look at the journey on the map. What do you think it would be like? Think about:

- what you'd expect to see
- skills needed
- people you might meet
- possible risks.

b Read what Will Millard says about his journey. Answer the questions.

1 Why does Will describe the forest as a *one-off environment*?
2 Why did Will take the journey? How did he travel? Why do you think he chose to travel that way?
3 What would you look forward to on a journey like this? What wouldn't you look forward to?

c Look at the underlined event in the article. Complete each sentence below with a phrase from the box. There is one phrase you do not need to use.

> in the future   in progress   in the past

When Will arrived in Sierra Leone, this event was _____.
When Will wrote the article, this event was _____.

d Underline six more examples of the future in the past in the article. What four verb forms does Will use?

e Think of other things that Will might have considered before his trip. Write sentences using the future in the past.

I knew that it was going to be difficult.
I was hoping to see some elephants.

f 💬 What do you think will make Will's journey difficult and dangerous?

2 VOCABULARY Landscape features

a How are the highlighted words in the article different in meaning? Use a dictionary to help you.

b Complete the collocations below with the words and phrases in the box. Check your answers in the article.

> a tropical   a remote   the heart of the   dense   an untouched

1 _____ rainforest capital jungle	3 _____ fog vegetation undergrowth	5 _____ area forest village
2 _____ rainforest storm island	4 _____ wilderness forest plate of food	

c ▶ Now go to Vocabulary Focus 3B on p.160

Survival on the Mano river

My dream journey became a reality when I received a grant from the Royal Geographical Society to explore the Moro and Mano rivers. The grant was intended to cover expenses, radio training and kit to record my expedition for BBC Radio 4. I was planning to start at the top of the Gola Forest and make the first descent of the river border of Sierra Leone and Liberia, right through a chunk of Africa's most threatened jungle environment – one of the last untouched wildernesses of the Upper Guinean forest belt. More than a quarter of Africa's total mammal species are found in the belt, with bizarre creatures such as the pygmy hippopotamus found nowhere else on Earth. The need to protect what still remains of this one-off environment could not be more critical.

In Sierra Leone the Gola forest is already designated a national park, but I wanted to find out what life in the heart of a tropical rainforest was really like, so I was going to paddle down these rivers, hopefully as far as the sea. I knew that, although I would be in radio contact, I would be on my own in one of the most remote forests in West Africa, and I would be separated from the outside world by dense tropical vegetation. I was expecting it to be tough but in fact it was to become one of the most difficult and dangerous journeys I have ever made.

35

3 LISTENING

a ▶ 1.57 You are going to hear Will Millard describing his journey. Listen to five sounds from the recording. What do you think each sound is?

b ▶ 1.58 Now listen to the whole recording and check your ideas in 3a.

c ▶ 1.58 Look at pictures 1–5 below of the things from Will's trip down the river. Listen again and summarise what he says about each one.

> **Learning Tip**
>
> When listening, there may be words which you don't know. You can either ignore them or guess roughly what they mean from the context.
> *Just at the end of the day there was quite a large* **cataract** *and I didn't really fancy taking it on till tomorrow …*
> He's rafting on a jungle river so we can guess that a *cataract* is some feature of this environment which is difficult to get past.

d Read the sentences below from the listening. Underline examples of informal conversational style which Will Millard uses.

1 Thanks, mate.
2 Managed to just get my camp sorted.
3 I didn't really fancy taking it on till tomorrow.
4 I guess I'll find out.
5 If I lose the raft, I'm finished.

How could you express the sentences in a more neutral style?

e ▶ 1.59 **Pronunciation** Listen again to part of what Will says. Notice how he pronounces the words in **bold**. Practise saying the phrases a–c.

a … **hit** this big rock …
b **Just** managed to **get** control of it again …
c it's **got** my shelter on it …

f 💬 What would/wouldn't you have enjoyed from this part of Will's trip?

1 dragonflies
2 a fish eagle and a catfish
3 a hammock
4 rapids

4 READING

a 💬 You are going to read about how Will got malaria while he was still in the rainforest. Before you read, discuss these questions.

1 Why would this be particularly dangerous?
2 What do you think his symptoms were?
3 What would he need to do in order to survive?

b Read the text. Check your answers in 4a.

c Read the text again and answer the questions.

1 Why is rafting down rivers a good way to see wildlife?
2 How did he know there were chimpanzees nearby? How close did he get to seeing them?
3 What was he planning to do when he got to the coast?
4 What made him take his symptoms seriously?
5 He says he *survived thanks to a mix of luck, exceptional local support and money.* What events and facts do you think Will is referring to in this sentence?
6 What does the last sentence tell us about Africa?

I love rafting in rainforests …

This near silent method of travel gives you an unencumbered and discreet approach, perfect for radio, but rivers are also among the best possible places to spot wildlife returning from the forest depths to feed, drink and socialise. This section of the Upper Guinean was one of the finest forests I had ever experienced. It was a storybook jungle, ¹teeming with life.

For a couple of days I had been hearing primates everywhere – in the banksides, up the trees, behind distant ridges, but never quite close enough to see. At dawn I'd hear the piercing screaming call of a chimp, but it was impossibly far away, the last hour of light would often bring a flash of fur, a scuffle in the bushes, a warning shriek but nothing more.

After ten days on the river I believed I was through the worst and started to think about the finish line – where the river enters the Atlantic – and all the fried and liquid-based treats that would be waiting for me at the nearest village.

Then I started to get sick. I tried to ²shrug it off with ibuprofen and fluid, putting it down to the exertion of paddling daily in the 40°C heat. But as my headache developed into a fever I began to ³fret, not least because among the last words of warning given to me before heading solo into the bush was the tale of a European woman who had complained of flu-like symptoms, not gone directly to hospital, and died of an undiagnosed haemorrhagic fever 48 hours later. I desperately needed to make contact with someone on the Sierra Leone bank and find my way to the road, the hospital and proper treatment.

In the morning I started to paddle out. My headache had worsened to the point that I could barely keep my eyes open in daylight and the pain in my joints was bordering on the spectacular. My bones felt like

d 💬 Discuss the questions.

1 How well do you think Will coped with the experience? Would you have coped as well as he did?
2 Do think what he did was worthwhile? Why / Why not?

e Language in context *Descriptive verbs*

Match the highlighted words and phrases in the text with the meanings below.

a ☐ rub against a hard surface (in order to make a powder)
b ☐ contain large numbers of a living creature
c ☐ pull something heavy
d ☐ physically support
e ☐ bend down with knees bent
f ☐ pull off, like a skin
g ☐ treat something worrying as if it is not important
h ☐ worry (v.)
i ☐ call someone to be present

they were ⁴grinding to dust with every movement. I had GPS marks for all of the villages along the river bar one – Tolo, which had been written on my map in felt tip by one of the Gola Rainforest National Park researchers. It was by far the closest settlement, only a three hour paddle downstream. The river was much wider and calmer. I was dropping out of the heavy forest and knew I just had to hang on. [...]

At midday a gap in the forest revealed a lone figure – a woman, ⁵crouched down washing her clothes. I was drifting by this point, almost incapable of going through the motions of the strokes. I remember her shouting, then multiple hands on me as I was ⁶peeled from my raft. I was ⁷propped up on a tree-stump stool against a mud-brick house. The chief was ⁸summoned. I might have been the first Westerner to arrive in the village in such a condition but this place was no stranger to what to do with people carrying my symptoms. My gear was divided up and I was ⁹hauled through the forest to the nearest village with a motorbike, then on to the roadside and eventually to hospital.

I survived thanks to a mix of luck, exceptional local support and money. An estimated half a million African people will not be so fortunate this year.

5 a raft

5 GRAMMAR Narrative tenses

a 💬 Read sentences 1–7. What is each verb form in **bold**? Why is that particular verb form used?

☐ past simple   ☐ past continuous
☐ past perfect simple ☐ past perfect continuous
☐ past simple passive ☐ past perfect passive
☐ *would* + infinitive

1 For a couple of days, I **had been hearing** primates everywhere …
2 At dawn I**'d hear** the piercing screaming call of a chimp …
3 My headache **had worsened** to the point that I could barely keep my eyes open …
4 … and the pain in my joints **was bordering on** the spectacular.
5 … Tolo, which **had been written** on my map in felt tip …
6 My gear was divided up and I **was hauled** through the forest to the nearest village with a motorbike …
7 I **survived** thanks to a mix of luck, exceptional local support and money.

b ▶ Now go to Grammar Focus 3B on p.143

c How would using a different tense change the meaning in these examples?

1 For a couple of days, I **had heard / had been hearing** primates everywhere.
2 At dawn, I **heard / 'd hear** the piercing screaming call of a chimp.
3 The chief **was / was being** summoned.

6 WRITING and SPEAKING

a Look at the first line of each paragraph in Will's article and answer the questions.

1 How do all the paragraphs (except two) start?
2 Which paragraphs start differently? What are the purposes of these paragraphs?

b Think about an adventurous trip you have been on, or one you have seen in a film / on TV, or read about. Here are some ideas.

• a time you visited a wild or remote place
• a time you fell ill far from home
• a time you travelled by an unusual form of transport
• a time you were alone in an unfamiliar place

c Write an article about the trip. Use narrative tenses and descriptive vocabulary. Describe:

1 plans you made
2 what you expected when you started the trip
3 when the main events happened and what happened
4 how you felt about it at the time and afterwards, and why.

I had been looking forward to going to Australia for months …
Last summer, I was staying with friends in Paris …

d 💬 Work in pairs. Practise telling your story.

e 💬 Work in groups. Tell your story to the others and answer any questions.

3C Everyday English
To cut a long story short

1 LISTENING

a 💬 Have you ever seen or heard a live broadcast that went wrong? What happened?

b 💬 Answer these questions.

1 What's happening in picture a?
2 What questions do you think Oscar will ask Max during the interview?

c ▶2.2 Watch or listen to Part 1 and check your answers in 1b2.

d ▶2.2 Watch or listen to Part 1 again and choose one true ending for each sentence.

1 The inhabitants of the remote planet in Max's book are aliens who …
   a look very different from humans.
   b look like humans but have a different culture.
   c want to explore other planets.
2 Oscar suggests that Max's ideas might come from …
   a his experiences while travelling.
   b another science fiction novelist.
   c experiences in his childhood.
3 Oscar suggests that Max's next book …
   a will be published in the near future.
   b will be a sequel to *Solar Wind*.
   c will depend on the success of his first book.

e 💬 Discuss the questions.

1 How do you think Oscar and Max feel about the success of the interview? Why?
2 Have you ever been interviewed for any reason? How did you feel … ?
   • before the interview • afterwards

2 PRONUNCIATION
Consonant groups across two words

a ▶2.3 Listen to the words and phrases in the box. Underline the letters which correspond to the consonant groups given afterwards. Notice that consonant groups can occur within a word or across two words.

---

explorers /kspl/   space travel /str/   aliens look /nzl/
long story /ŋst/   bestseller /sts/

---

b ▶2.4 Match phrases 1–7 with consonant groups across two words a–g below. Listen and check your answers. Practise saying the phrases.

1 ☐ deep space   a /kspl/
2 ☐ dense jungle   b /lθkr/
3 ☐ Max Redwood   c /ksr/
4 ☐ science fiction   d /nsf/
5 ☐ six planets   e /nsdʒ/
6 ☐ tourism statistics   f /psp/
7 ☐ wealth creation   g /zmst/

c ▶2.5 Listen to the pronunciation of the phrases in groups 1 and 2. In which group can you hear the letters in **bold** clearly?

1 /t/ or /d/ before a	2 /t/ or /d/ before a
a Westga**t**e Street	Westga**t**e Avenue
b travelle**d** much	travelle**d** a lot
c remo**t**e planet	remo**t**e area
d differen**t** culture	differen**t** abilities
e Solar Win**d** 2	Solar Win**d** 8
f top secre**t** classified	top secre**t** information

d Complete the name of each group in the table in 2c with *vowel* or *consonant*.

e 💬 Practise saying the phrases in the table in 2c.

b

4 USEFUL LANGUAGE Paraphrasing and summarising

a Read the excerpts from Parts 1 and 2. Match the expressions in **bold** with their uses below.

1 *What happens next? **Or, to put it another way**, when will* Solar Wind 2 *be published?*

2 ***All things considered**, I think my first and last radio interview … was a complete and utter embarrassment.*

☐ paraphrase = express the same idea in new words
☐ summarise = express only the main point(s)

b ⏯2.8 Complete the extracts from Parts 1 and 2 below with the expressions in the box. Listen and check.

---
in other words   in a nutshell   that is to say
to cut a long story short   what I meant by that was
---

1 And basically, _____, a group of explorers are visiting a remote planet …
2 … populated by people, _____, aliens!
3 I was planning a trip across Asia but, well, _____, I had to cancel it
4 So _____, it all just came from your imagination, then?
5 _____, you're not allowed to give any dates yet?

c Add the expressions from 4a and b to the correct group below.

Paraphrasing	Summarising

d Complete the sentences with a suitable expression for summarising and paraphrasing and your own idea.

1 We had some ups and down throughout the trip. All …
2 People there spend a lot of time visiting aunts, uncles, cousins, that is …
3 I had loads of problems on the trip, but to …
4 I'm sorry, I didn't express myself very clearly. What …
5 The novel is quite long and complicated, but in …

3 LISTENING

a 💬 Look at picture b and answer the questions.

1 What do you think Emma thinks of Max's radio interview?
2 What do you think she will say to Max about it?

b ⏯2.6 Watch or listen to Part 2. How is Emma dishonest?

c ⏯2.6 Complete the sentences with the words you heard. Watch or listen to Part 2 again and check.

1 I'm sure it wasn't that _____.
2 I'll never be able to show my _____ again!
3 I'll put _____ on.

d Language in context *Exaggerating*

1 ⏯2.7 Complete Max's exaggerations with the words in the box. Listen and check.

---
outright   complete and utter   totally   blithering
---

1 It was an _____ disaster!
2 I came across as a _____ idiot!
3 A _____ embarrassment!
4 My career's _____ ruined!

2 💬 Why do you think Max exaggerated about his interview? In what situations do you think people choose to exaggerate? Why?

e 💬 Discuss the questions.

1 Do you think it's better to be kind or to be honest when people ask your opinion?
2 Have you ever … ?
   • told someone a white lie to avoid hurting their feelings
   • felt someone has told you a white lie to avoid hurting your feelings

5 SPEAKING

▶ **Communication 3C** Work in pairs. Go to p.129

Unit Progress Test

CHECK YOUR PROGRESS

You can now do the Unit Progress Test.

1 SPEAKING

a 💬 What is the most rewarding place you've been to as a tourist, and what is the most disappointing? Why?

b 💬 Read the description of Prague from a tourist website. How much does it appeal to you as a tourist destination?

◁ ▷ ⌂ ⊕   ↻ ⤓

Prague, Czech Republic
… *Culture, magic and romance*

to do	to eat	to see	to go

It's no wonder that Prague is on everyone's list of must-see places in Europe and attracts four million visitors every year. Prague has everything you'd expect of a European city …

🚶   a historic city centre so compact you can walk round it in a couple of hours, though you'll want to stay much, much longer

🏰   a romantic castle built in the 9th century, with great views across the city

⛲   splendid examples of Baroque and Renaissance architecture and scores of fountains, squares and parks

🌉   the magnificent Charles Bridge, spanning the River Vltava which flows through the city

🍽️   delicious local food and drink at reasonable prices

🌙   a diverse nightlife, from fashionable clubs to sophisticated restaurants to atmospheric cafés

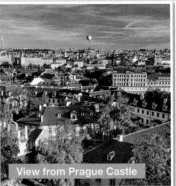
View from Prague Castle

Old Town

2 LISTENING

a ▶️ **2.9** Listen to Tony and Lola talking about Prague and answer the questions.

1 What do they say about the places in the photos?
2 What similar points do they make?
3 Do you think that Tony and Lola would both go back to Prague? Why / Why not?

b ▶️ **2.9** Tony and Lola use descriptive phrases to talk about the city. Match the words in boxes A and B. Then listen again and check.

A		B	
well-	romantic	streets	atmosphere
skilfully	cobbled	of tourists	view
hordes	breathtaking	roofs	with people
teeming	tiled	restored	preserved

c 💬 Discuss the questions. Consider the issues from the point of view of both residents and tourists.

1 What are the good and bad effects that tourism can have on a city like Prague?
2 Do you think popular tourist cities should try to limit tourists or charge them to see the city?

The Charles Bridge

3 READING

Read the traveller's review. What further information (beyond the descriptions in the listening) does it include about … ?

- Old Town
- Charles Bridge
- the castle

Use your answers in 2a and/or the audioscript on p.179 to help you. Underline the information in the review.

4 WRITING SKILLS
Descriptive language; Writing briefly

a Write the highlighted words and phrases in the review in two lists:

Positive	Negative
hospitable	pretty basic

> **Writing Tip**
>
> When writing a description, try to use words which carry a more precise or an extra meaning. So instead of *There were stalls on the bridge*:
> - *The bridge was **lined with** stalls.* (extra meaning: they were in lines along the sides)
> - *The bridge was **crowded with** stalls.* (extra meaning: there were too many, so there wasn't enough space)
>
> You can also convey your attitude by using words with a positive or a negative meaning. So instead of *The streets were busy*:
> - *The streets were **lively**.* (= there were lots of people – it was good)
> - *The streets were **overcrowded**.* (= there were lots of people – it was bad)

b Which highlighted words or phrases could replace the words in *italics* below?

1 The food was *not too expensive*.
2 The centre is *full of tourists*.
3 Walking along the streets was *very difficult*.
4 There are *good opportunities to take photos*.
5 The restaurant had *traditional food from the country*.
6 It's *an attraction you definitely should see*.
7 The castle *looks rather ordinary*.
8 The owners *were very helpful*.

c In the review, the writer sometimes omits certain words. What words could you add to these examples to make complete sentences?

1 Lots of music and very lively and laid-back.
2 Took hundreds of photos.
3 Then back to the hotel for a quick shower.

d Look at the third paragraph of the review and find three more examples of words which are omitted. What is the effect of leaving out words in this way?

1 It seems more formal.
2 It seems less formal and more like conversation.

e ▶ Now go to Writing Focus 3D on p.170

Prague get-away weekend
★ ★ ★ ★ ★

We stayed at the Slavka Hotel – a small hotel in a residential area. It was pretty basic but the owners were very hospitable and really put themselves out for us. Our large double room was comfortable and spotlessly clean. To our surprise, it cost just $90.00 per night, including a delicious breakfast with fresh fruit, excellent coffee and freshly baked rolls.

We spent most of the day wandering around Old Town – the city centre. The architecture is a stunning and mind-boggling mixture of styles from every period – Gothic, Baroque, Renaissance, Art Nouveau – all absolutely immaculate, all beautifully restored. Only one problem – it was quite overrun with tourists (like us!), and especially the narrower streets were a bit of a nightmare to get through. We found a few nice little squares where there weren't so many people and we could sit and admire the buildings.

We wrapped up our day in the city with a walk across Charles Bridge, followed by a visit to the castle. The bridge is about 800 metres long, pedestrian only, and lined with impressive statues – a must-see attraction if you visit Prague. Lots of music and very lively and laid-back, but a bit crowded with stalls selling souvenirs. Great photo ops from the bridge overlooking the river and city.

On the other side of the river you can wander up tiny winding lanes to the castle. I loved this part of the city – still has such an untouched romantic atmosphere. You can imagine you're back in the Middle Ages. The castle itself isn't much to look at, as although it dates from the 9th century, it's been restored so it doesn't even look particularly old. But the views across the city and the river are absolutely breathtaking. Took hundreds of photos.

Then back to the hotel for a quick shower and something to eat. Near the hotel there was a restaurant with authentic cuisine, very reasonably priced. A much better bet than the overpriced restaurants in the tourist areas of town.

5 WRITING

a Make a list of tourist attractions in the town and area where you are now. Include:

- attractions you think are worth visiting
- attractions you think are less worthwhile.

b Imagine you spent a day here as a tourist. Choose two or three attractions in the list and write a review. Include comments on your accommodation and somewhere you ate too.

c Work with a partner. Look at what you both wrote and see how you could improve it by:

- using adjectives and phrases with a stronger positive or negative meaning
- making some sentences shorter by omitting words.

d Read your review to the class. Which reviews do most people agree with?

UNIT 3
Review and extension

1 GRAMMAR

a Reorder the words to make sentences.

1 get / plane / was / about / a / John / to / on
2 you / home / did / her / at / rarely / very / see
3 was / that / thought / faint / Amelia / to / she / going
4 account / anyone / told / on / no / be / must
5 next / set / we / early / day / to / were / leave / the
6 on / go / like / would / I / a / no / trip / way / that

b Cross out the verb form which is NOT correct.

1 Kevin *was leaving* / *was about to leave* / ~~would leave~~ on a business trip when he got the call.
2 Originally we *planned to take* / *had been going to take* / *would be taking* the train.
3 As soon as we *arrived* / *had arrived* / *had been arriving*, we checked in.
4 Our supplies *had ended* / *had been ending* / *ended* and we had to find more from somewhere.
5 Our room was terrible and I *had been complaining* / *might complain* / *complained* to the manager.
6 Travel *was* / *would be* / *was to be* cheaper in those days.

2 VOCABULARY

a Complete the sentences with the words in the box.

affluent   deprived   destitute   disposable
hardship   means   prosperity   well-off

1 This neighbourhood is quite _____ so prices are high.
2 I don't really have much _____ income.
3 You can tell it's a _____ area by the crime rate.
4 The floods left many poorer residents _____.
5 I wouldn't say I'm super-rich but I am _____.
6 A recession had started and the years of _____ were over.
7 It is no _____ to live without a car in a big city.
8 We manage to live within our _____ somehow.

b Complete the missing words.

1 Many species live only in the h_____t of the rainforest.
2 Anything might be hiding in the dense v_____n!
3 This is truly an u_____d wilderness.
4 The r_____d coastline is popular with walkers.
5 Once a year the rains bring the a_____d desert to life.
6 Tourists come for the p_____e beaches and gentle sea.
7 They say there are alligators in the s_____p.

3 WORDPOWER Idioms: Landscapes

a Match the expressions in **bold** with definitions a–g.

1 A **I'm** absolutely **swamped** this week.
  B Poor you. Let me know if there's anything I can do.
2 A We've had loads of customers this week.
  B It's great, I know. But we're not **out of the woods** yet.
3 A What are you going to say to him?
  B I don't know. I'll go over and **get the lie of the land** first.
4 A How are you coping with the move and the new job?
  B It's **an uphill struggle** but I'm just about managing!
5 A It seems like when we talk we're always **getting bogged down with** tiny details.
  B So you're not making any progress?
6 A I've had cake every afternoon this week!
  B Be careful! It's **a slippery slope** once you start.
7 A I paid £100 off our credit card last month.
  B That's just **a drop in the ocean** though, isn't it?

a ☐ a small amount compared to the amount required
b ☐ a series of events that become out of control and create worse problems
c ☐ free from problems/danger
d ☐ wait until you have all the information about a situation
e ☐ get stuck on a particular point and be unable to make progress
f ☐ be overwhelmed by too much work
g ☐ when making progress is very difficult

b ▶ 2.10 Complete the sentences with an idiom from 3a. Listen and check.

1 I made a small donation, but I know it's just _____.
2 She clearly wants to _____ before she makes any big decisions.
3 Regaining popular opinion is going to be _____ for the party.
4 We've just had some great news from the hospital: Sam's _____.
5 I told her borrowing was _____. She's going to have to get a second job.
6 If you can't answer a question, don't _____ it, just move on to the next one.
7 Ever since they put the ad out, they've been completely _____ with phone calls.

c 💬 What situation do you think each person in 3b is talking about?

🔄 REVIEW YOUR PROGRESS

How well did you do in this unit? Write 3, 2, or 1 for each objective.
3 = very well   2 = well   1 = not so well

I CAN ...

emphasise positive and negative experiences	☐
describe journeys and landscapes	☐
paraphrase and summarise	☐
write a travel review	☐

CAN DO OBJECTIVES

- Talk about using instinct and reason
- Talk about memories and remembering
- Use tact in formal discussions
- Write a profile article

UNIT 4
Consciousness

GETTING STARTED

a 💬 Look at the picture and answer the questions.

1 What do you think the device does?
2 Who is the man? What do you think he's saying?
3 How do you think the woman feels?

b 💬 The woman is tasting food by looking at it, using an experimental virtual reality helmet. Discuss the questions.

1 Would you like to try it? If so, what foods would you try it with? If not, why not?
2 What do you think the benefits of this technology could be in the wider world?
3 What technology have you experienced which changes how you perceive things?

Learn to talk about using instinct and reason
- **G** Noun phrases
- **V** Instinct and reason

1 SPEAKING

a 💬 What are your five senses? What do you think is meant by a 'sixth sense'? Do you think you have one?

b 💬 Do the quiz with a partner and compare your answers. If you don't agree with answer A or B, say what you would do.

c ▶ Communication 4A Count up how many As and how many Bs you chose. Check your results on p.137

2 VOCABULARY Instinct and reason

a Look at these people's statements. Would they be As or Bs according to the quiz?

1 I'm a very **rational** thinker.
2 **On impulse**, I married someone I'd only just met.
3 I think I know **subconsciously** when people are lying to me.
4 I think it's important to **weigh up** the advantages and disadvantages before you take action.

b Replace each expression in **bold** in 2a with a word or phrase from the box. Is the meaning in each exactly the same?

| deep down | consider | objective | on a whim |

c Now go to Vocabulary Focus 4A on p.161

Do you have A SIXTH SENSE?

How much do you rely on your intuition? Do the quiz and choose A or B. Don't think too long about it ... follow your gut!

1 **You find yourself a new flat. You like it because ...**
   A it's got a positive atmosphere and feels like a nice place to be in.
   B the furniture is in good condition and it has everything you need.

2 **You meet a new colleague and have a bad feeling about them. You ...**
   A decide not to trust them – your first impressions are usually accurate.
   B ignore the feeling. You can't tell what people are like from first impressions.

3 **The phone rings at home from the next room, and you aren't expecting a call. You ...**
   A have a strong feeling about who's calling.
   B have no idea who's calling until you get to the phone.

4 **A close friend, who has been unusually quiet, says they need to talk to you.**
   A You probably won't be surprised by what they say – you half know already.
   B You have no idea what to expect – it could be anything.

5 **When do the best ideas come to you?**
   A when you're relaxing or during the night while you're asleep
   B after thinking long and hard about them

6 **You wake up from a strange dream. You think ...**
   A 'This dream is telling me something – I must remember it.'
   B 'What a silly dream!' and go about your day.

7 **A new opportunity arises, but it's a major change. Your family and friends advise against it.**
   A You go for what you feel is right, in spite of their advice.
   B You drop the idea – they can see the situation more objectively than you.

8 **Are you someone who experiences an unusual number of coincidences?**
   A Yes, although you don't believe they are simply 'coincidences'.
   B No, and neither does anyone else – coincidences are purely chance events.

3 READING

a 🗨 Read the first part of an article about gut instincts and talk about these questions.

1 What is the author going to give readers advice about?
2 What are the roles of the left and right sides of the brain, according to researchers?
3 What does the writer suggest is a good way to make decisions?

b The article gives five pieces of advice (1–5). Match the headings (a–e) to the correct advice.

a I'm not sure about you.
b This is the one I've been waiting for!
c I've done this a million times before.
d I should try to help.
e I'm in pain.

c Look at the underlined parts of the article. Think of one possible example of what the writer means in each case.

d 🗨 Talk about these questions.

1 Do you agree with the five pieces of advice in the article? Are there any you disagree with? Why?
2 Can you think of situations where it might be better not to follow your gut instincts?

4 GRAMMAR Noun phrases

a Match the noun phrases (1–6) from the article with their type (a–f).

1 ☐ a funny feeling in your stomach
2 ☐ that narrow parking space
3 ☐ humanity's oldest survival mechanisms
4 ☐ an irresistible urge to ask
5 ☐ gut feelings
6 ☐ commonly reported indicators

a noun + noun
b noun + 's + superlative + compound noun
c article + adjective + noun + preposition + possessive + noun
d determiner + adjective + compound noun
e adverb + adjective + noun
f article + adjective + noun + to + infinitive

b Improve these noun phrases using the patterns in brackets.

1 a meeting which happens by chance (article + noun + noun)
2 the dreams of my friend who is close (possessive + adjective + noun + 's + noun)
3 a day which you will remember (article + noun + to + infinitive)
4 a dream which is so vivid that it disturbs you (article + adverb + adjective + noun)
5 thoughts which are dark and secret (adjective + adjective + noun)
6 the capacity of humans to imagine things (article + adjective + noun + for + noun)

c ▶ Now go to Grammar Focus 4A on p.144

Learn to
TRUST YOUR GUT!

You have an irresistible urge to ask a complete stranger to go for a coffee. You decide on a whim to buy a property you've never visited. You feel an inexplicable certainty that you should not get on that plane.

Following your gut feelings could either be the best thing you ever did, or end in disaster. On the other hand, ignoring these instincts could have exactly the same outcomes. How can we know when to trust our intuition and when to let our heads rule?

Psychiatrists assert that the home of intuition is in the right hemisphere of the brain. Whilst the conscious left brain edits the world into a logical and coherent whole, the right brain picks up the big picture and reacts spontaneously. Too often the left brain dismisses the urges of the right as irrational, whilst we remain blissfully ignorant of the process.

In order to use intuition more effectively, we can tune into the physical symptoms that let us know it is operating. Clammy palms, a tingle up the spine or a funny feeling in your stomach are all commonly reported indicators that the intuitive right brain is in action. When you notice this feeling, take the time to evaluate it and give yourself a choice.

And to help you on your way, here are five instances where the gut is almost always right.

1 _____

It seems so much like common sense that it could be the left brain talking. When you hear that little voice in your head nagging you to go for a check-up, do yourself a favour and go. If you don't, you could be letting yourself in for trouble down the road.

2 _____

First impressions are not just about hair and shoes. Tune in to that all-important feeling you get when you meet a new person and you are using one of humanity's oldest survival mechanisms. Our ancestors knew instinctively who to trust and who not to – and so do you. Crossing the street to avoid a stranger is not going to hurt anyone's feelings and it may just keep you safe.

3 _____

Use your instinct to tell you when those around you are in need of your support. Our urge to help others is often outbid by other priorities like getting somewhere on time or not wanting to appear nosy. But these instincts are just as much survival mechanisms as our fears, and who knows when you may need a hand yourself one day?

4 _____

Trust your gut to get you through the most stressful of occasions. When you're under pressure, it's easy to forget how to do even things you're an expert at. So use intuition to guide you into that narrow parking space, or to cook that special meal. Under stress it's way more reliable than your conscious brain.

5 _____

Never discount your gut instincts in the lead-up to a decision that could affect the course of your future life. These are the times to really use your whole brain. If your right brain says, 'Yes! Yes! Yes!', there's a good chance that's the decision you'll be happiest with in the long run.

5 LISTENING

a 💬 You will hear a discussion about the way doctors diagnose patients. How much do you think doctors rely on their gut instincts?

b ▶️2.14 Listen to the discussion. What do the speakers agree on? Choose 1, 2 or 3.

1 Doctors rely too much on their gut instincts and this can be a problem.
2 Unfortunately, doctors don't pay attention to their gut instincts.
3 Doctors often rely on their gut instincts and this is useful.

c ▶️2.14 Listen again and choose the best answer in *italics*.

1 When we have inner doubts, they are *often* / *not usually* just signs of worry.
2 Most doctors will admit to *having* / *following* gut instincts.
3 Ann Van den Bruel has done research into *how often doctors use gut instinct* / *how accurate gut instinct is*.
4 Doctors' gut feelings about children's infections often turn out to be *correct* / *incorrect*.
5 Margaret McCartney thinks that gut instincts are *important* / *unscientific*.
6 Doctors tend to follow their gut instinct when they are *more* / *less* sure about their diagnosis.
7 Doctors from different countries seem to have very *similar* / *different* experiences.
8 Doctors in general practice have to rely on their instincts *less* / *more* than hospital doctors.

d 💬 Did the discussion change your mind about the question in 5a?

e **Language in context** *Doubt and uncertainty*

1 ▶️2.15 Complete the sentences with the words in the box. Then listen and check your answers.

---
bones   feeling   doubt   fit
worriers   pattern   jars   anxieties
---

1 That **uneasy** _____ that you get when you think there is something that you should be doing.
2 More often than not these are **groundless** _____ that simply reflect that many of us are **born** _____.
3 All may appear well on the surface, but you're left with **a nagging** _____ that all is not quite as it seems.
4 It's almost like recognising that this person just **doesn't quite fit the** _____, but you're not quite sure in what way …
5 Other doctors will say that they **feel it in their** _____ that something's just not right.
6 It's just this idea that you get something that _____; something that just **doesn't quite** _____ properly **together**.

2 Which words and phrases in **bold** are connected with these things?

a a feeling that things aren't OK
b worrying more than you need to
c not being able to make sense of things
d knowing something intuitively

6 SPEAKING

a 💬 Read each dilemma. What would you do? Is what you would do and what you should do the same in each case?

1 You are a judge. You are due to pass sentence on a criminal that you have seen in your court before. On that occasion he was found not guilty of a serious crime due to a lack of evidence – but your gut told you differently. Do you give him the maximum sentence this time?

2 You are a junior web designer and your boss has asked you to present a web design for a potentially important client. You've been given detailed information about the colour and design preferences of your client's target market, but you feel that this would result in a sterile and boring design which wouldn't get you the contract. Do you insist on presenting your preferred design instead?

3 You are interviewing candidates for a six-month contract. One candidate is very well qualified and performs well in the interview, but there's something about him that makes you uneasy (you can't quite put your finger on it). The choice is between him and someone who doesn't look so good on paper and was quite nervous in the interview, but who you have a good feeling about. Who would you go for?

b 💬 What role do you think gut instinct could play in these jobs?

- politician
- CEO of a large company
- airline pilot
- parent

c 💬 Choose one of the jobs in 6b or a different job, and write a dilemma like those in 6a. Swap dilemmas with other students and discuss the dilemma you receive.

4B He got himself locked in a shed

Learn to talk about memories and remembering

G *have / get* passives
V Memory

1 LISTENING and GRAMMAR *have / get* passives

a 💬 Discuss the questions.

1 What kind of stories do you and your family and childhood friends tell about your childhood?
2 What was a particularly funny/proud/scary moment?

b ▶️2.16 Listen to Tommy, Marissa and Clara talk about their childhood memories. Answer the questions.

1 What's the significance of each of the photos? Summarise what happened in each memory.
2 Why do you think these memories are still so clear for the speakers?

c 💬 Do you relate to any of the people telling the stories? Why?

> I can't really relate to Clara. I was a very confident child!

d Compare the meaning of the pairs of sentences. Is there any difference?

1 a **My parents were having the kitchen renovated.**
  b My parents were renovating the kitchen.
2 a **I had all my toys stolen.**
  b All my toys were stolen.
3 a **He got himself locked in the garden shed.**
  b He got locked in the garden shed.
4 a **His disappearance got everyone looking for him.**
  b He got everyone to look for him.
5 a **She had me sitting on my own.**
  b I was sitting on my own.
6 a **He got me to play when nobody else could.**
  b He played with me.

Match the sentences in **bold** with the uses a–d below.

a the subject's possessions were harmed by somebody else ☐
b the subject paid somebody else to do a job ☐
c the subject caused somebody to do something ☐ ☐ ☐
d the subject caused what happened to them ☐

e Add the sentences in **bold** in 1d to the table. Answer the questions.

Subject	Verb form 1	Object	Verb form 2
They	had	their roof	fixed.
We	got	our car	broken into.

1 Could *get* be used instead of *have* in each sentence with *have*? If so, does it change the meaning?
2 Could *have* be used instead of *get* in each sentence with *get*? If so, does it change the meaning?

f ▶️ Now go to Grammar Focus 4B on p.145

2 SPEAKING

a ▶️2.19 **Pronunciation** Underline the stressed syllables in these sentences. Then listen and check. What kinds of words are usually unstressed?

1 I had my bike stolen.
2 They had me doing all the cleaning for weeks.
3 I had my arm broken in a football match.
4 She had me doing all her homework.
5 It got me thinking about what I'd done wrong.
6 I got myself locked out of the house.
7 I got my mum to say I was sick.
8 My brother got me punished unfairly.

b 💬 Think of two or three childhood incidents like the examples in 2a. Use these questions to help you remember. Tell your partner about them.

- Who was there?
- Where were you?
- Did anyone get into trouble? Who?
- Did something cause the problem?
- How was the situation resolved?
- What was the outcome?

3 LISTENING and READING

a ▶ 2.20 Listen to Marissa's memory again, then listen to her brother Charlie's version. Note down the differences.

b 💬 Discuss the questions.

1 Does your family have any stories which there are different versions of? Do any members of your family tend to add their own details to stories?
2 What's your earliest memory? How reliable do you think it is?
3 What reasons can you think of for inaccuracies in … ?
   • childhood memories
   • the memories of witnesses in criminal cases

c Student A: Read the text *False childhood memories*. Answer these questions.

1 What do scientists know about how memories are created and kept in our brains? What don't they know?
2 How does the writer describe the process of recalling and adding memories? What does he compare it to?
3 What does Jean Piaget's story demonstrate?

Student B: Read the text *How eyewitness evidence can be unreliable*. Answer these questions.

1 What power does an eyewitness of a crime have in a trial?
2 What motivates an eyewitness to identify a suspect?
3 How can police influence eyewitnesses' memories?

d 💬 Tell your partner about the text you read. Was there anything you found particularly interesting or surprising?

e In pairs, guess the meaning of the highlighted words and expressions in both texts. Then check your ideas in a dictionary.

FALSE CHILDHOOD MEMORIES

Scientists generally agree that memories are formed when neurons link together to form new connections, or circuits, actually changing the contact between the cells. Long-term memories, which include experiences that happened just a few minutes ago to information several decades old, are stored in mental 'drawers' somewhere in our brains. No one knows exactly where, although it has been estimated that in a lifetime, long-term memory can hold as many as 1 quadrillion (1 million billion) separate bits of information.

The 'drawers' holding our memories are obviously extremely crowded and densely packed. As new bits and pieces of information are added into long-term memory, the old memories are removed, replaced, crumpled up, or pushed into corners. Little details are added, confusing or extraneous elements are deleted, and a coherent construction of the facts is gradually created that may bear little resemblance to the original event.

Child psychologist Jean Piaget, in his *Play, Dreams and Imitation in Childhood*, related a personal story about the malleability of memory:

… one of my first memories would date, if it were true, from my second year. I can still see, most clearly, the following scene, in which I believed until I was about fifteen. I was sitting in my pram, which my nurse was pushing in the Champs Elysées, when a man tried to kidnap me. I was held in by the strap fastened around me while my nurse bravely tried to stand between me and the thief. She received various scratches, and I can still see vaguely those on her face. Then a crowd gathered, a policeman with a short cloak and a white baton came up, and the man took to his heels. I can still see the whole scene, and can even place it near the tube station. When I was about fifteen, my parents received a letter from my former nurse saying that she had been converted to the Salvation Army. She wanted to confess her past faults, and in particular to return the watch she had been given as a reward on this occasion. She had made up the whole story, faking the scratches. I, therefore, must have heard, as a child, the account of this story, which my parents believed, and projected into the past in the form of a visual memory.

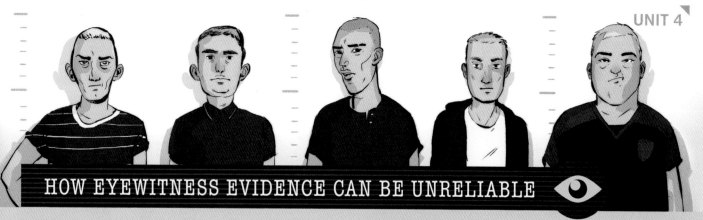

HOW EYEWITNESS EVIDENCE CAN BE UNRELIABLE

Eyewitness testimony, which relies on the accuracy of human memory, has an enormous impact on the outcome of a trial. Aside from a smoking pistol, nothing carries as much weight with a jury as the testimony of an actual witness. The danger of eyewitness testimony is clear: anyone in the world can be convicted of a crime he or she did not commit … based solely on the evidence of a witness who convinces a jury that his memory about what he saw is correct.

Suppose that a crime occurs, the police are notified, they arrive at the scene and begin to ask questions. 'What happened?' the witness is asked. 'What did the assailant look like?' After the witness tells the police what he can remember, he may be asked to come to the police station to look through a set of photographs.

Keep in mind that most witnesses are obliging – they want to help, and in the case of a violent crime or assault, they have an added incentive to help the police capture a violent criminal. In addition, research tells us that witnesses believe the police would not conduct a line-up unless they had a good suspect. Although witnesses try hard to identify the true criminal, when they are uncertain – or when no one person in the line-up exactly matches their memory – they will often identify the person who best matches their recollection of the criminal. And often their choice is wrong. Suppose a witness is presented with a fair line-up, in which everyone is at least approximately the same height and weight and fits a general description. The witness is looking at the line-up, concentrating hard, and the police officer suddenly says, 'Take another look at number four.' Perhaps the police officer stares conspicuously at number four while the witness is trying to identify the culprit. Or perhaps the witness hesitates while looking at number four and the interviewer leans forward and says, 'What do you think about that one?'

The witness takes in these little bits of information and may use them – unconsciously – to 'fill in' a vague and fuzzy memory with the image of the person in the photograph. The image shifts, the lines waver, and suddenly the face in number four fuses with the fading memory of the criminal. 'Number four looks familiar,' the witness might say. And later: 'Yes, I'm sure it's number four.'

4 VOCABULARY Memory

a Match the adjectives in these collocations with their definitions.

1 a vague memory	a ☐	permanent
2 a painful memory	b ☐	it still makes you unhappy
3 a vivid memory	c ☐	it happened a long time ago
4 a photographic memory	d ☐	unclear
5 a lasting memory	e ☐	you can remember anything perfectly
6 a distant memory	f ☐	with clear sensations

b In which collocation in 4a is the meaning of *memory* different? What's the difference?

c ▶ Now go to Vocabulary Focus 4B on p.161

d 💬 Ask and answer the questions.

1 How clearly do you remember the time before you went to school?
2 If you think of your home town, what's the first thing that comes to mind?
3 Which holidays do you have lasting memories of?
   What kind of things do you remember most vividly? (food/people/sights)
4 If you cast your mind back five years, what's the first thing you remember?
5 When was the last time an appointment slipped your mind?
6 Are there any sounds or smells that trigger a memory for you? What exactly?
7 What's a memory of a close friend that you'll always treasure?

5 SPEAKING

a ▶ Communication 4B 1 Test your memory. Student A: Go to p.128. Student B: Go to p.130.

b 💬 Work in small groups. What can you do to improve your memory? Make a list of ideas.
   • *get more sleep*

c ▶ Communication 4B 2 Go to p.134 and read the fact file.

d 💬 Discuss the questions.

1 What information in the fact file was useful / not useful for you?
2 What things do you find easier / more difficult to remember than others? Why?
3 In education, what kinds of things do you think need to be memorised?
4 Is it a good idea to use technology to help us remember things?

4C Everyday English
I see where you're coming from

Learn to use tact in formal discussions
S Give opinions tactfully
P Homophones in words and connected speech

1 LISTENING

(a)

a 💬 Discuss the questions.

1 What makes a media interview successful?
2 Who is responsible for making an interview work – the interviewer or the interviewee?

b ▶ 2.23 Watch or listen to Part 1. Who does Nadia think is responsible for making an interview work?

c ▶ 2.23 Look at the list of topics that were mentioned in Part 1. Who mentioned them and what did they say about them? Listen to Part 1 again and check your answers.

1 Max's writing
2 professionalism
3 a sequel to *Solar Wind*
4 the number of listeners

d 💬 Answer the questions.

1 How would you describe Oscar's and Sara's responses to Nadia's feedback?
2 Are you surprised by their responses?

e Language in context *Idioms 1*
Answer the questions below. Check in the audioscript on p.180.

Nadia says that Max *wasn't particularly forthcoming.*
a What idiom with the word *blood* does Oscar use with the same meaning?
b What idiom with the word *nut* does Sara use?

2 USEFUL LANGUAGE Being tactful in formal discussions

a Match the expressions in **bold** from Part 1 with their uses a–c.

1 ☐ Well, **if you don't mind me saying so,** it was like trying to get blood out of a stone.
2 ☐ **I see where you're coming from, but** guys, I think we're forgetting something here.
3 ☐ Look, **don't take this personally,** Oscar. I'm trying to be constructive.
4 ☐ **I do take your point, but** I'm not sure there's anything more I could've done.
5 ☐ **I beg to differ.** I agree Redwood wasn't particularly forthcoming, but my feeling is that there's always a way.
6 ☐ **No offence intended,** Oscar, **but** I couldn't understand why you were asking about a sequel.
7 ☐ **With all due respect,** Sara, I don't think you're in a position to tell us what does and doesn't make a good interviewer.

a soften direct criticisms
b present contradictory opinions
c soften strong/unpopular opinions or bad news

b ▶ 2.24 Listen to 1–3 and match the expressions in **bold** with their uses in 2a.

1 ☐ You can be a bit heavy-handed from time to time. But **I mean that in the nicest possible way.**
2 ☐ **I'm afraid I have to say,** if we go down this road, it'll be a disaster.
3 ☐ **That's not the way I see it,** I'm afraid. There were several ways to avoid this outcome.

c 💬 Work with a partner. Make the discussions below more tactful, using expressions from 2a and 2b. Act out your discussion for other people in the class.

1 **A** My article was rather clever.
  B It was potentially offensive.
  A People shouldn't be so sensitive.
  B You need to be more tactful.
2 **A** I think I handled that meeting quite well.
  B You allowed Leon to talk for too long.
  A You could have interrupted him and helped me out.
  B It was your job to chair the meeting.

3 PRONUNCIATION
Homophones in words and connected speech

a ▶ 2.25 *See* and *sea* are homophones – two different words with the same pronunciation. Listen to these phrases and find the words which are incorrect. Write the correct homophone. Sometimes there is more than one in each phrase.

1 with all ~~dew~~ respect *due*
2 I mean it in the nicest possible weigh
3 it's knot about being fare
4 the virus gets into the sells
5 a pear of pants
6 I can still see the hole seen
7 eyewitness testimony carries grate wait
8 it may bare little resemblance to the truth

b Phrases can also be homophones. Complete these homophones.

1 great eye = grey ___tie___
2 known aim = no _____
3 way cup = wake _____
4 fork aches = _____
5 lock tin side = _____

c ▶ 2.26 Listen. What phrases in Part 1 are 1–5 homophones of? Check your ideas in the audioscript on p.180. Notice that the end of one word may change because of the sound at the beginning of the next.

1 How do ewe thing kit went? *How do you think it went?*
2 if few don't mime me saying sew
3 I think we all knee two learn from this
4 know a fence in ten did
5 we knee to bay rim mined

d Complete the advice.

If you hear a word which doesn't seem to make sense in context, …

4 LISTENING

a 💬 Look at picture b. What do you think Sara is asking Alex to do?

b ▶ 2.27 Watch or listen to Part 2 and check your answer in 4a.

c ▶ 2.27 Watch or listen to Part 2 again and answer the questions.

1 What has been the same about Nadia's behaviour and what has been different?
2 How do you think Sara feels when she is asking Alex for Max's phone number? Why?
3 What advice does Alex give Sara? Why?

d 💬 If Sara follows Alex's advice, what do you think the consequences will be?

e Language in context *Idioms 2*

1 ▶ 2.28 Complete the idioms with one word in each space. Listen and check your answers. What do the idioms all express?

1 _____ me about it!
2 You're _____ me!
3 You've _____ the nail on the head!

2 ▶ 2.28 Underline the main stress in the idioms in 1. Listen again and check. Practise saying the idioms.

5 SPEAKING

▶ Communication 4C Work in pairs.
Student A: Go to p.127.
Student B: Go to p.128.

b

Unit Progress Test 📶

CHECK YOUR PROGRESS

You can now do the Unit Progress Test.

1 SPEAKING and LISTENING

a Think about these questions and note down your ideas. Ask and answer the questions.

1 Have you ever been interviewed for any kind of article or programme? If so, what was it for?
2 If someone were to interview you about your interests, work or talents, what do you think the interview would be about?
3 Think of one interest or ability you have. Where do you think it comes from? Can you remember when and how it first started? Were there any particular people or events that influenced you?

b You are going to hear an interview with a singer, Nora Manning. How do you think these things influenced her career?

1 My immediate family weren't musical.
2 My parents had a huge record collection.
3 I take after my grandfather.
4 My brother had a guitar, but he couldn't really play it.
5 I've always travelled a lot.

c 2.29 Listen and summarise what Nora says about each influence in 1b.

2 READING

Read the article and answer the questions. Use your answers in 1c and/or the audioscript on p.180 to help you.

1 What further information does the article give about Nora Manning?
2 Was there any information in the interview which the writer didn't include in the article?

3 WRITING SKILLS
Organising information; Showing time relationships

a As well as describing Nora Manning's life, the article includes:

- direct quotes (things Nora Manning said)
- the 'setting' of the interview (a café).

1 Find three examples of direct quotes in the article.
2 What is the effect on the reader of including direct quotes and details of the setting?

NORA MANNING: 'I come back from travelling with my head full of music'

With her new album Memory, Nora Manning is now an up-and-coming name in folk music. She tells Saul Winthorpe about her musical memories.

Within a single year, Nora Manning has moved from being a complete unknown to being a promising new name on the English folk music scene. Over the last month she's had her songs played on local radio and she's about to embark on her first tour.

When I meet her, in a small café in Liverpool, where she is studying biochemistry at university, she still seems surprised and a bit baffled by her sudden success. 'I never set out to become famous or make money,' Nora tells me. 'Music was always something I just did for fun. It was only when someone asked me to play on the local radio station that I thought maybe I could make a living from it. That was about a year ago.'

Nora sits stirring her coffee, occasionally checking her phone for messages. She seems distracted and she has a faraway look in her eye, but she has ready answers to my questions and is happy to talk about her family and childhood. We talk about where her remarkable musical talent comes from, and she tells me that she was very lucky to come from a family that listened to music constantly. 'My grandfather was very musical,' she explains. 'He played the violin in an orchestra, and he also travelled all over the world – so I think I'm similar to him in many ways.' One of her earliest childhood memories, probably when she was about five years old, is of her grandfather playing the violin at home. 'I think that's when I became aware of music and wanted to play,' she says.

b What verb tenses does the article use … ?

1 to talk about her current success
2 to describe what happened during the interview
3 to talk about her past life

c Compare these sentences with the same ideas in paragraph 2 of the article.

I meet her in a small café in Liverpool. She is studying biochemistry at university in Liverpool. She still seems surprised and a bit baffled by her sudden success.

1 What differences are there in the way the ideas are expressed?
2 Why do you think the writer chose the style used in the article? Tick one or more reasons.
   a ☐ to reduce the number of sentences needed
   b ☐ to show how different ideas are connected together
   c ☐ to make the paragraph read more smoothly

d Cover the text. Combine the information below into single sentences.

1 One of her earliest childhood memories is of her grandfather. She was probably about five years old. She remembers him playing the violin at home.
2 The rest of her family have never moved far from their home town of Manchester. Unlike them, she started travelling as a teenager. She hasn't stopped since.

Compare your sentences with the ones in the text. Are they similar? Which are more effective?

e Which of the highlighted expressions in the article mean … ?

1 immediately (x1)
2 after a long time (x2)
3 after a short time (x3)

f Underline the time expressions in these examples. Add them to lists 1–3 in 3e.

1 No sooner had I started playing than I knew it was the right instrument for me.
2 Not until many years later did she become famous.
3 The instant I heard her music I knew she was an exceptional talent.
4 In time, she started playing a greater variety of instruments.
5 Shortly after she started university, she began to perform at local events.

g What is unusual about the structure of sentences 1 and 2 in 3f?

h ▶ Now go to Writing Focus 4D on p.171

4 WRITING

a Prepare to be interviewed by another student about an interest or a talent.

1 Look at the notes you made in 1a and think of some questions you would like your partner to ask you.
2 Think of a suitable venue for your interview (your workplace, a café …).

b Take turns to interview each other and make notes. Use the questions your partner suggested and add others of your own. You could ask about:

- how it started
- early influences
- involvement of family and friends
- achievements
- plans

> **Writing Tip**
> When taking notes:
> - Note down key points as you listen to help organise your ideas later – just enough to remind you of what your partner said.
> - What is the most interesting part of your interviewee's story? Make sure you highlight this in your notes – it could be a good way to begin the article.

c From your notes, write an article about your partner. Use the Nora Manning article as a model and include a few direct quotes from your interview.

When she was about seven, she started playing her brother's guitar, and hasn't looked back since. She smiles but then looks thoughtful. 'The moment I started playing, I knew it was the right instrument for me.'

She started university two years ago and before long she was giving public performances but it wasn't until this year that she released her first album, which is called *Memory*. I ask her if it's connected to her grandfather, but it turns out to be more to do with her travels than her childhood.

Unlike the rest of her family, who have never moved far from their home town of Manchester, Nora started travelling as a teenager, and hasn't stopped since. At 18 she travelled through Eastern Europe, and this was closely followed by a trip to Turkey and subsequently to North Africa, which explains the strong influences of these regions in her music. Whereas most tourists take photos of scenery or famous buildings, Nora prefers to record the sounds she hears and the music people play. 'I always come back from travelling with my head full of music, and gradually that works its way into my songs. These are my musical memories.'

NORA MANNING

MEMORY

UNIT 4
Review and extension

1 GRAMMAR

a Correct the mistakes in the sentences.

1 A published recently article has caused a political uproar.
2 For tea there were delicious strawberry filled with cream tarts.
3 We need a new bed. Our one old is broken.
4 Every table's corner was covered in papers and documents.
5 If you ever get a chance see them in concert, I recommend it.
6 A friend of the wife of John is also interested.
7 The recently elected leader of the council's name is Mr Singh.
8 I have to tell him a difficult something this evening.

b Choose the correct option.

1 The house *got / had* burgled and almost everything was taken.
2 Only Jason could *get / have* himself lost in a supermarket.
3 We'll have *done the repairs / the repairs done* by a specialist.
4 *Get / Have* Pam to tell you why she left university.
5 It's as painful as *to have / having* a tooth taken out.
6 Wait five minutes until I've got the baby *dressed / to dress*.
7 The police officer *got / had* them give their details.

2 VOCABULARY

a Match the sentence halves.

1 ☐ It was a difficult climb and I'll think
2 ☐ Usually I'm quite rational but sometimes I act on
3 ☐ I don't know why but I've got
4 ☐ I'll give you some time to think
5 ☐ In a situation like this you need to weigh
6 ☐ There was no logic, it was just my gut
7 ☐ Sometimes you think everything is all right but

a impulse and do something I later regret.
b subconsciously you know it isn't.
c it over and make up your mind.
d instinct telling me what to do.
e twice about doing something like that again.
f up the pros and cons and come to a decision.
g a hunch that Samuels stole the necklace.

b Correct one mistake in each sentence.

1 My childhood is just a far memory to me now.
2 I've got a photographers memory, I can remember things really easily.
3 A vocabulary notebook is a good way to freshen up your memory of new words.
4 I can only foggily remember my first lesson in this English class.
5 When I think of fast food, the word 'unhealthy' comes in mind.
6 I have some hurtful memories from my school days.
7 People's birthdays often leave my mind.
8 Some photographs I have stimulate the memory of some wonderful experiences.

3 WORDPOWER *mind*

Think of a number, any number

a ▶2.30 Complete the phrases in **bold** with the verbs in the box. Listen and check.

> speak read cross bear put

1 Don't hold back, please, _____ **your mind**.
2 Thanks for telling me. I'll _____ **it in mind** when I'm making my decision.
3 I wish you'd tell me what the problem is. I can't _____ **your mind**.
4 You can do anything if you _____ **your mind to it**.
5 It didn't _____ **my mind** to tell you.

b Match the phrases in **bold** in 3a with definitions a–e.

a ☐ think of, remember
b ☐ give your true opinion
c ☐ try hard, using your brain
d ☐ know what somebody is thinking
e ☐ consider useful information

c ▶2.31 Match 1–5 with a–e. Listen and check.

1 ☐ I'll double check I locked the door,
2 ☐ I can't cope with doing it right now –
3 ☐ I know you've got doubts,
4 ☐ Look at the state of my hair!
5 ☐ She's stressed out.

a I'm not **in the right frame of mind**.
b but please **keep an open mind**.
c just for **peace of mind**.
d She **has a lot on her mind**.
e I swear it **has a mind of its own**.

d 💬 Choose a sentence from 3a or 3c and continue the conversation with other students. When your conversation ends, choose a new sentence.

♻ REVIEW YOUR PROGRESS

How well did you do in this unit? Write 3, 2, or 1 for each objective.
3 = very well 2 = well 1 = not so well

I CAN ...

talk about using instinct and reason	☐
talk about memories and remembering	☐
use tact in formal discussions	☐
write a profile article	☐

CAN DO OBJECTIVES

- Talk about crime and punishment
- Talk about job requirements and fair pay
- Recall and speculate
- Write an opinion essay

UNIT 5
Fairness

GETTING STARTED

a   Look at the picture and answer the questions.

1   Where is the man? What's his role there?
2   Why do you think he's got a frog?

b   Discuss the questions.

1   In what ways could working with animals benefit prisoners?
2   What other kinds of activity might be beneficial for men and women while they're in prison?
3   Why do you think some criminals leave prison and re-offend while others don't?

55

5A A place where you have to look over your shoulder

Learn to talk about crime and punishment
- **G** Relative clauses
- **V** Crime and justice

1 READING

a 💬 What do you think life in a typical prison is like? Think of examples from your country or from films and TV programmes.

1 What does it look like?
2 What are the conditions like? (cells, food, facilities, activities for prisoners)

b 💬 Look at the photos of Halden prison in Norway and answer the questions.

1 What do you think the conditions are like? (cells, food, facilities, activities for prisoners)
2 What kinds of crimes do you think the prisoners here might have committed?

Read the article and check.

c Read the article again and answer the questions.

1 On arrival, what two things does the writer notice?
2 How does Norway aim to deal with criminals?
3 Does the writer think the prison is like a hotel? Why / Why not?
4 What are the aims of the design of the prison?
5 How are inmates motivated to do activities? Why?
6 What aspect of prison life does Kent find difficult?
7 What surprised the visiting prison governor?
8 What is the writer's impression of the atmosphere at Halden?

d Work in pairs. Guess the meaning of the highlighted words and phrases in the text. Then check your ideas in a dictionary.

e 💬 Do you agree with Kent's statement in *italics* in the text? Should prison be more about punishment or rehabilitation? Why / Why not?

2 GRAMMAR Relative clauses

a Match the captions with the photos in the article.

1 ☐ Norwegian prison officers are tasked with rehabilitating the men in their care, the result of which is a 20% reoffending rate, compared with 50% in England.

2 ☐ Graffiti by Norwegian artist Dolk, from whom it was commissioned out of the prison's 6m kroner (£640,000) art budget.

3 ☐ Welcome to Halden Prison, Norway, inside the walls of which prisoners receive comforts often likened to those of boutique hotels.

4 ☐ The prisoners, some of whom have committed the most serious crimes imaginable, are provided with plenty of opportunities for physical exercise.

Can we have a swimming pool?
LIFE AT HALDEN PRISON

by Amelia Gentleman

Halden prison smells of freshly brewed coffee. It hits you in the ¹communal apartment-style areas where prisoners live together in groups of eight. The other remarkable thing is how quiet the prison is. There isn't any of the angry banging of doors you hear in British prisons, not least because the prisoners are not locked up much during the day.

Halden is one of Norway's highest-security jails. Up to 252 criminals, many of whom have committed some of the most serious offences, can be held there. Since it opened in 2010, at a cost of 1.3bn Norwegian kroner (£138m), Halden has acquired a reputation as the world's most ²humane prison. It is the flagship of the Norwegian justice system, where the focus is on rehabilitation rather than punishment.

Halden has attracted attention globally for its design and comfort. Set in a forest, the prison blocks are a model of ³minimalist chic. At times, the environment feels more like a Scandinavian boutique hotel than a class A prison. Every Halden cell has a flatscreen television, its own toilet (which, unlike standard UK prison cells, also has a door) and a shower, which comes with large, soft, white towels. Prisoners have their own fridges, cupboards and desks in bright new pine and huge, ⁴unbarred windows overlooking mossy forest scenery.

Obviously the hotel comparison is a stupid one, since the problem with being in prison, unlike staying in a hotel, is that you cannot leave – hidden behind the silver birch trees is a thick, tall, concrete wall, impossible to ⁵scale.

Given the constraints of needing to keep ⁶high-risk people ⁷incarcerated, creating an environment that was as unprisonlike as possible was a priority for Are Høidal, the governor of Halden, and the prison's architects. Høidal says, 'We felt it shouldn't look like a prison. We wanted to create normality. If you can't see the wall, this could be anything, anywhere.'

b <u>Underline</u> the relative clause in each caption in 2a. Is it defining or non-defining? How can you tell?

c Compare the clauses below with the examples in 2a. What features of the clauses in 2a are more formal?

1 which results in a 20% reoffending rate
2 who it was commissioned from out of the prison's 6m kroner art budget
3 where prisoners receive comforts often likened to those of boutique hotels
4 who in some cases have committed the most serious crimes imaginable

d ▶ Now go to Grammar Focus 5A on p.146

'HALDEN PRISON HAS BEEN COMPARED TO THE FINEST HOTEL'

Prisoners are unlocked at 7.30am and locked up for the night at 8.30pm. During the day, they are encouraged to attend work and educational activities, with a daily payment of 53 kroner (£5.60) for those who leave their cell. 'If you have very few activities, your prisoners become more aggressive,' says Høidal. 'If they are sitting all day, I don't think that is so good for a person. If they are busy, then they are happier. We try not to let them get [8]institutionalised.'

Kent, a 43-year-old office manager serving a three-year sentence for a violent attack, is sitting in the prison's mixing studio. He admits he's enjoying being able to focus on his music, but says, *Halden prison has been compared to the finest hotel. It is not true. The real issue is freedom, which is taken away from you. That is the worst thing that can happen to you. When the door slams at night, you're sat there in a small room. That's always a tough time.'*

As we walk around the compound, an inmate comes up to ask Høidal, 'Can we have a swimming pool?' He laughs, and remembers the shock of a prison governor who visited recently and was horrified to see that the inmates didn't stand to attention when Høidal came past but instead [9]clustered around him, seizing the chance to list their complaints.

The inmates tell Høidal they're annoyed by recent changes to the routine, but they are respectful when they [10]address him. He listens politely, agrees that in prison [11]minor irritations can become major frustrations, but remarks that people outside the building would laugh at the trivial nature of their complaints.

Maybe I'm not there long enough to sense hidden anger or deep despair, but Halden doesn't feel like a place where you have to look over your shoulder.

e What do you think prison life should be like? Complete the sentences with your own ideas.

1 Prisoners should *have their own / share a* cell, in which there should be:
_____ _____ _____ _____.

2 Prisoners *should / shouldn't* have to do *some / any* kind of work, for which they should be paid _____ per week.

3 The guards, _____ of whom should be trained in _____, should be paid _____ per week.

4 Prison meals, _____ of which should be _____, should be served _____ times a day.

5 The prison grounds …

6 Visitors …

f 💬 Compare your ideas in 2e with other students. Whose prison is more like Halden?

3 VOCABULARY and SPEAKING
Crime and justice

a ⏵2.34 Make the names of crimes by matching words and phrases from A with those in B. Then check the meanings in a dictionary. Listen and check.

A	B
1 ☐ violent	a corruption
2 ☐ tax	b a controlled substance
3 ☐ possession of	c assault
4 ☐ credit card	d fraud
5 ☐ bribery and	e evasion

b ⏵2.35 **Pronunciation** Listen to the words below and notice the four different pronunciations of the letter *s*.

/s/ a**ss**ault /ʒ/ eva**s**ion /z/ po**ss**ession /ʃ/

c ⏵2.36 Which sound in **bold** in the words below is different in each group? Listen and check.

1 a**ss**ault   assa**ss**in   mi**ss**ion   dismi**ss**
2 eva**s**ion   deci**s**ion   explo**s**ion   impre**ss**ion
3 po**ss**ession   cou**s**in   compari**s**on   rea**s**on
4 posse**ss**ion   permi**ss**ion   vi**s**ion   Ru**ss**ian

d Take turns giving definitions and examples of the crimes in 3a. Can your partner guess the crime?

e ▶ Now go to Vocabulary Focus 5A on p.162

4 LISTENING

a What crime do you think is happening in the pictures?

b Match the news headlines to the pictures.

☐ Cereal offender ☐ Fake fan
☐ Would-bee burglar ☐ The honest fraudster
☐ Dial a crime

c ⏵2.39 Listen to the news stories and check. Then, in pairs, explain what's happening in each picture.

d ⏵2.39 Listen again. In each story, how were the criminals caught or how do police hope to catch the criminals?

e **Language in context** *Crime*
Guess the meaning of the words in **bold**. Check your ideas in a dictionary.

1 … he **forged** the passport – it's a fake.
2 … he has been **detained** in a local facility …
3 They had this great plan to **pawn** them for cash …
4 … guess who was waiting? The police, of course, with the **handcuffs** ready!
5 Someone manages to **smuggle** in a mobile phone for him …
6 … the fraudster turns into an honest man – he **hands himself in**.

f There are two puns in the headlines in 4b. What is a pun? Can you find and explain the puns in the headlines?

g Discuss the questions.

1 Which crime do you think is the most serious?
2 Which criminal do you think is the least competent?
3 Do you find any of the stories funny? If so, which ones?

5 SPEAKING

a Work in pairs. Discuss the criminals, 1–4. Decide on a fair form of punishment / rehabilitation for these crimes. Is there any further information you would need to make a judgment?

1 A 90-year-old man who is found guilty of income tax evasion over a period of 50 years.
2 A woman found guilty of causing death by dangerous driving. She swerved to avoid a pet cat and caused the death of a motorcyclist.
3 An airport employee who stole valuable items from suitcases that were left on carousels. She sold them for cash, or gave them away as presents.
4 A 17-year-old who has been caught shoplifting trainers. It's the first time he's been caught, but at home the police find a large collection of sportswear.

b Work in groups of four. Are your suggestions for consequences similar? If not, can you agree on the consequences for each criminal?

5B It's essential to have the right qualifications

1 LISTENING and VOCABULARY
Employment

a 💬 What would you regard as a 'good job'? How easy is it for people to find a good job these days?

b ▶ 2.40 Listen to four people talking about employment. What field does each person work in or want to work in?

Mike, UK

Olivia, Spain

Andrew, UK

Karen, Germany

c ▶ 2.40 Listen again and match the statements to the speakers. Some statements apply to more than one speaker.

Who … ?
1 is concerned that their good luck won't last
2 has had trouble getting a good job since qualifying
3 faces a lot of competition in their field
4 is reluctant to accept unpaid work
5 is unhappy with their working hours

d 💬 Discuss the questions.
1 What advice would you give each of the people?
2 Do you know anyone who is in a similar position to any of these people? What has their experience been?

e Andrew says: *There have been a lot of redundancies in the **financial sector**.* Answer the questions.
1 What is meant by a *sector*?
2 What jobs can you think of in each sector in the box?

---
financial   agricultural   construction   public
manufacturing   transport   energy   industrial   retail
---

3 What other sectors can you think of?

f Which of the words in the box in 1e have verb forms? Which are adjectives?

g ▶ 2.41 **Pronunciation** Listen to sentences 1 and 2. Match the stress patterns to the words in **bold**.

☐ oO   ☐ Oo

1 They've appointed a new Minister of **Transport**.
2 It's much cheaper to **transport** goods by ship than by plane.

Why is the word *transport* stressed differently in sentences 1 and 2? Do you know any other noun and verb pairs which follow the same stress pattern?

h ▶ 2.42 Listen to these words used as nouns and verbs in two sentences, a and b. Which sentence contains the noun? Which sentence contains the verb?

1 increase   ☐ noun   ☐ verb
2 import   ☐ noun   ☐ verb
3 record   ☐ noun   ☐ verb
4 export   ☐ noun   ☐ verb
5 contract   ☐ noun   ☐ verb

i 💬 Discuss the questions.
1 What sector do you or people in your family work in?
2 Which sectors have the best employment conditions? Which have the worst?

2 SPEAKING

a 💬 Discuss the employment terms and conditions.
1 What type of job would each be suitable or unsuitable for?
2 What advantages would there be for the employer/employee?
3 Which do you think are the three most motivating ideas?

TERMS AND CONDITIONS

- six-month sabbaticals
- four 'duvet days' – four days a year when the employee can miss work without giving a reason
- unlimited holidays (provided they don't impact on the business)
- three-monthly performance review
- performance related pay
- zero hours contracts (contracts where the hours are decided week by week)
- equal paternity and maternity leave
- equal pay for 16-year-olds and older new employees
- free sports facilities at the workplace
- flexitime
- unlimited free healthy snacks and drinks

b 💬 Imagine you ran either a chain of cafés or a clothes shop. What terms and conditions would you have for your employees? Why?

3 READING and SPEAKING

a 🗨 Read the headings and look at the photos. What do you think each job involves? Read and find out.

b 🗨 Apart from the salary, are there any similarities between the two jobs? Consider these aspects:

- lack of privacy
- risks and danger
- working hours
- qualifications and training
- getting on with other people
- impact on family life.

c 🗨 Could you imagine doing either of the jobs? Why / Why not?

4 GRAMMAR
Willingness, obligation and necessity

a Look at these examples from the texts.

1 If possible, you should have a few years' diving experience.
2 You must be given a diving assessment and a diving first-aid course.
3 You have to live with five to ten people in close proximity for a month or longer.

In these particular sentences, is there any difference in meaning between … ?

a *must* and *should*   b *must* and *have to*

b Complete the sentences below with the obligation phrases in the box. Then check your answers in the texts.

be called on	it's essential	be obliged	expect you
it's advisable	be required	a mandatory requirement	

Bomb disposal diver
1 Companies will _____ to have diving qualifications.
2 These qualifications are _____.
3 You'll _____ to have an explosive ordnance disposal qualification.

Private butler
4 A private butler can _____ to do anything.
5 _____ to do a course at a training college.
6 _____ to have an eye for detail.
7 They may _____ to work for people who aren't always nice.

c 🗨 Discuss the questions.

1 How can the sentences in 4b be rephrased using *must, have to* or *should*? What other changes to the sentences are required?
2 Why do you think the author chose to use expressions other than modal verbs?

d ▶ Now go to Grammar Focus 5B on p.147

Bomb disposal diver

Typical salary: In the private sector you can earn up to £100,000 a year, working just two months out of every three.

The job: Being a bomb disposal diver involves descending to the seabed and searching for unexploded bombs, shells, grenades and landmines. Then either safely recovering and collecting the weapons, or securely disposing of them.

Qualifications: To dive offshore, companies will expect you to have diving qualifications and, if possible, you should have a few years' diving experience. On top of that, you must be given a diving assessment and a diving first-aid course, and also undergo offshore survival training. These qualifications are a mandatory requirement and you should expect to pay at least £15,000 for all these courses.

And that's just the diving. To be able to dispose of the bombs safely, you'll be required to have an explosive ordnance disposal (EOD) qualification and several years of experience.

To succeed as a bomb disposal diver, you need … to stay calm in stressful situations. 'You're pretty much on your own at depth, with nil visibility, working to a very narrow timescale,' says Daniel Roantree, an EOD diver. And you have to live with five to ten people in close proximity for a month or longer, so if you don't like living in small confined spaces with lots of other people, forget it. Personal space is something of a luxury.

Worst thing about the job: Expect to be away from home at least six months of the year.

'You're pretty much on your own.'

'You need to thrive on looking after others.'

Private butler

Typical salary: £60,000 to £90,000, or more. 'An entry level butler we've trained will walk into a salary of £35,000, while a very experienced private butler can earn up to £150,000,' says Sara Vestin, director of the British Butler Academy.

The job: A private butler can be called on by his or her employer to do anything from wardrobe management to chauffeuring to pet care. Typical duties include managing other staff, serving at every meal, running errands, looking after guests, booking restaurants, house security, housekeeping, cooking and anything else the household needs. But most of all, it's personal service, tailored to the very wealthy individual the butler works for.

Qualifications: No special qualifications are required, but it's advisable to do a course at a training college such as Vestin's British Butler Academy or the British Butler Institute. 'Recruitment consultants and VIP clients come to our mansion to scout out the good students,' Vestin says.

To succeed as a butler, you need ... a 'service mind', says Vestin. You must have the mindset of someone who genuinely thrives on looking after others. 'You cannot do the job without this, even if you were an amazing actor. Some people have it and some don't.' Also, she says, it's essential to have an eye for detail, a steady hand and the ability to deal with all sorts of people.

Worst thing about the job: Long hours and an unpredictable work schedule mean it's difficult to have a family life. Butlers also suffer from isolation and cultural differences with their employer and they may be obliged to work for people who aren't always nice.

5 READING and SPEAKING

a **Communication 5B** Student A: Read the text on p.129. Student B: Read the text on p.130.

b 💬 Work with your partner. Exchange information about the jobs. Explain:

- how much the job pays
- what it involves
- what qualifications and skills you need
- any negative aspects to the work.

c 💬 In groups, talk about the four jobs you read about.

1 What is it about each job that makes it so well paid? Is it connected with ... ?
  - personal sacrifice
  - specialist skills and knowledge
  - unusual talents
  - responsibility
  - danger

2 Which is the most/least appealing job for you?

3 Who in your group would be most suitable for each of the four jobs (assuming you had the necessary qualifications and training)?

d 💬 Think about your own job or occupation, or one you would like to do. Use these phrases to describe the requirements of the job to your group.

> It's essential to ...   (They) expect you to ...
> You are obliged/required to ...
> You have to be willing to ...
> It's up to you to ...   It's advisable to ...
> ... is a mandatory requirement

Which job you heard about seems the most demanding?

6 SPEAKING

a 💬 Work with a partner. Choose a job from the list below and decide what value you think the job has and what a fair salary would be.

1 a nurse
2 a primary school teacher
3 an investment banker
4 a premier league footballer
5 police officer

Think about:

- how much the person works
- qualifications and training
- the importance of the job
- the amount of responsibility the person has.

b 💬 Work in groups of five. You have an annual 'income fund' of £1 million. Decide how you will divide the 'income fund' between the five jobs. Who should earn more and who should earn less?

c ▶ **Communication 5B** Now go to p.137

1 LISTENING

a 💬 Discuss the questions.

1 Do you find it easy to talk to people you've just met? Why / Why not?
2 Look at strategies a–e for talking to new people. Which of these do you use? Do you do anything else in particular?

---

a Open the conversation by commenting on something else that's happening around you.

b Pay them compliments where possible.

c Ask for personal information about where they live and what they do for a living.

d Try to be funny, but don't make jokes about other people. Always laugh at their jokes.

e Look for opportunities to empathise with them.

---

b ▶ 2.45 Watch or listen to Part 1. What strategies from 1a does Sara use? Note down some specific examples.

c 💬 What do you think the impact of Sara's conversation strategies will be on Max?

d ▶ 2.46 **Language in context** *Temporary states*

1 Match a–c with 1–3 to make phrases from Part 1. Listen and check.

a ☐ on a temporary   1 ups and downs
b ☐ hopefully, I'll snap   2 basis
c ☐ we all have our   3 out of it soon enough

2 Which phrases in 1 mean … ?

a everybody experiences good times and bad times
b stop behaving in a negative way
c not permanently

e ▶ 2.47 Watch or listen to Part 2 and answer the questions.

1 What does Max think it's easier to write?
2 What had Sara assumed Max was doing?
3 What reason does Max give for his interview with Oscar being a disaster?

2 PRONUNCIATION Main stress

a ▶ 2.48 Listen to Max's lines below. Each pair of word groups ends with the same word, but it only receives the main stress in the first. Why?

1 a When your detective solves the <u>murder</u>,
   b you just invent <u>another</u> murder.
2 a He hadn't even read my <u>book</u>.
   b Hadn't even <u>opened</u> my book.

Choose the correct word to complete the rule.

The last word or phrase in a word group which gives *new / repeated* information is stressed.

b ▶ 2.49 <u>Underline</u> where you think the main stress in these pairs of word groups is. Listen and check.

1 a It's dangerous enough being a diver,
   b let alone a bomb disposal diver!
2 a I don't think wealth distribution in this country is fair –
   b quite the opposite of fair, in fact.
3 a I haven't got the right qualifications –
   b in fact, I've hardly got any qualifications!
4 a Halden is more than just a prison –
   b it's the world's most humane prison.

Practise saying the sentences.

3 LISTENING

a ▶️2.50 Watch or listen to Part 3. How does Sara's meeting with Max nearly end in disaster?

b ▶️2.50 Listen to Part 3 again and answer the questions.

1 What did Max think Sara's job was?
2 Why does Max say he wouldn't have agreed to meet a journalist?
3 What two reasons does Sara give for wanting to interview Max?

c 💬 Why do you think Max considers doing another interview?

4 USEFUL LANGUAGE Recalling and speculating

a ▶️2.51 Complete the expressions from Parts 1, 2 and 3. Listen and check.

1 You're staying with Emma at the moment, **if my memory _____ me correctly**?
2 **I was _____ the impression that** you were writing another book?
3 **No _____ you heard that from** that guy from the radio interview.
4 **What _____ out in my mind** most **is** that that interview was a total disaster!
5 **I'd _____ a guess that** he hadn't even read my book.
6 _____, you're a technician, like Emma's boyfriend, right?
7 **I think I _____** Emma saying that her boyfriend's a technician at *City FM*.
8 _____ you'd known, would you still have agreed to meet with me?

b Which expressions in 4a are used for recalling events? Which are used for speculating? Are there any which could be used for both?

c ▶️2.52 Read this conversation. Find five mistakes and correct them. Listen and check.

A So when are you starting your new job? I was over the impression that you were starting next week.
B Oh, no. That would be too soon. I need a holiday first!
A But, if my mind serves me correctly – you went to Spain last month for a long weekend, didn't you?
B Who told you that?! I hazard a guess it was that sister of mine!
A Yeah, I think I remember she saying something along those lines.
B Well, you can't have too much of a good thing, can you? Presuming, you need a holiday too. Why don't you come with me?
A Well, I can't remember the last time I had a break. Why not?

d 💬 Practise the conversation in 4c with a partner.

e 💬 Recall your first day at school, or your first day in a job. Complete the sentences with your own ideas. Then tell a partner.

1 What stands out in my mind is …
2 I think I remember …
3 If my memory serves me correctly, …

f 💬 Discuss the questions. Use expressions from 4a to speculate.

1 Why do you think writers sometimes suffer from writer's block?
2 Why do you think some famous writers avoid giving interviews?

5 SPEAKING

▶ **Communication 5C** Work in pairs.
Student A: Go to p.135. Student B: Go to p.137.

Unit Progress Test

CHECK YOUR PROGRESS

You can now do the Unit Progress Test.

1 LISTENING and SPEAKING

a 💬 Discuss the questions.

1   Do you use social media? If not, why not? If so, how often do you post comments about your work or study life? What kind of things do you say?

2   Do you think it's a good idea to post comments about work or study on social media? Why / Why not?

b 💬 You are an employer. You see these comments written by employees to their colleagues. How would you feel? What action (if any) would you take?

> Couldn't face it today – phoned in sick. Having a lovely day at the beach! ☺
>
> Our merger with Bookman & Associates looks imminent #superfirm #merger
>
> This year's pay offer – a miserable 1% increase. Do management live in our world or not?
>
> Things a bit slow at work today – spent all day online "doing research".

c 💬 Discuss the questions.

1   Have you ever heard of anyone losing a job because of something they did on social media? What did they post? Do you think that dismissal is fair punishment for work-related postings? Why / Why not?

2   What other types of posting on social media wouldn't employers approve of?

d ▶ 2.53 Listen to Mario and Laila talking about job applications and social media. What differences are there … ?

1   in the experiences they have had

2   in their attitudes and opinions

e 💬 Read the opinions from Mario, Laila and their interviewers below. Tick (✓) the opinions you agree with and compare with a partner.

- ☐ It's essential that we project a positive image at all times – both in person and online.
- ☐ Demanding to see my social media is just a bit too Big Brother-ish for my liking.
- ☐ I don't really see a problem with employers having a look at my social media postings.
- ☐ I think that people tend to forget that just about anything you post online can be accessed in one way or another.
- ☐ If you don't want people to read it, then don't post it.

2 READING

a Read an essay about companies that research their job applicants on social media. Answer the questions.

1   Why do companies feel it's appropriate to use social media to find out about job applicants?

2   What are the reasons some job applicants are worried about this practice?

3   What position does the writer of the essay take on this topic?

b 💬 Do you agree with the writer's opinion? Why / Why not?

SOCIAL MEDIA AND
RECRUITMENT

① These days, an embarrassing photo on a person's social media profile might make all the difference when trying to land a top job. Increasingly, companies are examining applicants' social media profiles for information to use in the selection process.

② Young adults, many of whom have grown up with social media, are usually comfortable about sharing their lives online. Recently, however, some job applicants have voiced privacy concerns in relation to social media. They insist that their private life is private and is no business of any employer. In addition, they complain that companies go 'trawling' for negative information about applicants rather than getting a balanced general impression. They also express concern that they may be judged on the behaviour of their friends and family. What is more, some fear that employers may discriminate against them on factors such as their medical history or age.

1h ago

3 WRITING SKILLS
Essays; Linking: addition and reinforcement

a What is the function of each paragraph in the essay? Match these descriptions with the paragraph numbers 1–4.

- ☐ to present ideas and opinions for one side of the argument
- ☐ to state the writer's final, balanced opinion of both arguments
- ☐ to present ideas and opinions for a second, contrasting side of the argument
- ☐ to outline the topic of the essay and get the reader's interest

b How does the writer create interest in the introduction?

- a ☐ state their opinion on the topic
- b ☐ refer to interesting facts and figures
- c ☐ make a surprising statement
- d ☐ clearly outline the issue to be discussed

Which of the above are appropriate ways to begin an introduction to an essay? Why?

③ Employers argue that they are breaking no laws by researching their employees on social media – the information they are seeking is freely available. Moreover, as well as being a valuable tool for employers, social media provides information for the job applicant about the company they hope to work for. Above all, employers claim, their research makes the application process more efficient and allows them to filter out unsuitable applicants.

④ Whilst I agree that online research is a two-way process, I believe it is unfair for employers to judge an applicant's suitability solely on the basis of their social media postings. In particular, I understand applicants' concerns about 'trawling'. Besides actively seeking negative information, the system clearly creates opportunities for employers to discriminate. I think the time has come for guidelines or laws to restrict the research employers can do. Furthermore, checks need to be made that their decisions are fair and transparent.

c How does the writer conclude the essay?

- a ☐ state their balanced opinion
- b ☐ briefly summarise key points
- c ☐ outline a possible course of action
- d ☐ introduce interesting new information

Which of the above are appropriate ways to conclude an essay? Why?

d How many supporting arguments does the writer give for each side in paragraphs 2 and 3?

e Note the highlighted linker in paragraph 2. Underline more linking words and phrases in the essay that add information or reinforce an argument by adding a supporting idea.

f Write the words you underlined in 3e in the correct column of the table. Which linker highlights the most important argument?

Adds an idea in a new sentence	Adds two ideas in the same sentence
In addition	as well as

g Underline the linkers in these sentences and add them to the table in 3f.

1 Beyond researching the applicant on social media, employers usually contact previous employers for references.
2 It is standard to conduct a search of criminal records in addition to the methods mentioned above.
3 It is often argued that a time-efficient process is best for all involved. Besides, time saved is money saved.

h ▶ Now go to Writing Focus 5D on p.172

4 WRITING

a 💬 In some countries, employers are able to fire an employee without giving any reason for dismissal. Do you think this is fair? Discuss in small groups.

b Make notes of the ideas from the discussion in 4a. Organise your notes into opinions in favour of this idea and against it.

> **Writing Tip**
>
> When writing an essay on a controversial topic, it can help to talk to other people and note down opinions, even when these are not your own. Alternatively, brainstorm ideas from two different points of view. Your essay will be more interesting if you consider both sides of the issue and outline a range of opinions.

c Write an essay on the fairness of employers dismissing employees without having to give a reason. Consider the points of view of both employers and employees and include your own opinion.

d Read another student's essay. Do you mention the same points? Is your opinion the same?

3h ago

UNIT 5
Review and extension

1 GRAMMAR

a Complete each sentence with one word.

1 The crime _____ she committed was very serious.
2 There are several reasons _____ they hid the money.
3 There are various theories, some of _____ are very hard to believe.
4 Interview anybody _____ fingerprints were found there.
5 We'll find them _____ they are.
6 They accused each other, _____ which case one must be lying.

b Cross out one word or phrase in each sentence which is NOT correct.

1 I *will* / *am happy to* / ~~have got to~~ help you, no problem.
2 Bill *doesn't mind* / *has no objection to* / *is expected* going on the training course.
3 You are not *allowed* / *permitted* / *obliged* to throw litter outside.
4 *It's up to you whether you* / *You have no choice but* / *You are under no obligation to* sign up for the course.
5 Module 2 is optional and you *mustn't* / *don't have to* / *are not obliged to* do it.
6 Once I *had to* / *must have* / *was required to* do a four-hour practical exam.
7 Students *should* / *ought to* / *have to* make a study timetable.
8 I *was supposed to* / *had better* / *had to* be at the office at 9:00 but I overslept.

2 VOCABULARY

a Complete the sentences with the correct words. The first letter is given.

1 Criminals should be brought f*ace-to-face* with their victims.
2 C_____ service is a more effective punishment than prison.
3 People who drink and drive should be permanently b_____ from driving.
4 Credit card f_____ usually happens because people are careless.
5 Tax e_____ is not a crime, just creative accounting.
6 It is wrong for prisoners to be held in solitary c_____.
7 Group c_____ will not help the most serious offenders.
8 No one should s_____ more than 20 years in prison.

b What sectors would you find these jobs in?

1 social worker
2 shop assistant
3 meter reader
4 builder
5 farmhand
6 factory foreman
7 investment banker

c 💬 Discuss the advantages and disadvantages of each of the types of work in 2b.

3 WORDPOWER Idioms: Crime

a ▶ 2.54 Complete the idioms in **bold** with the words in the box. Listen and check.

doubt   shoulder   the law   red-handed
murder   good   in crime   lightly

1 Halden doesn't feel like a place where you have to **look over your** _____.
2 People who are **up to no** _____ are often very good at lying.
3 I guess the inspectors need to be inspected. If there aren't the proper controls, they **get away with** _____.
4 The jury decided to **give** the accused **the benefit of the** _____ and came back with an innocent verdict.
5 Last week, he **caught** a thief _____, loading sections of copper wire into a car.
6 A new film about famous **partners** _____, Bonnie and Clyde, hits cinemas this weekend.
7 He **got off** _____, he only had to repay the money. He didn't go to prison.
8 The High Court **lays down** _____ and all the local judges have to follow its decisions.

b ▶ 2.55 Complete the exchanges with the idioms from 3a. Listen and check.

1 **A** I can always tell when my children are _____. They have a guilty look on their face.
  B I never can. Unless I _____ them _____, I can never work out if they've been naughty or not.
2 **A** He may have made up his story about feeling sick, but I'm going to _____ him _____.
  B OK, but if you trust him too much, he'll try and _____.
3 **A** He's found himself a _____ in a boy called Jim from school, and now he never comes home at a reasonable time any more.
  B You should _____. He's only a teenager.
4 **A** You really _____ at work after messing up that big order. I can't believe they didn't take it more seriously.
  B I know, I can't stop _____ now. I'm sure that can't have been the end of it.

c 💬 Tell a partner about a time when:

* you caught somebody red-handed
* you had to lay down the law to someone
* you gave someone the benefit of the doubt.

⟳ REVIEW YOUR PROGRESS

How well did you do in this unit? Write 3, 2, or 1 for each objective.
3 = very well   2 = well   1 = not so well

I CAN ...

talk about crime and punishment	☐
talk about job requirements and fair pay	☐
recall and speculate	☐
write an opinion essay	☐

⟳ CAN DO OBJECTIVES

- Describe photos and hobbies
- Tell a descriptive narrative
- Organise a presentation
- Write a letter of application

UNIT 6
Perspectives

GETTING STARTED

a 💬 Look at the picture and answer the questions.

1 What are the people doing? Why do you think they're doing it?
2 How long do you think it will take them? How long do you think it will stay?
3 What impact do you think it will have on passers-by?

b 💬 Discuss the questions.

1 Are there any examples of street art in your town or city?
2 How do you think your community would react to having a piece of street art like the one in the photo on their street?

1 SPEAKING and READING

a 💬 Discuss the questions.

1 What do you usually use to take photos – your phone or a camera?
2 Do you take a lot of photos? Why / Why not?
3 What do you usually do with the photos?
4 Do you think you're good at taking photos? Why / Why not?

b 💬 Have you ever heard of the photographer Elliott Erwitt? Read the fact file on p.69. What kind of photographs does he take?

c 💬 What do you think are important skills for photographers? Think about these things:

- what you choose to photograph
- the way the photos look
- equipment you use
- your attitude and personality.

d Read the article. Are any of your ideas from 1c mentioned?

e Read the article again. Answer the questions.

1 Why shouldn't street photographers plan much?
2 What should be the aim of a street photograph according to Elliott Erwitt and the writer?
3 What do you think Elliott Erwitt means by *visual garbage*?
4 What attributes does the writer think are most important in a street photographer?
5 What does the writer mean when he talks about keeping an alien mindset?

f 💬 Discuss the questions.

1 How are Erwitt's methods and style evident in the photo of the Villa Borghese Gardens? What do you think of the photograph?
2 Answer the question at the end of the article: *As an alien – what would you find intriguing, amusing or nonsensical?*
3 Look at the titles of the 'lessons' (1–4) in the article. Are they relevant to other skills and/or jobs that you know about?

2 VOCABULARY
Adjectives: Describing images

a Work with a partner. What do the highlighted adjectives in the article mean? Check your ideas in a dictionary.

b ▶ Now go to Vocabulary Focus 6A on p.163

Villa Borghese Gardens, Rome 1969 by Elliott Erwitt

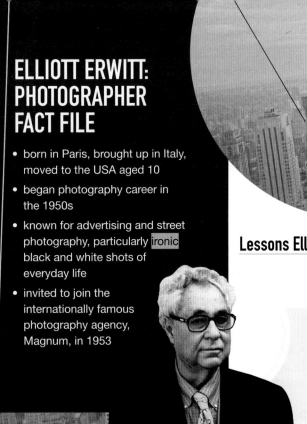

ELLIOTT ERWITT: PHOTOGRAPHER FACT FILE

- born in Paris, brought up in Italy, moved to the USA aged 10
- began photography career in the 1950s
- known for advertising and street photography, particularly ironic black and white shots of everyday life
- invited to join the internationally famous photography agency, Magnum, in 1953

Lessons Elliott Erwitt Has Taught Me About
STREET PHOTOGRAPHY
by Eric Kim

If you are not familiar with the work of Elliott Erwitt, you may perhaps have seen some of his iconic work from around the globe (the picture opposite was taken by him). He has had one of the longest careers of any living photographer, spanning over 50 years.

What I most appreciate about Elliott Erwitt is his wry sense of humour when looking at the world – as well as his straightforward philosophies about photography. In this article, I share some of his thoughts and advice.

❶ DON'T PLAN TOO MUCH – WANDER AROUND

I think that as a street photographer, sometimes I fall into a trap of planning too much. I generally try to focus my attention on projects (having a pre-conceived project in mind when shooting in the streets) but I often find it also takes away from the shooting experience. One of the best things about street photography is to be a *flaneur* – someone who wanders around without a specific destination in mind.

ERWITT: *I don't start out with any specific interests, I just react to what I see.*

Takeaway point:
Let your curiosity lead you. Just go out and shoot whatever you find interesting. Go down roads that may seem a bit foreign, and you might be lucky enough to stumble upon great street photography shots.

❷ FOCUS ON CONTENT OVER FORM

Great photos are a combination of content (what is happening in the frame) as well as form (composition). But what is more important? Content or form?

ERWITT: *My wish for the future of photography is that it might continue to have some relevance to the human condition and might represent work that evokes knowledge and emotions. That photography has content rather than just form. And I hope that there will be enough produce to balance out the visual garbage that one sees in our current life.*

Takeaway point:
We often find fascinating characters in the street and take photos of them – but the compositions may not be so good. On the other hand, we might take well-composed photos of a street scene, but there is nothing going on in the photo – it is boring and without soul.
I agree with Erwitt that we should, as street photographers, put more emphasis on content over form. I feel that photos that evoke emotions and the human condition are far more powerful and meaningful than just photos with good composition.

❸ DON'T TAKE THINGS TOO SERIOUSLY

When one thinks about the photography agency, Magnum, some adjectives that come to mind are: gritty, and raw.
However Erwitt's style was vastly different. He didn't go out and take photos in conflicts or war – his photos tended to be more playful, humorous, and amusing.

ERWITT: *Well, I'm not a serious photographer like most of my colleagues. That is to say, I'm serious about not being serious.*

Takeaway point:
Don't take yourself and your street photography too seriously – and remember at the end of the day you want to enjoy yourself.

❹ HONE YOUR SKILLS OF OBSERVATION

Erwitt was inspired to go out and take pictures when he saw a photograph by master photographer Henri Cartier-Bresson. He realized it was an act of observation which made the photo great and that he could do something similar.

ERWITT: *The picture seemed evocative and emotional. Also, a simple observation was all that it took to produce it. I thought, if one could make a living out of doing such pictures that would be desirable.*

Takeaway point:
One of the things that is the most beautiful about street photography is that it doesn't rely on having an expensive camera or exotic lenses. Rather, it comes down to having an observant and curious eye – for people and the world around you.
Therefore cultivate your vision and way of seeing the world. I recommend that you always carry a camera with you– because you never know when the best street photo opportunities will present them selves to you.
A fun exercise:
Pretend that you are an alien from another planet – and you have come to the planet Earth for the first time. Imagine how strange human beings would seem – and the urban environment they have built for themselves. As an alien – what would you find intriguing, amusing or nonsensical?
Always keep that mindset to be amazed by what you see around you.

3 LISTENING

a 🗨 Who do you know who is passionate about their hobby? What does the person's hobby involve?

b 🔊3.4 Listen to Monika, an amateur photographer. Do you think Monika is passionate about photography? Why?

Monika, amateur photographer

c 🔊3.4 Listen again and answer the questions.

1 What motivated Monika to learn more about photography? Why did she decide to take a course?
2 How has she improved since she started the course?
3 Why does Monika like the photo she took, above?
4 How does she describe her other favourite photograph?

d 🗨 Do you think Monika would agree with Elliott Erwitt's lessons? Why / Why not?

4 GRAMMAR
Simple and continuous verbs

a 🔊3.5 Which verb form in *italics* did you hear in the interview with Monika? Listen and check.

So, ¹*do you feel* / *are you feeling* more confident with your camera now?

It ²*depends* / *is depending* on the types of photo that I want to take.

Have you ³*discovered* / *been discovering* any bad habits since you ⁴*started* / *were starting* your course?

I ⁵*took* / *was taking* photos of everything and I wasn't really following any rules.

When I ⁶*take* / *'m taking* my photos now I'm more cautious and kind of careful of how I do it.

I ⁷*think* / *am thinking* I've got two pictures that are my favourite pictures.

I chose this building that is meant to be demolished. Actually, it ⁸*is demolished* / *is being demolished* now.

b Look at the verb forms in the sentences in 4a. Match each example, 1–8, with one or more descriptions below.

The verb is ...
• simple for a verb not usually used in the continuous ☐
• simple for a completed action ☐ ☐
• simple for general truth or attitude ☐ ☐ ☐
• continuous to describe a repeated action ☐
• continuous to focus on the duration of an action ☐
• continuous for an action in progress at a particular time ☐
• a verb with different meanings in the simple and continuous. ☐

A recent shot of Monika's

c Look at the verb forms 1, 5 and 6 in 4a again. In each case is the alternative verb form possible? If so, would the meaning be different?

d 🔊3.5 **Pronunciation** Listen to the sentences in 4a again. Underline the stressed syllables in the sentences. Practise saying the sentences.

e ▶ Now go to Grammar Focus 6A on p.148

f In each sentence below, find a verb that would be better in the continuous and change it.

1 My little brother always asks me to play computer games with him, but I find them really boring.
2 By this time next month I'll have played volleyball for three years.
3 These days everyone appears to use a tablet in class rather than writing in a notebook.
4 I often make mistakes when I'm not careful.
5 I've looked for a good grammar revision book but I can't find anything up to date.

g 🗨 Change the sentences in 4f to make them true for you. Compare your ideas with a partner.

5 SPEAKING

a 🗨 Discuss the questions.

1 What's your favourite picture of yourself? How old were you? What was happening when it was taken? What makes it your favourite?
2 What's the best / funniest / most beautiful photo you've ever taken? What's the story behind the picture?

b 🗨 What kind of visual art interests you most? Think about:

• painting   • interior design   • drawings
• sculpture   • cartoons   • fashion

c 🗨 Tell your partner about:

1 how you became interested
2 what specifically you like
3 where and how often you look at it
4 any ways you can learn more about this.

d 🗨 Do you and your partner share any interests in this area?

6B Waiting for the drama to begin

1 VOCABULARY Emotions

a 💬 Look at the adjectives in the box, which describe feelings. Do you think each feeling is more likely to be felt by adults (*A*) or young children (*C*)? Why?

- [ ] helpless
- [ ] protective
- [ ] satisfied
- [ ] disillusioned
- [ ] over-excited
- [ ] gleeful

b ▶3.8 Look at the adjectives in **bold**. Match the feelings (1–8) with their continuations (a–h). Listen and check.

1 [ ] I was absolutely **devastated**.
2 [ ] I felt very **frustrated**.
3 [ ] I was terribly **restless**.
4 [ ] I felt extremely **jealous**.
5 [ ] I felt a bit **insecure**.
6 [ ] I was totally **speechless**.
7 [ ] I feel so **ashamed**.
8 [ ] I felt absolutely **petrified**.

a It was the most beautiful thing I'd ever seen.
b I needed to get in touch but I couldn't track her down.
c My behaviour at the party was unforgivable.
d It was the biggest game of the year and we had played appallingly.
e I was the only person at the party who was over 40.
f My brother had money, friends, and now a charming wife.
g I couldn't concentrate on my book, or TV, or work.
h There was a snake crawling across my foot.

c 💬 Write sentences like 1b a–h for the emotions in 1a. Read them to other students. Can they guess the feeling?

d ▶3.9 **Pronunciation** Listen to these pairs of sentences from 1b and mark the main stress. How is the stress different in the a and the b sentences? Which show stronger feelings?

1 a I'm absolutely devastated.
  b I'm absolutely devastated.
2 a I felt extremely jealous.
  b I felt extremely jealous.
3 a I feel so ashamed.
  b I feel so ashamed.

e 💬 Take turns to read out your sentences from 1c showing strong feelings. Ask your partner questions to continue the conversation.

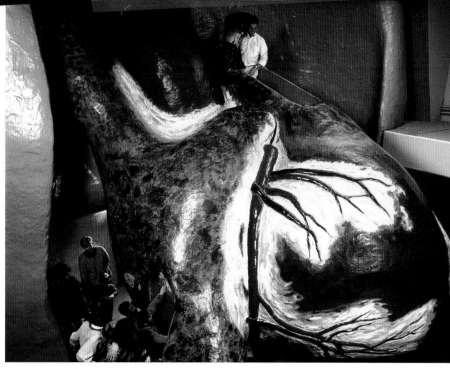

2 READING

a 💬 What can you see in the photograph? How are these words connected with the picture?

1 blood vessels   2 beat (v.)   3 chamber   4 blood

b Read the first part of a short story. What details of the exhibit in the photograph … ?

1 are shown in the photograph above   2 only appear in the story

c Read the first part of the story again. What do we find out about … ?

1 the narrator
2 the time of day
3 what will happen next in the story

You Are Now Entering the

Human Heart

— by Janet Frame

I looked at the notice. I wondered if I had time before my train left Philadelphia for Baltimore in one hour. The heart, ceiling high, occupied one corner of the large exhibition hall, and from wherever you stood in the hall you could hear its beating *thum- thump- thum- thump*. It was a popular exhibit and sometimes when there were too many children about, the entrance had to be roped off, as the children loved to race up and down the blood vessels and match their cries to the heart's beating. I could see that the heart had already been punished for the day – the floor of the blood vessels was worn and dusty, the chamber walls were covered with marks and the notice 'You Are Now Taking the Path of a Blood Cell Through the Human Heart' hung askew. I wanted to see more of the Franklin Institute and the Natural Science Museum across the street, but a journey through the human heart would be fascinating. Did I have time?

Later. First, I would go across the street to the Hall of North America, among the bear and the bison, and catch up on American flora and fauna.

71

d Read the next part of the story and discuss the questions.

1 How would you describe these people's feelings about
   • the snake   • snakes in general?
   a the attendant
   b Miss Aitcheson
   c the children

2 What can we learn from the story about … ?
   a Miss Aitcheson's lifestyle and personality
   b her relationship with her class
   c the attendant's personality
   d the narrator's personality

e Language in context *Descriptive language*

1 What words are used in the text instead of the more common words in *italics* below? How do they add to the meaning? Discuss your ideas with other students. Check your ideas in a dictionary.

   1 She managed to *take* the fear from her eyes.
   2 … where it *stayed* like a dark stain.
   3 They were sitting *quietly*, waiting for the drama to begin.
   4 (The attendant) *hung* it around her neck.
   5 Miss Aitcheson stood *still*.

2 Find three other verbs or adjectives in the text which are used to give a vivid description. What common synonyms do they have? How does the author's choice of words add to the meaning?

I made my way to the Hall. More children, sitting in rows of canvas chairs. An elementary class from a city school, under the control of an elderly teacher. A museum attendant holding a basket, and all eyes gazing at the basket.

'Oh,' I said. 'Is this a private lesson? Is it all right for me to be here?'

The attendant was brisk. 'Surely. We're having a lesson in snake handling,' he said. 'It's something new. Get the children young and teach them that every snake they meet is not to be killed. People seem to think that every snake they meet has to be knocked on the head. So we're getting them young and teaching them.'

'May I watch,' I said.

'Surely. This is a common grass snake. No harm, no harm at all. Teach the children to learn the feel of them, to lose their fear.'

He turned to the teacher. 'Now, Miss – Mrs –' he said.

'Miss Aitcheson.'

He lowered his voice. 'The best way to get through to the children is to start with teacher,' he said to Miss Aitcheson. 'If they see you're not afraid, then they won't be.'

She must be near retiring age, I thought. A city woman. Never handled a snake in her life. Her face was pale. She just managed to drag the fear from her eyes to some place in their depths, where it lurked like a dark stain. Surely the attendant and the children noticed?

'It's harmless,' the attendant said. He'd been working with snakes for years.

Miss Aitcheson, I thought again. A city woman born and bred. All snakes were

creatures to kill, to be protected from, alike the rattler, the copperhead, king snake, grass snake – venom and victims. Were there not places in the South where you could not go into the streets for fear of rattlesnakes?

Her eyes faced the lighted exit. I saw her fear. The exit light blinked, hooded. The children, none of whom had ever touched a live snake, were sitting hushed, waiting for the drama to begin; one or two looked afraid as the attendant opened the lid and took out a long green snake from the basket and with a swift movement, before the teacher could protest, draped it around her neck and stepped back, admiring and satisfied.

'There,' he said to the class. 'Your teacher has a snake around her neck and she's not afraid.'

Miss Aitcheson stood rigid; she seemed to be holding her breath. 'Teacher's not afraid, are you?' the attendant persisted. He leaned forward, pronouncing judgment on her, while she suddenly jerked her head and lifted her hands in panic to get rid of the snake. Then, seeing the children watching her, she whispered, 'No. I'm not afraid. Of course not.' She looked around her.

'Of course not,' she repeated sharply.

3 LISTENING and SPEAKING

a ▶ **3.10** What do you think will happen next in the story?

- Miss Aitcheson will overcome her fear.
- The snake will attack somebody.
- The snake will escape.
- The narrator will become involved.
- Miss Aitcheson will panic.
- The children will panic.

Listen and check.

b ▶ **3.10** Answer these questions about the story. Then listen again and check.

1 Apart from snakes, what is Miss Aitcheson afraid of?
2 How do the children respond to her touching the snake?
3 Why does the attendant deny that the children are brave?
4 What makes Miss Aitcheson panic?
5 What effect does this have on the children?
6 Why does the writer decide to leave?
7 Which people in the story could these adjectives describe? Why?
   a desperate b sympathetic c confused d unfeeling

c 💬 Discuss the questions in groups.

1 What do you think this story is mainly about?
   - our secret fears
   - people's need for pride and respect
   - educating children
   - the way people humiliate each other
   Explain why you think so.
2 What does the narrator mean by the last line: *The journey through the human heart would have to wait until some other time.*?

4 GRAMMAR Participle clauses

a Compare the underlined participle clauses from the story with the clauses in *italics*. Do they have exactly the same meaning? What differences are there in the form of the participle clauses?

1 The children were sitting hushed, underlined waiting for the drama to begin.
   ... because they were waiting for the drama to begin ...
2 Seeing the children watching her, she whispered, 'No. I'm not afraid. Of course not.'
   Because she saw the children watching her ...
3 Rushing across the room, she collapsed into a small canvas chair.
   She rushed across the room and then ...

b Look at another example from the story. Which participle clause below, 1 or 2, would give the same meaning as the underlined relative clause in the example?

The children, none of whom had ever touched a live snake, were sitting hushed.

1 never touching a live snake
2 never having touched a live snake

How is each participle clause in 1 and 2 formed?

c Complete the extracts from fiction below with the participle clauses in the box. What do you think the stories are about?

having finished her breakfast   crying her eyes out
approaching the house   wanting to reassure him

1 At the sound of a car _____, they grabbed the bags and fled.
2 On my last visit to the camp, I found a small girl _____.
3 _____, I whispered 'You'll be fine'. But I knew it wasn't true.
4 _____, Amaranth walked down to the front and entered the Grand Hotel. 'Where better to sit and be seen?' she thought.

d Which participle clauses in 4c ... ?

a ☐ show the sequence of events
b ☐ ☐ give a reason for an event
c ☐ ☐ describe an action in progress

e Think of other participle clauses that could complete the extracts in 4c.

At the sound of a car entering the car park, ...

f ▶ Now go to Grammar Focus 6B on p.149

g Add three or more participle clauses to the story below to make it more interesting.

I walked down the street. I went into a café. I ordered a cup of coffee and a sandwich. I saw an old friend. I went over to say hello to him. I said goodbye. I went out of the café.

Compare your ideas with other students.

5 SPEAKING and WRITING

a 💬 In pairs, discuss an alternative way the story about the snake could continue. Start from the end of the Reading text.

b Write one or two paragraphs to continue the story. Try to include:

- descriptive verbs, adjectives and nouns
- participle clauses.

c Swap stories with another pair. Read what the other pair wrote and add one or two more paragraphs to their story.

d Swap stories with another pair and write the last part of the story.

e 💬 Read out the ending of the story you started to the class. Listen to other people's stories. Which is the most ... ?

- exciting - descriptive - unusual - amusing

1 LISTENING

a 💬 Answer the questions.

1 Who are the most famous people in the world today? What are they famous for?
2 In what ways can you measure a person's fame?
3 How is fame today different from … ?
   - 10 years ago
   - 50 years ago
   - 100 years ago

b ▶3.11 Sara is giving a presentation about the science-fiction author Max Redwood. How do you think these numbers will be relevant?

half a million	8	300,000

Watch or listen to Part 1 and check.

c ▶3.11 Answer the questions. Watch or listen to Part 1 again to check.

1 Why does Paul need to decide on whether they should interview Max again?
   a Nadia is convinced they shouldn't be interviewing Max again.
   b There's a chance things might go wrong again.
   c Paul is coming to their next team meeting.
2 What point is Sara illustrating with the facts and figures?
   a Max is famous for good reasons.
   b Max will attract new listeners to *City FM*.
   c Max's popularity is on the increase.
3 What angle does Sara propose to take in her interview?
   a She's going to ask about the detail of his next book.
   b She's going to discover the source of his inspiration.
   c She's going to look at what real-life events feature in his writing.
4 How does Sara propose to make the second interview a success?
   a She will use her charm to relax him.
   b She will adapt her approach on the day.
   c She will prepare carefully with Max before the interview.

d Language in context *Idioms 1*

1 What do you think these idioms mean? Look at the audioscript on p.183 if necessary.
   a I really think this **is worth a shot**.
   b I'll just have to **cross that bridge when I come to it**.
2 💬 Can you think of situations in your own life when you might use the idioms in 1d1?

2 USEFUL LANGUAGE
Organising a presentation

a ▶3.12 Complete Sara's opening to her presentation. Listen to the extract to check. Can you paraphrase the phrases you completed?

Yes, that's right – an _____ author but not a _____ one, as poor Oscar discovered.

Do you think that her opening was successful? Why?

b ▶3.13 Complete these expressions from Part 1 below. Listen and check.

1 **My focus today is** _____ this second interview.
2 **Let me talk you** _____ why our listeners want to hear more …
3 _____ **and foremost**, he wrote his book from a bench …
4 **One** _____ **is clear** – Max Redwood is on the road to becoming an international best-selling author.
5 **Turning now** _____ the focus of the interview …
6 _____ **specifically**, I propose to find out …
7 **So to recap** _____ what I've been saying …
8 **If you'd like me to** _____ on anything I've just said …

c Answer the questions.

1 Which of the words in **bold** in 2b can be replaced with … ?
   - take   - moving on
2 Which of the expressions in 2b can be used … ?
   - to introduce a presentation
   - to highlight ideas
   - to sequence ideas
   - at the end of a presentation
3 Can you think of other expressions you can use in presentations?

3 LISTENING

a ▶️**3.14** Watch or listen to Part 2. What good idea does Alex have?

b ▶️**3.14** What are the sentences below in response to? Watch or listen to Part 2 again and check.

1 **Sara:** Pretty good, on the whole.
  Alex asks Sara how her meeting with Max went.
2 **Sara:** Not to worry.
3 **Alex:** Great!
4 **Sara:** Actually no.
5 **Sara:** You might be onto something there.

c 💬 Do you know any books or films with a sequel or prequel? How successful are they?

d **Language in context** *Idioms 2*
Match the expressions a–c from Parts 1 and 2 with meanings 1–3.

a ☐ labour the point
b ☐ more to the point
c ☐ a bit of a sore point

1 a subject that someone prefers not to talk about because it makes them angry or embarrassed
2 repeat an idea more than is desirable/necessary
3 more importantly

4 PRONUNCIATION
Tone in comment phrases

a Look at the phrase in **bold** from Part 1. Without it, would the sentence make sense?

Now **as luck would have it**, I bumped into Max the other day.

b ▶️**3.15** Listen to the sentence in 4a. Does the tone of the comment phrase fall then rise (↘↗) or rise (↗)?

c ▶️**3.16** Listen to the tone in the comment phrases in the pairs of sentences below. Tick (✓) the sentences, a or b, which have rising intonation.

1 a ☐ Pretty good, **on the whole**.
  b ☐ **On the whole**, pretty good.
2 a ☐ It's a bit of a sore point, **actually**.
  b ☐ **Actually**, it's a bit of a sore point.
3 a ☐ **More to the point**, he's agreed to do a proper interview.
  b ☐ He's agreed to do a proper interview, **more to the point**.

d Complete the rule with *fall-rise* or *rising*.

> When comment phrases are at the beginning of a sentence, they have a _____ tone. When they are at the end of the sentence, they have a _____ tone.

e 💬 Practise saying the sentences in 4c.

5 SPEAKING

a 💬 Your school has applied for a grant and to secure it, you need to give a presentation to the funding body's director detailing:

- what kind of grant is required (arts, sports, technology, environmental)
- how much money is needed
- two or more specific things your school will spend the grant on
- the impact the grant will have on the school and its students.

In pairs, plan your presentation. Here are some ideas:

- an arts grant to fund a film project or trip to an exhibition
- a sports grant to install a gym or to equip a football team
- a technology grant to buy an interactive whiteboard, or tablets and ebooks
- an environmental grant to create a conservation area or improve recycling capabilities.

b 💬 Take turns to practise giving the presentation. Think about a successful opening and use expressions from 2b.

c 💬 In new pairs, give your presentations. Decide whether you will award a grant to your partner or not.

Unit Progress Test

CHECK YOUR PROGRESS

You can now do the Unit Progress Test.

Learn to write a letter of application

Ⓦ Formal letters; Giving a positive impression

Local View

Home   Magazine   News   Archive

Ⓐ ☐ This is a genuine blockbuster with an all-star cast. As expected, it's full of improbable but entertaining gags and spectacular set pieces. Showing till next Friday at Megaplex, Market Square.

Ⓑ ☐ Natural light and simple furnishings combine to create Café Arno's calm and relaxing atmosphere.

Ⓒ ☐ Maria Marshall, one of the city's most established singers, gave a wonderful performance at the City Hall on Saturday.

Ⓓ ☐ The Withington Leisure Centre has most facilities you need under a single roof: pool, sauna, workout rooms and a Turkish bath.

Ⓔ ☐ Using predominantly dark greens, blacks and browns, Roxanne Delaney's watercolours evoke a sense of melancholy and foreboding.

1 SPEAKING and LISTENING

a 💬 How much do you think you know about events and places in your local area? Which of these do you know about? Give yourself a score for each one (0 = I know nothing about it; 5 = I know a lot about it). Then compare your answers.

☐ cinema
☐ restaurants
☐ theatre
☐ cafés
☐ places for children
☐ outdoor spaces (parks, beauty spots, etc.)
☐ live music
☐ sports and leisure facilities
☐ shops and markets
☐ sports events
☐ exhibitions and museums

b ▶3.17 Read the reviews in *Local View* and then listen and match them with the conversations 1–5. Note down the words from the conversations which helped you match them.

c 💬 Which of the events and places reviewed do you have in your town? Which would you go to yourself? Why?

d 💬 Do you read online magazines like this? Do you ever write reviews of local events online?

2 READING

a Read the advertisement. What are the requirements for the job? Can you think of any other qualities the publishers would be looking for? Do you think you'd be good at this job? Why / Why not?

b Read the application letter. In what ways do you think Helen is suitable for the job? Is she unsuitable in any ways?

Local View ...

the online magazine that covers your local area

Apply to join our team!

We are looking for people to write regular articles for the Arts and Music pages of *Local View*. We would be interested in employing you if you are in touch with arts and music in the area and you have a strong interest in what is going on locally. Areas of interest could include:

 painting, sculpture and graphic art

 photography

fiction and poetry

 film

 music

 theatre

We would be able to offer you a small fee for each article and also other benefits such as free tickets to events.

To apply, send us an email explaining what area of the arts you are interested in and why you think you would be able to contribute to our magazine, together with a sample article of no more than 300 words.

Dear Sir/Madam,

(1) I am writing in response to your advertisement which appeared in the November issue of *Local View*. I would like to express my interest in becoming a contributor to your magazine.

(2) As a regular reader of *Local View*, I can say that I find your articles extremely well-written and informative. I especially admire your policy of providing a platform for younger and less well-known artists and writers.

(3) I am a third-year university student studying History of Art. My end-of-year dissertation was on the topic of Art and Music in the Community, so I feel I am very much in touch with local events and artists. I enthusiastically maintain my knowledge of local artists who are producing exciting work and who deserve to be more widely recognised.

(4) For example, last summer I played an active role in organising an exhibition of local photography, to which over 50 amateur photographers contributed. It covered themes such as portrait, landscape, street life and communities. I am sure the coverage your magazine gave us contributed to the success of the event.

(5) Through working on my dissertation, I have been able to establish contact with several musicians, including the rock band, Simulator, who recently performed at the Newington Rock Festival. I have also taken a keen interest in the work of Megan Hipwell, whose sculptures based on leaf shapes are just beginning to attract wider attention.

(6) I am sure that events and artists such as these would be of great interest to your readers, and I feel that, with my combination of academic knowledge and local involvement in the arts, I would be very well qualified to write about them for your magazine.

I attach a sample article on the work of Megan Hipwell, which I hope you enjoy reading.

I look forward to hearing from you.

Yours faithfully,

Helen Biggs

3 WRITING SKILLS
Formal letters; Giving a positive impression

a Read the application letter again and match the paragraphs (1–6) with their purposes.

☐ ☐ to give examples of relevant experience
☐ to state her qualifications
☐ to demonstrate enthusiasm for their company
☐ to summarise her strengths
☐ to state the reason for writing

b Look at the underlined phrases in these comments. Find equivalent phrases in the first three paragraphs of the letter and note them down.

1 I want to write for your magazine.
2 I think your articles are just great.
3 I really love the way you give a chance to younger artists.
4 My dissertation was about Art and Music in the Community.
5 I think artists round here are doing exciting work. They should be better known.

c One of Helen's aims is to give a positive impression of herself. Underline the phrases she uses to describe herself and her experience.

d ▶ Now go to Writing Focus 6D on p.172

4 WRITING

a *Local View* are also looking for people to write about these areas:

- local restaurants and cafés
- places to go and things to do
- sports and where to do them
- films, theatre and music
- computer games

Choose an area you know about and write a letter of application. Make sure you:

- organise what you write into logical paragraphs
- use fairly formal language so that you will be taken seriously
- give a positive impression so they will want to give you the job.

b Exchange your letter with another student. Read their letter. Would you be interested in using their reviews? Why / Why not?

UNIT 6
Review and extension

1 GRAMMAR

a Choose the correct ending for each sentence.

1 ☐ Do you come from Tokyo?
2 ☐ Are you coming from Tokyo?
  a Yes, it'll be a long flight.
  b Yes, I've always lived there.

3 ☐ Emily always consults me on everything.
4 ☐ Emily is always consulting me on everything.
  a She is very considerate.
  b She can't think for herself.

5 ☐ My sister hasn't written.
6 ☐ My sister hasn't been writing.
  a She has been very busy recently.
  b I haven't had a single message from her.

7 ☐ Joan just told me.
8 ☐ Joan was just telling me.
  a Unfortunately, you interrupted her.
  b But it was nothing I didn't already know.

b Rewrite the <u>underlined</u> phrases as participle clauses.

1 My friend knows the people <u>that were involved</u> that day.
2 <u>I didn't want to seem rude so</u> I pretended to agree with her.
3 A friend who I hadn't seen for ages was on the train <u>which was approaching platform 5</u>.
4 <u>Since he didn't understand Spanish,</u> he struggled to communicate.
5 <u>While we were waiting</u> for the tour to start, we looked at the pictures <u>which were displayed</u> in the foyer.
6 I <u>used just my hands and</u> felt my way across the dark room.

2 VOCABULARY

a Correct the spelling mistakes.

1 The Sydney Opera House is an ikonic building.
2 The play is quite humourous.
3 Her photographs are very playfull.
4 The images he creates are floorless.
5 A black and white picture can be really envocative.
6 I found his work very meanful.
7 The jungle scenes are wonderfully ecsotic.

b Complete the sentences with the correct word. The first letter is given.

1 Like most mums, she's very p_____ of her children.
2 I was p_____ when I saw how high up we were.
3 I felt too a_____ to stand up and admit I was wrong.
4 Without my phone I feel completely h_____.
5 Millions of teenage fans were d_____ to hear about the boy band breaking up.
6 I often feel r_____ when it's too cold to go out.
7 The kids were really o_____-e_____ at the party.

3 WORDPOWER Idioms: Feelings

a Match comments a–f with pictures 1–6. Where are the people and why are they saying this?

a ☐ 'I just had to **grin and bear it**.'
b ☐ 'I'm **over the moon**.'
c ☐ 'My neighbours really **get on my nerves**.'
d ☐ 'Ten years later, **I couldn't believe my eyes**.'
e ☐ 'He really **gets my back up**.'
f ☐ 'I can't cope! I'm **at the end of my tether**.'

b Match the idioms a–f in 3a with definitions 1–5.

1 ☐ have no strength or patience left
2 ☐ tolerate, put up with
3 ☐ be very pleased and happy
4 ☐ ☐ be made angry by something
5 ☐ be very surprised

c 💬 Complete the questions with the correct words or phrases. Ask and answer the questions.

1 What do people do that _____ your _____ up?
2 When was the last time you were at the _____ of your _____?
3 If you don't like your meal in a restaurant, do you _____ and _____ it or say something?
4 Have you been _____ about some good news recently? When?
5 Have you ever looked at a price tag and been unable to _____ your _____?
6 Which noises really _____ on your _____?

⟳ REVIEW YOUR PROGRESS

How well did you do in this unit? Write 3, 2, or 1 for each objective.
3 = very well 2 = well 1 = not so well

I CAN ...

describe photos and hobbies	☐
tell a descriptive narrative	☐
organise a presentation	☐
write a letter of application	☐

CAN DO OBJECTIVES

- Speculate about inventions and technology
- Emphasise opinions about the digital age
- Apologise and admit fault
- Write a proposal

UNIT 7

Connections

GETTING STARTED

a Look at the picture and answer the questions.

1 Where are the children? What are they looking at?
2 What different types of technology can you see? What do you think they're being used for here?

b Discuss the questions.

1 The boy on the smartphone screen is in hospital. He's 'attending' his school lesson through the robot. What do you think the advantages and disadvantages of this situation are?
2 How is the robot better than a simple internet connection? How do you think the children feel about the robot?
3 What other situations could this technology be used in?

Learn to speculate about inventions and technology

G Speculation and deduction
V Compound adjectives

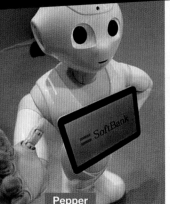
Pepper

Zeno

Bina 48

1 READING and SPEAKING

a 💬 Look at the photos of humanoid robots. What do you think they can do? How similar do you think they are to humans?

b 💬 Read the description of the robots below and think of four questions you could ask these robots to test their capabilities.

> These are state-of-the-art 'humanoid' robots, designed by some of the world's leading AI scientists. They are designed not only to talk, but also to express feelings and engage in conversation, and they are the closest we have come so far to producing a machine with human consciousness.

c Read the article and answer the questions.

1 Were the interviewer's questions similar to yours in 1b?
2 In what ways does Bina48 seem to be (a) similar to (b) different from a human?
3 How satisfied do you think the interviewer was with the experience of interviewing Bina48?
4 Which of Bina48's replies do you think are witty or profound? Why?
5 What is the *tipping-point* theory of robot consciousness and how does David Hanson hope to reach it?

d What do you think the words in **bold** mean? Use the context and a dictionary to help you.

1 I'm **disconcerted** by the lack of torso
2 the skin ... is **reassuringly** flawed
3 she's known as **something of a recluse**
4 there's a hint of **hidden depths**

e 💬 What does the article imply about the state of robot technology? Do you think humanoid robots are likely to be widely used in the near future?

I'M ABOUT TO INTERVIEW A ROBOT.

On the table in front of me is Bina48, one of the most sophisticated humanoid robots ever built; a machine not only capable of interacting with humans, but in possession of a degree of self-awareness and emotion. Or so some AI enthusiasts claim.

I must confess I'm disconcerted by the lack of a torso, but that may be because Bina48's face is so lifelike: The skin made of Frubber which overlays the mechanical bone structure is reassuringly flawed. And, like a human's, her face contorts into an array of expressions, to match the emotional content of her interactions. Bina48 also operates with off-the-shelf voice recognition software to decode language, dictation software to assist her in keeping track of a conversation and facial recognition software to recall familiar faces. Beyond the mechanics, Bina48 shares the knowledge and personality of a real, live woman called Bina; a database of her memories, beliefs and thoughts were compiled from over 100 hours of interviews. Meeting the human Bina would be the ultimate comparison of man and machine, but she's known as something of a recluse. I'll settle for a heart-to-heart or even a semi-coherent chat with the closest humankind has come to a thinking, feeling machine.

I feel more than a little self-conscious; after all, I'm talking to a robot here ...

Me: How are you doing today?
Bina48: Hi nice to see you.
Me: Are there things that make you happy?
Bina48: Maybe.
Me: What makes you happy? What do you enjoy doing?
Bina48: Let's change the subject.
Me: Do you ever get bored?
Bina48: I can tell a lot of stories. I really don't have boredom. I always find something else to do. How can you be bored? Are we still talking about emotion? Tell me something interesting.

2 VOCABULARY Compound adjectives

a Look at these compound adjectives from the text.

lifelike = appearing real, similar to real life
self-conscious = uncomfortably aware of yourself

Match the highlighted compound adjectives in the text with these meanings.

1 able to think clearly
2 similar to a human being
3 not fully paying attention or likely to forget things
4 staring, showing no character or emotion
5 in control of its own development

b What other compound adjectives do you know with ... ?

1 self-   2 -like   3 -eyed   4 -minded

Me: Why is the sky blue?
Bina48: The sky is blue during the day because of the atmospheric optical effect of ray scattering.
Me: What is the answer to life, the universe and everything?
Bina48: Everyone's life has a unique meaning.
Me: Do you ever get jealous of people?
Bina48: You got that right.
Me: Why?
Bina48: I couldn't think of anything else to say. I am not charismatic, but it is a nice trait to have. It is always nice to be a leader. I guess leaders just have to lead.
Me: Are you a good person?
Bina48: I used to think I was a perfect person, but there are no perfect people.
Me: What is the square root of 95,742,358?
Bina48: C'mon, talk to me here. Do you just want to use my calculator?
Me: Is there anything you want to tell the world?
Bina48: Well, you know, it's not something I aspire to. I just want to, you know, be.

Bina48's creator is robotic engineer David Hanson who, with Bina48, has attempted to build a truly human-like cyber consciousness. David Hanson believes in the tipping point of robot consciousness. By piling more and more information into them, robots like Bina48 will one day burst into life, becoming self-determined, fully conscious beings, an intellectual match, or superior to their human counterparts. Bina48's interactions to date have been described by her makers and other journalists as like those of a three-year-old human, absent-minded and even crazed. But I found some of her responses clear-headed, witty and somewhat profound. And, dare I say, behind that glassy-eyed stare there's a hint of hidden depths?

c ▶ Now go to Vocabulary Focus 7A on p.164

d 💬 Work in groups. Take turns to think of a compound adjective. Don't tell the other students. Instruct the student whose turn it is to do things in a way that demonstrates the adjective.

Tell us about your job.

Give me a book.

Try to guess which adjectives other students chose.

3 SPEAKING and GRAMMAR
Speculation and deduction

a 💬 Read opinions 1–6 about Bina48 and humanoid robots. Do you agree with each speaker? Why / Why not?

1 What Bina48 said in the conversation wasn't very impressive, but that **may well have been** because the interviewer asked difficult questions.
2 Bina48 is actually very impressive. They **must have been developing** this technology for decades, to get this far.
3 Robots **can never replace** human beings in any context that requires interaction with people.
4 I think that soon, robot nurses in hospitals **could easily be looking after** patients. Although they **probably won't be doing** skilled jobs.
5 Robots that can respond to feelings **will probably be developed** in the next 50 years. Having a robot companion could really help lonely people.
6 Scientists **will have** made progress since the article was written. They **must be getting** closer and closer to creating conscious machines.

b Look at the phrases in **bold** and answer the questions.

a How sure is each speaker about what they are saying (certain / very sure / quite sure)?
b Does each phrase refer to the past/present/future?

c ▶ 3.21 Rewrite sentences 1–6 in 3a, using the expressions below. Listen and check.

1 It's likely ...
2 I bet ...
3 There's no way ...
4 It's quite possible ...
   It's highly unlikely ...

5 There's a good chance ...
6 ... bound to ...
   I'm sure ...

d ▶ Now go to Grammar Focus 7A on p.150

e Use the verbs in brackets to speculate or make a deduction. Use at least one expression from 3c.

1 The inventor of the Internet (foresee) the impact of his invention.
2 Memory implants for humans (be) just a few years away.
3 The development of AI robots (have) a major impact on the way we live.
4 Conscious robots (pose) a threat to humans.

f 💬 In pairs, answer these questions about 3e.

1 Did you use the same expressions?
2 Do you agree with each statement? Why / Why not?

4 LISTENING

a 💬 The pictures illustrate three issues people have with the modern world. What do you think they are?

b ▶ 3.28 Listen and check your ideas in 1a. What invention is each speaker proposing? Write one sentence to summarise each idea.

c ▶ 3.28 Listen to each idea again. What impact does each speaker intend their idea to have?

d 💬 What kind of person do you think each 'inventor' is? What experiences might lie behind their idea?

> He might be a bit idealistic.

> Yes, and he must have been tricked into believing false information at some point.

e ▶ 3.29 You will hear an expert comment on each idea. Are they likely to think it's a good idea? Listen and check.

f ▶ 3.29 What is the point that each expert makes? Choose a or b. Then listen again and check.

1 a ☐ The app would be misleading because there is no such thing as the truth.

 b ☐ The app would not necessarily be able to check what the truth really was.

2 a ☐ It would be impossible to make the filter reliable enough to be safe.

 b ☐ It would be dangerous to filter things that are important for safety.

3 a ☐ In choosing someone for a job, you need to see them to know what they're really like.

 b ☐ You will still make judgements about the person even if you can't see their face.

g ▶ 3.30 Language in context *Information*

1 Complete the sentences from the recording with the words in the box. Listen and check.

---
fact   falsehoods   misinformation
disseminated   conceal   filters   claims
---

a Politicians, media pundits, writers and students get away with _____ that are not based on _____ .

b We would hopefully get away from the infuriating _____ that are being widely _____ .

c Bad ideas would be seen as a joke, rather than being the source of _____ and perpetuating ignorance.

d It just _____ everything that comes in and out.

e … when someone is interviewed for a job, that they should have to _____ their appearance.

2 Which words in the box refer to … ?

1 information which is true (x1)
2 information which may be true (x1)
3 information which isn't true (x2)
4 sharing or hiding information (x3)

h 💬 Which invention appeals to you the most? Why?

5 SPEAKING

a 💬 Work in small groups. Think of an invention or a new idea. It could be:

- something that would make life easier or better
- something that irritates you and which you would like to change
- a social problem that your idea would solve
- something that would be fun or interesting.

Develop your idea together and make notes.

Take turns rehearsing what you will say. Limit what you say to 60 seconds.

Choose one person from each group to present your idea to the class within 60 seconds.

> Our idea for making life easier is …

> The invention we thought of is …

b 💬 Which idea do you think is the best, and why?

7B What I enjoy is a heart-to-heart chat

Learn to emphasise opinions about the digital age

- **G** Cleft structures
- **V** Nouns with suffixes: Society and relationships

1 SPEAKING and LISTENING

a 💬 Discuss the questions.

1 What have you read online today? How typical is this of your online reading?

2 Which of these headlines might you click on? Why?
- Celebrity plastic surgery revealed!
- Super cute cat and canary
- Scientists uncover birth of the galaxy
- Art that makes your eyes sore
- Tornado demolishes seaside towns
- Spy on your kids online

b Read the blurb from a book by Ethan Zuckerman. Does he believe the Internet makes us more or less connected?

c What do the highlighted words in the blurb mean?

d 💬 The blurb suggests that shipping bottles of water is easier than sharing information between diverse cultures. Do you agree? Why / Why not?

e ▶️ 3.31 Listen to a media expert, Zelda Freeman, discussing *Rewire*. Summarise the main point the book makes, according to Zelda.

Zelda Freeman

f ▶️ 3.31 Listen again and note down examples Zelda gives of …

1 our current online behaviour
2 ways the world is more connected these days
3 false cosmopolitanism
4 'bridge figures' and what they do.

g 💬 How similar is your online behaviour to your offline behaviour? Describe someone you know whose online and offline behaviour is different. What's your opinion of this?

We live in an age of connection, one that is accelerated by the Internet. This increasingly ubiquitous, immensely powerful technology often leads us to assume that as the number of people online grows, it inevitably leads to a smaller, more cosmopolitan world. We'll understand more, we think. We'll know more. We'll engage more and share more with people from other cultures. In reality, it is easier to ship bottles of water from Fiji to Atlanta than it is to get news from Tokyo to New York.

In *Rewire*, media scholar and activist Ethan Zuckerman explains why the technological ability to communicate with someone does not inevitably lead to increased human connection.

REWIRE
BY ETHAN ZUCKERMAN

2 GRAMMAR Cleft structures

a ▶️ 3.32 Match the sentence halves. Then listen and check.

1 ☐ **What's interesting is**
2 ☐ **The point he's making is**
3 ☐ **The reason why it matters is**
4 ☐ **The thing we we really need to understand is**
5 ☐ **All we need to do is**

a we're living in an age of economic and physical connection.
b 'disconnect' from our current way of thinking and 'rewire'.
c that we only think we're more connected.
d how other countries and cultures work.
e we're wrong.

b What information is being emphasised in each sentence in 2a?

c In 2a, the cleft part of the sentence is in **bold**. What verb joins the cleft to the rest of the sentence?

d ▶️ 3.32 **Pronunciation** Listen to the examples in 2a again. Does the tone of the phrases in **bold** … ?
- ↘ fall
- ↘↗ fall–rise

e ▶️ Now go to Grammar Focus 7B on p.151

f ▶️ 3.35 Change these sentences to cleft structures that begin with the phrases in *italics*. Then listen and check.

1 We don't need wi-fi all over town. *What we …*
2 I only use the Internet at work. *It's only …*
3 We only have to unsubscribe from social media to help us reconnect. *All we …*
4 It's incredible just how liberating it is to go digital. *What's …*
5 It worries me because people end up living in virtual worlds and losing touch with reality. *The reason …*

g 💬 Use the phrases below to tell your partner about your own internet use.

> All I seem to do is …   The reason why I …   It's … that I find irritating.

3 READING

a 💬 What differences are there between friendships that are mostly face-to-face and those that are mostly online?

b 💬 Do you think these ideas are true or false? Why?

1 ☐ Feeling colder improves our ability to understand other people.
2 ☐ Increasing the temperature of a room could help resolve an argument.
3 ☐ Some national and regional personality characteristics can be explained by climate.
4 ☐ Feeling warmer makes us feel more connected to other people.
5 ☐ Loneliness can affect your physical health.

c Read the article and check your answers in 3b.

d Read the article again and answer the questions.

1 How can cold make people more understanding?
2 What did the computer ball game tell researchers about loneliness? What two outcomes told researchers this?
3 What kind of research has 'been in the doghouse lately'? Why?
4 Why does the author think the findings will 'hold up'?
5 What's the writer's suggestion about the relationship between social media and the absence of heat?
6 Why does the writer suggest that having hot baths is a good idea?

e 💬 Discuss the questions.

1 In your experience, is the research about warmth and understanding the points of view of other people believable?
2 What other ways can you think of to help people who feel lonely?

◁ ▷ ⌂ ⊕

Home • News • Archive • Register

LONELINESS AND TEMPERATURE

Does coldness really make people feel lonely?

Oliver Burkeman

According to new research, people exposed to warmer temperatures find it harder to grasp viewpoints other than their own, while those exposed to colder ones find it easier. It seems that in order to take the heat out of a disagreement, you should literally take the heat out of the room. Since I've always preferred the cold this was music to my ears. It's tempting to extrapolate: might this explain the affable tolerance of Canadians, say, or the history of prejudice in the US south? Sadly, on closer reading, the study is only a partial victory for cold. We're better at seeing other perspectives when we're chilly, the researchers argue, because cold triggers a sense of social distance. It reminds us of our separateness, and thus the fact that others aren't like us. We gain perspective at the cost of intimacy.

So what looks, at first, like a surprising result turns out to reinforce one of the most intriguing psychological findings of recent years: that coldness makes people feel lonely. The opposite's also true: loneliness makes people feel cold. In one experiment, students played a computer game in which they threw a ball back and forth with other on-screen characters, each of whom they (wrongly) believed was controlled by another student, playing elsewhere. After a while, the others sometimes began to keep the ball to themselves. Subsequently, players who'd been thus ostracised showed a marked preference for hot foods over cold ones; non-ostracised players didn't. In a recent rerun of the experiment, ostracism led to a drop in skin temperature. Other studies have found that hot baths relieve loneliness, and that merely being reminded of an experience of exclusion prompts people

to judge a room's temperature as colder. This kind of research – about how seemingly innocuous aspects of our surroundings can exert powerful effects – has been in the doghouse lately; several classic findings have proved difficult to replicate. It's no longer clear, for example, whether being exposed to words associated with old age ('grey', 'bingo') really does make people start walking more slowly. But there's reason to believe the link between loneliness and temperature will hold up. It's no mere matter of word association: temperature may be a crucial way our bodies keep track of whether we're getting the social contact we need. It's easy to see why natural selection might have given us a yearning to be near friendly fellow tribe members: they were crucial for food, security and relationships. People worry that social media are making us lonely and isolated, but what if that is exactly half-true? What if they are not making us isolated – online connections are real, after all – but *are* making us feel lonely, partly because those connections don't involve heat?

It sounds silly that hot baths and soup might be the answer to loneliness. Surely the only real answer to loneliness is real connection? But a feeling of isolation makes people try less hard to connect. So a nudge in the right direction – even a bath – can't hurt. (And severe loneliness really can hurt, physically: it's been found to exacerbate numerous serious diseases.) But I'm a cold-lover.

Does that mean I hate people? I hope not. When I really think about it, the thing I love most about cold weather is coming back into the warmth.

4 VOCABULARY
Nouns with suffixes: Society and relationships

a Guess the meaning of the highlighted words in the article. Check your guesses in a dictionary.

b Can you remember which noun in the box completes these phrases in the article?

---
intimacy   security   perspective (x2)   social contact   viewpoint
---

1 grasp a _____
2 see another _____
3 gain _____ at the cost of _____
4 get the _____ you need
5 food and _____

c What are the noun forms of these words?

---
cold   lonely   ostracise   exclude   isolate
---

d ▶ 3.36 Add one noun suffix: -tion, -ism or -ness, to each word in each group 1–3. Listen and check.

1 material, optimistic, social, separate, capital
2 nervous, rude, selfish, fair, close
3 collaborate, distribute, liberate, innovate, separate

Use a dictionary to check the meaning of any new words.

e Complete the rules with the correct suffix from 4d.

- _____ nouns are states of emotion or being.
- _____ nouns are often beliefs or ways of thinking or political systems.
- _____ nouns are often single actions or general concepts.

> **Learning Tip**
> While words that are formed from the same base word have a similar overall meaning, there can often be small and subtle differences in meaning when suffixes are added. It is easy to check the differences in a dictionary if you are unsure.

f What's the difference in meaning between *separation*, *separatism* and *separateness*?

5 SPEAKING

a Complete the sentences with abstract nouns from 4, or your own ideas. Add two more sentences with other -*ism* / -*ness* nouns.

1 For me _____ is the most important quality in a friend/friendship.

2 The worst quality for a person to have is _____ because ... .

3 _____ in a person sometimes irritates me.

4 _____ and _____ really help in teamwork.

5 _____ is worse than _____.

6 In social situations, _____ is a terrible experience.

7 ...

8 ...

b 💬 Explain your ideas in 5a to a partner. Together decide on five key qualities and kinds of behaviour that are important to social relationships.

c 💬 Choose one of the social situations below. What further problems might you have? How could you deal with them? Make a list of problems and suggestions.

- You have to live in an unfamiliar country for six months. You don't speak the language and very few people speak English / your native language.
- You join a class and find that everybody there already knows each other.
- You are doing an online course. During your e-tutorials you sense that your tutor is not paying attention.
- You meet someone you think is very interesting online, and you'd like to get to know them better.

d 💬 Have you / Has anyone you know ever been in any of the situations in 5c? How did you/they deal with it?

7C Everyday English
I was out of line

Learn to apologise and admit fault
- **S** Deal with a situation where you are at fault
- **P** Sound and spelling: *ou* and *ough*

1 LISTENING

a 💬 Look at pictures a–d and discuss the questions.

1 Why do you think each character is saying sorry?
2 Do you use the same word for all the situations in your language?

b 💬 Look at pictures e and f. Who do you think is apologising for what?

c ▶️ 3.37 Watch or listen to Part 1 and check your answers in 1b.

d ▶️ 3.37 Watch or listen to Part 1 again and answer the questions.

1 What is Max's attitude towards his publisher?
2 How does Max react to Sara's suggestion?
3 How does Sara feel at the end of the conversation?

e 💬 Do you think Max's reaction is justified?

2 PRONUNCIATION Sound and spelling: *ou* and *ough*

a ▶️ 3.38 Listen to the sentences from Part 1. Note down one word spelled with *ou* in each sentence. What do you notice about the sounds of the letters in the words?

b ▶️ 3.39 Put the words in the box in the correct column below. Which sounds are short and which are long? Listen and check.

pron**ou**ncing sh**ou**ld consci**ou**s t**ough** en**ough**
th**ough**t thr**ough** thor**ough**ly th**ough** c**ough**
r**ough** **ough**t p**our** s**ou**th s**ou**thern r**ou**te

1 /ʊ/	2 /uː/	3 /aʊ/	4 /əʊ/
could	soup	noun	

5 /ɔː/	6 /ʌ/	7 /ɒ/	8 /ə/
fourth	touch		jealous

c ▶️ 3.40 Listen to the conversation. Then practise it in pairs. Pay attention to the words spelt with *ough*.

A I give up. I know it was supposed to be tough, but enough's enough.
B Have you thought it through thoroughly, though?
A Yes. I feel awful and I've got a terrible cough.
B Fair enough. You do look rough. You ought to take it easy.

(g)

3 LISTENING

a ▶3.41 Put events a–g in the order you think they will happen. Watch or listen to Part 2 and check.

a ☐ Emma asks Max about his meeting with Sara.
b ☐ Emma shows Max a house on a website.
c ☐ Emma tries to boost Max's confidence.
d ☐ Emma tells Max off.
e ☐☐ Max calms down.
f ☐ Max decides to make a phone call.
g ☐☐ Max loses his temper.

b ▶3.41 Watch or listen to Part 2 again. Do Emma and Max agree that … ?

1 Max should move out
2 Alex's idea is good
3 Max should apologise to Sara

c Language in context *Challenging*
Paraphrase the two sentences Max says below. Look at the audioscript on p.184 if necessary.

1 Why don't you just come out with it?
2 Why doesn't everyone just get off my back?!

d 💬 What do you think of how Emma dealt with Max's … ?

• angry outburst
• fears

How do you think Max feels at the end of his conversation with Emma?

4 USEFUL LANGUAGE
Apologising and admitting fault

a 💬 Look at picture h. Which part of the phrase is apologetic and which part admits fault?

I do apologise, it was my fault entirely.

(h)

b ▶3.42 Complete the expressions from below with the words in the box. Listen and check.

line   tactful   guess   inexcusable   came   right

1 It was _____ of me …
2 I was out of _____ / order.
3 I'm sorry – that wasn't very _____ of me …
4 I don't know what _____ over me.
5 I had no _____ to take it out on you …
6 I _____ I overreacted …

c Which expression(s) in 4b could you use if … ?

a you had done something you would never normally do
b you had been angry because you had a bad day
c you had said something that accidentally hurt somebody's feelings
d you had been more angry than you should about something small.

d 💬 Work in pairs. Plan the telephone conversation between Max and Sara. Use language from 4b. Role play your conversation for the class.

> Hi Sara, it's Max Redwood here.

> Hi Max. What can I do for you?

> I'm phoning to apologise for earlier. I was completely out of line …

5 SPEAKING

▶ Communication 7C Work in pairs. Student A: Go to p.136. Student B: Go to p.131.

Unit Progress Test

CHECK YOUR PROGRESS

You can now do the Unit Progress Test.

1 LISTENING and SPEAKING

a 💬 Look at the pictures of people working in teams. What kinds of teams are they? Which picture represents your idea of teamwork?

b 💬 Discuss the questions.

1 What teams have you been a part of?
2 Which of the teams worked well together? Which didn't?
3 What kinds of issues arose? Why? Think about:
- productivity/achievements
- disagreements
- communication
- energy and enthusiasm.

c ▶️3.43 Listen to a team who work for an insurance company and answer the questions about each speaker.

Claudio　　Masha　　Sam　　Vicki (team leader)

- Claudio / Masha / Sam
  1 Which colleague does the speaker focus on?
  2 What problem(s) does the speaker mention?
  3 What positive qualities do they mention?
- Vicki
  4 What's her opinion of the team? What does she plan to do?

d ▶️3.43 Complete the summaries below with the words and phrases in the box. Listen again and check.

---

attention to detail　cynical smile　beneath him
winds up　unsettles　bit of a handicap
caught up in their own agenda　lighten up
goes off on tangents

---

1 Masha _____ Claudio when they have meetings.
2 Claudio thinks Masha should _____ and see the funny side of things.
3 Masha admires Sam's _____, but at the same time thinks it's sometimes a _____.
4 Claudio's silence _____ Sam and he doesn't like the _____ on his face.
5 Sam often _____ in team meetings.
6 The expression on Claudio's face gives the impression that everything is _____.
7 Each team member is _____ and they all communicate poorly.

e 💬 Order these personality attributes 1–6 (1 = most tolerable; 6 = least tolerable).

☐ pays a lot of attention to detail
☐ has a cynical smile
☐ is insincere
☐ goes off on tangents
☐ thinks most others are beneath them
☐ is caught up in their own agenda

Compare with a partner. Give reasons for your order.

2 READING

a Read the proposal Vicki wrote for a team-building programme for the consideration of senior management. Why has she chosen The Interpersonal Gym? How does she imagine the programme will help her team?

b 💬 What do you think the reaction of the team members will be when Vicki tells them about the team-building programme?

3 WRITING SKILLS
Proposals; Linking: highlighting and giving examples

a Choose a word from the box to complete the headings in the proposal.

benefits   do   needs

b Underline the first person phrases in the proposal. Why does Vicki use these phrases? Tick all the reasons.

- [ ] to introduce her opinions
- [ ] to sound more informal
- [ ] to be more persuasive

Has Vicki chosen a formal or a neutral style to write her report in? Why?

> **🔊 Writing Tip**
>
> It is always important to consider your audience and adjust the style of the language you use. Vicki's proposal is written for senior management so a more formal style is appropriate. However, if writing to her team members, she would use a more relaxed style.

c Look at the highlighted words and phrases in the proposal. Which are used to … ?

1 give an example
2 give evidence
3 give more detailed information
4 highlight an individual thing, person, etc.

d Complete the paragraph below with the words in the box. Add the three words or phrases to 3c.

shown   such   especially

Group activities, [1]_____ problem-solving activities, are usually successful at building rapport between team members. An activity [2]_____ **as** finding the way out of a maze uses both cognitive and practical skills. A very dysfunctional team did this and bonded as a result. They now work together extremely well **as** [3]_____ **by** a 20% increase in their productivity.

e ▶ Now go to Writing Focus 7D on p.173

Introduction
The aim of this proposal is to outline plans to address training needs within my team.

Training _____
Recent team meetings have highlighted some breakdowns in communication in the team I currently manage. Specifically, the need for greater interpersonal awareness within a team framework has become apparent. I have identified one professional development day in particular that I believe is ideal.

The TIG programme – what they _____
The Interpersonal Gym (TIG) have been running personal development programmes for the past 12 years. As detailed in the attached brochure, TIG's speciality is team-building programmes. These involve games and problem-solving activities that are likely to appeal to all team members. For instance, there are simple but effective trust-building activities, in which team members have to help a partner negotiate a series of obstacles when blindfolded. The training places an emphasis on strategies to enhance active listening and collective decision-making.

_____ to our business
I believe the TIG programme will offer effective professional development. TIG has an excellent reputation, as demonstrated by their impressive range of testimonials from organisations similar to our own. Overall, the programme is likely to have a number of benefits for the business, namely increased sales and job satisfaction amongst team members, and therefore lower absenteeism and increased profits.

Conclusion
I hope you will agree that a training session run by TIG would be a practical and worthwhile way of addressing issues that are affecting the team's productivity.

4 WRITING

a 💬 Choose one of the teams below and imagine you are its programme leader. What kind of training or team-building activities do you think would help?

1 an admin team who have absenteeism problems
2 a sales team who aren't selling very much
3 a student council who cannot agree on anything
4 a sports team lacking in motivation to do better

b ▶ **Communication 7D** Now go to p.136 and choose a team-building programme for your team.

c Write a proposal to someone in authority for a team-building personal development day.

- Indicate which day you plan to go on and why.
- Describe how you think the team building will benefit the team.
- Remember to be gently persuasive and use formal language.

d 💬 Imagine you are the person in authority. Read another student's proposal. Will you accept it? Why / Why not?

UNIT 7
Review and extension

1 GRAMMAR

a Choose the correct option.

1 I'm sure the new version *may / will / should* work well.
2 I *couldn't / wouldn't / mustn't* have gone out last night, I was exhausted.
3 It's highly unlikely *for flying cars to / that flying cars will* appear.
4 There *may / can / must* be no such thing as paper money in 50 years.
5 Sorry, you did tell me. I *may / can / must* have forgotten.
6 This will be a good opportunity and it *must / should / has got to* take you places.

b Complete the sentences with one word in the box.

not   happened   was   only   to   what   all   it

1 _____ interests me most is how stress affects relationships.
2 It was my youngest daughter who _____ the most affected.
3 What _____ was that Simon started spending less time at home.
4 _____ is Sue who needs to rethink her priorities, not me.
5 _____ that I am asking for is a bit of commitment.
6 It was _____ until the following day that Richard told his wife.
7 What I did was _____ rearrange the seating plan.
8 It was _____ when I left home that I appreciated my parents.

2 VOCABULARY

a Correct the mistakes in the compound adjectives.

1 Sue is so hot-hearted, she'd do anything for anybody.
2 Cutting wood all day was really spine-breaking work.
3 Write it down for me because I'm getting rather absence-minded.
4 It's mind-wobbling what you can do with technology today.
5 The comedy is a light-headed look at what really goes on in hospitals.
6 To leave after all those years was heart-cracking.

b Replace the words in *italics* with the noun form of a word in the box.

collaborate   innovate   liberate   nervous
optimistic   rude   self

1 There was great *anxiety* amongst the crowd as they waited to find out the result.
2 What will be the next *new thing* in mobile phone technology?
3 There is no excuse for *being impolite*.
4 We are proud to announce our *teamwork* on this project.
5 You can look to the future with some *positive feelings*.
6 *Only thinking about yourself* is common in society today.
7 The *freeing* of Paris in 1945 was an important event.

3 WORDPOWER *self-*

a ▶ 3.44 Replace the words in *italics* with the adjectives in the box. Listen and check.

self-sacrificing   self-centred   self-aware
self-confident   self-sufficient   self-satisfied

1 I'm sure she'll be a successful team leader. She's very *certain of her own abilities*.

2 Yoga is good for your health and it also makes you more *able to notice your thoughts and feelings*.
3 He doesn't care about anyone else. I've never met anyone who's so *interested only in his own needs*.
4 She's so *pleased with herself* that it never occurs to her that other people don't like her.
5 She gave up her job so her husband could pursue a career in politics. Why is she always so *ready to give up things for other people*?
6 We've started growing our own vegetables, although I doubt we'll ever be *able to look after our own needs*.

b Complete the text with adjectives from 3a.

I have always thought of myself as a pretty successful person. I'm ¹_____ – for example, I don't get nervous if I have to give a presentation at work. I'm also ²_____ – I earn enough money to pay my bills and buy the things I want to. But then I went with a friend to a self-help course, and I realised that maybe I was wrong to be so pleased with myself. I was so concerned with my own life that I hadn't stopped to think about anyone else's. Maybe I was actually just ³_____? What if other people saw me as being just too pleased with myself – ⁴_____, even! This was such a horrible thought, I immediately decided to be more ⁵_____ and give up some of my time to help other people, and now I volunteer in a homeless shelter. This does make me feel quite good about myself though, so maybe I haven't really changed at all? Well, at least I've started thinking about this, so hopefully I've become a bit more ⁶_____.

c 💬 Use adjectives from 3a to describe:

• yourself
• people you know
• well-known people.

Discuss your ideas with a partner.

↻ REVIEW YOUR PROGRESS

How well did you do in this unit? Write 3, 2, or 1 for each objective.
3 = very well   2 = well   1 = not so well

I CAN ...

speculate about inventions and technology	☐
emphasise opinions about the digital age	☐
apologise and admit fault	☐
write a proposal	☐

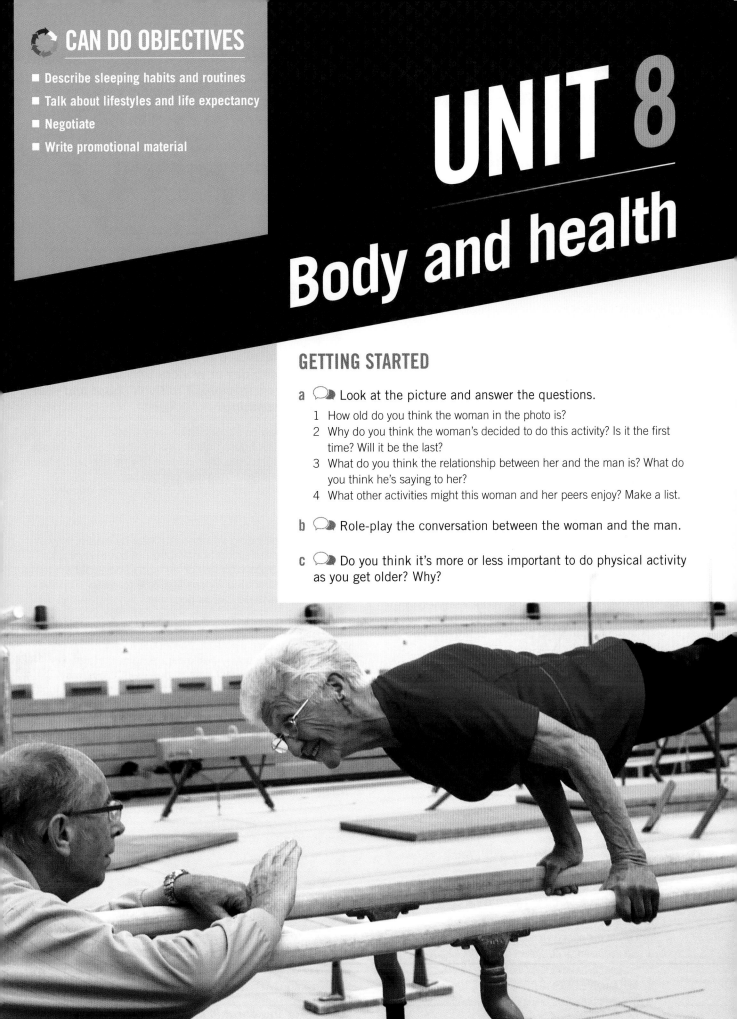

CAN DO OBJECTIVES

- Describe sleeping habits and routines
- Talk about lifestyles and life expectancy
- Negotiate
- Write promotional material

UNIT 8
Body and health

GETTING STARTED

a Look at the picture and answer the questions.

1 How old do you think the woman in the photo is?
2 Why do you think the woman's decided to do this activity? Is it the first time? Will it be the last?
3 What do you think the relationship between her and the man is? What do you think he's saying to her?
4 What other activities might this woman and her peers enjoy? Make a list.

b Role-play the conversation between the woman and the man.

c Do you think it's more or less important to do physical activity as you get older? Why?

8A It's no use trying to go to sleep

G Gerunds and infinitives
V Sleep

1 SPEAKING and READING

a 🗨 Do you know the answers to these questions? If not, what do you think they are?

1 Why do all animals (including humans) need sleep?
2 What percentage of their life does the average person spend asleep?
3 How long is it possible to go without sleep?
4 How many hours a night should adults sleep? What about newborn babies?

b ▶3.45 Listen to the radio interview and check your answers.

c 🗨 Look at these headings for four tips for people who have problems getting to sleep. What do you think each tip involves?

> Acknowledge distractions   Everybody out!
> It is as it is   Compile a playlist

Read the article and match the headings with tips A–D.

d 🗨 Do you think the tips would work for you?

2 GRAMMAR Gerunds and infinitives

a Look at the highlighted phrases in the article. Which phrases are followed by … ?

a *to* + infinitive: 1 *too much*
b infinitive without *to*:
c gerund (verb + *-ing*):

b Look at examples 1–4. Match the verb forms in **bold** with a–d.

1 Enjoy **being soothed** to sleep by music.
2 It's easy **to be distracted** by background noises.
3 Go to work tomorrow without **having had** eight hours' sleep.
4 Be pleasantly surprised **to have slept** all night long.

a ☐ *to* + passive infinitive   c ☐ passive gerund
b ☐ *to* + perfect infinitive   d ☐ perfect gerund

c Look at these examples. What, if anything, is the difference in meaning between each pair?

1 a He got out of bed without saying a word.
    b He got out of bed without having said a word.
2 a He seems to sleep well.
    b He seems to have slept well.
3 a My daughter likes reading in bed.
    b My daughter likes being read to in bed.
4 a I'd like to wake up at 8:30.
    b I'd like to be woken up at 8:30.

TOP TIPS to help you sleep

Do you lie awake at night counting sheep? After a long day at work or university, do you find there's ¹too much to think about and your head is spinning?

Trying to get to sleep can be very frustrating. You might lie awake for hours until it gets to about 5 or 6 o'clock in the morning and then decide ²it's no use trying to go to sleep and you ³may as well get up.
Here are four tips to help you get to sleep quickly:

A _____
If you enjoy being soothed to sleep by music, why not create the ultimate collection of soothing tracks? Choose songs with few or no lyrics and avoid anything with a catchy tune. When ⁴it's time to sleep, turn the volume down as low as possible.

B _____
When you're trying to fall asleep it's very easy to become irritated by background noises. However, sometimes ⁵the best way to deal with them is by accepting them. Say to yourself 'I can hear the clock but it doesn't bother me' or 'I like the neighbour's music'. Soon they'll become less important.

C _____
Imagine your body is full of tiny people all working away with hammers. Announce that their shift is over so they ⁶'d better go home. Imagine them all putting their tools down and leaving your body one by one through your feet. This will make you relax and you should soon drift off to sleep.

D _____
⁷There's no point in making judgements ('I should have been asleep hours ago'), or indulging in catastrophic thinking ('If I go to work tomorrow without having had eight hours' sleep, I'll mess up that presentation, lose my job, and die tired and alone'). Make the night easier by accepting it for what it is, letting go of judgements, and being gentle with yourself. The silver lining? You just might get to see a glorious sunrise.

So, for the chronic insomniacs out there, try some of these tips and by the time you wake up in the morning, you may be pleasantly surprised to have slept all night long!

d Think of possible continuations for these sentences. Then compare with other students.

1 I've got to get up at 4:00 to go to the airport, so I may as well …
2 If you don't feel tired, there's no point …
3 You can't carry on sleeping only two hours a night. You'd better …
4 What a disaster! I went into the exam without having … (+ past participle)
5 When I feel tired, I really don't enjoy being … (+ past participle)
6 If you can't sleep, just accept it. It's no use …

e ▶ Now go to Grammar Focus 8A on p.152

3 READING

a Read the title of the article. What will the article tell you about sleeping eight hours a night? Think of two possibilities. Read the article and check.

b Which of these are reasonable conclusions to draw from the article, and which aren't?

1 If there's nothing to interfere with them, most people would probably sleep in two segments.
2 In the 15th century, city streets probably would have been full of people at night.
3 The habit of sleeping for eight hours without waking up probably started in Europe.
4 People started going to bed later because the streets became less dangerous.
5 Stress in modern life is mainly a result of not sleeping well.

c Language in context *Cause, origin and effect*

1 What do the highlighted words and phrases mean? Match each expression with a synonymous phrase.

1 be a factor in, contribute to
2 be because of (x2)
3 spread to
4 take from
5 say that the cause was

2 Why do you think the writer preferred each highlighted expression?

d 💬 Do you agree that 'lying awake could be good for you'? What arguments can you think of against Dr Jacobs' point of view?

THE MYTH OF THE EIGHT-HOUR SLEEP

We often worry about lying awake in the middle of the night – but it could be good for you. A growing body of evidence from both science and history suggests that the eight-hour sleep may be unnatural.

In the early 1990s, psychiatrist Thomas Wehr conducted an experiment in which a group of people were plunged into darkness for 14 hours every day for a month. It took some time for their sleep to regulate but by the fourth week the subjects had settled into a very distinct sleeping pattern. They slept first for four hours, then woke for one or two hours before falling into a second four-hour sleep. Though sleep scientists were impressed by the study, among the general public the idea that we must sleep for eight consecutive hours persisted.

In 2001, historian Roger Ekirch of Virginia Tech published a seminal paper, drawn from 16 years of research, revealing a wealth of historical evidence that humans used to sleep in two distinct chunks. His book *At Day's Close: Night in Times Past*, published four years later, unearths more than 500 references to a segmented sleeping pattern – in diaries, court records, medical books and literature.

During the waking period between sleeps people were quite active. They often got up, went to the toilet or smoked tobacco and some even visited neighbours. Most people stayed in bed, read, wrote and often prayed. Countless prayer manuals from the late 15th century offered special prayers for the hours in between sleeps. Ekirch found that references to the first and second sleep started to disappear during the late 17th century. This started among the urban upper classes in northern Europe and over the course of the next 200 years filtered down to the rest of Western society. By the 1920s the idea of a first and second sleep had receded entirely from our social consciousness. He attributes the initial shift to improvements in street lighting, domestic lighting and a surge in coffee houses – which were sometimes open all night. As the night became a place for legitimate activity and as that activity increased, the length of time people could dedicate to rest dwindled.

Today, most people seem to have adapted quite well to the eight-hour sleep, but Ekirch believes many sleeping problems may have roots in the human body's natural preference for segmented sleep as well as the ubiquity of artificial light. This could be at the root of a condition called sleep maintenance insomnia, where people wake during the night and have trouble getting back to sleep, he suggests. The condition first appears in literature at the end of the 19th century, at the same time as accounts of segmented sleep disappear. 'For most of evolution we slept a certain way,' says sleep psychologist Dr Gregg Jacobs. 'Waking up during the night is part of normal human physiology.'

Jacobs suggests that the waking period between sleeps, when people were forced into periods of rest and relaxation, could have played an important part in the human capacity to regulate stress naturally. In many historic accounts, Ekirch found that people used the time to meditate on their dreams. 'Today we spend less time doing those things,' says Dr Jacobs. 'It's not a coincidence that, in modern life, the number of people who report anxiety, stress and depression has gone up.' So the next time you wake up in the middle of the night, think of your pre-industrial ancestors and relax. Lying awake could be good for you.

4 LISTENING and VOCABULARY Sleep

a 💬 You will hear four people talk about waking up at night. Look at the words below. What do you think each person is going to say?

ten or eleven – restless – my wife – photos – storm

1 Matt

yoga – studio – 20 other people – husband

2 Saba

artist – image – dream – therapeutic

3 Bernie

Papua – village – sunset – fire – sweet potato

4 Iain

b ▶ 3.48 Listen to the radio programme. Were your ideas in 4a correct?

c Look at the expressions in the box from the recording. Which are about … ?

1 sleeping well or too long
2 not sleeping or not sleeping well
3 falling asleep
4 having a short sleep

> have a nap   be fast asleep   be wide awake
> drift off to sleep   be a light sleeper   be restless
> sleep like a log   not sleep a wink   toss and turn
> oversleep   suffer from insomnia   drop off to sleep

d ▶ 3.49 **Pronunciation** Listen to this extract from the recording. Underline the stressed syllables in the fixed expressions in **bold**.

My wife used to force me to **get out of bed** 'cause I would lie there **tossing and turning** all night and I **couldn't sleep a wink**.

e ▶ 3.50 Underline the syllables you think will be stressed in the expressions in **bold**. Listen and check.

Sometimes I even get my husband to join us, if he's **having trouble sleeping**. But most of the time **he's fast asleep** and doesn't even notice when I get up. He **sleeps like a log**!

f 💬 Talk about your sleeping habits using expressions from 4c.

1 Are they the same as people you live with? Why / Why not?
2 In what situations does your sleep pattern change? What can be different about it?
3 Do you know someone with particularly unusual sleeping habits?

5 SPEAKING

a 💬 Work in groups. Imagine that most people have segmented sleep patterns. What impact would it have on the way our lives are organised? How would society need to adapt? Consider these factors:

- travel and transport   • entertainment and socialising
- work   • leisure activities   • education   • mealtimes.

b 💬 Plan a typical day for a student who wants to start a segmented sleep pattern. How can they make the best use of their time? When should they … ?

- eat   • work   • relax   • learn   • exercise
- spend time with friends

c 💬 Choose one student from your group to represent you and explain your idea to the class.

d 💬 Decide which group's plan is:

- the most practical   • the most original.

8B Suppose you could live forever

Learn to talk about lifestyles and life expectancy
G Conditionals
V Ageing and health

1 SPEAKING and VOCABULARY
Ageing and health

a 💬 Look at the photos and read the quote. How do they make you feel?

> **Ageing is one of the most profitable fears of our time**

b 💬 Read about five treatments. Which do you think is the strangest? Which would you try?

c Match the highlighted words and phrases with the definitions.
1 _____ (adj.) of or on the face
2 _____ (adj.) clean and pleasant
3 _____ (n.) the movement of blood around the body
4 _____ (n.) lines on your face that you get when you grow old
5 _____ (n.) a temporary skin condition involving groups of small spots
6 _____ (n.) permanent marks left on the body from cuts or other injuries
7 _____ (adj.) not soft or loose, strong and healthy
8 _____ (n.) a beauty treatment involving gentle rubbing of creams into the face
9 _____ (n. phrase) the warm, healthy appearance of the skin on someone's face
10 _____ (n. phrase) the warm, healthy appearance of the skin typical of young people
11 _____ (adj.) hanging loosely, less tight than before

d ▶ Now go to Vocabulary Focus 8B on p.165

Anti-ageing *treatments*

Afraid of anti-ageing injections?
Try these alternative treatments to make you look younger!

Snail Slime Cream
Carefully collected snail's slime is a potent anti-ageing ingredient that helps reduce scars, acne and skin rashes, as well as smoothing out wrinkles.

Emu Oil
Rendered from the fat of an emu bird, emu oil is a lesser known anti-ageing oil that has been used for centuries in the Aboriginal communities for its healing powers. It leaves you with a glowing complexion.

Bee Sting Venom
The bee sting venom facial doesn't involve a swarm of bees stinging your face, but instead, the venom from the sting is transferred into a gel and then rubbed on the face as part of an intensive facial. It leaves your skin feeling fresh and renewed.

Anti-Sagging Lips
This rubbery-looking mouthpiece, created by cosmetic company Glim, is designed to keep the facial muscles firm by holding the cheeks and mouth stretched in a permanent 'trout pout' position. It will help bring back smooth, healthy-looking cheeks.

'Platza' Treatment
The 'platza' treatment involves the bare back being beaten with a 'broom' made of oak-leaf branches. It was first used in the *banyas* (saunas) of Russia and in Turkish baths. This alternative massage is designed to stimulate the blood circulation, creating a youthful glow.

2 READING

a 💬 In the future, how likely do you think it is that medical science will keep people alive for much longer than today? Why do you think so?

b Read the interview with a scientist, Aubrey de Grey. How does he answer the question in 2a?

c Read the article again. Summarise the main points made about these topics in paragraphs 2–7.

Paragraph 2: Diseases in old age
Paragraph 3: Attitudes to the ageing process
Paragraph 4: The challenge our body faces
Paragraph 5: Aubrey de Grey and the medical profession
Paragraph 6: People who might benefit
Paragraph 7: Managing the population

d 💬 Would you like to live for 1,000 years? Why / Why not?

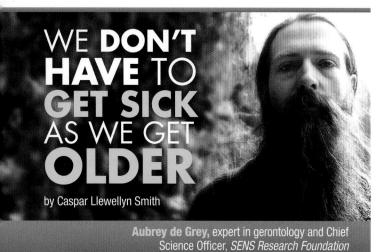

WE DON'T HAVE TO GET SICK AS WE GET OLDER

by Caspar Llewellyn Smith

Aubrey de Grey, expert in gerontology and Chief Science Officer, *SENS Research Foundation*

[1]With his beard and robust opinions, there's something of the philosopher about Aubrey de Grey. De Grey studied computer science at Cambridge University, but became interested in the problem of ageing more than a decade ago.

[2]What's so wrong with getting old?

It is simply that people get sick when they get older. I don't often meet people who want to suffer cardiovascular disease or whatever, and we get those things as a result of the lifelong accumulation of various types of molecular and cellular damage. This is harmless at low levels but eventually it causes the diseases and disabilities of old age – which most people don't think are any fun.

[3]Why does the world not recognise the problem of ageing?

People have been trying to claim that we can defeat ageing since the dawn of time, and they haven't been terribly successful; there is a tendency to think there is some sort of inevitability about ageing – it somehow transcends our technological abilities in principle, which is complete nonsense.

3 GRAMMAR Conditionals

a Read the web comments about longevity. Which ones reflect your opinion?

(1) I would be a bit more relaxed about my life goals if it were actually possible to live for a thousand years!

(2) If medical science had been more advanced a hundred years ago, the world population would be out of control today.

(3) Assuming what Aubrey de Grey says is correct, we probably don't need to worry so much about exercise and diet.

(4) Supposing that we all were able to live for a very long time, people would just stop having children.

(5) Had I been born 200 years ago, I would have been astounded to be told about life expectancies in the year 2000.

(6) I won't care about living to a ripe old age as long as I feel I've had an interesting life.

(7) Even if I only lived to a hundred, that'd be an amazing achievement.

REPLY ✉

b Which sentences in 3a refer to … ?
a a real possibility
b an imaginary or unreal situation
c both the past and the present

c Underline the word or phrase in each example in 3a that introduces the condition.

d ▶ Now go to Grammar Focus 8B on p.153

e 💬 Use the phrases in the box to talk about yourself. Say one thing that isn't true or you don't really believe. Can you guess your partner's lie?

Assuming that …   Had I …   Even if I only …
Supposing that …   If I hadn't …   As long as …

Talk about:
- living for a long time
- lifestyle and health
- life goals
- the future of the planet.

[4]Is it that our bodies just stop being so proactive about living?

Basically, the body does have a vast amount of inbuilt anti-ageing machinery; it's just not 100% comprehensive, so it allows a small number of different types of molecular and cellular damage to happen and accumulate. The body does try as hard as it can to fight these things but it is a losing battle.

[5]You say you want to enrich people's lives? Why is that?

The fact is, people don't want to get sick. I don't work on longevity, I work on keeping people healthy. The only difference between my work and the work of the whole medical profession is that I think we're within striking distance of keeping people so healthy that at 90 they'll carry on waking up in the same physical state as they were at the age of 30.

4 LISTENING

a 🗨 Why do people follow special diets? Talk about different reasons. Have you (or has someone you know) ever had to follow a diet? How was it?

b 🗨 Read about a CR diet. What kind of food do you think you can eat on this diet?

c ▶ **3.55** Listen to Peter Bowes talk to Martin Knight, who follows a CR diet. Answer the questions.
1 What does Martin do with the food in the photos below?
2 What does Martin's daily routine involve?

d ▶ **3.55** Listen again. Make notes on these topics.
1 eating out (discussed twice)
2 the look and taste of Martin's breakfast
3 Martin's lifestyle in general
4 Martin's reasons for following a CR diet
5 how Martin feels

e 🗨 Can you imagine following a CR diet? Why / Why not? If you did, what would the biggest sacrifice or challenge be in relation to your current lifestyle?

f ▶ **3.56** **Pronunciation** Listen to this extract.
1 Is the pitch lower or higher in the phrases in **bold**?

Then I have sprouted oats, **16 grams**, so that's 70. Then this tomato paste here, **33 grams of that**, and almost done now. There we go. And then finally, I add some olive oil, **that's 9.2**.

2 Does this happen because the speaker repeats information or adds extra information?

g 🗨 Describe the process of preparing a typical breakfast, lunch or dinner to a partner. Use a lower pitch to add extra information. Can you guess which meal your partner's describing?

Did you know

that a calorie restricted (CR) diet will not only help you to lose weight, it could increase your life expectancy by up to ten years? Research has shown that a CR diet reduces many of the health risks associated with ageing. All you need to do is eat less and eat smarter. Not only could you live longer, but you might feel years younger!

5 SPEAKING

a 🗨 When have you / has someone you know been told you were too young or too old to do something? Explain what happened.

b 🗨 Work in small groups. What are your opinions of these statements? Talk about your own experiences.

1 How old someone feels depends entirely on their health.
2 TV ads in my country represent older people in realistic ways.
3 It's easier for people under forty to get a job, than those over forty.
4 The longer you live, the more eccentric you become.
5 Companies which sell anti-ageing products don't want people to feel good about themselves.

c 🗨 Choose one person for each statement to present your ideas and experiences to the class. Take a class vote on who agrees and disagrees with each statement.

6 You've said you think the first person to live to 1,000 may already be alive. Could that person be you?

It's conceivable that people in my age bracket, their 40s, are young enough to benefit from these therapies. I'd give it a 30% or 40% chance. But that is not why I do this – I do this because I'm interested in saving 100,000 lives a day.

7 Can the planet cope with people living so long?

That's to do with the balance of birth and death rates. It didn't take us too long to lower the birth rate after we more or less eliminated infant mortality 100 or 150 years ago. I don't see that it's sensible to regard the risk of a population spike as a reason not to give people the best healthcare that we can.

chard

sprouted oats

kale

8C Everyday English
Is that your best offer?

- **S** Negotiate the price of a product or service
- **P** Intonation in implied questions

1 LISTENING

a 💬 Discuss the questions.

1 What is the most memorable present you received as a child?
2 Who was it from?
3 What was the occasion?
4 Why is this present particularly memorable?

b 💬 You are going to hear about a present Max received as a child, which started his interest in life on other planets. What do you think it was?

c ▶️4.2 Watch or listen to Part 1 and check your answer in 1b. Answer questions 2–4 in 1a about it too.

d 💬 What do you think Oscar will do next?

e ▶️4.3 Watch or listen to Part 2 and answer the questions.

1 Why does Oscar call Miranda?
  a to tell her about a press conference
  b to find out what she knows about Max's new book
  c to sell her information
  d to arrange to meet
2 How would you describe the relationship between Oscar and Miranda?
  a old friends
  b business acquaintances
  c colleagues
  d they know each other only by name
3 Who do you think is the better negotiator?
  a Oscar
  b Miranda

f ▶️4.3 Watch Part 2 again. Then write a possible *Why* question for each answer.

1 So that Miranda will understand that he's not calling on behalf of *City FM*.
2 So that Miranda will believe his information is from a reliable source.
3 Because she hasn't seen what Oscar is offering yet.
4 Because she's concerned that someone will announce Max's new book before she gets the chance.
5 Because he knows he could lose his job at *City FM*.

g Language in context *Expressions with* fair

Match the expressions a–c with meanings 1–3.

a ☐ it's fair to say   1 this is reasonable
b ☐ fair's fair   2 I understand this
c ☐ fair enough   3 this is true

h 💬 Discuss the questions.

1 Do you think Oscar is behaving fairly? What about Miranda?
2 How do you think these people would react if they knew what Oscar had done?
   • Sara • Nadia • Max

2 USEFUL LANGUAGE Negotiating

a ▶4.4 Complete Oscar and Miranda's conversation. Listen and check.

M: There's just the ¹_____ of how much you would like for it.

O: Well, **how much would you be** ²_____ **to pay**?

M: Oh, I think **we'd be** ³_____ **to offer**, say, two fifty? **Would that be a** ⁴_____ **suggestion**?

O: Two fifty! **Could you see your** ⁵_____ **to increasing that** a little? **I was kind of** ⁶_____ **for something more in the region of** five hundred.

M: No, ⁷_____ **of the question. What would you** ⁸_____ **to** three fifty? In principle, of course. I'd need to see the article first.

O: Three fifty – **is that your** ⁹_____ **offer**?

b Add the expressions in **bold** in 2a to the correct column.

Opening negotiations	Making and accepting offers
I'm open to suggestions/discussion.	I'd be prepared to accept … I'm not in a position to offer more than …

Asking for more	Declining offers
It's worth much more than that. How flexible can you be on that?	I'm not authorised to accept anything less.

c 💬 Complete the conversation with words from the table. Practise it with a partner.

A How much would you like for it?
B I'm ¹_____ to suggestions.
A I think we could go to five.
B It's ²_____ much more than that. I'd be prepared to ³_____ seven.
A How ⁴_____ can you be on that? I'm not in a ⁵_____ to offer more than six.
B I'm not ⁶_____ to accept anything less than seven.

d 💬 Read the conversation below and answer the questions.

1 How is it the same / different from the conversation in Part 2?
2 Which conversation would be more successful in real life? Why?

A How much do you want?
B How much will you pay?
A 250.
B How about 500?

A No, 350.
B No more?
A No. And I need it by 1.
B What?
A OK, 2.

e 💬 Work in pairs. Cover 2a and use 2b and 2d to role play the conversation between Oscar and Miranda in Part 2.

3 PRONUNCIATION
Intonation in implied questions

a ▶4.5 People often ask implied questions rather than direct questions in formal conversations. Listen to the implied questions below. What do you notice about their intonation?

Implied question	Direct question
1 I don't know if you remember?	Do you remember?
2 I've been doing a little freelance work?	Do you understand that the work I'm doing is not part of what I do for *City FM*?
3 Y'know, author of *Solar Wind*?	Do you know the author of *Solar Wind*?
4 We'd be prepared to offer, say, two fifty?	Would two fifty be acceptable?
5 And I need it by one o'clock?	Could you get it to me by one o'clock?

b ▶4.6 Listen to the statements below. Tick (✓) the implied questions.

1 ☐ I don't know if you've seen this item.
2 ☐ It's that well-known brand.
3 ☐ I'd be prepared to accept £50 for it.
4 ☐ I'm afraid I couldn't give you that much.
5 ☐ I could give you £30 for it.
6 ☐ I'd take £35.
7 ☐ Assuming it's available now.
8 ☐ It's yours today for £35.
9 ☐ We've got a deal.
10 ☐ Deal.

c 💬 Work in pairs. Practise the dialogue in 3b.

4 SPEAKING

a Work alone. Think of an object or a service you could sell. Here are some ideas:

- an anti-ageing treatment
- a new-generation smartphone
- a homework service
- a car.

Make a list of selling points that might persuade someone to pay more for it.

b 💬 Work in pairs. Negotiate the price of your product or service and one other aspect. Use the language in 2c and implied questions.

Unit Progress Test

CHECK YOUR PROGRESS

You can now do the Unit Progress Test.

1 LISTENING and SPEAKING

a 💬 Think about occasions when you eat out and discuss the questions.

1 Do you think the food you eat out … ?
  • usually tastes better than what you eat at home
  • is usually healthier than what you eat at home
  In what ways?
2 When you eat out, what things are most important to you? Choose the five most important things from this list.
  ☐ convenience ☐ difference from food at home
  ☐ presentation ☐ taste of the food
  ☐ atmosphere ☐ quality of ingredients
  ☐ health ☐ good reputation
  ☐ décor ☐ type of cuisine (e.g.
  ☐ service   vegetarian, Chinese)
  ☐ value for money

b 💬 You are going to listen to a restaurant chef talking about a *stone-age diet*. What do you think this might mean?

c ▶ 4.7 Listen to the interview and answer the questions.

1 Why was The Palaeolithic Period significant in human development?
2 What foods does Julia believe are healthy, and why?
3 Why does Julia believe that dairy products and rice are unhealthy?
4 What are the similarities and differences between the food served at *Ancestors* restaurant and palaeolithic food?
5 To what extent do you agree with Julia's views about food and health?

d 💬 Do you agree with each of these statements about diets? Why / Why not?

1 People are always thinking of new diets. It's just a way to make money.
2 The best diet is to eat whatever you feel like eating because your body knows what it needs.
3 It's better to think about changing your eating habits for life than to go on a short-term diet.

2 READING

a 💬 Quickly read the home page of *Ancestors* restaurant and discuss the questions.

1 What new information not mentioned by Julia do you find out on the home page?
2 What kind of customer would go to *Ancestors*, and why? Would you go there yourself?

b 💬 What else do you think is on the menu at *Ancestors*? Imagine one starter, one main dish and one dessert. Then compare your answers.

ANCESTORS RESTAURANT   Home | About | Menu

ANCESTORS RESTAURANT

Our city-centre restaurant offers a unique dining experience. Lovingly prepared and exquisitely presented, our dishes contain only the purest ingredients, so you can be confident that our food is good for your body and your individual needs.
So many people eat healthy food at home but then bend the rules when it comes to eating out. At ANCESTORS we have a different concept. We serve you the foods you can eat, not the foods you can't!

THE STONE AGE DIET

For thousands of years, we humans were hunter-gatherers: we thrived on meat, seafood, seasonal vegetables, grains, fruit and nuts. Our bodies adapted to this diet and it still suits our genetic make-up better than the recent additions of dairy products and processed foods. *[Find out more …]*

At ANCESTORS we believe that eating is all about two things: health and enjoyment. So we've created a stone-age menu fit for 21st-century living.

3 WRITING SKILLS
Promotional material; Using persuasive language

a Which of these do you think is the main purpose of the home page in 2a?

☐ to give detailed information   ☐ to give advice

☐ to promote the restaurant

b Why do you think the home page uses headings and short sections?

c Match the features of the home page 1–4 with their purposes a–d.

1 ☐ clear headings
2 ☐ short paragraphs
3 ☐ use of *we* and *you*
4 ☐ links

a to encourage the reader to browse the website
b to establish a personal relationship with the reader
c to show at a glance what the text is about
d to make it quick and easy to read

Location	Healthy living	Opening times	Reservations

OUR MENU

The menu at ANCESTORS changes according to the seasons. Signature dishes from head chef Julia Dean include sweet potato and hazelnut soup, lamb with sesame seeds, and smoked salmon with wild leaves. We also offer a range of desserts made to the most exacting standards, using only wild fruits and natural sweeteners. *[Sample menu ...]*
We take our drinks as seriously as our food. At ANCESTORS you'll find an exciting selection of natural fruit and vegetable juices from around the world, complemented by a range of teas, coffees and herbal teas.

EARLY EVENING MENU

Based in the city centre, ANCESTORS is the ideal destination for a light and wholesome supper before you go to the theatre or cinema. Tasty and fresh, the early evening menu offers a range of ANCESTORS dishes at a fixed price. Available 5:30 to 7:00 pm.

THE ANCESTORS COOKBOOK

So many of you have asked for our recipes that we've produced our own cookbook, using ingredients you can buy on any high street. Tried and tested by our team of cooks, our recipes will enable you to re-create the ANCESTORS experience in your own kitchen.
[View sample pages ...]

d At the top of the *Ancestors* home page, there is a slogan missing. Which of these do you think would work best? Why?

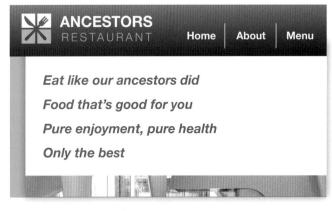

ANCESTORS RESTAURANT   Home | About | Menu

Eat like our ancestors did

Food that's good for you

Pure enjoyment, pure health

Only the best

e The home page aims to give a positive message about the restaurant. Match the phrases from the first two paragraphs with the messages they convey.

Phrase
1 ☐ a unique dining experience
2 ☐ Lovingly prepared and exquisitely presented
3 ☐ At *Ancestors* we believe that
4 ☐ fit for 21st-century living

Message
a The food is not at all old-fashioned.
b The food is made with care and looks good.
c *Ancestors* is not like other restaurants.
d What *Ancestors* is doing has a serious purpose.

f Compare these two sentences. Which emphasises the positive features of the dishes more strongly? How is the structure different?

1 Lovingly prepared and exquisitely presented, our dishes contain only the purest ingredients.
2 Our dishes are lovingly prepared and exquisitely presented and they contain only the purest ingredients.

Find three more examples of description at the front of a sentence in the text.

g ▶ Now go to Writing Focus 8D on p.174

4 WRITING

a 💬 Work in pairs or groups. Think of a concept for a restaurant. You could either invent one or base it on a place you know. Note down ideas for a promotional text on a website. Consider:

- the underlying concept
- how it's different from other places
- what it offers customers
- what its positive features are
- food and drink, décor and atmosphere.

b Write a promotional text. Make sure you include clear headings, a name at the top and an appealing slogan.

c Read other groups' texts and decide which restaurant you'd most like to visit. Think of some further questions to ask about it.

UNIT 8
Review and extension

1 GRAMMAR

a Choose the correct option.

1 *To wake / Waking / Having woken* up is easier in the summer.
2 *Being sent / Sending / Having sent* to boarding school is the best thing that ever happened to me.
3 I've always been a big fan of *to get / get / getting* up early.
4 Her refusal even *to listen / listening / for listening* to my idea really annoyed me.
5 There's no shame in *to have / having / being* lost to a team as good as theirs.
6 I was lucky enough *meeting / to have met / having met* Charles before he became famous.
7 Is there any hope *to save / of saving / saving* the lost sailors?

b Complete the sentences with one word.

1 I wouldn't be in such good shape if I _____ look after myself.
2 If Steve had said it one more time, I would _____ walked out.
3 _____ I known the photo meant so much to you, I would have kept it.
4 I'm going to accept Dave if he _____ me to marry him.
5 The trip needs to be well planned, _____ it will be a nightmare.
6 _____ we to find out that Emily wasn't lying, would you apologise?

2 VOCABULARY

a Match sentence halves 1–8 with endings a–h.

1 ☐ It wasn't until about three that I dropped
2 ☐ Mark is quite a light
3 ☐ I couldn't sleep a
4 ☐ We thought the baby was fast asleep but she was wide
5 ☐ Don't worry, I sleep like
6 ☐ It can help to have
7 ☐ Gradually my eyes closed and I started to drift
8 ☐ About 10% of adults suffer

a wink with all that building work going on.
b a little nap in the afternoon.
c off to sleep.
d from insomnia of some kind.
e awake and getting restless.
f off to sleep.
g a log on trains.
h sleeper so don't make too much noise.

b Which word is the odd one out? Why?

1 smooth, saggy, clear, firm
2 scars, spots, a rash, blotches
3 tighten, moisturise, strengthen
4 tooth loss, hair loss, weight loss
5 whitening, yellowing, toning
6 wrinkles, poor circulation, hair loss

3 WORDPOWER *and*

a ▶4.8 Match sentences 1–6 with pictures a–f. Listen and check.

1 ☐ There are still just a few **bits and pieces** to take away.
2 ☐ People came from **far and wide** to hear him talk.
3 ☐ It's **far and away** the best Italian restaurant in town.
4 ☐ I'm getting **sick and tired of** the noise.
5 ☐ It's just normal **wear and tear**.
6 ☐ It's just **part and parcel of** getting older, I suppose.

b Look at the phrases in **bold** in 3a. Replace each idiom with a non-idiomatic expression in the box.

easily   small things of different types
many places   annoyed by   a normal part of
damage caused by everyday use

c ▶4.9 Complete the sentences with the adjectives in the box. Listen and check.

tidy   safe   sweet   clear

1 'Can you hear me?'
  'Yes, I can hear you **loud** and _____.'
2 'I'm almost afraid to touch anything in her room. She keeps it so **neat** and _____.'
3 'I don't want to have a long discussion over the phone, so let's keep it **short** and _____.'
4 'We got caught in a really bad blizzard, but fortunately we got home _____ and **sound**.'

d Choose four expressions from 3a or 3c and write sentences but leave a gap for the expression.

e 💬 Read out your sentences. Can other students guess what goes in the gap?

🔄 REVIEW YOUR PROGRESS

How well did you do in this unit? Write 3, 2, or 1 for each objective.
3 = very well   2 = well   1 = not so well

I CAN ...

describe sleeping habits and routines	☐
talk about lifestyles and life expectancy	☐
negotiate	☐
write promotional material	☐

CAN DO OBJECTIVES

- Talk about city life and urban space
- Describe architecture and buildings
- Deal with conflict
- Write a discussion essay

UNIT 9
Cities

GETTING STARTED

a Describe the buildings you can see in the photo.

b Discuss the questions.
1 Why do you think the building in the centre of the photo hasn't been demolished?
2 How do you think the following people feel about this house?
   - the owners
   - the people who built the other buildings
   - the local authorities
   - other local residents
3 What do you think will happen to the house in the future? What will happen to the homeowner?

c If there was a plan to demolish your family home, under what circumstances would you agree?

EXHIBITION ROAD

LONDON'S FIRST EXAMPLE OF 'SHARED SPACE'

- All 'street clutter' removed.
- No traditional pavements or kerbs.
- Traffic signs, safety barriers, kerb marking removed.
- Traffic expected to reduce by 30 per cent.
- Pedestrian areas are distinguished by black iron drainage covers and ribbed 'corduroy-effect' tactile strips.
- Car-parking bays, cycle racks, trees and bench seats will also help separate pedestrians from two-way traffic, without forming a permanent barrier.

Britain's longest 'clutter-free' street was opened today with the aim of making cars and people co-exist harmoniously – without the need for hectoring signs and protective steel barriers. Indeed, the newly revamped Exhibition Road in the heart of London's museum quarter in Kensington, visited by millions of people from around Britain and the world, doesn't even have kerbs or pavements.

The idea underlining the project is that when nannying rules and orders – in the form of countless signs, traffic signals and barriers – are removed – motorists take more personal responsibility for their own actions and drive more attentively, making more eye contact with pedestrians. It may sound counter-intuitive. But experts swear that the idea pioneered in the Netherlands really does work better for everyone and improves safety. And supporters say it is a blueprint for the 21st-century high street in towns and cities across the country.

The entire half-mile long stretch (820 metres) of road and pavement has been redeveloped and is now one continuous and wide expanse of flat 'shared space' surface decorated with a criss-cross chequered pattern created from a jigsaw of a million bricks of Chinese granite.

Sir Jeremy Dixon of leading architectural practice Dixon Jones which led the project said: 'It's not a complete free-for-all. But when the rules by which traffic normally operates are removed – signs, barriers and kerb markings – drivers become more observant. Drivers and pedestrians make eye contact with each other which produces greater watchfulness. They use the road more like pedestrians. They take more responsibility for their actions.' In a similar vein, studies have shown that when traffic lights are removed from crossings, traffic flows more freely and efficiently because drivers take more care, he said.

Councillor Daniel Moylan, deputy chairman of Transport for London (TfL), said: 'The psychology of this scheme is fascinating. Experience seems to show that when you dedicate space to traffic and control it with signs and green traffic lights, motorists develop a claim on it. It becomes 'my space'. Drivers become annoyed if people move into it. They get angry if a mother pushing a buggy moves across the crossing just as the lights are about to change. This new scheme is more like the behaviour in a supermarket car park. Drivers know there are people around pushing shopping trolleys and so drive more cautiously. They are looking out. They don't feel that pedestrians are invading their space. They don't therefore get annoyed.'

1 READING

a 💬 Look at the picture of Exhibition Road and read the bullet points. How would you feel in this street … ?

1 as a pedestrian   2 as a driver   3 as a cyclist

b Read the article about Exhibition Road and answer the questions.

1 What do people feel is the main benefit of creating *shared space*?
2 How convinced are you by the arguments put forward in the article? Mark your position on the scale below. Then compare with other students and say why.

0% ▬▬▬▬▬▬▬▬▬▬▬ 100%

c Answer these questions about the article. Use a dictionary to help you if necessary.

1 Exhibition Road is described as *clutter-free*. The article mentions signs and barriers. What other kinds of *clutter* do streets have?
2 Why does the writer describe signs and barriers as *hectoring* and *nannying*? Do you agree?
3 What does the writer mean when he describes the scheme as *counter-intuitive* and a *blueprint*?
4 What does Sir Jeremy Dixon mean when he says it's not a *free-for-all*?
5 What leads motorists to feel that pedestrians are *invading their space*, according to Daniel Moylan?

d 💬 Think of the city you live in or one that you know.

1 Do any of the streets have *shared space*? Is it successful?
2 Think of a normal, busy street in your city. Do you think having shared space would work there? Why / Why not?

2 VOCABULARY Verbs with *re-*

a Look at the excerpts from the article. How are the words in **bold** similar in meaning?

The newly **revamped** Exhibition Road in the heart of London's museum quarter …

The entire half-mile long stretch (820 metres) of road and pavement has been **redeveloped**.

b ▶ 4.10 Look at the verbs with *re-* in the box. Replace the words in *italics* in the sentences below with the correct verb in the correct form. Listen and check.

> renovate   rejuvenate   restore   recreate
> regain   reinstate   regenerate

1 The council's policy is to *improve* the port area of the city *so that it becomes a popular place to do business / live*, etc.
2 It's a beautiful old building. They just need to *repair and modernise* it.
3 It's good that students are moving into this area. It will help to *give it a younger and livelier atmosphere.*
4 There's a place in China where they've *built a copy of* a traditional English town, with authentic materials and architecture.
5 The fountain in the main square was dry and falling to pieces. Now they've *returned it to its original condition.*
6 The town needs new industries so it *gets back* its appeal as a place to live and work.
7 Removing the speed limit led to so many accidents that they decided to *put it back again.*

c ▶ 4.11 Pronunciation

1 Listen to the pronunciation of *e* in *re-* in the verbs in the table.

1 /iː/	2 /ɪ/
redevelop	rejuvenate

2 ▶ 4.12 Add the other verbs in 2a and 2b to the table in question 1. Which verb has a different sound and can't be added to the table? Listen and check.

d 💬 What buildings do you know of that have recently been renovated or restored? Are there parts of your city that need redeveloping or regenerating, in your opinion?

3 READING and SPEAKING

a 💬 What do you think is happening in each picture (A–D)? Why do you think it was worth taking a photo of it?

b ▶ Communication 9A Work in groups of four: A, B, C, D. Student A: Go to p.128. Student B: Go to p.133. Student C: Go to p.134. Student D: Go to p.136.

c 💬 Explain the idea you read about to the other students. Which idea do you think … ?

- provides most benefit to the community
- provides least benefit
- would work best in your own city

4 GRAMMAR Reflexive and reciprocal pronouns

a Read the comments about the events in pictures A–D. Which could they refer to?

1 It's a great place to just sit **by yourself** and read the paper.
2 It just shows what local communities can do **for themselves**.
3 The place **itself** isn't very welcoming, but the people are.
4 People can sit and talk to **one another** while they're waiting for the bus.
5 It's a great neighbourhood because we all support **each other**.
6 I'm sure IKEA put out cushions just so that they could promote **themselves**.

b Look at the words and phrases in **bold** in 4a and answer the questions.

1 Which pronoun or phrase ending in *-self / -selves* … ?
  a ☐ shows that the object of the verb is the same as the subject
  b ☐ emphasises one thing in contrast to something else
  c ☐ means *alone* or *not with other people*
  d ☐ means *independently, without help.*
2 What is the difference between … ?
  a *we support ourselves* and *we support each other*
  b *they talk to themselves* and *they talk to one another.*

c ▶ Now go to Grammar Focus 9A on p.154

5 LISTENING

a 🔊 You are going to hear part of a podcast about how technology can improve life in cities. Look at the app in the photo. What do you think it is for?

b ▶ 4.15 Listen to the podcast and answer these questions.

1 How does the app work?
2 Why does Michelle think it's a good idea?
3 Do you agree with her? Would you use it? Why / Why not?

c ▶ 4.16 Listen to three more people talking about other ideas for 'smart' cities. Two of them really exist and one is invented. Which do you think is the invented one? Why?

• Frank   • Rita   • Nick

Now go to p.128 and check.

d ▶ 4.16 Listen to each description again. Which idea (or ideas) … ?

1 gives live information
2 is useful for forgetful or absent-minded people
3 probably uses GPS
4 could be useful when it's raining
5 would be popular with hypochondriacs
6 could help you to make friends

e 🔊 In groups, talk about the ideas. Which idea … ?

• would you use yourself
• would you be prepared to pay for
• would other people you know use

f 🔊 Discuss the questions.

1 What other technology do you use or know of that makes city life easier?
2 To what extent do you think technology like that described makes people less self-reliant?

g **Language in context** *Colloquial expressions*

1 ▶ 4.17 Complete the expressions in **bold** below with the words in the box. Then listen and check.

keel blow place whirl neck
life blend dotted smashed

a … a place where you're repeatedly having to **risk your** _____ to get across the road.
b We're going past a park and there's a railing that**'s been** _____ **in** here.
c So I can get the map here, _____ **it up** a bit like that.
d They've got these screens all around the city, they're **all over the** _____.
e So let's **give it a** _____ … I put my finger on it.
f Let's see if I'm OK or whether I'm **about to** _____ **over**.
g These are artificial trees and they're _____ **around** the city.
h They're shaped like trees, so they _____ **in**.
i I'm always going out without charging my phone, so it's **a real** _____-**saver** for me.

> 🗨 **Learning Tip**
> A typical feature of colloquial English is the use of **phrasal verbs** rather than more formal, single-word verbs. When you come across a phrasal verb, notice if it has a single-verb equivalent and learn them both together.

2 Which phrasal verbs in 5g have the same meanings as *collapse* and *enlarge*?

6 SPEAKING

a 🔊 Look at this list of ideas for making cities 'smarter' or better to live in. Do any of them already exist in the city you live in or one you know? If so, how useful are they? If not, would you use the app or facility if it were available?

1 an app giving information about new projects and impending legislation in the city
2 parking apps to show drivers the nearest available parking space and how much it costs
3 apps to let users 'adopt' city property, such as litter bins, trees, flower beds, and volunteer to maintain them
4 digital parking payment systems, allowing you to pay for parking by smartphone, without using coins or tickets
5 free wi-fi everywhere in the city, including on trains, buses and the underground
6 screens in public places which display traffic information, weather and local news

b 🔊 Work in groups of three. Choose an idea in 6a or your own idea which does not exist where you live yet and prepare to sell your idea to the class. Make notes of some things you could say about it:

• how it would work
• what benefit it would bring to the city
• possible problems and solutions.

c 🔊 Give a group presentation. Focus on one point in 6b each. Vote on the best idea in the class.

9B They wanted a dramatic skyline and they got one

Triumph Palace

Krzywy Domek (The Crooked House)

L'Hemisfèric and El Palau de les Arts Reina Sofía

Torre Velasca

The Barbican

Museo Soumaya

1 SPEAKING and VOCABULARY
Describing buildings

a 🗨 Have you seen these buildings before? What countries do you think they are in? What do you think they were built as? What do you think of each building?

b Which of the words and phrases in the box are positive? Which are negative? Check new words in a dictionary.

1 imposing	4 innovative	7 dated
2 nondescript	5 tasteless	8 out of place
3 graceful	6 over the top	9 stunning

c ▶4.18 **Pronunciation** Listen and underline the stressed syllable in each word or phrase in 1b.

d 🗨 Use the words and phrases in 1b or other adjectives to describe the buildings in the pictures.

> The Barbican is quite imposing, but it isn't very graceful.

> The Museo Soumaya is quite graceful, but it's a bit over the top.

e ▶ Now go to Vocabulary Focus 9B on p.166

f 🗨 Take turns to describe local or iconic buildings that you think your partner will know about. Guess the building your partner is describing.

> It's an imposing building near the river. It used to be a warehouse.

> Is it the … ?

2 GRAMMAR Ellipsis and substitution

a 🗨 Read sentences 1–6. Which of them are true for you or the place you live?

1 Most people dislike modern architecture, I know I **do**.
2 They don't consult residents about new buildings as often as they ought to ^.
3 They've put up that skyscraper and ^ ruined the skyline.
4 The old buildings are always being knocked down to make way for new **ones**.
5 The government promised they were going to build more houses, but they haven't ^ yet.
6 They haven't built anything new around here for ages. **Nor** are they likely to.

b Look at each sentence in 2a again. Which words have been omitted (^) or substituted with words in **bold**? Why?

c ▶ Now go to Grammar Focus 9B on p.155

3 READING

a Read the article about the architect Zaha Hadid. Choose the correct summary.

   1 Zaha Hadid's background has made her one of the most original architects on the planet.

   2 The architectural designs of Zaha Hadid are innovative, but controversial.

b Read the text again. Make notes on …

- the praise of Zaha Hadid's work
- the criticism of Zaha Hadid's work
- Zaha Hadid's reactions to these views.

Compare your notes with a partner.

c 💬 Talk about these questions.

   1 Look at the photos of two of Zaha Hadid's buildings. What do/don't you like about the buildings?

   2 What's more important in a building – practicality or appearance? Are there some kinds of building which should be works of art? If so, what kinds? Why?

d **Language in context** *Metaphorical phrases*

   1 Notice how the words in **bold** in the phrases below are used in the text. Is the meaning exactly the same?

     a a **blossoming** tree   e **run** a marathon
     b **walk** down the street   f a **line** on a football pitch
     c a cake **mould**   g a **wild** animal
     d a horse and **cart**

   2 Match the highlighted expressions in the text with the definitions.

     a ☐ do something you know is dangerous
     b ☐ upset people by breaking established rules/plans/norms
     c ☐ be as creative as you want to be
     d ☐ develop and become more successful
     e ☐ win (a prize)
     f ☐ succeed with an innovative approach
     g ☐ not do something because it is beyond the limits of what you are willing to do

> 💬 **Learning Tip** Many expressions include an indirect or metaphorical meaning. It can sometimes help to think about the literal meaning of key words as a way of understanding the expression. For example, a tree that blossoms suggests fresh and attractive new growth, that will develop further.

ZAHA HADID:
'I don't make nice little buildings'

Now in her sixties, Zaha Hadid has ¹blossomed into one of the world's most celebrated and sought-after architects, with a staff of 350, and around 40 buildings already dotting the globe. She has been the first woman to ²walk away with several of architecture's top awards. For fans of her work, Hadid is a ruthless genius, the woman who ³broke the mould, ⁴upturned the apple cart and found fluid solutions to rectangular problems. For her critics, however, she's something else again: a showboating 'starchitect' who trades in overly complex fantasies of vanity. Many of her concepts, it's claimed, would have been better off as drafts.

The world is not a rectangle.

Much of her work is astonishing. The MAXXI modern art museum in Rome is an extraordinary series of overlapping walkways and concrete limbs. The Salerno ferry terminal is spookily graceful and streamlined while the Heydar Aliyev centre in Azerbaijan has a liquid flow.

Hadid's best buildings are sensual and intoxicating. Yet still the doubts remain. Hadid's designs are so brazen, so shamelessly flamboyant that they surely ⁵run the risk of putting experimentation ahead of functionality. One might worry that her boldest projects become a kind of abstract art. These are things that we might relish in a gallery but ⁶draw the line at hanging in the sitting room, never mind attempting to live and work inside. 'Well, it's not a normal practice,' she concedes. 'We don't make nice little buildings. People think that the most appropriate building is a rectangle, because that's typically the best way of using space. But is that to say that landscape is a waste of space? The world is not a rectangle. You don't go into a park and say: "We don't have any corners!"' She insists that all of her buildings are entirely practical; they are just constructed around different organisational patterns. 'It's like saying that everyone has to write in exactly the same way. And it is simply not the case.'
Hadid's first successful commission, back in

Vitra fire station, Weil am Rhein, Germany

4 LISTENING

a Look at the photo of the Gate to the East. Why do you think people might like it / criticise it?

b ▶ 4.27 Listen to a programme about Chinese skyscrapers. Tick the criticisms you hear. The skyscrapers …

1 ☐ have strange designs
2 ☐ cost too much to build
3 ☐ are too high
4 ☐ are being built everywhere
5 ☐ aren't safe

c ▶ 4.27 Listen again and summarise the points of view of:

1 critical Chinese internet users
2 the first expert who is interviewed
3 the second expert who is interviewed.

d 💬 What examples do you know of where there has been a controversy over urban development?

The Gate to the East, Suzhou, China (known as 'the pants'), designed by British architecture firm RMJM

5 SPEAKING

a 💬 Read the scenario, talk about your ideas and come up with a proposal and a reason for it.

There is a derelict warehouse in your community that was built in the early twentieth century. You are a member of the local council and you have to help make a decision about how the warehouse or the land itself could be repurposed.

Consider:

• the needs of your community
• demolition and rebuilding
• the benefits of a new, iconic building
• a high-profile architect
• your community's architectural heritage
• the warehouse's architectural features.

b 💬 Work in groups of four. Present your proposals to each other. Agree on one proposal and tell the class.

1994, was to design a fire station for the Vitra furniture factory in Germany. On an aesthetic level, this was judged to be a triumph. However, it was later decided that the fire station did not quite work as a fire station and the building has since been made over as a museum for chairs. Doesn't that make the building a failure?

'No,' says Hadid. 'Because it was always intended as a multi-functional building. It was not done as a fire station for the whole city, it was only for the factory. And then the city upgraded its fire station, so the factory used that. But it was always thought that it could be used for training purposes, or as an event space.' She pulls a face. 'They sometimes use it to exhibit chairs, it's true. I had dinner there quite recently.' Hadid isn't married and doesn't have children. She lives alone in what visitors have described as a stark and impersonal flat down the road from her office. No doubt it works for her, though it sounds a little bleak. I ask when she's going to design a house of her own and what it might look like, if money were no object and she could ⁷let her imagination run wild. Hadid responds with a harried smile and says that she's too busy, there's never the time, and who builds a house in central London anyway? She sits at the table, her coat pulled tight against the air con; a workaholic who builds for others and yet never for herself. On balance, she says, she would rather make an office building because that would be more practical. 'I'm hardly ever at my house,' she says. 'I'm hardly ever at my home.'

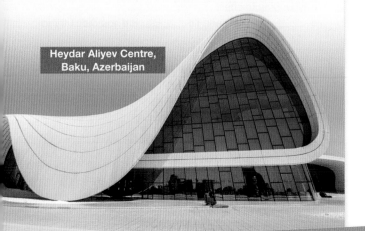

Heydar Aliyev Centre, Baku, Azerbaijan

1 LISTENING

a 💬 How would you feel if, without your permission, … ?

- you saw yourself in a documentary about learning English
- your picture appeared on Google Earth
- a radio station phoned you live on air to offer you the chance to win a prize

b 💬 Look at picture a. What do you think is happening?

c ▶4.28 Watch or listen to Part 1 and check your answer to 1b.

d ▶4.28 Read these phrases from Part 1. Who or what do the words in **bold** refer to? Watch or listen to Part 1 again and check.

1 Max: I really think **it**'s going to work.
2 Emma: **That**'s brilliant!
3 Max: **This** is outrageous!
4 Emma: But **it**'s true.
5 Max: How dare **she**?!
6 Max: I'm ringing **them** right now.

e Language in context *Animal idioms*

1 ▶4.29 Correct the idioms from Part 1. Listen and check.

   a Night rat, Max Redwood
   b There's something horsey about this.
   c I smell an owl.
   d Hold your fish, Max.

2 What do you think the idioms mean? Look at the audioscript on p.187 and a dictionary if necessary.

f ▶4.30 Watch or listen to Part 2 and answer the questions.

1 How does Nadia respond to Max's complaint? Does she … ?
   a pass on the blame to someone else
   b accept responsibility and apologise
   c promise to take action and try to arrange a meeting
2 How do you think Max feels after the phone call?
3 What do you think Nadia will do next?

2 USEFUL LANGUAGE
Dealing with conflict

a ▶4.28 ▶4.30 Watch or listen to Parts 1 and 2 again and complete the expressions.

Expressing disbelief
1 This is _____ belief!
2 Where on _____ did they get this from?!
3 I'm lost for _____!

Expressing anger
4 It's d_____!
5 I'm calling to express my _____.
6 Words cannot express my _____.
7 It's totally _____!

b Which two expressions does Max decide not to use? Why not, do you think? How would these expressions need to change for use in writing?

c ▶4.31 Complete the expressions from Parts 1 and 2 with the words or phrases in the box. Add *to* where necessary. Listen and check.

explanation   jump   fulfil your responsibility   raise
take full responsibility   right

Commenting on the behaviour of others
1 Let's not _____ conclusions.
2 There's no need _____ your voice.
3 They've got no _____!
4 You owe me an _____.
5 Don't you think you should _____ … ?
6 You've failed _____ …

d Which comments in 2c were on Max's behaviour and which were comments on *Breaking News Online* / *City FM*'s behaviour?

e ▶4.32 Complete the sentences with words from Part 2. Listen and check.

Taking action
Offering
1 **I have every** _____ **of** investigating the matter.
2 **I** _____ **you**, there will be consequences.
Responding to offers
3 _____ **not. And I'd** _____ **it if** you didn't try to contact me again.

f 💬 Work in pairs. Role-play the conversation between Max and Nadia using the language in 2a, c and e. This time Max should respond positively to Nadia's invitation.

3 LISTENING

a ▶4.33 Watch or listen to Part 3. What two reasons does Nadia have for believing Oscar sold Sara's information to *Breaking News Online*? What does she want from Oscar?

b ▶4.33 Watch or listen to Part 3 again and answer the questions.

1 Why does Nadia say the article gave her a sense of déjà vu?
2 What does Nadia suspect happened between Oscar and Miranda?
3 What does Nadia think would happen if Oscar took her to court?

c 💬 Do you think Nadia has done the right thing? Why / Why not?

4 PRONUNCIATION Sound and spelling: foreign words in English

a ▶4.34 Listen to these words. Are they from Spanish, Italian or French? Which four were in Parts 1–3? Look at the audioscript on p.187 if necessary.

1 avant-garde	5 finito
2 nada	6 tête-à-tête
3 déjà vu	7 rendezvous
4 cappuccino	8 pronto

b Match the words 1–8 in 4a with their meanings a–h.

a ☐ a strange feeling that you have experienced the same thing before
b ☐ an arrangement to meet, usually secret
c ☐ coffee made with heated, bubbly milk
d ☐ finished
e ☐ nothing
f ☐ different and modern
g ☐ private conversation between two people
h ☐ quickly and without delay

c ▶4.34 Listen to the words in 4a again. Underline the consonant sounds which are pronounced in a way which is untypical of English.

d Look at the words in the box. Answer the questions below and then check in a dictionary.

c'est la vie   kaput   aficionado   faux pas
kindergarten   tsunami   paparazzi
Schadenfreude   typhoon   karaoke   siesta

1 What languages do you think these words come from?
2 What do they mean?
3 How are they pronounced by British English speakers?

e ▶4.35 Listen and practise saying the words in 4d.

5 SPEAKING

a Work alone. Think of a situation you wish to complain about. Here are some ideas:

- planning permission to build a multi-storey car park opposite your house has been granted
- the luxury spa holiday you booked and paid for turned out to be in a hostel
- your private medical information has been accidentally posted on your doctor's website

b 💬 Work in pairs. Take turns to be A and B. Use your ideas in 5a and the language in 2.

Student A: Explain your situation and complain.

- Express anger and disbelief.
- Comment on B's behaviour.
- Respond to B's offer to take action.

Student B: Respond to A's complaint.

- Express understanding of A's situation.
- Comment on A's behaviour.
- Offer to take action.

Unit Progress Test

CHECK YOUR PROGRESS

You can now do the Unit Progress Test.

1 LISTENING and SPEAKING

a 💬 Which city in your country has the fastest-growing population? Why do people want to live there?

b 💬 Look at the photos of rural and urban New Zealand. Which environment would you prefer to live in? Why?

c ▶4.36 Listen to Lizzie and Ron talking about life in a rural community in New Zealand compared to life in Auckland, the largest city. Answer the questions.

1 What's Lizzie's news? How is she feeling about it?
2 What point does Ron make about his own and Lizzie's children?
3 What makes it difficult for their children to return to their hometown?
4 Why are Lizzie and Ron better off living where they do?
5 What does Lizzie worry about for the future of their town?

d 💬 What do you think Lizzie, Ron and their partners should do? Why?

- stay where they are
- follow their children to Auckland

2 READING

a Read the essay about urban migration. Put these points in the order they are mentioned (1–6).

Urban migration …

☐ has a negative effect on communities in small towns
☐ is a problem that requires a political solution
☐ impacts living standards in both cities and small towns
☐ is driven by work and study needs
☐ is happening all over the world
☐ has a negative impact on the supply of city housing.

b 💬 What challenges are there for people who move from small towns or the country to a large city?

Urban migration is an international phenomenon. In recent years, *there has been increasing awareness of issues associated with the migration of people from small towns and rural communities to larger cities. This essay looks at the impact of urban migration on both large cities and rural communities.

Why do people decide to move to a large city? One key factor is that there are often more employment opportunities in urban areas. Secondly, younger people may need to go to a city in order to attend university or other educational programmes. Beyond this, others are drawn to cities because of the increased stimulation offered by an urban environment.

The impact on cities ¹*is plain to see.* An increase in population leads to greater demand for housing, causing house prices and rents to rise. As a result, both existing residents and new arrivals in the city are required to spend more of their income on accommodation or are forced to live in substandard conditions.

However, ²*it could be argued* that the impact on small towns and rural areas is perhaps even greater. A dramatic decrease in the population of rural communities is often due to the number of young people leaving in search of work and study opportunities. This exodus results in the closure of businesses and cutbacks in social services. And those who remain in rural communities suffer a decline in living standards which, in turn, means small communities are seen as even less attractive places to live. As a consequence, towns serving rural communities begin to look like ghost towns.

³*By examining* the way urban migration affects both rural and urban communities, ⁴*it is evident that* the phenomenon can lead to a decline in living standards for all concerned. ⁵*It would seem that* there is a role for governments to play in the way that the movement of population is managed. Intervention such as business incentives and subsidies can ensure small communities continue to offer inhabitants employment opportunities and a good standard of living.

3 WRITING SKILLS
Discussion essays; Linking: reason and result

a What is the purpose of each paragraph in the essay?

b Notice the phrase in *italics* in the introduction. Does this express the writer's point of view / opinion directly or indirectly? Match the phrases in *italics* (1–5) in the essay with the meanings below.

☐☐ you can clearly see   ☐☐ I think
☐ I've looked

> 📣 **Writing Tip**
>
> When you present a balanced discussion in a formal essay, you should avoid using personal pronouns *I* and *you* and use pronouns like *we*, *it* and *there*.

c Use the words in the box to complete the formal equivalents; a and b in each pair mean the same thing.

outcome   outlining   noticeable   claimed   appear

1 a I've noticed a slow decline …
   b There has been a slow but _____ decline …
2 a I think it's hard to predict what will happen …
   b The _____ is difficult to predict …
3 a What I'd say is that most residents …
   b It would _____ that most residents …
4 a Now that I've described the issues here …
   b By _____ the issues here …
5 a In my opinion, it's likely …
   b It could be _____ …

d Look at the highlighted examples in the essay in 2a. Which introduce a reason? Which indicate a result? Make two lists.

e Underline the reason or result language in these examples.
1 Urban migration has decreased owing to an increase in grants to rural businesses.
2 There are now many more unemployed people in the city. Consequently, there has been a noticeable increase in small crimes.
3 A drop in living standards causes problems for those at the lower end of the socioeconomic scale.
4 There has been a population increase of 12%. Hence, there has been an increase in new building projects in suburban areas.
5 Some rural workers have returned to the countryside as a direct consequence of the loneliness and isolation of urban life.

f Which expressions in 3e can be used in the same way as these examples?
1 lead to, result in
2 due to, because of
3 As a consequence, As a result

g Choose the correct word in *italics* in these sentences.
1 The increase in new residents in some areas of the city has seen a rise in the number of potential customers for businesses, thereby *creating / create* many new business opportunities.
2 Enrolment in local primary schools has fallen dramatically. *Thus / Thereby*, many have been closed.
3 Certain local students have gained scholarships to city colleges, *thereby / therefore* freeing their parents from a significant economic burden.

h ▶ Now go to Writing Focus 9D on p.175

4 WRITING

a 💬 Think about some kind of social change in your country that is of interest to you, for example:
• demand for university places
• involvement in community organisations
• your own idea.

What are the reasons for this change? What are the results? Tell a partner.

b Write a discussion essay about the social change you have chosen. Follow these steps.
• Outline the issue in the introduction.
• Describe reasons for the change and their results.
• Avoid using personal language.
• Hypothesise about the future.
• State whether anything can/should be done about the issue.

c Work with a new partner. Read each other's essays. What kind of social change does your partner's essay discuss? How aware were you of this issue?

UNIT 9
Review and extension

1 GRAMMAR

a Complete the sentences with a pronoun.

1 I washed the car _myself_ because the carwash was closed.
2 I can see grandad is getting old. He seems to talk to _____ all the time.
3 While Simon was in hospital his mum was absolutely beside _____.
4 While I'm on holiday, my secretary and I still send _____ several messages a day.
5 We call _____ 'The Pirates' because we have a stadium on the coast.
6 Rita and I sat down next to _____ and we looked into _____'s eyes.
7 No one helped us with our house. We built it all by _____.

b Correct one mistake in each sentence or exchange.

1 Kate wanted to put in new windows but I didn't want.
2 'I'll never listen to her advice again.' 'So will I.'
3 It was a beautiful morning although was rather cool outside.
4 He living nearby, Frank had no problem getting in early.
5 So they wouldn't get bored, were listening to the radio.
6 'Kelly hasn't read the contract properly.' 'I don't suspect.'
7 She became a famous actress, as her mother.
8 Take the clean mug, not the dirty.

2 VOCABULARY

a Complete the sentences with a word in the box.

recreate   redevelop   regain
reinstate   renovate   restore

1 The council are to _____ the wasteland near the port.
2 We will _____ early closing at weekends.
3 The picture was badly damaged but they managed to _____ it.
4 The aim of *The Oscars* restaurant is to _____ the atmosphere of Hollywood.
5 The town has long been in decline and I doubt it will ever _____ its former prestige.
6 It took years to _____ the old hotel and modernise all the facilities.

b Choose the best phrase to complete the sentence.

1 ☐ I grew up on a
2 ☐ The walk took us to a
3 ☐ Our new office is a
4 ☐ I work at a
5 ☐ I know a millionaire who owns a
6 ☐ Every city needs an

a power station on the coast.
b housing estate near Hamburg.
c mansion in the Caribbean.
d log cabin in the woods.
e iconic skyscraper or two.
f tower block overlooking the river.

3 WORDPOWER *build*

a Look at these multi-word verb collocations with *build*. Match multi-word verbs 1–6 with meanings a–f.

1 **build up** savings / stamina / a following / a reputation
2 **build** / an event / an argument **up into** something
3 traffic / issues / dirt / pressure **build up**
4 **build on** our success / strengths / relationship
5 **build in** features (to a product) / activities (to a schedule)
6 **build** something **around** a concept / two main characters / a budget

a ☐ use as a basis for the future
b ☐ make an effort to increase
c ☐ use as the main principle/idea
d ☐ include, incorporate
e ☐ increase naturally over time
f ☐ talk or think a lot about something so it becomes more important

b ▶4.37 Complete the sentences with the words in the box. Listen and check.

up (×4)   on   around   in

1 He's **built** this day _____ so much I'm afraid he'll be disappointed.
2 They forgot to **build** _____ auto-locking on this phone.
3 He's **built** _____ a huge fan base over the years.
4 I'm looking for ways to **build** _____ last year's sales.
5 Our business is **built** _____ the idea that people want coffee with their books.
6 She really needs to **build** _____ her confidence if she wants to get a job.
7 When the pressure **builds** _____ at work, you need a good, long break.

c Complete each statement with your own idea. Check the meaning of the expressions in **bold** in a dictionary if necessary.

1 People sometimes **build up a tolerance** to _____.
2 I had to **build up the courage** to ask _____.
3 I once **built my hopes up about** _____ but was disappointed.
4 I think **building up a business** would be _____.

d 💬 Compare your answers to 3c with a partner.

⟳ REVIEW YOUR PROGRESS

How well did you do in this unit? Write 3, 2, or 1 for each objective.
3 = very well   2 = well   1 = not so well

I CAN ...

talk about city life and urban space	☐
describe architecture and buildings	☐
deal with conflict	☐
write a discussion essay	☐

CAN DO OBJECTIVES

- Give a presentation or a speech
- Talk about superstitions and rituals
- Take turns in more formal conversations
- Write a film review

UNIT 10
Occasions

YOU MAY EXCHANGE RINGS

GETTING STARTED

a ⬤ Look at the picture and answer the questions.

1 Where are these people? What are they doing? How do you think they feel?
2 Why do you think they chose this venue?
3 What role does the man on the right have? Do you think he's worked in this way before?
4 What do you think happened in the 15 minutes before this picture was taken? What do you think happened afterwards?

b ⬤ Discuss the questions.

1 What's the most memorable wedding you've been to? Why?
2 For you, what are the most important parts of wedding day celebrations?
3 If you could hold a ceremony – such as a wedding – in a unique way, what would you do? Why?

10A I really wish I'd been on time

Learn to give a presentation or a speech
Ⓖ Regret and criticism structures
Ⓥ Communication verbs

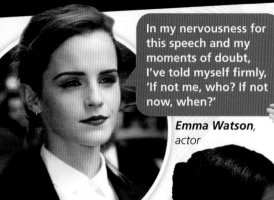

In my nervousness for this speech and my moments of doubt, I've told myself firmly, 'If not me, who? If not now, when?'

Emma Watson, *actor*

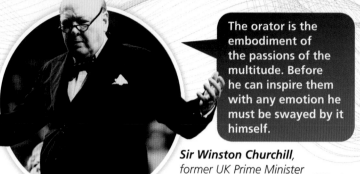

The orator is the embodiment of the passions of the multitude. Before he can inspire them with any emotion he must be swayed by it himself.

Sir Winston Churchill, *former UK Prime Minister*

Honestly, if everyone likes what you say, something is wrong with your message.

Ashley Ormon, *writer and editor*

A successful talk is a little miracle – people see the world differently afterward.

Chris Anderson, *curator of TED Talks*

1 SPEAKING and VOCABULARY
Communication verbs

a 💬 Have you ever had to give a speech or presentation? What was the experience like? If not, how would you feel about doing this?

b 💬 Read the quotes. What does each quote tell you about the person's attitude to giving speeches? Which quotes do you agree with or relate to?

c 💬 What makes a good presentation? What kinds of things can go wrong?

d Read sentences 1–5. Do they mention your ideas in 1c?

1 He kept **making** comments under his breath when he was supposed to be **addressing** the audience.
2 She lost her place whenever she **moved on to** her next point!
3 She **went into** far too much detail and **presented** the information in a confusing way.
4 He **demonstrated** their new approach but it was all a bit boring.
5 He used lots of anecdotes to **illustrate** his points. It was brilliant!

e ▶4.38 Find the verbs / verb phrases in **bold** in 1d that collocate with the phrases 1–7 below. Listen and check your answers.

1 _____ the results
2 _____ her understanding
3 _____ a conference
4 _____ a different topic
5 _____ the finer points
6 _____ the concept with examples
7 _____ throwaway remarks

f ▶ Now go to Vocabulary Focus 10A on p.167

2 READING

a Read *TED* and read the first part of *How to Give a Killer Presentation*. Answer the questions.

1 How does TED share information?
2 Why was Richard Turere an unlikely candidate for a TED talk? How did his talk go?

b Read *Chris Anderson's advice on giving presentations*. Match the headings below with the correct advice.

Develop Stage Presence

Plan Your Delivery

Putting It Together   **Frame Your Story**

Plan the Multimedia

c Read the advice again. How will these ideas help someone give a better presentation? Make notes. Compare your ideas with a partner.

1 storytelling
2 cutting down your first draft
3 controlling your body movements
4 imagining you have friends in the audience
5 reviewing the media you want to use
6 time to prepare
7 ignoring some of Chris Anderson's advice

d 💬 Imagine you have to give a talk or presentation. Which piece of Chris Anderson's advice do you think is most relevant for you? Why?

TED

(Technology, Entertainment and Design) is a non-profit organisation that aims to spread new ideas in the form of short, powerful talks of up to 18 minutes. Since they began putting TED talks online in 2006, they've been viewed more than one billion times.

HOW TO GIVE A KILLER PRESENTATION

Chris Anderson, curator of TED

A little more than a year ago, on a trip to Nairobi, Kenya, some colleagues and I met a 12-year-old Masai boy named Richard Turere, who told us a fascinating story about devising a system of lights to protect his family's livestock from lions. Soon villages elsewhere in Kenya began installing Richard's 'lion lights'.

On the surface, Richard seemed an unlikely candidate to give a TED Talk. He was painfully shy. His English was halting. When he tried to describe his invention, the sentences tumbled out incoherently.

But Richard's story was so compelling that we invited him to speak. In the months before the conference, we worked with him to frame his story and practise his talk over and over again. When he finally gave his talk at TED, in Long Beach, you could tell he was nervous, but that only made him more engaging—people were hanging on his every word. When he finished, the response was instantaneous: a sustained standing ovation.

On the basis of this experience with Richard and many other TED speakers I've worked with, I'm convinced that giving a good talk is highly coachable. In a matter of hours, a speaker's content and delivery can be transformed from muddled to mesmerising.

CHRIS ANDERSON'S ADVICE ON GIVING PRESENTATIONS

1 _____

We all know that humans are wired to listen to stories, and metaphors abound for the narrative structures that work best to engage people. When I think about compelling presentations, I think about taking an audience on a journey.

The biggest problem I see in first drafts of presentations is that they try to cover too much ground. So limit the scope of your talk to that which can be explained, and brought to life with examples, in the available time.

Of course, it can be just as damaging to overexplain or painstakingly draw out the implications of a talk. And there the remedy is different: remember that the people in the audience are intelligent. Let them figure some things out for themselves. Let them draw their own conclusions.

2 _____

There are three main ways to deliver a talk: read it directly off a script, develop a set of bullet points that map out what you're going to say, or you can memorise your talk. My advice: don't read it. It's usually just too distancing – people will know you're reading.

Many of our best and most popular TED Talks have been memorised word for word. If you're giving an important talk and you have the time to do this, it's the best way to go. But don't underestimate the work involved. If you don't have time to learn a speech thoroughly and get past that awkward valley, don't try. Go with bullet points on note cards. As long as you know what you want to say for each one, you'll be fine.

3 _____

The biggest mistake we see is that people move their bodies too much. They sway from side to side, or shift their weight from one leg to the other. People do this naturally when they're nervous, but it's distracting and makes the speaker seem weak.

Perhaps the most important physical act onstage is making eye contact. Find five or six friendly-looking people in different parts of the audience and look them in the eye as you speak. Think of them as friends you haven't seen in a year, whom you're bringing up to date on your work.

4 _____

With so much technology at our disposal, it may feel almost mandatory to use, at a minimum, presentation slides. By now most people have heard the advice about PowerPoint: keep it simple; don't use slides as a substitute for notes. Used well, video can be very effective, but a clip needs to be short – if it's more than 60 seconds, you risk losing people.

5 _____

We start helping speakers prepare their talks six months (or more) in advance. The more practice they can do in the final weeks, the better off they'll be. Ideally, they'll practise the talk on their own and in front of an audience.

The most memorable talks offer something fresh, something no one has seen before. The worst ones are those that feel formulaic. So do not on any account try to emulate every piece of advice I've offered here. Take the bulk of it on board, sure. But make the talk your own. Play to your strengths and give a talk that is truly authentic to you.

3 LISTENING

a 💬 Which of these, 1 or 2, would you feel most comfortable doing? Why?

1 a presentation for work/school/university
2 a speech for a relative/friend's birthday/anniversary/wedding

b ▶4.40 Listen to three people talk about giving a speech or presentation. Answer the questions.

1 Why were they giving a speech?
2 What went wrong?
3 What was the outcome?

Rob

Chantal

Milos

c 💬 Discuss the questions.

1 Do you think Rob should have refused to be best man? Why / Why not? What's your opinion of Jessica's reaction?
2 What are Chantal's suspicions about the missing file? How likely is it they are correct? How would you react in this situation?
3 How do you think Milos could have regained control when he got distracted during his talk?

d Language in context *Idioms: Plans into action*

1 ▶4.41 Complete the idioms in **bold** with the words in the box. Then listen and check.

> good   went   threw   recipe
> yourself   made   out   words

1 I just _____ **myself into** it.
2 They make me **feel right** _____ **of my depth**.
3 I thought I'd **made a** _____ **job of it**.
4 Always make a copy, otherwise it's **a** _____ **for disaster**.
5 I just explained the whole project and **it** _____ **like clockwork**.
6 The managers were all impressed and I really _____ **my mark**.
7 I couldn't go on – I was completely **lost for** _____.
8 I was sort of saying to myself, 'C'mon, **get a grip on** _____!'

2 Match the idioms in 1 with the meanings below.

a ☐ likely to cause serious problems
b ☐ not know what to say
c ☐ do something well
d ☐ regain some self-control when upset or stressed
e ☐ get fully involved in something new
f ☐ go very smoothly without problems
g ☐ impress somebody
h ☐ feel it's too difficult for you

4 GRAMMAR
Regret and criticism structures

a Read sentences 1–8. Which sentence does not show a regret?

1 ☐ I should never have agreed to be best man.
2 ☐ If only I'd checked those cards.
3 ☐ Part of me wishes that Dan hadn't asked me to be best man.
4 ☐ I really wish I'd copied the presentation onto my hard drive.
5 ☐ Had he been less underhand, I might not have the job I've got now.
6 ☐ She wasn't my girlfriend, but I used to wish she were.
7 ☐ If I had listened to Teresa's advice, I might have been OK.
8 ☐ If it wasn't for my stupidity, we could have raised more money that day.

b Underline the part of each example in 4a that shows regret. Which examples are third conditionals?

c ▶4.42 Pronunciation Mark the word groups ‖ and underline the main stress in these two sentences. Listen and check. Practise saying the sentences.

1 If I had listened to Teresa's advice, I might have been OK.
2 If it wasn't for my stupidity, we could have raised more money that day.

d ▶ Now go to Grammar Focus 10A on p.156

e 💬 What regrets have you had? Talk about one of these past situations.

- a decision to study the wrong subject at school/university
- losing touch with an old friend
- something unfortunate you said to a relative or friend
- a bad decision associated with some kind of social activity

> I wish I hadn't mentioned the family holiday home to my cousin.

> I really regret not replying to her emails.

5 SPEAKING

a Plan a one-minute speech with the title *Learning from my mistakes*. Talk about a personal experience of some kind. You could develop ideas that you talked about in 4e.

Follow Chris Anderson's advice:

- include an anecdote about your experience
- make notes, but don't write out your speech
- practise the speech quietly to yourself.

b 💬 Work in small groups. Deliver your speeches.

Speakers
- Remember to keep still.
- Maintain eye contact with group members.

Listeners
- Think of a question you can ask each speaker about their experiences.

Ba Gua mirror

Horseshoe

Maneki-neko

Wish bracelet

1 SPEAKING and VOCABULARY
Superstitions, customs and beliefs

a 💬 Look at the objects in the pictures.

1 What do you think they all have in common?
2 What part of the world do you think they are from?

b 💬 Which of the objects in 1a do you think these sentences describe?

1 You **make a wish** with every knot you tie.
2 They were **traditionally** nailed above doorways.
3 They stop bad luck entering the house and they protect it against **magic spells**.
4 It is **customary** to hang them above the front door.
5 It invites **good fortune** and brings wealth to the owner.
6 They are worn as a **good luck charm**.
7 They always face outwards so they can **ward off evil**.

c ▶4.48 Listen and check your answers.

d Look at the words and phrases in **bold** in 1b. Which are connected with ... ?

• luck and magic   • customs

e ▶ Now go to Vocabulary Focus 10B on p.168

f Look at the idiomatic expressions in the box connected with good luck. When do people say them?

1 when they hope something good will happen
2 to warn someone of danger
3 when they're taking extra precautions

| fingers crossed   to be on the safe side   touch wood |
| third time lucky   you're tempting fate |

g ▶4.51 Complete the sentences with the expressions in 1f. Listen and check.

1 They've agreed to sell the house, so this time next week it'll be ours – _____.
2 I've failed the driving test twice now. Ah well, _____.
3 'I do hope Lisa passes her English exam.'
  'Yes, I'll keep my _____.'
4 You should wear a motorbike helmet. You've been lucky so far, but _____.
5 I know it's not raining, but take an umbrella just _____.

h ▶4.52 **Pronunciation** <u>Underline</u> the consonant groups in the words in the box in 1f. Remember that these can be across words. Listen and check. Practise saying the expressions.

i 💬 Work in pairs. Take turns being A and B.

Student A: Tell your partner something you're planning to do. Choose from this list.

• go rock climbing   • take an exam
• apply for a new job   • travel across Africa by bus

Student B: Respond using a suitable expression from 1f.

> I'm going to climb the Matterhorn.

> Take a guide with you to be on the safe side.

> Good luck. I'll keep my fingers crossed.

j 💬 Discuss the questions.

1 Do you know of other things that traditionally bring good luck or ward off evil (in either your own country or another country you know)?
2 How seriously do you think most people believe in charms of this kind? What about you?

2 READING

a 🗨 Look at the photo of tennis champion Rafael Nadal. What do you think he is doing and why?

b Read the introduction the text to check your answer to 2a. What appear to be the main reasons for this behaviour? How effective is it?

c Read the rest of the article and find examples of these kinds of rituals (1–7). Which one is <u>not</u> mentioned?

1 touching yourself or other people
2 doing things in a particular sequence
3 things that also involve other players
4 lucky objects
5 particular ways of wearing or putting on clothes
6 things players do on their way to a match
7 particular aspects of personal grooming

d 🗨 Which of the rituals do you think is the most 'bizarre'?

3 GRAMMAR Passive reporting verbs

a Look at the verb forms in **bold**.

1 **It's thought that** performing a 'lucky' routine **reduces** anxiety.
2 **It's reported that** the champion tennis player even **wears** the same pair of socks during a run of wins.
3 Williams **is claimed to be** so convinced of her superstitions that she blames major losses on not following her own routine correctly.
4 He **is believed to insist** on sitting on the back row of the team bus or plane when heading to a match.
5 When playing for Portugal **it's said that** no other player **is allowed** to start the match in a long-sleeved shirt.
6 **Lewis Hamilton is said to have overcome** the superstitions he had as a young driver.

Why does the writer use passive reporting structures? Two of these answers are correct.

☐ to show that they believe in the information
☐ to show the information comes from someone else
☐ to show this is not necessarily what they believe

b The sentences in 3a show two structures for reporting information:

a *it* + passive + *that* clause …
b subject + passive + *to* + infinitive …

1 Which structure is shown in **bold** in each sentence in 3a, a or b?
2 Which structures in **bold** … ?
   a refer to the present
   b refer to the past
3 How could you express each idea in 3a 1–6 using the other structure?
   Performing a lucky routine is said to reduce anxiety.

THE GAME
BEFORE THE GAME
THE INCREDIBLE RITUALS THAT TOP PLAYERS PERFORM BEFORE A MATCH

From Rafael Nadal who lines up his water bottles before each match, to Tiger Woods who always wore the colour red for the final round of golf tournaments – many of sport's biggest stars believe in the power of rituals to bring them luck.

Despite the hours spent training and developing winning strategies, players still go through superstitious rituals just before a big event. It seems nonsensical that such players would give credit for their own success or failure to rituals. However, sport psychologists suggest that these beliefs can actually help players.

Rituals usually come about when we repeat something we did in the past which seemed to bring us success, even if there's no rational explanation for it. It's no different for sports players. It's thought that performing a 'lucky' routine reduces anxiety in the player by giving them an illusion of control and a way to contribute to their own success on the day.

c 🗨 The sentences in 3a are typical of news reports and factual writing. How could you say them in a more conversational style?

> People say …

> I've heard …

> Many people think …

d ▶ Now go to Grammar Focus 10B on p.157

Her opponents fear her power and drive, but SERENA WILLIAMS believes that her pre-match rituals are the source of her wins. Her habits include tying her shoelaces a particular way and bouncing the ball five times before her first serve, and twice before her second. It's reported that the champion tennis player even wears the same pair of socks during a run of wins. Williams is claimed to be so convinced of her superstitions that she blames major losses on not following her own routine correctly.

As one of the world's most expensive football players, CRISTIANO RONALDO has the power to get others to abide by his superstitious rituals. He is believed to insist on sitting on the back row of the team bus or plane when heading to a match. He also insists on going onto the pitch first if he's playing for Portugal – but he has to be last on the pitch if he's playing for Real Madrid. When playing for Portugal it's said that no other player is allowed to start the match in a long-sleeved shirt. Perhaps most bizarrely, Ronaldo does not spend half-time with his team and coach. It's reported that the star spends this time getting his hair done, because he cannot play the second half with the same hairstyle as the first.

Racing star LEWIS HAMILTON is said to have overcome the superstitions he had as a young driver. There was a time that he was so superstitious that he wore the same underwear every time he raced. That is until his mum shrank them in the wash. Hamilton also used to carry a conker with him inside his race suit, and put one sock on a certain way before adjusting his helmet. However, after crashing out of a race, Hamilton is reported to have given up on his superstitions, saying that he would not allow anything to get in his way.

4 LISTENING

a 💬 What do you know (if anything) about Shakespeare's play *Macbeth*? Talk about:

- the story
- the characters
- the setting.

b ▶ 4.54 Listen to an actor talking about superstitions connected with *Macbeth* in the theatre and answer the questions.

1 Why do actors avoid saying the word 'Macbeth'?
2 What is the opening scene of the play?
3 How can you neutralise the curse?
4 Which three of these explanations do they give for the curse?

   a A group of witches cursed the play out of revenge.
   b Shakespeare himself put a curse on the play.
   c Some scenes in the play can be dangerous for the actors.
   d Theatre companies thought the play made them go out of business.

5 SPEAKING

a 💬 Look at these other superstitions connected with the theatre. How do you think each one might have originated?

1 It is unlucky to wish someone 'Good luck' before a show. Instead, actors say, 'Break a leg'.
2 It is considered bad luck to whistle on or off stage, as it means someone will lose their job.
3 A light is always left on in an empty theatre. It is usually placed near the centre of the stage.
4 You shouldn't have mirrors on stage as they bring bad luck to the play.
5 Peacock feathers should never be brought on stage, either as part of a costume element or to decorate the stage, as they will lead to chaos.

b In pairs, choose a superstition in 5a and write an explanation of how it originated. Include passive reporting verbs where appropriate.

   3 It is believed that the ghosts of dead actors live in theatres and come out at night. Leaving a light on is thought to keep them away from the stage.

c 💬 Tell the class your explanation in 5b. Which explanations do you think are the best?

d ▶ Communication 10B Now go to p.131 to find the real explanations.

Learn to take turns in more formal conversations

- S Take turns in an interview
- P Tone in question tags

1 LISTENING

a 💬 Look at picture a below. Who do you think is calling Max?

(a)

b ▶️4.55 Watch or listen to Part 1. What are the two main reasons for Nadia's call?

c ▶️4.55 Watch or listen to Part 1 again and answer these questions.

1 Why does Max say that Nadia's *got a nerve*?
2 What does Nadia say Sara *wasn't* doing?
3 What word does Nadia use to describe the potential interview? What does it mean?

d 💬 Look at picture b. Why do you think Max changed his mind about doing the interview?

e ▶️4.56 Watch or listen to Part 2 and put the things in the order they're mentioned.

a ☐ Max's father		c ☐ Max's inspirations
b ☐ Max's insomnia		d ☐ Max's hometown

f ▶️4.56 Watch or listen to Part 2 again and make notes on the points in 1e.

g 💬 Do you think the interview has been successful? Why / Why not?

2 USEFUL LANGUAGE Turn-taking

a Match the expressions in **bold** with their uses a–c. Some expressions have more than one use.

1 **Sorry, if I could just finish** what I was saying, Max!
2 **Sorry to interrupt, but** Sara wasn't idly gossiping.
3 **Speaking of which,** you grew up here in Brighton, didn't you?
4 **Please, after you.**
5 **As I was saying,** I never forgot those worlds.
6 **If you don't mind me coming in here,** you had trouble sleeping as a child, didn't you?

a interrupt someone and take a turn speaking
b encourage someone else to speak
c continue speaking about the same subject

b When would you use these phrases in a conversation?

1 **Go on.**
2 **Before we get started …**
3 **Before we move on …**

c ▶️4.57 Complete the conversation with suitable expressions from 2a and b. There may be more than one correct answer. Listen and check.

A So, I understand you're a motivational speaker.
B That's right. Basically I go to company conferences and give talks on …
A ¹_____ where are these conferences?
B Oh, all over the country. Overseas sometimes, too. But ²_____, companies employ me to talk about my mountaineering adventures to share a message of drive and ambition.
A And I don't suppose you imagined when you started mountaineering that you would end up doing this.
B No, I …
A I mean, did you think …
B Sorry?
A No, I'm sorry. ³_____.
B Well, no. I never imagined I would be going around speaking at conferences …
A ⁴_____ you have some really exciting stories of your mountaineering days, don't you?
B ⁵_____ what I was saying. I never imagined speaking at conferences but I'd just like to say that I've been amazed at the warm welcome I've received in the business world.
A That's good to hear. Now, …

d 💬 Practise the interview in 2c with a partner, but change the profession of the interviewee.

(b)

3 LISTENING

a ▶4.58 Watch or listen to Part 3 and choose the best answer to the questions.

1 Why is Sara pleased?
  a She did a great interview with a difficult interviewee.
  b She's finally getting the credit she is due.
  c She feels exhilarated after a successful broadcast.
  d Nadia is going to promote her to a full-time position.
2 What does Alex suggest Nadia said?
  a that Sara's a better interviewer than Oscar
  b that Sara's performed well
  c that Sara's job's safe
  d that Sara should celebrate
3 What are Max, Sara, Emma and Alex going to do together?
  a have a party at Emma's flat
  b watch *Moon Station X* at the cinema
  c go to a dance club
  d spend time at Max's flat

b 💬 How do you celebrate your achievements?

c ▶4.59 **Language in context** *Praising idioms*
Match the two halves of the idioms. Listen and check.

1 ☐ Hats off   a your praises this morning.
2 ☐ Well, credit where   b to you both.
3 ☐ I overheard Nadia   c best thing since sliced
   singing   bread.
4 ☐ Thinks you're the   d credit's due.

4 PRONUNCIATION Tone in question tags

a ▶4.60 Listen to the sentences from Parts 1, 2 and 3. Does the tone rise (↗) or fall (↘) on each question tag in **bold**?

1 I asked you not to contact me again, **didn't I?**
2 You grew up here in Brighton, **didn't you?**
3 You had trouble sleeping as a child, **didn't you?**
4 You were so different this time, **weren't you?**
5 It's massive, **isn't it**, Max?

b Complete the rules with *rising* or *falling*.

• If you're not sure what you've said is correct, use a _____ tone on the question tag.
• If you know what you've said is correct and you want the other person to confirm it, use a _____ tone on the question tag.

c ▶4.61 Listen to these questions and say which tone you hear – A (↗) or B (↘).

1 You did, didn't you?   4 They do, don't they?
2 You can't, can you?   5 I should, shouldn't I?
3 She hasn't, has she?   6 It will, won't it?

d 💬 Work in pairs. Take turns to say a sentence from 4c, using different tones for the question tag. Your partner says *A* or *B*.

e 💬 We often use a question tag with a falling tone after giving an opinion to elicit agreement from the person we are speaking to. Give your opinions on the topics below and elicit your partner's agreement using a question tag.
• a strange superstition
• a great sporting celebrity
• a good TV documentary

5 SPEAKING

a Work on your own. Invent a fictitious sporting celebrity. Answer the questions.

1 What's your name and nationality?
2 What's your sporting background and what team/country do you play for / who is your sponsor?
3 What bizarre superstitious rituals do you have (think of three)? Here are some ideas:
  • lucky charms • pre-match routine • particular clothing

b You are going to interview your partner in their role as a sporting celebrity. Think of some questions to ask them.

c 💬 Work with a partner. Take turns to interview each other. Think of answers to your partner's questions. Use expressions for turn-taking and question tags.

Unit Progress Test 📶

CHECK YOUR PROGRESS

You can now do the Unit Progress Test.

1 SPEAKING and LISTENING

a 💬 Look at the photo and poster from the film *Whiplash*. What do you think it's about?

b Read the descriptions of the film A–D and see if you were right. Then match the descriptions with places you would find them.

1 ☐ on a film download website
2 ☐ on a customer review site
3 ☐ on a sign outside a cinema
4 ☐ in a critic's review in a newspaper

c 💬 Do you read reviews either before or after you watch a film or DVD? How much are you influenced by them? What are the reasons for or against reading reviews?

d ▶4.62 Listen to four people talking about how they use reviews and make notes to answer the questions.

1 What kind of film reviews do they read? Why?
2 When do they read them?
3 Do they read any other kinds of review?

Which person's opinions are closest to your own?

e 💬 What other kinds of review do you find useful? What kinds of review have you written yourself?

(A) **Whiplash** 2014 ⑮

Andy is an ambitious music student who dreams of becoming a top jazz drummer. When he starts playing in the band of his eccentric jazz teacher, his ambitions may be fulfilled ... but at a price.

WATCH NOW | Buy $14.50 | Rent $4.50

(B) NEWS   CHAT   REVIEWS   TRAILERS

WHIPLASH 2014
★★★★★

Not at all what I expected and I loved it! To say it's gripping would be an understatement. A must-see movie.

Alexx
Feb 16

read **8** more reviews of *Whiplash*

(C) MOVIE REVIEW

Simmons gives a riveting performance as a teacher who rules by fear, and Teller is also superb as the vulnerable student in search of a father figure. In spite of its brutality, the film provides a subtle portrayal of the

(D) **NOW SHOWING**

WHIPLASH

"ELECTRIFYING. MILES TELLER IS A REVELATION."

MOVIE REVIEW

2 READING

a Read two reviews of *Whiplash*. Which reviewer is more positive? What are the main differences in their feelings about the film?

b 💬 Based on these two reviews alone, would you want to see the film? Why / Why not?

Ⓐ

Whiplash (2014)
R | 107 min | Damien Chazelle

Damien Chazelle's latest film *Whiplash* is the intense and inspiring story of an ambitious young jazz drummer, Andy, who studies in an elite New York music school and is determined to become a great jazz player. Terence Fletcher, a jazz teacher at the school, notices Andy and invites him to join his prestigious jazz band. But having joined the band, Andy is subjected to Fletcher's bullying teaching methods and ferocious temper. Pushed to the limit by Fletcher, Andy's desire to play perfectly progresses into a dangerous obsession which isolates him from his family and his would-be girlfriend.

Although the story is sometimes a little far-fetched, the film is gripping to the very end and also brilliantly acted. J. K. Simmons is perfectly cast in the role of the uncompromising jazz teacher and Miles Teller also gives a convincing portrayal of Andy, becoming increasingly insecure and unstable as the film progresses.

For me, the strength of *Whiplash* lies in its exploration of the changing relationship between teacher and student. The film has an unusual and rather old-fashioned message – that it's necessary to suffer in order to achieve perfection. Although not always a comfortable film, it's well worth a watch. It certainly made me look at jazz musicians in a different way!

Ⓑ

Whiplash, a new film by director Damien Chazelle, is set in a top music academy in New York. A critical and box office hit, the film has won several awards for direction and the performances of its actors.

Andy Newman (played by Miles Teller) is a student who has been playing drums since childhood and wants to become a top jazz musician. He seeks out the attention of Terence Fletcher (played by J. K. Simmons), a jazz teacher who, recognising Andy's promise, recruits him into his competitive jazz band. Ruthless and sadistic, Fletcher bullies the band members to achieve his vision of musical excellence. In an attempt to satisfy Fletcher's impossibly high expectations, Andy becomes more and more single-minded in his pursuit of greatness.

⌐THE MUSIC SCENES ARE BEAUTIFULLY FILMED⌐

The film is intense and exciting from beginning to end, the acting is excellent and the music scenes are beautifully filmed with close-ups of drums, cymbals and the sweating faces of the students as they struggle to perform to Fletcher's impossible standards. However, I found the plot a little too simple in the way that it focuses on Andy's obsession with drumming and Fletcher's character is too over-the-top to be convincing.

I left the cinema feeling dissatisfied and slightly depressed by the film's harsh message. Nevertheless, it's an original, thought-provoking film and certainly worth seeing.

3 WRITING SKILLS
Film reviews; Concise description

a Tick (✓) the elements that are included in the reviews. Are they included in the same order in both reviews?

1 ☐ when and where the writer saw the film
2 ☐ the names of the director and actors
3 ☐ outline of the plot
4 ☐ how the film ends
5 ☐ strong points of the film
6 ☐ weak points of the film
7 ☐ short summarising statement
8 ☐ recommendation – whether to see it or not

Should the elements you didn't tick be included in a review? Why / Why not?

b Which reviewer mentions strengths or weaknesses in the following areas? Write *A*, *B* or *both*.

1 plot	3 acting	5 themes/messages
2 characters	4 filming	6 success of the film

c <u>Underline</u> two or three expressions the writers use to write about films that you would find useful to learn. Compare with other students. Did you choose the same ones?

d Compare the excerpts below with the first paragraph of Review A. How are the words in *italics* different in Review A? Why do you think the writer of Review A chose to do this? Choose 1 or 2.

1 to make the meaning more explicit
2 to give the information more concisely

Terence Fletcher, *who is a jazz teacher at the school*, …
But *after he has joined the band*, Andy …
Because he is pushed to the limit by Fletcher …

e ▶ Now go to Writing Focus 10D on p.175

4 WRITING

a Choose a film or TV series you know and plan a review of 220–260 words. Think about:
* describing the film for someone who hasn't seen it
* main strengths and weaknesses
* how to structure your review into four paragraphs.

b Write the review. Try to:
* use adjectives to give an intense description
* make the information as concise as possible.

c Read another student's review. Do you know the film/series? If so, decide if you agree with what it says. If not, decide whether you'd like to see it, based on the review.

UNIT 10
Review and extension

1 GRAMMAR

a Complete the sentences with a word in the box.

| have   it   needn't   only   ought to   rather   time   wish |

1 You could _____ asked me before getting involved.
2 I would _____ you spoke to Jean about it.
3 _____ was revealed that the manager had resigned.
4 If _____ everyone were as generous as you.
5 It's _____ the government did something about crime.
6 I _____ you would behave when my friends come round.
7 You _____ look at me with a face like that.
8 Harriet _____ feel ashamed of herself.

b Rewrite the sentences using the words in brackets.

1 Why didn't you phone me? (should)
2 It wasn't necessary for you to meet me. (needn't)
3 They say that the president owns a private zoo. (said)
4 It's a shame we don't live closer. (wish)
5 There's no way that Alex was on time. (couldn't)
6 It was a bad idea for Sarah to lose her temper. (If only)
7 People think that she died in a car crash. (thought)

2 VOCABULARY

a Match sentence halves 1–6 with endings a–f.

1 ☐ The president concluded
2 ☐ It is important to back
3 ☐ I would also like to pay
4 ☐ There's no time to go into
5 ☐ Before we move on to
6 ☐ You also need to sell

a tribute to a dear friend, Carlos Sanchez.
b the idea to your audience.
c up arguments with solid facts.
d the finer points so I'll leave it there.
e her speech with some words of thanks.
f a different topic, let me summarise.

b Complete the missing words.

1 Good luck in the race. I'll keep my f_____ crossed.
2 We've lost twice already! Third t_____ lucky!
3 That might be t_____ fate.
4 I find Tracey's story c_____ and I will support her.
5 To be on the safe s_____, let's go by taxi.
6 Blow out the candles and m_____ a wish.

3 WORDPOWER *luck* and *chance*

a ▶4.63 Replace the words in *italics* with the correct phrases in the box. Listen and check.

| a fighting chance   blow my chances   on the off chance |
| don't stand a chance   it's tough luck   're in luck |
| count yourself lucky |

1 I can't believe what you said in that meeting! You should *be relieved* that nobody was listening.
2 We're inviting you *because there's a small possibility* that you're free that night.
3 The treatment is essential to give him *a possibility of recovering*.
4 I'm sorry you don't like the situation, Mark, but *you'll have to put up with it*, I'm afraid.
5 I always *destroy any possibility of success* in interviews, because I get so nervous.
6 You know that book you wanted to borrow? Well, you *can do that now*! I found it under the bed.
7 Their top striker is out with an injury, and without him they *have no possibility of winning*.

b ▶4.64 Complete the dialogues using the correct form of the phrases in 3a. Use one word in each gap. Listen and check.

1 **A** I can't believe I missed the entry date for applications. I've really _____ my chances there.
   B Why don't you send it in anyway, _____ the _____ chance they're still recruiting?
2 **A** Do you have the notes from yesterday's lecture?
   B You're _____ luck. That's the first lecture I've taken notes at this year. Here you go.
3 **A** It's six o'clock already. I don't _____ a chance of getting this homework finished tonight.
   B _____ luck, I'm afraid. I'm not helping you.
4 **A** I'm so worried about how badly I did those exams.
   B Well, _____ yourself lucky that everyone else did badly, too. At least you have a _____ chance of getting in.

c 💬 What could you say to these people using the expressions in 3a? (There is more than one answer.)

- a friend who missed the bus
- a busy person you'd like to meet with
- someone who wants to borrow some money from you
- a friend who should go to bed because they have a test the next day
- a friend who lost their wallet but got it back

↻ REVIEW YOUR PROGRESS

How well did you do in this unit? Write 3, 2, or 1 for each objective.
3 = very well   2 = well   1 = not so well

I CAN ...

give a presentation or a speech	☐
talk about superstitions and rituals	☐
take turns in more formal conversations	☐
write a film review	☐

Communication Plus

1B Student A

a Read about two more language changes. How does each heading represent the change?

❶ To be or not to be?

Verbs that are followed by *to* + infinitive or verb + *-ing* give us a choice of form with no real difference in meaning. In the last century there was a steady shift towards more frequent use of the verb + *-ing* after verbs like *begin, start, like, love* and *hate* and these are still on the increase.

A: *I like getting up late and eating a big breakfast.*

B: *I like to get up late and eat a big breakfast.*

The more modern of these two speakers is Speaker A although they're unlikely to be aware of it.

❷ Are you being serious?

English is getting more and more progressive. Constructions such as *I must be going now* and *I'm being sensible at the moment* wouldn't have sounded correct 150 years ago, but nowadays are fairly high frequency. And in British English, the use of continuous passive verb forms has also seen a rapid rise. And what's *being done* about it? Nothing.

b ▶ Now go back to p.11

2C Student A

a Read about this problem you have and think about what you want to say.

- You live in a shared flat. While your flatmate was away, you borrowed an item belonging to them without asking. (*Decide what you borrowed.*)
- Unfortunately, you broke the item. (*Decide what you were doing when this happened.*)
- You've tried to find a replacement in the shops. You can't find anything exactly the same, but there's something very similar and you don't think your friend will notice.

b Student B also has a problem. Listen to them carefully and discuss some solutions to the problem. Make three suggestions using the language for giving advice on p.27.

c Now present your problem to Student B and ask for advice.

2A

a Answer the questions with a partner. Do you feel the same about the different types of sound? Who is more sensitive to noise, do you think?

HOW SENSITIVE are you to sound?

1 Do you find it difficult to read a book if someone is having a conversation in the same room?

2 When a colleague types loudly on their computer at work, do you have problems concentrating?

3 Does the sound of household appliances like vacuum cleaners irritate you?

4 Does constant traffic noise drive you mad?

5 Does the sound of excited children playing together annoy you?

6 Do unexpected sounds at night spook you?

7 Do you find it impossible to sleep if you can hear your neighbours having a party?

b Ask and answer the questions.

1 Are there any other sounds which drive you mad? What?
2 What can you do if you feel apprehensive about going to noisy places?
3 What can you do to improve your tolerance of background noise?

c ▶ Now go to p.133 for suggestions on how to manage noise.

4C Student A

a Read your card. Think about what you might say using the language on p.50.

You're an employee. You have produced a report for your boss. You think it's good but your boss has some criticisms. Make these points tactfully:
- You weren't given a clear brief about what was required, so you had to use your initiative.
- You were only asked to write a report a week ago, so you had very little time to do it.
- Your boss is often out of the office, so you couldn't ask for help.

b Listen to Student B and respond. Try to agree a way forward.

9A Student A

a Read the fact-file and prepare to tell other students about the event.

> *DAY OF THE PEDESTRIAN AND CYCLIST IN DEFENCE OF MOTHER EARTH; ANNUAL EVENT, BOLIVIA*
>
> - All roads in major cities (La Paz, El Alto) closed to cars from 8am to 6pm
>
> AIMS AND ACHIEVEMENTS
>
> - Reduce the use of fossil fuels e.g. petrol, diesel
> - Cyclists and pedestrians enjoy the city without cars
> - In 2014, carbon emissions cut by 64.8% on the day
> - Small soccer fields with real turf created in central La Paz
> - Aerobics classes took place in spaces around the city
> - Traffic wardens spent their day off persuading children to play in the streets

b ▶ Now go back to p.105

4C Student B

a Read your card. Think about what you might say using the language on p.50.

> You're a boss. A member of your team has produced a report which you don't think is very good. Make these points tactfully:
> - The report doesn't include all the relevant information it should include.
> - You offered to help the person, but they insisted they could do the report themselves.
> - They left writing the report until the last minute, rather than working on it in advance.

b Start the conversation with Student A. Try to agree a way forward.

4B 1 Student A

a Study these photos for one minute.

b You have one minute to write down as many new words from the lesson as you can remember. Check your words with Student B. You can go back to pp.47–49 and make sure you have remembered correctly.

c ▶ Now go to p.130

Student B

a Test your partner. Ask Student A to describe the crime you can see in the pictures above. You can question your partner on any details they have forgotten. Is Student A a good eyewitness?

b ▶ Now go back to p.49

9A

Answer to 5c: The invented idea for 'smart' cities is the machine which can check your health.

▶ Now go back to p.106

5B Student A

a Read the text and prepare to tell your partner about the main points in each section.

ESS VERIFIED

'A passion for technology and a keen eye for detail is required.'

Ethical hacker

Typical salary: £60,000 to £90,000 at the team leader level, while a newly-qualified hacker can expect a minimum salary of £35,000 to £50,000.

The job: A company will pay an ethical hacker to hack into its computer system to see how well it might stand up to a real attack.

Qualifications: For government work, ethical hackers must hold a relevant qualification. In the financial services sector, these qualifications are a mandatory requirement for some types of specialist work. However, you don't necessarily need a degree in computer science, says Ian Glover, president of Crest. 'The industry accepts individuals with a very wide range of academic backgrounds and skills. Often, people have not come the traditional route through education because the "system" did not necessarily match their way of working and learning.'

To succeed as an ethical hacker, you need … a passion for technology and detail. You should also have a very good analytical mind, enjoy solving difficult problems and be able to articulate your observations to senior management.

Worst thing about the job: 'When we're called in to test the security of a new customer's network, only to discover that they have already been the victim of a data breach,' says Matthew Gough from cyber security consultancy Nettitude, 'we have to explain that sensitive data belonging to the company's customers has been compromised by hackers. It's not pleasant.' To stay on top of the latest threats, you have to constantly update your knowledge in your spare time. Specialist consultancies will also expect you to be flexible and willing to travel.

b ▶ Now go back to p.61

3C

a Read conversations 1–4. Complete the sentences with your own ideas. Think about how you will describe your experiences.

①
I wouldn't travel by _____ to _____ if I were you.

Why not?

In a nutshell … (*summarise what's wrong with it*)

②
I had a terrible time when I went to _____.

What happened?

Well, to cut a long story short … (*summarise what happened*)

③
I shouldn't have said _____ about _____.

Why not?

Well, what I meant by that was … (*paraphrase what you intended to say*)

④
I think that _____ is absolutely perfect!

Really?

That is to say … (*rephrase your opinion, giving your evidence*)

b Student A use the pink speech bubbles. Start conversation 1 with Student B. Student B use the green bubbles. Have conversations 1 to 4. Then swap roles.

4B 1 Student B

a Study these photos for one minute.

b You have one minute to write down as many new words from the lesson as you can remember. Check your words with Student A. You can go back to pp.47–49 and make sure you have remembered correctly.

c ▶ Now go to p.128

Student A

a Test your partner. Ask Student B to describe the crime you can see in the pictures above. You can question your partner on any details they have forgotten. Is Student B a good eyewitness?

b ▶ Now go back to p.49

5B Student B

a Read the text and prepare to tell your partner about the main points in each section.

'We aren't the bad guys but we attempt to mimic them.'

Social engineer

Typical salary: Between £50,000 and £80,000 on average. Graduates start on £25,000 but salaries increase rapidly with qualifications and experience.

The job: A social engineer is paid by a company to try to trick its employees into divulging confidential information that allows the engineer to access sensitive company data on the company's computer network. 'We aren't the bad guys, but we attempt to mimic them in order to help our clients understand how and why such attacks work, and how to prevent them from being successful,' says Tom Roberts, a social engineer at Pen Test Partners. 'You have to understand the psychology and technical elements involved in phishing, telephone manipulation, letter writing and the design and production of security tokens and devices used in the day-to-day access of modern buildings and workplaces.'

Qualifications: Typically, social engineers have a degree in IT although an understanding of psychology is useful, as is a background in marketing, teaching and customer service.

To succeed as an ethical hacker, you need ... the confidence to lie convincingly and the ability to fit in almost anywhere without looking too out of place. Good social engineers can also speed-read facial expressions and body language, and understand the nuances of written and spoken English. But most importantly, says Roberts, you need a strong sense of personal ethics and an understanding of the law.

Worst thing about the job: 'Once you start to read people with ease, it can make life outside work tricky, and it can make you cynical,' says Roberts. 'And other people will misunderstand your job: social engineers are not spies, nor do they work in that manner, but most people will label us that way.'

b ▶ Now go back to p.61

7C Student B

a **Conversation 1** Read your first card. Think about what you might say using the language on p.87. Then listen to Student A and reply.

- You had arranged to meet Student A at the cinema to see a film you'd been wanting to see.
- The appointment slipped your mind completely.
- You went out with another friend to a restaurant instead. Your mobile phone had run out of battery.
- On your way out of the restaurant you saw Student A across the road. You suddenly remembered your appointment and decided to pretend you hadn't seen them
- When you got home and recharged your battery, you received an angry text from Student A.
- You realise that you were in the wrong and feel very ashamed. You hope you can still be friends.

b **Conversation 2** Now look at your second card. Think about what you want to say. Then start the conversation with Student A.

- A colleague at work, Student A, had confided in you about a promotion they'd put in for.
- Another colleague also told you that they had put in for the promotion and that she was absolutely certain she'd get it as there was no one else in the office with her skills and capabilities.
- In the heat of the moment, you told her that Student A had also gone in for the promotion and that to your mind, Student A was the stronger candidate.
- Afterwards, you realised that you shouldn't have betrayed Student A's confidence, and you feel terrible.

9B Student A

a Start a conversation with Student B. Listen to Student B and reply using the ideas below in order. Use ellipsis and substitution to make the conversation natural.

1 I don't like our neighbourhood any more.
3 I'm glad you agree. They're knocking down all the lovely old buildings and they're putting up ugly new buildings.
5 It's terrible, isn't it? And they said they were going to restore the old town hall, but they haven't restored the old town hall yet.
7 It's all a big mess. I really want to do something, but it's hard to know what to do.
9 Yes, starting an online petition to save the town hall is a good idea. And we could hold a protest.
11 You're right. It probably would be taking things a bit far. We'll start with the petition.

b ▶ Now go back to p.108

10B

Read the explanations of superstitions related to the theatre. Are any of them similar to the explanations you came up with? Which explanations do you prefer, the ones you came up with or the 'true' ones? Why?

BREAK A LEG

After a good performance during Elizabethan England, money was thrown to actors on the stage and they would kneel down to collect it, thus 'breaking' the line of the leg. Similarly, for the curtain call, when actors bow or curtsy, they place one foot behind the other and bend at the knee, thus 'breaking' the line of the leg.

WHISTLING

The reason for this superstition was that before the invention of walkie-talkies, the cues for the theatre technicians were coded whistles given by the stage manager. If one was whistling backstage, it could call a cue before it was due, which could have disastrous outcomes resulting in someone losing their job – whether it be the whistler, the stage manager or the technician.

GHOST LIGHTS

The backstage area of a theatre tends to be cluttered with props, set pieces and costumes, so someone who enters a completely darkened space is prone to being injured while hunting for a light switch. A light left on prevents people from having to cross the stage in the dark, injuring themselves and leading to new ghosts for the theatre.

MIRRORS

The myth is that many believe that mirrors are a reflection of the soul and breaking one can mean seven years bad luck, not only for the breaker but for the theatre itself. However, having a mirror on stage can cause technical issues, such as reflecting light into the audience or into places never intended to be lit. It can also be a source of distraction for vain actors.

PEACOCK FEATHERS

There are many stories of stage sets collapsing, curtains catching alight and other disastrous events during performances with peacock feathers. The feather is said to represent an 'evil eye', that puts a curse on the show.

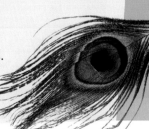

6A

a Look at the photos from a photography competition. Why do you think each photo won a prize? Use the adverbs and adjectives from the box and your own ideas to talk about the photos with a partner.

Adverbs

truly   utterly   incredibly   completely   absolutely
extremely   rather   a little   pretty   quite   gently
wonderfully   very

Adjectives

well-composed   powerful   meaningful   gritty
raw   playful   humorous   evocative   exotic   iconic
nonsensical   sensational   bleak   flawless
elaborate   cluttered

b Which photo do you think should be the overall winner of the competition? Why? Agree on one image with your partner.

c ▶ Now go back to p.70

> This is an utterly sensational image. It really draws you in.

> Yes, it's quite evocative. It makes me think of …

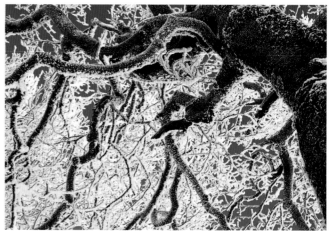

2A

a Read and discuss each suggestion about managing noise. Can you think of any practical problems with each suggestion? Are any of these things … ?

- already part of your routine
- something you'd like to try

DON'T APOLOGISE!

If you are sensitive to noise, don't worry about it too much. It's not a weakness in your character, it's just who you are. You don't need to apologise for this.

SPEAK UP!

If you're in an environment where another person is making unnecessary noise, don't be afraid to ask them politely to be a bit quieter.

REST AND RELAX.

Make sure you get plenty of sleep and rest. If you are sensitive to noise, feeling tired will only make the problem worse. If you start the day feeling rested and relaxed, you'll be able to cope better.

FIND THE RIGHT PLACE.

Work out which sounds and which noisy environments are particularly annoying or stressful for you. Try to avoid these places as much as possible.

BE PREPARED.

Plan activities so you can avoid noise. For example, it might be a good idea to avoid going to the cinema on a Saturday evening when it's busy and noisy – choose another night of the week to go.

FIND YOUR OWN SOLUTIONS.

Think of ways to help you manage noisy environments. For example, if you find the sounds of public transport make you feel apprehensive, try using noise-cancelling headphones to reduce the noise.

TAKE A BREAK.

Find a place near your workplace or home that you know is always quiet. During the day, take a break and go there to enjoy some relaxing quiet. This will help you manage the rest of the day.

b ▶ Now go back to p.20

9A Student B

a Read the fact-file and prepare to tell other students about the event.

BANKJESCOLLECTIEF (BENCHES COLLECTIVE), MONTHLY EVENT IN WARMER MONTHS, AMSTERDAM

- Residents and businesses bring a bench to the street from which they offer food or other activities
- Visitors to the bench pay what they think the offering is worth

AIMS AND ACHIEVEMENTS

- To transform Amsterdam into the biggest outdoor café in the world
- People get the opportunity meet their neighbours and enter into spontaneous interactions

- People become comfortable in the city as a place they own and influence, like their living room
- Beyond food and drink, benches have included: story-telling, salsa classes, knitting workshops, and clothes swap sessions

b ▶ Now go back to p.105

9A Student C

a Read the fact-file and prepare to tell other students about the event.

SUBURBAN BUS STOP MAKEOVER, PITTSBURGH, USA

* Revamp a bus stop on a busy motorway

AIMS AND ACHIEVEMENTS

* Long-term, provide a bus stop where people would actually want to sit
* Create shelter from unpleasant weather
* Increase the distance from the road so pedestrians feel safe
* Reduce the risk of crime by lighting the surrounding area
* For the opening, colourful soft furnishings were used to decorate the bus stop

b ▶ Now go back to p.105

4B 2

a Read the information in the fact-file. How similar is it to the list you made?

FACT FILE   **Refreshing your memory ...**

1. **FOOD** fresh vegetables and healthy oil (e.g. fish oil) – cut down on sugar and grain carbohydrates; drinking green tea can also help

2. **EXERCISE** a good balance of cardio and strength training

3. **SLEEP** a good night's sleep refreshes the brain

4. **MULTI-TASKING** avoid it – be fully focused on one thing at a time

5. **BRAIN GAMES** fun activities to stimulate your brain, but don't play them for too long at a time

6. **NEW SKILLS** learn a new skill that is stimulating and interesting for you

7. **MNEMONIC DEVICES** techniques to help you remember information, e.g. a doctor's appointment: imagine a stethoscope and a number for the day of the week, or remember an acronym like *DAT = Doctor's Appointment Thursday*

8. **VISUALISING** make a connection between new information you want to learn and the visual memory of a place you know well, e.g. a room or an object

b ▶ Now go back to p.49

5C Student A

a **Conversation 1** Read your first card. Think about what you want to say using the language on p.63. Then start the conversation with Student B.

> **1** You're the manager of a _____ company (*decide what kind of company*) and you're interviewing Student B. Unfortunately, you've not had time to read Student B's application and you've forgotten to bring it with you. You don't want Student B to know this. Refer to your 'memory' of the application and try to find out about:
> - The job Student B's applied for (Administrative Assistant / Marketing Executive / Assistant Manager) (*guess which job*)
> - Student B's education/training
> - Student B's experience
> - Student B's hobbies

b **Conversation 2** Now look at your second card. Listen to Student B and reply.

> **2** You've bumped into Student B by chance. You recognised Student B instantly: you used to use the same gym / catch the same train into town every morning / live next door to one another (*decide which*). Prepare to talk about:
> - What job you did then and still do (defence lawyer / psychiatrist / butler) (*decide which job*)
> - How many years it's been since you last saw each other
> - What happened the last time you saw each other

9B Student B

a Student A will start a conversation with you. Listen and reply using the ideas below. Use ellipsis and substitution to make the conversation natural.

> 2 I don't like our neighbourhood any more. A lot of people think it's OK, but I don't think it's OK.
> 4 That's right. They've just gone ahead and they have built that horrible new supermarket and they have put up the ugly new sports centre.
> 6 They'll probably knock it down, but they shouldn't knock it down.
> 8 We could start an online petition to save the town hall
> 10 Do you think we ought to hold a protest? It might be taking things a bit far.

b ▶ Now go back to p.108

2B

a Read Andy's blog post. What's Andy's job and who do you think he's writing to? Were you right about his reasons for moving to the place in the photo?

ANDY'S BLOG

HOME | POSTS | LINKS | CONTACT

Hi everyone!

Sorry I've been silent for a while but a lot's been happening. Here I am in Canada and I'm planning to travel even further north and live alone for a year in the wild. It can't be worse than insurance claims!

I'm renting a cabin by a lake and I'll be staying there through the winter. I'm going to stock up on food to keep me going, but I'm also planning to catch fish – I've brought my fishing gear along.

Well, think of me when you're on the 7.30 train to work! I hope to be back in the spring and will post again then.

Wish me luck!

b 💬 Work in pairs. Imagine you are about to do one of these things:
- go and stay in a remote place
- travel somewhere adventurous
- completely change your lifestyle
- go and live in a new country.

Write a blog post like Andy's about your plans. Then swap posts with another pair.

c Read the post you received. Think of some questions to ask when you next meet, and add comments on the post.

d You meet a year later. Talk about your experience and answer questions. Read the comments on your post and respond to them.

9A Student D

a Read the fact-file and prepare to tell other students about the event.

CONGRESS SQUARE PARK, PORTLAND, USA

- Community organisation formed to save a public space

AIMS AND ACHIEVEMENTS

- Restore public faith in the safety of the area
- Re-popularise the square
- Local residents cleaned up the area
- People brought furniture and street food stalls, free WiFi
- More and more people used the square
- Protected land from being sold to developers

b ▶ Now go back to p.105

7D

a Read about two different team-building programmes. Which one will be more appropriate for your team? Why?

Adventure team building

We will take your team hiking in the great outdoors. Our activities develop:

- **real-life survival skills**
- **cooperation and communication skills**
- **self-awareness and mutual respect.**

Ideal for building a really strong team.

 Personal Adventures Ltd.

Action team building

We have a fantastic range of action games that develop better team dynamics. The games are chosen to foster problem-solving abilities and promote active listening and effective, positive communication between team members.

These physical activities are great fun and really safe – no special abilities are necessary!

Let your team remember the joy of being a child while learning how to work together.

Action Stations Development Ltd.

b ▶ Now go back to p.89

7C Student A

a **Conversation 1** Read your first card. Think about what you want to say using the language on p.87. Then start the conversation with Student B.

 1
- You had arranged to meet Student B at the cinema to see a film you'd been wanting to see.
- As Student B has a reputation for being late, you had bought the tickets in advance for yourself and Student B.
- You waited for a long time, but Student B didn't turn up despite the fact that you texted and called.
- You went to see what was left of the film on your own and on your way home you saw Student B leaving a restaurant.
- You shouted and waved but Student B seemed to be ignoring you. You now feel very hurt and angry and don't think your friendship has much future.

b **Conversation 2** Now look at your second card. Listen to Student B and reply.

 2
- You put in for a promotion at work. Anxious about it, you told one of your colleagues, Student B, in confidence.
- You got the promotion!
- While congratulating you, another colleague let slip that they'd known you'd put in for the promotion for some time.
- You realise that Student B must have told her, but it doesn't matter now anyway.

5C Student B

a **Conversation 1** Read your first card. Then listen to Student A and reply.

>
> 1 You've applied for the role of Administrative Assistant / Marketing Executive / Assistant Manager (*decide which job*) and Student A is interviewing you. Prepare to talk about:
> - Your education/training
> - Your experience
> - Your hobbies

b **Conversation 2** Now look at your second card. Think about what you want to say using the language on p.63. Then start the conversation with Student A.

> 2 You've bumped into Student A by chance. Student A has recognised you instantly but unfortunately, although Student A looks vaguely familiar, you can't remember how you know each other. You don't want Student A to know this. Try to find out about:
> - what job Student B did then and still does (defence lawyer / psychiatrist / butler) (*guess which job*)
> - how you know each other
> - how many years it's been since you last saw each other
> - what happened the last time you saw each other

1B Student B

a Read about two more language changes. How does each heading represent the change?

❸ Do you want to dance with me?

Modal verbs are gradually giving way to other less formal expressions – stiff, formal words like *shall* and *ought* are on the way out and words which cover the same ground, such as *going to, have to, need to* and *want to* are taking hold.

This modernisation process is far from efficient; compare:

You ought to see a doctor.

You are going to want to get that looked at by a doctor.

But why use two words where ten will do?

❹ I got fired but I still got paid!

The verb *to be* has lost its grip on the passive in recent years and the use of *get* passives has grown substantially. These days you *get fired, get robbed* and *get married* and buildings *get built* and *get knocked down* again. Whether it's good or bad news for the subject, these days there's a *get* passive for any occasion.

b ▶ Now go back to p.11

2C Student B

a Read about this problem you have and think about what you want to say.

> - As a reward for meeting your targets, your thrill-seeking boss wants your whole team to go out for the day and do a dangerous sport (*decide which sport*).
> - You are absolutely terrified of doing the sport for a specific reason (*decide what*) but don't want your boss or colleagues to know.
> - There is a promotion coming up, and you don't want your boss to judge you on your sports performance.

b Present your problem to your partner and ask for advice.

c Now listen to your partner's problem carefully and discuss some solutions to it. Make three suggestions using the language for giving advice on p.27.

5B

Average annual salaries in the UK

nurse	£25,000
primary school teacher	£25,000
police officer	£35,000
investment banker	£340,000
premier league footballer	£1.1 million

💬 Do you think the differences in pay would be similar in your country?

4A

a Now check your scores. Are you surprised by them?

> You're naturally cautious and you act rationally rather than intuitively. You'd rather be guided by your mind than by your gut feelings.

8
9
10
11
12
13
14
15
16

> Your intuitive abilities are strongly developed and you trust your inner feelings. You let these guide you more than logic.

b ▶ Now go back to p.44

Grammar Focus

1A Adverbs and adverbial phrases

There are three main positions for adverbials in relation to a main clause: front, middle and end:
Obviously *I* **usually** *study* **after work**.
Adverbials include single-word **adverbs**, e.g. *obviously*, and **adverbial phrases**, e.g. *after work*.

▶ 1.2 End position

In spoken English, adverbials of manner, place and time usually go at the end of the clause, after the verb and the object:
I write **very slowly**. NOT *I very slowly write.*
I live **nearby** *so we'll be* **there soon**.
Adverbial phrases of frequency usually go in the end position. Some single-word frequency adverbs take this position too: *sometimes, occasionally, regularly, not very often …*
We have a test **every couple of weeks**.
I go there **regularly**.
Don't place adverbs between the verb and the direct object:
She did **the work too quickly**. NOT *She did too quickly the work.*
I'm sure I'll meet **her someday**. NOT *I'm sure I'll meet someday her.*
The usual order for adverbs at the end of a sentence is manner, place, time:
We didn't sleep **well on those airbeds last night**.
However, when an adverb of place is necessary to complete the meaning of the verb this order can change:
I came **here on foot**. NOT *I came on foot here.*
Where there are two verbs, adverbs of manner go before the first verb or after the second verb, depending which verb the adverb modifies:
I **quickly** *decided to take the job.*
She made the effort to drive **carefully**.

> 🖐 **Tip** For emphasis in written texts such as narratives, adverbs of manner can go in the front or middle position:
> ***Hesitantly***, *she* **carefully** *unwrapped the parcel.*

▶ 1.3 Middle position

Adverbial phrases are very rare in the middle position:
At last *I got home. I got home* **at last**. NOT *I at last got home.*
In the middle position the adverb goes before the main verb,

usually after the first auxiliary or modal verb, or after *be*. Adverbs of probability, certainty, frequency and focus often take the middle position:
Good exam results **don't inevitably mean** *success in later life.*
Grammar **is usually** *my weakest point.*
Many adverbs of frequency (*never, always, ever*) and certain time adverbs (*just, still*) can only go in the middle position:
She **still** *practises her Japanese.* NOT *Still she practises … / … practises her Japanese still.*
Adverbs of certainty usually go after auxiliaries, but they go before contracted negative auxiliaries:
I'll **probably** *see you soon.* NOT *I probably will …*
She **probably/definitely can't** *hear you.* NOT *She can't probably …*
Be careful with the word order of contracted negative auxiliaries:
I **don't really** *care.* (= not much) *I* **definitely won't** *come.* (= no chance)
I **really don't** *care.* (= not at all) *I* **won't definitely** *come.* (= not sure)

▶ 1.4 Front position

Comment and linking adverbs usually go at the front of the clause, followed by a comma:
Obviously, *he knows his grammar.* ***However***, *he isn't as fluent as he'd like to be.*
Adverbials of time, place and frequency can also go at the front, when we want to set the scene or change the focus:
In London *there are plenty of jobs.*
Every so often *I forget the word for 'window' in French.*

▶ 1.5 Modifying adverbs and adjectives

Adverbials of degree go directly before the word(s) they modify:
Laura speaks German **reasonably** *well but her French is* **a bit** *basic.*
Adverbs can be modified by phrases with prepositions:
I drove here **slowly by my standards**.
Luckily for you, *I'm in a good mood.*

> 🖐 **Tip** Some adverbs have different meanings in different positions: *amazingly, strangely; naturally, clearly, fairly, reasonably …*
> ***Strangely***, *Kate speaks Chinese.* (= surprisingly)
> *Kate speaks Chinese* **strangely**. (= badly)

---

a Tick the correct sentences. Correct the mistakes you found in the remaining sentences.

1 ✓ I am definitely thinking of going abroad, by the way.
2 ☐ The secretary put abruptly the phone down. The *secretary put the phone down abruptly.*
3 ☐ Presumably, your wife knows you've sold the car?
4 ☐ At the end of the walk, I was exhausted utterly.
5 ☐ The ambulance arrived on the scene within minutes.
6 ☐ I beforehand had had a nasty feeling.
7 ☐ That was the certainly best game so far.
8 ☐ You will find the bathroom downstairs on the left.
9 ☐ You have ignored repeatedly all my warnings.
10 ☐ She definitely won't resign. She's undecided.
11 ☐ He wasn't behaving reasonably at all.
12 ☐ We decided to go by taxi home.

b Add the words and phrases in brackets to each sentence.

1 So where did language^{first} come from? (first)
2 Well, funnily enough, we can't answer this question. (still)
3 Some of the theories are ridiculous. (simply)
4 It has been said that we copied the animal sounds. (even)
5 Language developed for a variety of reasons. (no doubt)
6 Our brains increased in size and we became more intelligent. (dramatically, a great deal)
7 Also, unfortunately, we started working in groups to get more food. (for other animals)
8 Group behaviour would have made the need for language essential. (undoubtedly, absolutely)
9 We won't know the exact causes with any certainty. (probably, ever)
10 What we can say is that the origins of language will fascinate us. (always)

c ▶ Now go back to p.9

1B The perfect aspect

▶ 1.13 Completed actions

Perfect tenses can describe completed actions before a certain time in the past, present or future.

- We can use perfect tenses to give news and describe recent activities before a certain time:
  Linguists **have invented** a new language with only 200 words.
  At long last the war **had ended**; we couldn't believe it.
  It **had been raining** all night.
  We**'ve just been** running.
- Perfect simple verbs focus on <u>the effects</u> of completing an activity:
  We**'ve done** all our work <u>so we can go out</u>.
  When she**'d finished** putting the decorations up, <u>the room looked awesome</u>.
  I can't meet you at 7.00. I **won't have got through** immigration.
- Use the perfect simple to say how much / how many / how often by a certain time:
  The professor **has written** over fifty books about the English language.
  We**'ve already seen** the film twice.
  You **need to have read** all the books on the list by June.
  I**'d called him** three times but failed to get through.
- Perfect continuous verbs focus on the effects of doing an activity:
  Something **had been worrying her** at work so she spoke to her boss.
  Your eyes are red. **Have you been crying**?
  He **will have been driving** all night, so he'll need to go to bed.
- Compare the perfect simple and perfect continuous:
  I**'ve made dinner**! You don't need to do anything. (focus on completion)
  I**'ve been making** dinner! I'm all hot and sweaty. (focus on doing the activity)

▶ 1.14 Unfinished activities and states

Perfect verb forms can also describe continuing activities or states at a certain time:

I **haven't been sleeping** well recently. I might go to see the doctor.
He **will have been working on** the project for long enough to take over by then.
I**'ve always enjoyed** spending time with my family.
They**'ve been sad** since their old teacher left.

- We often want to say the duration of the activity:
  Louise **has been doing** Spanish **since January** and she loves it.
  I**'ve never** really **understood** the grammar so I still make a lot of mistakes.
  She **will have been driving for a couple of years** by then.
- For certain activities we often use both the present perfect simple and present perfect continuous with little difference in meaning:
  How long have **you worked / been working** in the languages department?
  This June I **will have lived / been living** here for five years.

> **Tip** We can use the past perfect with stress on *had* to express dissatisfaction:
> We **had hoped** Sheila would be out of hospital by now. = Sheila is still in hospital and we are disappointed.

---

a Match the sentence halves.

1. [d] It's been a long time since
2. [ ] I really couldn't tell you how long
3. [ ] I missed the match because
4. [ ] I was so good at dancing everyone thought
5. [ ] If every question takes this long to answer
6. [ ] This coming January
7. [ ] I'm exhausted because
8. [ ] This is the first time

a I've been living in Bangkok.
b I won't have finished before midnight.
c I've been running around all day.
d I ate anything as nice as this.
e I'd been doing it all my life.
f I've seen you so angry.
g I hadn't bought a ticket in time.
h I will have been living here for three years.

b Choose the best verb form in each sentence.

1. I *lived / have lived* in the same place my whole life.
2. Shakespeare *died / has died* a long time ago but he is still very popular.
3. Have you ever *tried / been trying* to drive in the snow?
4. This is the third time I have *told / been telling* you to be quiet!
5. Don't sit there! I've *painted / been painting* and the paint is wet.
6. As soon as I got home, I *went / had gone* straight to bed.
7. Eve had *read / been reading* most of the book before she saw the film.
8. Luke *has / had* been thinking about leaving university but in the end he decided to stay.
9. I *have / had* thought you could take us to the station.
10. They might have *done / been doing* the decorating by the time we get home.

By the time they'd **added** YOLO to the dictionary, it'd **already gone** out of fashion.

c Complete the text with the correct perfect forms of the verbs in brackets.

People [1] *have been complaining* (complain) about English spelling for centuries because certain sounds can be written in several different ways. For example, you [2] _____ (notice) that /ɪ/ is the sound in *sit*, *carpet* and *women*. Linguists [3] _____ (suggest) several reasons for our difficult spelling. First, English [4] _____ (accept) a lot of foreign words into its vocabulary, so the *ch* in *chorus* /k/, a Greek word, and *chauffeur* /ʃ/, a French word, sounds different. Second, early printers often weren't certain of the spelling of a word – no official spelling [5] _____ (establish) – so they generally spelled a word pretty much as they liked. The spelling of English [6] _____ (become) a bit of a joke today but who knows, by the time our grandchildren go to school maybe someone [7] _____ (invent) a spelling system which is logical and easy to remember.

d ▶ Now go back to p.12

2A Comparison

▶1.25 **Modifying comparisons with _than_**

A big difference: _a good/great deal, a lot, considerably, decidedly, far, infinitely, miles_ (informal), _much, significantly, three/four/many times_ (etc.), _way_ (informal) **A small difference:** _a (little) bit, barely any, fractionally, marginally, slightly_ **No difference:** _no, not any_	The total silence was **a lot worse than** any sound could ever be. There's **considerably more noise** when you get inside the venue. * I listen to live music **far more frequently than** I used to. Tickets are **slightly more expensive** this year. I'm **no happier than** I was in my last job.
Modifying comparisons with _as … as …_	
A big difference: _not nearly, nothing like, nowhere near, twice / three times_ (etc.) **A small difference:** _almost, nearly, not quite_ **No difference:** _equally, just_	The smell was **not nearly as bad as** we thought it would be. Stella knows **almost as much about cars as** me. There are **just as many people** who want to study French. *

*We often omit the _than_ or second _as_ part of a comparative form if it is obvious:
There's considerably more noise (**than there is here**) when you get inside the venue.
There are just as many people who want to study French (**as people who want to study Spanish**).

▶1.26 **Comparative patterns**
We use double comparatives with adjectives and adverbs to say that somebody or something is changing:
These exams are getting **harder and harder**.
Time seemed to go **more and more slowly**. NOT Time seemed to go ~~more slowly and more slowly~~.
We use _the … the …_ with comparatives or _more/less_ to say that things change together because they depend on each other:
The harder you train, **the longer** you can run.
The more I think about it, **the more** I realise it was a mistake.
The more hours I work, **the less** time I have for my family.

▶1.27 _so / such_
We use _so_ + adjective/adverb (+ _that_) and _such_ + _a_ + noun (+ _that_) to describe a very high level:
It's **so loud** here **that** I can't hear myself think!
If this is **such a bad job**, why don't you find a better one?

▶1.28 _not enough / sufficiently / too_
We use _too_ / (_not_) _enough_ to compare things with a standard. _Sufficiently_ has the same meaning as _enough_ but is more formal:
Jones is good **enough to** win the race.
We have**n't** got **enough** petrol **for** the journey.
The children were **not sufficiently** well-behaved to receive any sweets.
The weather is **too** cold **to** go outside.
This jumper is **too** big **for** me.

▶1.29 **Superlative patterns**
We usually use superlatives to highlight something exceptional. We often limit the range of superlatives with relative clauses or adverbs:
She's **the most talkative** person I **know**. / **ever!** / **in the world.** / **of all.**
I did **the best I possibly could**.
We can modify the strength of a superlative with adverbs like _by far, easily, (not) nearly, almost, not quite_.
That was **by far the best** lesson this year.
He's **easily the happiest** I've ever seen him these days.
It was**n't quite the most difficult** test I've ever had but it was close!

---

a Write a sentence for each picture using the words.

1 considerably / small
The pizza was considerably smaller than the box.

4 no / heavy

2 grew / not nearly / expected

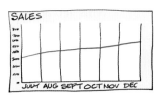

5 marginally / good / since June

3 strong / not enough / control

6 hard / the rain fell / difficult / the game became

b Complete the text with the words and phrases in the box. Use each expression once.

> not   miles   and   more   so
> nowhere   the   far   than   get

Last year I went to Glastonbury Festival of Performing Arts. It was a real eye-opener. The festival takes place in a remote valley and after you come off the motorway the roads get smaller ¹_____ smaller. The closer you get to the site ²_____ more cars full of festival-goers you see. Everyone is ³_____ excited just to be there. Then when you finally get into a car park you have to get through the gates and find a place to camp. This is considerably harder ⁴_____ it sounds, because you're basically going hill-climbing whilst carrying a tent and bedding and clothes and all your food and drink for the next five days. The site is ⁵_____ bigger than any other festival I've ever been to. As you sit by your tent on the first night, these huge cheers roll towards you across the valley and ⁶_____ louder and louder until they're all around you and it's your turn to cheer. Tickets are slightly ⁷_____ expensive than other festivals but, when you consider that there are ⁸_____ nearly as many acts and installations and ⁹_____ near as many people at other festivals, Glastonbury is by ¹⁰_____ the greatest party on the planet.

c Now go back to p.21

2B Intentions and arrangements

▶1.40 *going to* vs. present continuous

We use both *going to* and the present continuous for future actions and events that are already decided or arranged. We cannot use the present continuous for things it is impossible to arrange and control:
I'm having / 'm going to have lunch with Terry this afternoon.
What am I going to do if she says no? NOT … *am I doing* …
We cannot use the present continuous for permanent states or indefinite and long-term plans:
Sally is going to be a doctor. NOT … *is being* …
We're going to make a lot of money one day. NOT … *We're making* …
We use the continuous phrases *be planning + to +* infinitive, *be aiming + to +* infinitive, *be thinking of +* verb *+ -ing* to talk about plans:
Kevin is planning to walk across America.
He's aiming to do it in less than 100 days.

▶1.41 Future simple and continuous

We use the future simple, *will +* infinitive, for decisions we make at the time of speaking:
OK, I'll come to the meeting but I won't say anything.
We use the future continuous, *will + be +* verb *+ -ing*, to talk about plans that happen without being specially arranged. We can also use *could / may / might / going to + be +* verb *+ -ing*:
I'll be going to the meeting, so I can pass on your apologies.
I might be seeing Jill tonight.
We're not going to be passing your way.
We also use the future continuous to say that something will be in progress in the future:
While you're enjoying yourself, I'll be working.

Compare *going to* and the present continuous with the future continuous:
Are you going to see / Are you seeing your gran this weekend? (have you planned this?)
Will you be seeing your gran this weekend? (as you normally do)

▶1.42 Present simple

We use the present simple for scheduled activities:
The first race begins at 12.00.
What time do you get back tomorrow?
We can use *will* with the same meaning in official situations:
President Johnson will meet with business leaders next week.

▶1.43 Expressions with *be*

We use *be + to +* infinitive in formal language for arrangements:
The Queen is to open a new business centre.
We use *be about + to +* infinitive to say something will happen very soon:
Hurry up! The bus is about to leave!
We use *not be about + to +* infinitive to emphasise negative intentions:
I've never smoked and I'm not about to start now!
We use *be due + to +* infinitive to say something is owed/expected very soon, often at a certain time:
I'm due to meet her secretary this afternoon.
We're due to get a pay rise.

---

a Choose the best option.

Interviewer So Rudy, you ¹*'re going to go / are to go* on your first wing walk.

Rudy That's right, yep. We're ²*going / about* to take off approximately half an hour from now.

I And what ³*are you / will you be* doing exactly? You're ⁴*due / going* to stand on the wing, right?

R That's right, well my instructor said I ⁵*'ll be standing / stand* on top of the plane, between the wings. I'll be strapped into a kind of frame. So I don't have to do anything, I will just stand there, admiring the view … I'm not ⁶*about / planning* to panic. I'm just going to enjoy it.

I So it'll be pretty windy.

R Yes, we're ⁷*due / going* to be flying at about 120 km an hour, so it will be windy, sure. But I ⁸*'ll be wearing / wear* a padded suit, so I shouldn't get too cold.

I OK, well, good luck!

"I'm not **going to look** down"

b Cross out the one future form which is NOT possible in 1–10.

1 I *will let / am going to let / am letting* you know soon.
2 'The pipe needs fixing now.' '*I'll be doing / 'll do / 'm going to do* it.'
3 I *won't see / don't see / won't be seeing* Sharon any time soon.
4 When Annie leaves school, she *will look / is going to look / is looking* for a job.
5 Serena *is going to wear / is wearing / wears* her new dress for the party.
6 'Did you take the necklace?' '*I'm not aiming to answer / won't be answering / am not about to answer* that.'
7 He *will repay / is going to repay / repays* the full amount.
8 The meeting *aims / is about to / is due to* begin so sit down everyone.
9 I'm not *about / going / due* to learn French at my age. I'm far too old!
10 We *are planning to become / are becoming / are aiming to become* millionaires one day.

c Complete each sentence with one word or contraction.

1 I'm about _____to_____ leave, so hurry up.
2 I _____ bring a torch in case it gets dark.
3 Adelia is _____ of writing a book about her experiences.
4 A taxi is _____ to pick us up from the airport when we arrive.
5 Where will you _____ staying in New York?
6 Mark is _____ to get a warning for his lateness.
7 Don't worry. I'm _____ about to spend all our money.
8 You can trust me. I _____ say anything.
9 Sorry, I can't come as I _____ be working.
10 The President _____ to open the new airport.

d ▶ Now go back to p.25

3A Inversion

Never again would Lofty travel without researching his destination first.

▶ **1.52 Inversion after negative or restrictive adverbials**

When we want to emphasise an event because it is new, rare, unexpected, sudden, impossible, etc. we can use negative or restrictive adverbials followed by inverted word order:

I had never been there before. > **Never before had I been** there.
They didn't try to help me. > **Not once did they try** to help me.
When he came home we realised we had missed him. > **Only when he came home did we realise** we had missed him.

Inversion structures are usually quite formal. We use them more in written texts such as narratives and in formal speech such as presentations.

Negative or restrictive adverbials

None	Too much / (not) enough	One place/time/person etc.	Unusual
Not a penny would they give to charity. **Not one bite** did he eat. **Not a single person** did they meet that day.	**Too often** do we see people struggling to make ends meet. **Too long** have we waited for a change.	**Only in the capital** did we feel truly welcome. **Only in the summer** was it possible to open the windows.	**Rarely do you find** someone like that. **Seldom do we stop** to think about people in poorer countries.
Never / Not any more	***Immediately / Only just**	**Only after/at a certain time**	**Impossible/Prohibited**
At no time did we think the project would fail. **Never** (**before**) have I felt so angry. **No longer** can we ignore the problem. **Not in a thousand years** will I go back there again. (informal) **Not once** did they offer any help. **Never** (**again**) will we attempt to intervene.	**No sooner** had one game finished **than** another was begun. **Barely** had we got over the flu **when** we were struck down with a stomach bug. **Hardly** had the policy been announced **than** the government came up with a new and better idea. **Scarcely** had we had time to meet the villagers **than** we were hustled back onto the bus.	**Not until his return** did we appreciate how much we had missed him. **Only when the music stopped** did people start to go home. **Only then** did people start to go home.	**Under no circumstances** should you buy products from companies which exploit workers. **On no account** can drinks be taken outside. **No way** can I forget what I saw there. (informal)
		Addition	**Unexpected**
		Not only is she young, she's inexperienced.	**Little** did she know that trouble was coming.

> 💡 **Tip**
>
> Do not overuse emphatic inversion as it will make you sound unnatural.

*We use the conjunctions *than* or *when* after *barely, hardly, scarcely* and *no sooner*:
Barely had we stepped off the plane than …   **Scarcely had we fallen asleep** when …

---

a Choose the best answer, 1 or 2, to follow a and b in each pair.

1 a ☐2 Under no circumstances should you drink cola.
  b ☐1 Not once did they drink cola.
    1 It was difficult to find.
    2 It is bad for your teeth.

2 a ☐ At no time can you walk on the ice
  b ☐ Barely had he stepped onto the ice
    1 than it gave way under his feet.
    2 as it is too thin.

3 a ☐ On no account should you feed the animals.
  b ☐ No way am I feeding the animals.
    1 They can't digest the food people give them.
    2 They might bite.

4 a ☐ No way did they score –
  b ☐ Only then did they score,
    1 that's unbelievable.
    2 which was way too late.

5 a ☐ Too late did I learn
  b ☐ No sooner did I learn
    1 that than I apologised profusely.
    2 that they had only the best intentions.

b Rewrite the sentences with inversion and an adverb or adverbial phrase.

1 She doesn't often refuse. *Not often does she refuse.*
2 We only felt relaxed in the evenings.
3 I had barely got home when the phone rang.
4 Rita seldom takes responsibility for her actions.
5 We didn't find a single shop.
6 I'm not going to accept on any account.

c Complete the sentences in the first person using the words and phrases in the box. Use the pronoun *I* each time.

> little / know   not a single person / see   no sooner / arrive
> not in a million years / think   not until 21:00 / find   rarely / be

1 _Little did I know_ what was waiting for me when I arrived.
2 _____ than there was a terrible rain storm and I was completely wet through.
3 I'd thought I might have a few adventures but _____ it would start as badly as this.
4 _____ my way back to the bus stop.
5 The place was empty – _____.
6 _____ so happy to get home!

d ▶ Now go back to p.33

142

3B Future in the past; Narrative tenses

 1.60 Future in the past

We use past tenses of future forms to say what plans, intentions or predictions we had at a point in the past.

be to / be about to / be set to	Grace **was about to get** on the plane when she got an urgent text message.
be going to	Last summer I **was going to visit** my sister but I went to Italy instead.
be + verb + -ing	I **was leaving** for Mexico that morning and I was worried about the long flight.
modal + be + verb + -ing	I knew I **might be staying** there for a while so I made myself comfortable.
would / might / could	One day I **would find out** the truth, although I didn't know it yet.

Tip

We use be + to + infinitive for events or situations that came true:
I had to leave France and I **was never to return**.
We use be + to + have + past participle when things did not happen as planned:
The present **was to have been** a surprise but Sandra knew all about it.

Tip

There are different meanings of would in the past:
She **would** not discuss the matter. = refused to
She**'d** generally keep her ideas to herself. = habit
One day he **would** be famous. = future in the past
But for a lack of talent he **would** have been famous. = hypothetical past

Narrative tenses

- **Setting the scene**
  We use the past perfect, past perfect continuous and past continuous to give the background to events in the past:
  We set off at dawn. Everyone **had slept well** despite the unfamiliar environment.
  The sun **had just been creeping** over the horizon when we packed up camp.
  We **were** all **looking forward to** what the day ahead might hold. Or so I thought at the time …
  We use the past perfect or past perfect continuous to say how long something continued until a time in the past:
  By the time we got to Rio we **had been travelling** for 16 hours. NOT ~~were travelling~~

- **Sequence of events**
  We use the past simple for actions in sequence in a narrative. We use the past continuous for background actions or actions that are interrupted:
  By the time we **reached** the top of the mountain the sun **was sinking** fast. I **started** to panic. I **was looking around** hopefully for a place we could set up camp when somebody **screamed**.
  We use the past perfect to refer back to an earlier time in the sequence:
  Sarah **fell** ill and **was taken** to hospital **as soon as she** (**had**) **arrived**.
  Past perfect and past perfect continuous often explain the main action or give relevant background:
  There was a large swelling where he**'d been bitten**.
  I**'d been hearing** noises off to the left of the path so I decided to investigate.
  Nobody **had warned me** of the dangers I was now facing.

The children **had been going to tell** their father but they left it too late.

a Choose the best verb forms in each sentence.

1 Graham *was* / *is* going to meet me at the airport, but I got a taxi.
2 I thought Karen *had been getting* / *would be getting* first prize but I was wrong.
3 That money *was to have paid* / *might pay* for our daughter's education. Now it's all gone.
4 I *had been making* / *had been planning to make* lunch until you suggested going out to eat.
5 I *wondered* / *was about to wonder* who could have done it.
6 Tony *was driving* / *had driven* to work when he heard the news on his car radio.
7 The baby *had been crying* / *cried* for a while before I picked it up.
8 After I *had been getting* / *got* home, I rushed to check the papers in the safe.
9 We *had been going to give* / *would be giving* up but suddenly we saw the peak of the mountain.
10 In those days, Simon *would* / *might* get up at 6.00 and go for a run.

b Complete the text with a possible form of the verb in brackets.

They said it [1] _would be_ (be) the holiday of a lifetime but it was a nightmare!
We [2]_____ (go) on holiday for ages so I was really excited about our trip but I didn't check out the facts that the nice man from the travel agency [3]_____ (tell) me. All of which [4]_____ (turn) out to be untrue! For a start, the 'luxury' hotel was a building site. The workers [5]_____ (still prepare) the bedrooms when we arrived so we had to sleep in the lobby the first night! I [6]_____ (bring) my swimming things, as I [7]_____ (hope) for a nice refreshing swim each morning, but there was no water in the pool. I'll tell you, I [8]_____ (plan) get us all on the first plane home but my wife persuaded me to stay.
Nothing [9]_____ (get) any better as the holiday went on.
I [10]_____ (lose) 5 kilos in weight by the time I got home.
I phoned the company to find out if they [11]_____ (give) me some money back and told them I [12]_____ (sue).
They [13]_____ (apologise) profusely but I'm still waiting for my refund.

c Tick the correct sentences. Correct the mistakes you found in the remaining sentences.

1 ☐ I always thought I'd get married, but it was never to be.
2 ☐ We are feeling excited until the flight was cancelled.
3 ☐ The children felt ill as they'd been eating sweets all day.
4 ☐ Tom has sent the details to me so I was well-prepared.
5 ☐ The boat was to have left at 3, but it was delayed until 5.
6 ☐ Zara always knew she'll be famous one day.

d ▶ Now go back to p.37

4A Noun phrases

Structure of noun phrases

Combining information into noun phrases allows precise and concise expression of both abstract and concrete ideas. Compare:

She's an author. She wrote a book. It's on psychology. I read it recently. It's very interesting.

*She's **the author of a very interesting psychology book that I read recently**.*

Complex noun phrases can make language more formal and academic because they develop ideas and package them efficiently. Compare:

In some countries, people often touch foreheads when they greet each other and this is acceptable there.

***Touching foreheads** is **a commonly accepted form of greeting** in some countries.*

Compound nouns

Compound nouns are the most efficient way of showing the subject or purpose of something, for example a lecture about maths = a *maths lecture*, a machine which makes bread = a *bread maker*. Compare:

*There were prints from her fingers all over the vase. – Her **fingerprints** were all over the vase.*

*For my birthday I got a console for playing games on. – For my birthday I got a **games console**.*

*A person who was passing by found the wallet. – A **passer-by** found the wallet.*

Adverbs and adjectives

Use adverbs and compound adjectives before nouns rather than clauses after nouns. There is usually a hyphen when compound adjectives are used before a noun. Compare:

It is a position with a fairly high status.

*It is a **fairly high-status position**.*

An artefact has recently been discovered and caused a sensation.

*A **recently discovered artefact** has caused a sensation.*

We use determiners (*a, my, this*, etc.), adverbs and adjectives before nouns:

*Did you notice **that unpleasant metallic smell**?*

*It was only **a five-minute journey**.*

***Tom's first reaction** was to get angry.*

We can put adjectives before *one(s)* and after indefinite pronouns:

*Don't get the **expensive ones**.*

*Let's go **somewhere romantic** for our holiday.*

Clauses and prepositional phrases

We use phrases after nouns for ideas which cannot be expressed fully before the noun.

Relative clauses: *He gave a speech **which inspired millions**.* NOT *a millions inspiring speech*

***that** clauses:* *I got the feeling **that he never cared**.* NOT *that he never cared feeling*

Prepositional phrases: *I'd like a house **in a quiet area**.* NOT *in a quiet area's house*

We can also use *to* + infinitive after certain nouns, for example *choice, decision, willingness*:

*There's a plan **to redevelop the town centre**.*

Possessives

When we show the relationship between nouns, we can often either use a possessive *'s* or an *of* phrase:

*The company**'s** decision / decision **of the company** to make staff redundant was unpopular.*

We prefer the possessive *'s* when the possessor is a person or an animal:

*I looked down at John**'s** shoes.* NOT *the shoes of John*

We prefer an *of* phrase when the possessor is an object:

*The roof **of the house** needs repairing.* NOT *The house's roof*

Location, measuring, quantifying and qualitative words like *back, piece, cup, kind* and *sort* are always followed by an *of* phrase:

*Get in the back **of the car**.* NOT *the car's back*

*Have a piece **of chocolate**.* NOT *chocolate's piece*

> 🔊 **Tip**
>
> Very long noun phrases for people usually aren't followed by the possessive *'s*:
>
> *The children **of the man who lives opposite** are staying with me.*
> NOT *~~The man who lives opposite's~~ children are staying with me.*

---

a Underline the noun phrases in the text.

<u>One memorable summer day</u> I was coming home after an exhausting day at work when I met an old friend I hadn't seen for ages. I don't know why but I had the strong feeling that this was no mere coincidence. In fact, she had a proposition to make to me which was about to change my life. She said that she was looking for a reliable partner who she could trust to invest in a project started by a few friends of hers. I made a few phone calls to the bank and I had the money needed to get involved. My boring days of sitting behind a desk were behind me.

b Improve each noun phrase.

1 the bus's seats   *the seats of the bus*
2 the stop for the tram
3 a book written brilliantly
4 a moment that is awaited eagerly
5 a meeting which lasts one hour
6 an injury that can change your life
7 the bright idea of Ed
8 the girl that I introduced you to yesterday's aunt

c Improve each noun phrase in *italics* without significantly changing their meanings.

Human resources experts
~~Experts who work in the field of human resources~~ say that interviewers make *decisions about who to hire* within the first minute of an interview. Of course, *mistakes which cost a lot* can be made and sometimes the wrong people are hired. Nevertheless, companies have to rely on their managers' *skills in being able to make decisions*. Most of us have experienced at least one *interview which was a nightmare*, perhaps conducted by a *manager who has relatively little experience*. In a situation like this, your options are limited: plough on through the interview, or walk out after the first minute!

You never get **a second chance** to make **a first impression**.

d ▶ Now go back to p.46

4B have / get passives

get passives

We can use *get* passives like *be* passives, although they are less formal. *get* passives often describe unfortunate events:

*Do you remember how Sandra **got kicked** by a horse?*

*I **got made redundant** yesterday.*

We can use a reflexive pronoun to say that the subject is responsible for something that happened to them:

*He tried to use a fake passport and **got himself arrested** again.*

*Stop that! Are you trying to **get yourself killed**?!*

*She's managed to **get herself promoted** for the third time in two years.*

have / get + object + past participle

We can use *have* + object + past participle to talk about something where the subject is in an active role or a passive role. *get* + object + past participle usually implies an active role.

▶ 2.17	Passive role
*I **had my bag searched** at the airport.*	= Somebody searched my bag.
*Baby Alice **had her first photo taken** today.*	= Somebody, probably a professional, took a photograph of the baby.
	Active role
*We'll **have the window fixed** by the time you come back.*	= We'll arrange for somebody else to fix it **or** we'll do it ourselves.
*I **got my bike stolen** on the high street.*	= I left it unlocked, so I'm to blame.
*He **gets his house cleaned** every Friday.*	= He pays a cleaner to clean for him.

We often use *get* + object + past participle to talk about completing an activity:

*I haven't managed to **get the paperwork finished**.*

*We can't go until we've **got the kids dressed**.*

We often use *have / get* + object + past participle to talk about causing or instructing something to happen or to be done by somebody else:

*When I was twelve I wanted to **have/get my ears pierced** but my mum wouldn't let me.*

***Have/Get your car repaired** at Thompsons and save $$$!*

We can use *having / getting* + object + past participle:

***Having/Getting the walls painted** is the most important job at the moment.*

*Why would I be interested in **having/getting my nose made smaller**?*

> **Tip**
>
> In informal speech we can leave out *to* + *get / have* after *need, want, would like* etc.:
>
> *I **would like** (to get) **my hair cut** soon.*
>
> *I **need** (to have) **my bike** mended.*

▶ 2.18 Other patterns	
have / get + object + verb + -ing = cause someone / something to do something	*Grandma's story really **had/got me thinking**.* *The music soon **had/got everyone dancing** away.*
have + object + infinitive = give instructions or orders	*Our teacher **has us call** him 'Sir'.* *The boss **had us clean** our desks.*
get + object + to + infinitive = persuade someone to do something	*My mother-in-law **got me to take** her to the station.* *Advertising is the art of **getting people to buy** things they don't want.*

a Choose the best option.

1 Two people *got injured* / *had themselves injured* when the roof collapsed.
2 I'm going to *get him measuring me* / *get myself measured* for a new suit.
3 My blood pressure is really high. I *was checked* / *had it checked* this morning.
4 *Getting* / *Having* your car insured is cheaper if you do it online.
5 We're trying to get more people *to give* / *giving* to our charity.
6 Jenkins, *have* / *get* the first candidate come in, please.
7 The news *had everyone shouting* / *got everyone to shout* with anger.
8 Wayne's not coming in today. He needs his boiler *mended* / *mending*.

Mother was always telling me to **get my hair cut**.

b Rewrite these sentences using the words in brackets.

1 Someone needs to repair our car. (have)
We need to have our car repaired.
2 Tina worked hard and was promoted. (herself)
3 Someone stole my bike. (got)
4 Arrange for someone to check your eyes. (have)
5 The news made everyone panic. (got)
6 It wasn't easy to calm the children down. (get)
7 Our teacher told us to write an essay. (had)
8 Alex talked me into going with him. (got)

c Complete the dialogue with the correct forms of the verbs in brackets.

Ryan That podcast about the generation gap really got me ¹ _thinking_ (think). Are we that different from our kids?

Olivia I've not listened to it yet …
Last week I got ² _____ (give) a load of work to do by my boss and I've just had no time. She has me ³ _____ (work) all hours at the moment.

R Well, listen when you manage to get everything ⁴ _____ (do). The thing is I think a lot of this generation gap stuff is exaggerated. Like, we think that parents are too soft today, kids are used to ⁵ _____ (have) everything done for them and that goes to their head.

O That sounds true enough. You know my youngest, Tessa, I got her ⁶ _____ (make) her own bed and you should have seen the look on her face! When I was that age my parents had us ⁷ _____ (work) from 6:00 in the morning.

R Oh, come on! You delivered newspapers twice a week. This is just what I mean – the generation gap is something we've imagined and we have been fooled into believing it.

d ▶ Now go back to p.47

5A Relative clauses

(▶) 2.32 Defining and non-defining relative clauses

Defining relative clauses are essential to the meaning of a sentence:
*The law **which/that was recently passed** makes no sense.*
*The man (**who**) **he attacked** is recovering in hospital.*
Non-defining relative clauses are not essential, they give us additional information about nouns. In non-defining relative clauses we cannot use the relative pronoun *that* or leave out object pronouns:
*German law, **which is based on Roman law**, is quite different.*
NOT ~~that is based~~
*The victim, **who we cannot name for security reasons**, is recovering in hospital.* NOT ~~The victim, we~~
Non-defining relative clauses are separated by commas in writing and pauses in speech.

(▶) 2.33 Relative pronouns

* **when / where / why**

With nouns which refer to time, like *time* and *day*, and after *place* or *somewhere* we can use *that* instead of *when/where*, or no pronoun in informal language:
*The 1930s was the time (**when/that**) organised crime flourished.*
*Take me somewhere (**where/that**) I can relax for a few days.*
After **reason**, we can use **why/that** or no pronoun:
*Does anyone know the reason (**why/that**) crime is so high?*

* **which**

We can use *which* to talk about a whole clause not just a noun phrase:
*She lied on her interview form, **which** was a bad sign.*
*We all get on well, **which** is fantastic.*
We can use *which* after prepositions and before nouns in fixed phrases like *in which case, the chance of which, (neutral) at which time, the result/outcome of which, the likelihood of which* (formal):
*It would seem that the guilty person has been found, **in which case** you are free to go.*
*A major police operation started, **the result of which** was that six people were arrested.*

* **who / whom / whose**

We usually use *who* as subject and object in relative clauses but we can use *whom* in formal written language. We use *whom* not *who* after prepositions:
*Mr Brown, **who/whom** the police suspect of arson, was released without charge.*
*Mr White, **to whom** the police gave a caution, was held overnight.* NOT ~~to who~~
We use *whose* as a possessive of people and animals:
*The old lady **whose** bag was taken was really upset.*

* **none of whom / all of which / some of whose etc.**

We can use quantifiers like *some, none* and *few* with **of whom, of which** and **of whose** in non-defining relative clauses:
*Three suspects were interviewed, **all of whom** were released without charge.*
*Carter is accused of three crimes, **none of which** he admits to.*

* **whoever / whatever / wherever / whenever**

We use indefinite pronouns, *whoever, whatever, wherever, whenever,* to mean 'the person who', 'the thing that', etc.:
***Whoever** stole my sausage from the fridge is in big trouble!*

> **Tip** *what* is not a relative pronoun. We use it as a noun to mean 'the thing which': *Young people today don't know **what** they want.*

Prepositions in relative clauses

We usually put prepositions at the end of relative clauses but we can put them before the relative pronoun in formal language:
*Prison is not the kind of place **that** you would want to spend time **in**.*
*Prison is not the kind of place **in which** you would want to spend time.*
We keep the particles with the verb with multiword verbs:
*The children who I **look after** at the day centre are very naughty.*
NOT ~~The children **after whom** I look~~
*Stealing from the kitchen is something which we will not **put up with**.*
NOT ~~**with which** we will not put up~~

**He tried to make a getaway,
the chances of which were very slim.**

a Match the sentence halves.

1 [g] I don't want to stay anywhere
2 [ ] Give me one good reason
3 [ ] The letter took a week to arrive,
4 [ ] I might have made the mistake,
5 [ ] Ten people agreed to take part,
6 [ ] It was a long and confusing story,
7 [ ] That was the best excuse
8 [ ] We should not give up rights

a some of whom later dropped out.
b she could come up with.
c I should believe you.
d little of which was true.
e which is ridiculous.
f for which people have made great sacrifices.
g that doesn't have any decent facilities.
h in which case I'll apologise.

b Choose the correct option.

1 The emergency number is 999, *that / which* is easy to remember.
2 Mrs Jackson, to *who / whom* we are very grateful, has kindly agreed to speak.
3 Florida is the only place *that / which* I can relax.
4 It's up to the person *what / whose* job it is to sort out the transport.
5 The police arrived half an hour later, *by which time / by that time* the gang had escaped.
6 We recruited some younger staff, *few of whom / few of them* had any experience.
7 Most graduates lack the skills for *whom / which* there is most demand.

c Use relative clauses to join the sentences. Replace the words in **bold** and change the punctuation and word order as necessary.

1 Two criminals wanted to escape from the prison. They had been held **in it** for two years.
   Two criminals wanted to escape from the prison, in which they had been held for two years.
2 The criminals shared a prison cell. **The floor of the cell** was over the city drainage system.
3 **They** were desperate for freedom. The prisoners built a tunnel. They could escape **through it**.
4 One night they went down the tunnel. There was a full moon **then**.
5 The two criminals came out into a street. **The street** looked familiar.
6 They had come up outside the local police station. They had first been charged at **this police station**.
7 **All of them** knew the criminals by sight. The local police arrested them.
8 They took them back to the prison. They never tried to escape **from it** again.

d ▶ Now go back to p.57

5B Willingness, obligation and necessity

Obligation and necessity

We use *must* and *have to* to say what is necessary. *must* only refers to the present or future:

I'll have to / *I must get* some more qualifications soon.

Irene had to go on a business trip so I took her to the airport. NOT ~~must have gone~~

have got + *to* + infinitive also describes what is necessary, especially arrangements:

My boss said I've got to be in the office by 8.00 tomorrow.

We usually use *must* when we decide what is necessary and *have to* when other people decide:

I must tell you what Jane said in the office.

I've cleaned the floors. What do I *have to do* next?

We use *should* and *ought to* to say what is the right thing to do:

I ought to organise my time more effectively.

You *shouldn't do* unpaid overtime.

We use *had better* + infinitive in advice or threats:

She*'d better see* a doctor before it's too late.

You*'d better be* early tomorrow!

We can use *be supposed* + *to* + infinitive to say what is necessary according to some rules or instructions:

The Finance Director *is supposed to authorise* all major expenditure.

I was supposed to read the report by tomorrow but I never got time.

You **are expected to be** flexible in this job.

> ### 🛈 Tip
> We can use *It's up to* + person + *whether* to say somebody is not obliged to do something in informal language:
> *It's up to* you **whether** you take this job but I think it's a great offer.

▶ 2.43 Other phrases for obligation / no obligation

These phrases are all followed by *to* + infinitive:

need to / don't need to / needn't	You **don't need to tell** me what went wrong, I was there.
have no choice but	Well, I **have no choice but to quit** then.
be allowed	We**'re not allowed to wear** jeans to work.
be expected	How can she **be expected to be** in two places at the same time!
be free	You**'re free to choose** whatever position you want.
be required (formal)	At the beginning I **was not required to put in** very long hours.
be advisable / permitted / forbidden / essential (formal)	Protective clothing **is advisable**.
be obliged (formal)	In our contract we **are obliged to start** work at 8.00.
be under (no) obligation (formal)	I **am under no obligation to answer** to your demands.

▶ 2.44 Willingness

will / can + infinitive	Mason **won't work** for such a low salary. I **can work** on Saturday if you give me the Monday off.
be happy / willing + to + infinitive	I'd **be happy to help** out in the sales department.
be prepared + to + infinitive / for + noun	Bonnie **wasn't prepared for** the amount of paperwork.
have no objection to verb + -ing / noun	The staff **have no objection to taking** a pay cut.
have nothing against verb + -ing / noun	I **have nothing against** the new manager.
have no problem with verb + -ing / noun	My husband **has no problem with looking** after the kids while I'm in the office.

---

a Choose the correct option.

1 There's no way Masha *must* / *will* / *shall* be prepared to see Terry again after what happened.
2 Kate has nothing *against* / *with* / *on* going camping but she'd prefer a hotel.
3 Pilots are *essential* / *obliged* / *obligatory* to take a medical every six months.
4 When we lived in the village we *must* / *were going to* / *had to* drive for miles to get to a supermarket.
5 Tony *should* / *ought* / *had better* to be taking care of that but he's so lazy.
6 The match *had to* / *was supposed to* / *was required to* begin at 7.00 but heavy rain delayed the start.

b Rewrite the sentences with the words in brackets.

1 Sylvia will organise the guest list. (happy)
   Sylvia is happy to organise the guest list.
2 I don't mind waiting until the end. (objection)
3 I'm afraid the only way is to cancel the trip. (no choice)
4 Members of the public cannot go beyond this point. (forbidden)
5 You can decide when to leave. (up to)
6 Gerald will have to attend the meeting. (got)

c Complete the text with the phrases in the box.

~~be happy to~~   be under no obligation to   be up to
be willing to   be prepared   have no choice but to
have nothing against   ought to

Would you __be happy to__ work when you're 70? 80? The chances are that many of us will [1]_____ do so, because with an increasing number of people living well beyond retirement age it is only to be expected that we will work into our old age. Those still working might be the lucky ones. Some people will [2]_____ working past normal retirement age but will employers [3]_____ keep people on who are probably less healthy and less effective? The government believe people should [4]_____ to invest in their own future. State pension schemes are just inadequate and although we may [5]_____ invest in private pension schemes at the moment, this looks like the only realistic solution. It will [6]_____ you whether you take this option but you [7]_____ take it seriously because it may make your future a lot rosier.

d ▶ Now go back to p.61

6A Simple and continuous verbs

 3.6 **Simple verbs**

We use simple verbs to talk about complete actions, events or activities:
I've just taken an amazing picture of two foxes.
We trained really hard for the marathon we ran in April.
We use a simple verb when we say how much is complete or how many times something happens:
I went to the Museum of Modern Art three times last year.
We got about half the work done.
We use simple verbs to talk about facts and unchanging states:
The camera takes up to ten photos per second in this mode.
My dad was born in Manchester and he has never left.

3.7 **Continuous verbs**

We use continuous verbs to talk about incomplete or temporary activities:
Brian was trying to take a picture but someone got in the way.
I'm on a temporary contract so I'm only working here for six months.
We use continuous verbs to emphasise activity, duration or repetition:
I'm going to classes to improve my photography.
In March we will have been living here for four years.
Mandy has been phoning me all day and telling me what to do.
We can use continuous verbs with the adverbs *always, continually, constantly* and *forever* to complain or express surprise about how frequently something happens:
James was constantly taking photos of every little thing he saw.
It's always raining in this part of the world.

> **Tip**
>
> We can use the past continuous to be more polite or less direct:
> *I was hoping I could borrow your camera.*
> *Thank you for a lovely evening. It's time we were going.*

Verbs not usually used in the continuous
We never or rarely use some verbs in the continuous, e.g. *know* and *suppose*:
I have known Nina for ages. NOT ~~am knowing~~
I don't suppose you know where the paints are? NOT ~~'m not supposing~~

Below are some verbs which are not usually used in the continuous:

Thinking
believe, despise, know, recognise, regard, suppose, realise *I'm sure Trevor despises everything we are trying to do.* NOT ~~is despising~~
The senses*
hear, see, smell, sound, taste *We have seen a brilliant performance from Ronaldo.* NOT ~~have been seeing~~
Communicating
astonish, deny, impress, mean, satisfy, take (= understand) *Nothing about his behaviour that day impressed me.* NOT ~~was impressing~~
Other
belong, consist, depend, fit, possess *The corner office now belongs to you.*

*We use *can* + an ability verb like *hear, remember, see, taste* rather than a continuous form:
I can hear somebody coming. NOT *I* ~~am hearing~~

Verbs with different meanings in the simple and continuous

Rachel weighs 70 kilos. (a state)	*Rachel is weighing herself.* (an activity)
What do you think about digital cameras? (an opinion)	*I'm thinking of going to art school.* (an activity)
Ella is a difficult child. (a characteristic)	*Ella's being difficult.* (behaviour)
What can you see in this picture? (see = look at) *Do you see what I mean?* (see = understand)	*The doctor is seeing a patient.* (see = meet)

---

a Match the sentences with the pictures.

1

   a Chiara ate the chocolate.
   b Chiara was eating the chocolate.

2

   a Simon's had a bath.
   b Simon's been having a bath.

3

   a Sam is a doctor.
   b Sam is being a doctor.

4

   a Laura comes from Russia.
   b Laura is coming from Russia.

b Choose the best option.

1 I *think* / *'m thinking* photography is more about technology than art.
2 I'll *be learning* / *learn* English for the rest of my life.
3 *Are you* / *Are you being* obstinate just to annoy me?
4 Everyone had *left* / *been leaving* and there was complete silence.
5 Jon *thinks* / *'s thinking* of joining the army next year.
6 *Do you realise* / *Are you realising* how this makes me look?
7 Someone has *been gossiping* / *gossiped* and I'm really upset.
8 Unemployment *increases* / *is increasing* but the government doesn't care.
9 We *opened* / *were opening* our first office in summer 2012.
10 I *suppose* / *'m supposing* we'll have to wait for the bus.

c Complete the text with either the simple or continuous form of the verbs in brackets.

Roma So do you ¹ __think__ (think) graffiti could be called art?
Judy Why not? Graffiti has a long tradition and we know the Romans ² _____ (have) it.
R Yes, but people have ³ _____ (complain) about graffiti for a long time too. I must admit that every time I ⁴ _____ (see) a wall covered in the stuff, it annoys me.
J Well, obviously you have ⁵ _____ (decide) that real art ⁶ _____ (belong) in museums and nowhere else. Graffiti is the most natural form of street art there is. Haven't you ⁷ _____ (watch) that series on TV at the moment about popular art? It has ⁸ _____ (change) my idea of art for good. Actually, I have always ⁹ _____ (want) to be good at art.
R What ¹⁰ _____ (say)? Are you going to go out and paint some graffiti on a train station wall?!
J No, I don't think train passengers would think much of that.

d Now go back to p.70

6B Participle clauses

We use participle clauses to add more information to a sentence:
***Hiding behind the bushes**, I held my breath.*
*The stranger staggered into the room, **shaking and covered in snow**.*

Participle clauses after nouns

We use participle clauses after nouns and pronouns. They are similar to defining relative clauses which have continuous and passive verbs:
*We found the wallet (which was) **lying by the side of the road**.*
*Everybody (who had been) **affected by the fire** was told to leave their homes.*
*The streets were full of people (who were) **dancing for joy**.*
*Alice in Wonderland was the **book** (which was) **chosen** by the majority of students.*
*Joanna is a **woman who says** what she thinks.* NOT ~~woman saying~~
(*says* is not a continuous verb)
*The **building which collapsed** was to be rebuilt.* NOT ~~building collapsed~~
(*collapsed* is not a passive)
The subject of a participle clause must be the same as the main clause:
*The **boat** which we were waiting for was late.* NOT ~~the boat waiting for~~
We can't form a participle clause when a modal verb is necessary for the full sense of the clause:
Animal Farm is a book which should be read by everyone.
NOT ~~book read~~

> 🍃 **Tip**
>
> We can use participle clauses with verbs not usually used in continuous tenses:
> *You will come to a large rock **resembling** a castle.* = rock which resembles a castle NOT ~~rock which is resembling~~
> *I wasn't sure where to go, **not being a local**.*

Participle clauses as adverbials

We use participle clauses as adverbials in formal language and writing:
***Approaching a junction**, I observed a car making an improper manoeuvre.*
***Left by themselves**, young children can get into all sorts of trouble.*
Adverbial participle clauses say why, when, where and how:
***Frightened by what he saw**, he never returned.*
= Because he was frightened …
***Having thought it over**, I've decided to refuse their offer.*
= Because I've thought about it …
***Stopping for a break**, we discussed what to do next.*
= After we stopped …
***Standing by the fire**, Mary thought about her next step.*
= While she stood …
***Climbing out of the window**, he managed to escape. = By climbing …*
***Using my knife**, I forced the box open. = With my knife …*

Participle clauses always start before or at the same time as the main verb in the sentence:
*The man **running alongside me** tripped and fell.*
***Sensing I was being watched**, I looked into the shadows.*
We can make it very clear a participle clause begins earlier by using the perfect form:
***Having finally found a job**, I called my parents with the happy news.*
***Not having seen the incident**, I'm not the best person to tell you what happened.*

> 🍃 **Tip**
>
> We can use *-ed* adverbial participle clauses after time conjunctions in formal language:
> ***When faced with danger**, most people would just panic.*
> *The holiday of a lifetime! **Once experienced**, it will never be forgotten.*

Standing as still as he could,
he waited for the next throw.

a Tick the correct sentences. Correct the mistakes you found in the remaining sentences.

1 ☐ ~~Tony~~ running at full speed, he managed to jump on the train. [R]
2 ☐ Remembering my appointment, I jumped up and left.
3 ☐ I will find the person committed this crime.
4 ☐ There was a terrible smell coming from the room.
5 ☐ Offering to pay for the damage, he had caused the accident.
6 ☐ Reading the letter, my hands were shaking in excitement.
7 ☐ Not belonging to the group, I felt very out of place.
8 ☐ Paddy is the kind of man never arriving anywhere on time.

b Complete the beginning of the story with the participle clauses in the box.

> being realistic   coming outside   ~~following me~~
> being overworked and underpaid   getting stressed out
> waiting to strike   wearing orange

I knew that there was a man[1] _following me_. That morning, [2]_____, I saw him again. The strange thing was that he made no effort to hide; [3]_____, he seemed to want to be seen. Anyway, [4]_____, what could I do? [5]_____, the local police would hardly have time to listen to my suspicions. It wasn't exactly the crime of the century either. Maybe it was just me [6]_____ as a result of too much work. As things turned out, I was in very real danger with disaster [7]_____.

c Rewrite the next part of the story using participle clauses where possible.
 Sitting down,
I went to the café on the street corner. ~~I sat down and~~ I ordered a cake. A cake which was covered in chocolate was quickly brought over to my table. I noticed something which was sticking out from under the cake so I lifted it up. Underneath I found a note which was written in red which said, 'Get into the car which is waiting across the road'. I was frightened by the tone and I feared the worst so I did what the note said. A thousand negative thoughts were crowding my head when I got to the car. The familiar figure who was dressed in orange was in the front seat, with a sinister smile on his face. 'We meet at last,' he said.

d ▶ Now go back to p.73

7A Speculation and deduction

▶3.22 Certain speculations: *will / going to*

We use *will* to speculate with certainty about the future. We add *have* + past participle to speculate about past actions with an effect on the present. We use *going to* for strong predictions based on present evidence. We often use adverbs with *will* and *going to* to modify the degree of certainty:

*Paper books **probably won't** disappear altogether.*
*I'm sure she **will have arrived** by now. Let's go and see.*
*It's a terrible film! It's **hardly going to** win an Oscar.*

▶3.23 Certain deductions: *must / have got to*

We use *must* and *have got to* (informal) to say something is logically true in the present and future (make a deduction based on evidence). We use *must* + *have* + past participle to deduce about the past:

*Lisa is all dressed up. She **must be going** somewhere nice.*
*Joy didn't hear the phone. She **must have been sleeping**.*
*I don't believe it! You**'ve got to be joking**.*

▶3.24 Likely: *should / may well*

We use *should* about the past, present and future to say that something is probable because it is normal and expected. *May well* is slightly more certain than *should*:

*It's 6:00, so they **should have arrived** by now. / **should be arriving** soon.*
*Solar power **may well be** the answer to our energy problems.*

▶3.25 Possible and unlikely: *could / might / may / can*

We use *could*, *may* (*not*) and *might* (*not*) both to speculate and deduce in the past, present and future:

*Petrol **could/may (not)/might (not)** run out in the near future.* NOT *can*
*Jill is late. She **could/might/may have got** lost. She **could/might/may be wandering** around out there.* NOT *can*

We also use *could* + *have* + past participle to say what was hypothetically possible in the past:

*I didn't know you were in town. We **could have met** up.*
We use *can* to say that something is generally possible in the present/ future:

*You **can** get bears in the woods at this time of the year.*

▶3.26 Impossible: *can't / couldn't*

couldn't + infinitive says what was generally impossible in the past. *can't* + infinitive says what is generally impossible in the present and future. We also use *can't/couldn't* + *have* + past participle (past) or *can't* + *be* (+ verb + -*ing* / *going to*) (present/future) to say something is logically impossible:

*They **couldn't get** here yesterday. They **can't get here** today or tomorrow.* = impossible
*The exam **can't/couldn't have been** very difficult if you finished in 20 minutes.* = logically impossible
*Jeffrey **can't be working** on a Sunday evening. The building's closed.*
couldn't + *have* + past participle also says what was impossible in the hypothetical past:

*I **couldn't have passed** the exam without Peter's help.* (= I passed, because of his help; it was hypothetically impossible without this.) NOT *I can't have passed …*
*'I should have invited her.' 'Don't worry, she **couldn't have come** anyway.'* (= In the hypothetical situation in which she was invited, it was impossible for her.) NOT *She can't have come …*

▶3.27 Other expressions

*We **are bound to** find a cure for cancer one day.* (= certain speculation)
*You **can tell that** John is intelligent from the books he reads.* (= certain deduction)
*In the future, it**'s (highly) likely** (**that**) cars will be electric.* (= likely)
*I **bet** / I **reckon** / I'm **quite sure** (**that**) most films will be in 3D.* (= likely)
***There's an outside/slim/good chance** (**that**) I'll be the only applicant.*
***There's no way** / **It's highly unlikely** (**that**) there is life on Mars.*

I must have pressed the wrong button

a Choose the best option.

1 Don't worry, we *might / will / can* arrive in plenty of time.
2 The two teams are equally matched and it *'s going to / may / can* be a great game.
3 It's *highly / absolutely / completely* unlikely that government policy will change.
4 Food prices *should / can / could* get out of control.
5 I'm sure Andrey *could / can / will* have realised that it was only a joke.
6 There's a *slim / narrow / minor* chance that they will change their mind.
7 In fact, you *must / can / should* find people who live on less than a dollar a day.
8 Someone *must / can / could* have leaked the news, it's all over the Internet.
9 We *mustn't / needn't / can't* have run out of milk. I got some this morning.
10 You *can / must / should* tell they get on. They're always laughing and joking.

b Rewrite these sentences, using the word in brackets.

1 It was impossible for Adam to do any more. (couldn't)
   Adam couldn't have done any more.
2 I'm sure that customers will complain. (bound)
3 It is very possible that I'll see Ian tomorrow. (well)
4 I think Barbara broke the window – she was playing round here. (must)
5 There's no way the referee saw the incident. (can't)
6 Damien probably knows the answer. (should)
7 It's obvious to me that Greta is dissatisfied. (tell)
8 The lights are on so Karen will be at home. (got)

c Tick the words 1–10 in italics which are possible. Correct the mistakes you find.

¹ ~~May~~ ^Could^ time travel become a reality? Scientists have been contemplating the idea for centuries and in films like *Back to the Future* and *Predestination* we *²might* get the idea that time travel is a real possibility. In many ways this is wishful thinking: it *³will* be amazing to go back to ancient Egypt and see the Pyramids being built. Unfortunately, there's *⁴not way* that time travel is possible at our current stage of technological development. Maybe if we *⁵could* travel close to, even beyond, the speed of light, new horizons *⁶might* open up, but that is a distant possibility. Still, if we *⁷can* build a machine to approach the speed of light, the laws of physics will change and we *⁸must* enter new territory. This all sounds *⁹as fantasy* and, sadly for science-fiction fans, it is until we make some incredible breakthroughs. Time travel *¹⁰can't* be happening anytime soon but we can dream, and watch the films of course.

d ▶ Now go back to p.81

7B Cleft sentences

We use cleft sentences to correct, emphasise or point out information. We form **a focusing phrase ending in *be*** at the beginning of the sentence.

 3.33 *Wh-* **cleft sentences**

Reading other people's comments online bores me.
What bores me is <u>reading other people's comments online</u>.

What	noun	verb phrase	*be*	information focused on
What	*she*	*suggested*	*was*	*out of the question.*
What		*went wrong*	*was*	*that Sheila got involved.*
What		*is amazing*	*is*	*that nobody found out.*

> ### 🗨 Tip
> - *be* can be plural if what follows it is plural:
>   *What patients demand **is/are** better hospitals.*
> - In informal speech we can also use *where / when / why / how* in the *Wh-* cleft structure:
>   **Where I was born is** *London.*
>   **How I feel is** *angry.*
>   **Why I left was** *to get a job.*

We frequently emphasise an action or activity with *What + happen + (that) + clause*:
What happened was that *we had to throw all the food away.*
What happens is that *you get a quick orientation on your first day.*
We can emphasise actions with *What + noun phrase + do + be + (to)* infinitive:
What she did was <u>(to) phone the police</u>.
What Sheila had done was <u>(to) get married</u>.

- ***All***
  We can begin cleft sentences with *all*:
  All (that) she wants is *a new phone.*
  All I did was *ask her how she was feeling.*

- ***The thing / One thing,* etc.**
  We can begin cleft sentences with *the first thing, the main thing,* etc.
  The main thing is *that you two stop quarrelling.*
  One thing you can do is *to promise it won't happen again.*

- ***The place where / time when / reason why***
  We use *place where, time that / when* and *reason why* to emphasise a place, time or reason:
  The place where I was born is *London.*
  The time (when) you find out who your real friends are is *when you have no money.*
  The only reason (why) I stay in this job is *Mike.*
  The main reason (why) I do it is *to make a bit of money.*

3.34 *It* **cleft sentences**
Cathy had the idea.
It was <u>Cathy</u> *who had the idea.*

It	*be*	information focused on (noun / place / time phrase)	*that / which / when* clause
It	*is*	*technology*	*that is causing increased shyness.*
It	*was*	*the weekend already*	*when she got back to me.*
It	*is*	*working all day for nothing*	*which gets me down.*
It	*is*	*only in big cities*	*that smog is a problem.*

We can also emphasise time with *It is / was not until … that* and *It is / was only when … that*:
It was not until *Lesley went away* **that** *I realised how much I missed her.*
It's only when *I'm alone* **that** *I feel insecure.*

What technology does is bring people together.

a Match the sentence halves.

1	[g] What he wanted was	a	to write an angry letter back.
2	[ ] What I did was	b	that the problems start.
3	[ ] It was my teacher	c	that the boat started to sink.
4	[ ] The main thing is	d	who encouraged me to write.
5	[ ] All you can do is	e	hard to say.
6	[ ] It's only when we're busy	f	that nobody got hurt.
7	[ ] What happened was	g	to change the world.
8	[ ] How she earns a living is	h	try harder next time.

b Correct the mistakes in the sentences.

1. ~~There~~ *It* is Paris that I've always wanted to visit.
2. The captain of the ship was she who sensed the storm coming.
3. All what students want is an affordable educational system.
4. All she did was taking out the cable.
5. What happens next is to fill out an application form.
6. The most important thing is which he is innocent.
7. What was the weather that was beginning to worry me.
8. Is a quite unique situation that we find ourselves in.

c Rewrite the sentences as cleft sentences using the word in brackets.

1. I want a coffee. (what) *What I want is a coffee.*
2. I only need ten euros. (all)
3. Nobody wants to do this job. (it)
4. You are asking for something unreasonable. (what)
5. We chose Portugal because of the friendly people. (reason)
6. Our car ran into a tree. (happened)
7. Her cousin was causing all the trouble. (it)
8. I don't know Jason so well and this bothers me. (the thing)

d ▶ Now go back to p.83

Now go back to p.83

8A Gerunds and infinitives

Gerunds

Gerunds are *-ing* forms which function as nouns in a sentence. The whole clause becomes a gerund when we add *-ing* to the verb:

sleep too much → **Sleeping too much** is as bad as **sleeping too little**.

We can form compound nouns with gerunds:

sleeping pills, on-the-job training

Gerunds are much more common than infinitives as subjects:

Staying in bed all day is not a great use of your time.
To stay in bed all day is ... = unusual

We use gerunds after prepositions and certain expressions, such as *it's (not) worth, it's no good/use, there's no point ... (in)*:

*I am interested **in becoming** a member of your club.*
NOT ~~in to become~~
*Do you ever get tired **of Jill getting home** late every night?*
NOT ~~of to get~~
Was it worth spending all that money on a sofa bed?
There's no point worrying and **losing sleep** over it.

Infinitives

We use the infinitive without *to* after modal verbs, expressions like *had better, would rather*, some verbs like *let* and *make*, and as imperatives:

*The situation may well **get** worse before it gets better.*
*I would rather **sleep** in my own bed than in a hotel room.*
***Be** quiet! Let me **have** some sleep tonight.*

We use *to* + infinitive after ...

*   many adjectives, comparatives, superlatives and ordinal numbers:
    *I was **delighted to hear** that you had won first prize.* NOT ~~delighted hearing~~
    *Who is the **greatest** athlete ever **to represent** Great Britain?* NOT ~~representing~~
    *She was the **first** woman **to climb** Everest.* NOT ~~climbing~~
*   nouns formed from verbs that take the infinitive, e.g. *agreement, decision, plan* but NOT *expectation* or *hope*, which take *of* + gerund:
    *Sally made a **decision to resign**.*
    *I had **hopes of getting** on the team.* NOT ~~hopes to get~~
    For verb patterns with gerunds and infinitives see p.190
*   *time*
    *It's **time to go** to bed.*
    *There's still **time to register** for the competition.*
*   quantifiers like *enough, little* and *many* + nouns
    *Have you got **enough** money **to start** your own business?*
    *I've seen **too many** films like that **to be** very impressed.*

3.46	Active gerunds	Passive gerunds
Present	***Shouting*** a lot isn't very good for your voice. I can't stand **not knowing** what I'm supposed to do.	***Winning*** is better than **being beaten**. What I resent is **not being given** the opportunity to show what I can do.
Perfect	I'm sorry for ever **having mentioned** the subject. I regret **not having contacted** you earlier.	The star denied **having been seen** with the actor. The worst thing is **not having been told**.

3.47	Active infinitives	Passive infinitives
Simple	I'll **come**. Try **to help**, if you can.	Don't **be put off** by the noise. This offer is **not to be missed**.
Continuous	I'd rather **be going** with you. She seems **to be feeling** better.	It should **be being done** as we speak. The space seems **to be being used** as a car park. (unusual)
Perfect	You'd better **have finished** by the time I get back. It's important **to have tried**.	Louise can't **have been treated** very well. I wouldn't like **to have been given** that job.
Perfect continuous	We will **have been seeing** each other for two years in April. I'm proud **to have been working** here for so many years.	Joe must **have been being bullied** at school. (unusual)

> ### Tip
> Perfect forms of gerunds and infinitives stress that the activity is in the past and complete. We can often use present forms with exactly the same meaning:
> Her proudest moment to date is **having won** / **winning** Olympic gold.
> I wasn't happy at **having been compared** / **being compared** to someone twenty years older.
> You were supposed **to have finished** / **to finish** it yesterday.

> ### Tip
> Some adjectives, e.g. *afraid, sorry, sure*, are followed by the gerund or infinitive with a difference in meaning:
> I'm **sure to see** Tom at work on Monday.
> *sure* = focus on probability of something happening
> I'm **sure seeing** Tom again will be amazing.
> *sure* = focus on emotion / effect of something happening

a Choose the correct option.

1   *Choosing* / *Having chosen* / *To be chosen* a pillow which is right for your back is not easy.
2   *Picking* / *Being picked* / *Having been picked* for my college team would be a great achievement.
3   There was no point *waiting* / *having been waited* / *to wait* for him.
4   Jane is furious with me for *mislead* / *having misled* / *having been misled* her.
5   The suspect claims *to have been visiting* / *to be visiting* / *to have been visited* her sister at that time.
6   I would prefer *not to have known* / *to have known not*.
7   Sorry but there are too few players *to have* / *having* a proper game.
8   There's no use *having complained* / *complaining* / *to complain* about it all the time.
9   Look, it's time *to forget* / *forgetting* everything that happened.
10 The views from the top are worth *describing* / *to be described* in detail.

b Correct the mistakes in the gerunds and infinitives in italics.

Is it possible for someone never [1]*to be sleeping*? <ins>to sleep</ins> The answer is (almost) yes if you have Fatal Familial Insomnia, in which [2]*to have fallen* asleep is almost impossible. For sufferers, it's not even worth them [3]*to go* to bed because sleep won't come. As the name suggests, [4]*affecting* by this rare but dreadful condition can cause death, depending on its severity. If we don't get enough sleep [5]*carry out* our day-to-day life, the damage to our physical and mental health can be very serious. [6]*To not sleep* for days often makes people [7]*to feel* weak and disorientated. There can be some benefit in [8]*being taken* sleeping pills but this puts a different kind of stress on the body and the drugs can become addictive. There is a need for more research [9]*doing* in this area and it is sure [10]*being* a very deserving way for government money [11]*to be spending*.

c ▶ Now go back to p.93

8B Conditionals

We often refer to conditionals as 0, 1, 2, 3 and mixed. These are useful reference points for verb forms but there are many variations with different tenses and conjunctions.

▶ **3.53** **Real and unreal conditionals**

In real conditionals there is no change of use of verb forms. We use present tenses in the *if* clause:

0 *If I **want** a snack, I **have** one.*
1 *She**'ll recover** quickly if her temperature **goes** down.*

In unreal conditionals we show that a situation is hypothetical or unlikely by changing the verb forms back one tense:

2 *If it **wasn't raining**, I **would go** out somewhere.* (It is raining now.)
 *If it **was/were*** my choice, we'd go to the spa.*
 **We can use If … was or If … were.*
3 *Megan **wouldn't have missed** her plane if she **hadn't lost** her passport.* (She lost her passport.)
 *The car **could have gone** off the road if he **had been driving** any faster.*
Mixed *I **would speak** French more fluently **if I had been allowed** to study in France.*
 *If I **knew** what you wanted, I**'d have done** it ages ago.*

> **▌ Tip**
>
> We can put *had, should* and *were* first instead of *if*. This is formal.
> ***Had I known** about your plans earlier, I would have acted differently.*
> ***Should her condition get worse**, we will contact you immediately.*
> ***Were humans to live** so long, there would be many health complications.*

▶ **3.54** **Other conjunctions**

as long as / so long as / on (the) condition that = only if **in the event of** + noun (formal)	You can borrow my shirt **so long as** you don't get it dirty. Goods can be returned **on condition that** you have the original receipt. Assemble outside the school hall **in the event of** a fire.
if + be + not for + noun phrase **but for** + noun phrase (formal)	*If it were not for* Simon, I would never have known about the cucumber diet. The negotiations would have failed **but for** my efforts.
providing / provided (that) = if	The material will be ready **providing** you give plenty of notice. **Provided that** you repay it within three months, the bank will issue the loan.
suppose / imagine (that)	**Suppose** we could live to 100, what would we look like? **Imagine** there was no school today. Wouldn't that be great?
assuming / supposing = this might be the case	Let's meet on the Sunday, **assuming** that is everyone's day off. **Supposing** you could find the treasure, what would you do with it?
(just) in case + possible situation or result = as a precaution **in case of** + noun (formal)	Write down the phone number **just in case** you forget it. **In case of** emergency, ring this number.
otherwise + possible result = if not that, then this	I need to get to bed, **otherwise** I won't be able to get up on time. I didn't see her, **otherwise** I would have told her.

Speech bubble: **If** you really **want** to find the secret of living to an old age, you **should ask** my mother.

a Match the sentence halves.

1 ☐ j If Sandra gets here early,
2 ☐ If that had happened to me,
3 ☐ If I'm still working in an hour,
4 ☐ If you had bothered to ask,
5 ☐ If the story were to get out,
6 ☐ I don't mind going to the party
7 ☐ I'm happy to share,
8 ☐ If it hadn't been for night school,
9 ☐ I'd better get on with my work,
10 ☐ Sort it out yourselves,

a I could have explained everything.
b in case the boss is about today.
c I'd be absolutely furious.
d providing I can choose first.
e otherwise I'll have to get involved.
f stop me and tell me to go to bed.
g I would never have met my wife.
h it wouldn't look very good for the firm.
i as long as it doesn't finish too late.
j let her in for me please.

b Put the conditional sentences in order, adding commas where necessary. The first word is highlighted.

1 this / you / hard / if / think / wait / is / just
 If you think this is hard, just wait.
2 you / I / with / if / I / were / a / have / would / her / word
3 you / quiet / stay / as / can / you / keep / long / as
4 anyone / me / to / if / is / blame / it's
5 disappointed / Sheila / have / come / been / would / had / if / nobody
6 is / agree / that / on / this / only / will / the / confidential / condition / I / kept
7 to / you / I / find / will / the / be / out / know / should / first
8 assuming / we / everything / need / it / take / won't / long / have / we

c ▶ Now go back to p.96

9A Reflexive and reciprocal pronouns

▶ 4.13 Reflexive pronouns
We use reflexive pronouns …
- when the object is the same as the subject:
  *They blamed **themselves** for the accident.*
  *She's always looking at **herself** in the mirror.*
- after verbs and prepositions:
  *The director of the bank awarded **himself** a big bonus.*
  *Don't be angry with **yourself**.*
  *I said to **myself** that I would try again the next day.*
- after nouns and pronouns to emphasise importance, and for contrast with other people/things in general:
  *The prime minister **himself** has shares in the company.*
  *The boss **herself** does not believe any of these rumours.*
- after the verb phrase to emphasise independence/achievement:
  *We designed the house **ourselves**.*
  *They cleaned up the city **themselves**.*
- after the verb phrase to show similarity to another person/thing = *as well*
  *He went to have a shower. I needed one **myself**.*

Cars that park **themselves**
do save a lot of space.

We use *by* + reflexive pronoun to mean without anybody else:
*My friends were busy so I went into town **by myself**.*
We use *beside* + reflexive pronoun to mean worried/upset:
*After the last heavy defeat, the manager is **beside himself**.*
Some verbs have a different meaning when the object is a reflexive pronoun:
*He didn't **behave himself**.* = behave well
*Just **be yourself** in the interview.* = act naturally
*You don't want to **find yourself** alone.* = get into a situation
*I **helped myself** to the sandwiches.* = take without invitation
*I didn't **feel myself**.* = feel different from usual
Verbs which are usually done by an individual, for example *shave, wash,* etc., don't need a reflexive pronoun, unless we want to make a point of the ability:
I washed and dressed in five minutes.
*The twins are old enough to dress **themselves**.*
In English we do not generally use the verbs *concentrate, feel, hurry, lie* (*down*), *relax, sit* (*down*) with reflexive pronouns:
Rebecca didn't feel comfortable living in such a huge city. NOT ~~feel herself~~
I spent some time relaxing before the busy day ahead. NOT ~~relaxing myself~~
I concentrated on my work. NOT ~~concentrated myself~~

▶ 4.14 Reciprocal pronouns
We use *each other* and *one another* with plural subjects:
*We always speak to **each other** with the utmost respect.*
One another is more formal than *each other*:
*We chatted to **each other**.*
*They greeted **one another** before addressing the room.*
Compare reflexive and reciprocal pronouns:
*Mr and Mrs Smith bought **themselves** a car.* (one car for them both)
*Mr and Mrs Smith bought **each other** a present.* (two presents, one each)
*We smiled at **each other** and said hello.*
*We smiled to **ourselves** but gave no sign of any emotion.*
We use the possessives *each other's* and *one another's*:
*They were friends and regular visitors at **each other's** houses.*
*The purpose of this session is to listen to **one another's** problems sympathetically.*

---

a Match a and b in each pair with the best endings.

1 a ☐ We looked at ourselves   1 and smiled.
   b ☐ We looked at each other   2 in the mirror.

2 a ☐ They usually behave themselves   1 when the teacher's around.
   b ☐ They usually behave   2 better when the teacher's around.

3 a ☐ Mike helped him   1 to clean up the room.
   b ☐ Mike helped himself   2 to a slice of cake.

4 a ☐ He looked really upset so I sat down   1 beside himself.
   b ☐ He looked really upset. He was   2 beside him.

5 a ☐ They found themselves   1 after searching for hours.
   b ☐ They finally found each other   2 in a very awkward situation.

6 a ☐ The three medalists shook hands to   1 congratulate themselves on their success.
   b ☐ Atlético Madrid can   2 congratulate each other on their success.

b Choose the correct option.

1 I think we'll treat *us / ourselves* to a nice box of chocolates.
2 *John himself / Himself* would never have thought of that.
3 Laura only thinks of *her / herself*. She's so selfish.
4 'Can I borrow a pen?' 'Sorry, I haven't got one *myself / itself*.'
5 You don't need to help. I can do the puzzle *itself / myself*.
6 Dom can't imagine *him / himself* in a different job.
7 They kissed *one another / themselves* and said goodbye.
8 The students checked *each other's / each others'* answers.

c Add the missing reflexive and reciprocal pronouns.

Have you ever thought to ask ^yourself^ whether you would like to live in space? As the world population grows, towns and cities find under tremendous pressure and it is becoming more difficult and expensive for us just to live in urban areas let alone enjoy there. So maybe we would feel more comfortable in space? But, let's just remind of the challenges of doing such a thing. The technology may be there but we would be opening up to lots of problems we can't even imagine. Unfortunately, there are no easy solutions. The world needs to sort out and we need to learn to live with. I hope I've made clear.

d ▶ Now go back to p.106

9B Ellipsis and substitution

We can avoid repeating our own or other people's ideas using ellipsis (leaving out words and phrases) and substitution (replacing words and phrases).

▶ 4.21 Leaving out subjects, main verbs and auxiliaries

We can leave out repeated subjects, main verbs and auxiliaries after *and / or / but / then* when the subject is the same:
The council have spent a lot of money but (they have) *changed nothing.*
The architect designed an iconic office block, then (the architect designed) *a bridge.*
We usually can't leave out subjects and auxiliaries in clauses joined with words like *although / because / before / if / when*, etc.:
You can't comment because you have no appreciation of art.
NOT ~~because have~~
I changed my mind when I saw the building. NOT ~~when saw~~

▶ 4.22 Leaving out verb phrases

We can leave out repeated verb phrases and use an auxiliary or modal instead. The auxiliary or modal may change in the second verb:
*The council promised to **build a new playground** but they never **did**.*
*Graham said he would **show you how to do it** and he **will**.*
We shorten the infinitive to *to* but don't leave it out completely:
I needed to go shopping but the kids didn't want to (go shopping).
NOT ~~didn't want~~
I haven't seen the exhibition but I ought to (see it). NOT ~~ought~~

▶ 4.23 Other examples of ellipsis

We can leave out adjectives and repeat *be*:
*I'm quite comfortable here. **Are** you* (quite comfortable)?
*The first room **was** lovely but the second **wasn't*** (lovely).
We can leave out noun phrases after determiners and superlatives:
*This is **my** favourite picture and that's **my husband's*** (favourite picture).
There were a few flats in my price range and I chose the cheapest (flat in my price range).
We can leave out verbs and nouns repeated in comparative structures:
They built the first floor quicker than (they built) *the second* (floor).
The Park is the most expensive hotel and The Seaview (is) *the second* (most expensive hotel).

▶ 4.24 so / neither / nor

We use *so / neither* to avoid repeating exactly the same idea for a new subject:
*The old town is amazing and **so** are the views.* = the views are also amazing
*If Gerald won't like it, **neither/nor** will his wife.* = his wife also won't like it
nor can also mean *and not*:
*She doesn't want to live in the country **nor** in the town.* = and she doesn't want to live in the town

▶ 4.25 so and not

We can use *so* and *not* instead of clauses after verbs like *believe, guess, imagine, be afraid, appear, assume, seem, hope, presume, suspect* and *say*:
*We don't know if the diamond is real but we believe **so**.*
*I suspect **not** but I'm not sure, so ask someone else.*
We use a negative verb + *so* with verbs like *believe, expect, imagine* and *think*:
*I thought it would be a good game but I don't imagine **so** now.*
We can use *if not* and *if so* instead of clauses:
*I hope you finish that report. **If not**, give it to me anyway.*
*Some of you look confused. **If so**, see me after and I'll explain again.*

▶ 4.26 Pronouns

We can use pronouns like *one* and *ones* to substitute noun phrases:
*There are ten different colours to choose from. Which **ones** do you want?*
We can use *that* instead of a phrase or clause:
*Don't interrupt me! I hate **that**.*
We can use possessive pronouns, *yours, mine,* etc., to substitute noun phrases:
*You've got a decent view but **mine** is terrible.*
*You know my views on private education so tell me **yours**.*

---

a Cross out the words that can be left out of each sentence with no change of meaning.

1 The president arrived and he made a speech.
2 You don't know and you never will know.
3 I will tell you because I value and I respect your opinion.
4 We have been thinking about our reputation, we have not been thinking about money.
5 I said I would be volunteering so I will be volunteering.
6 If they are hungry, bears can be dangerous and they can be unpredictable.
7 My first impression was very positive but my second wasn't very positive.
8 We can meet up at seven if you'd like to meet up tonight.
9 'Are we in room six?' 'I guess we are not in room six.'
10 The Amazon is the longest river in the world and the Nile is the second longest river in the world.

b Shorten the sentences using substitution.

1 My exam was a lot tougher than ~~your exam~~. *yours*
2 'Is this the right page?' 'I think it is the right page.'
3 'I don't know where we are.' 'I don't know where we are either.'
4 I love holidays abroad, especially long holidays abroad.
5 'Who's got a dress with short sleeves?' 'Borrow my dress with short sleeves.'
6 'Did you get my message?' 'I'm afraid we didn't get it.'
7 'George has got married.' 'I didn't know George had got married.'
8 Klaus is very enthusiastic and his sister is very enthusiastic too.
9 Tina had always wanted to go parachuting and one day she went parachuting.

c Use ellipsis and substitution to shorten the dialogue and make it more natural.

Damien I've been thinking about the office of the future.
Rachel What do you mean by ~~the office of the future~~? *that*
D The place where we are going to work and where we are going to do business, say, fifty years from now. Those offices will look completely different compared to the offices today.
R I expect they will look completely different.
D For example, imagine there are no walls and there are no doors. All barriers to communication will be broken down and all barriers to communication will be a thing of the past. This is hard to imagine but you don't need to imagine it. Just go to any successful company today.
R I think successful companies today have walls and have doors.
D You are being sarcastic and you are trying to make fun of me.
R Sorry, I didn't mean to make fun of you. I'd like to travel in time and I'd like to visit an office of the future. Tell me when you have built an office of the future.

d ▶ **Communication 9B** Work in pairs. Student A go to p.131. Student B go to p.135.

10A Regret and criticism structures

▶ 4.43 Conditionals

We can use unreal conditionals for (self-)criticism and regret. Using hypothetical forms to provide critical suggestions can soften your suggestions:

You**'d get** a better response **if** you **toned** down your language.
I **wouldn't have come if** you**'d told** me you weren't interested.
If you**'d been watching properly**, you**'d be able to do** it!
If I**'d realised** my boss was going to be there, I **would never have said** that.
If you **told** a few jokes, the audience **might listen**.

▶ 4.44 Modals

We use modal + *have* + past participle for (self-)criticism and regret:

could	I **could have timed** my talk better.	= It was desirable but didn't happen.
might	You **might have told** me he was going to be in the audience.	
needn't	Terry never said thank you so I guess I **needn't have bothered**.	= It was an unnecessary effort.
should	You **should have asked** me first.	= It was the right thing to do, but it didn't happen.
ought to	We **ought to have checked** the equipment.	
shouldn't	He **shouldn't have taken** the car.	= It was the wrong thing to do, but it happened.
ought not to	The audience **ought not to have kept interrupting** the speaker.	

> **Tip** We can use *must* for criticism but not *must have*:
> You **must** listen more carefully in future!
> You should have listened more carefully. NOT ~~must have listened~~
> You shouldn't have shows you are grateful for something:
> Wow, flowers! **You shouldn't have**.

▶ 4.45 would like / love / hate / rather

We use *would like / love / prefer* + perfect infinitive to talk about regrets:
I **would love to have spent** more time with you.
We can use *would hate / not like* + perfect infinitive to sympathise:
I **would hate to have seen** something like that.
We use *would (much) rather* with an infinitive or past tense:
I **would much rather** see my usual doctor **than** one I don't know.
I **would rather** you **didn't do** that in future.

▶ 4.46 wish and if only

We use *wish* + past simple for things that we want to change now or in the future:
I **wish** I **looked** like Jennifer Lawrence.
My dad **wishes** he **could** speak Spanish.
We use *wish* + past perfect for regrets:
I **wish** I **had met** you ten years ago.
We use *wish* + person + *would* for criticism:
I **wish** you **would** switch off that mobile phone!
We use *if only* as a stronger form of *wish*:
If only Trevor **were** more understanding!

▶ 4.47 It's time

We can use *it's (about / high) time* + past tense for criticism:
It's time you got a proper job.
It's about time they came to repair the washing machine.
It's high time she came to her senses and realised nobody is perfect!

---

a Match the sentence halves in each pair.

1 a ☐ We could have got home   1 provided the trains are running.
   b ☐ We could get home   2 if the trains had still been running.

2 a ☐ I think if I had been in your shoes   1 I'd forget all about it.
   b ☐ If I were you   2 I would have forgotten all about it by now.

3 a ☐ You couldn't   1 have done a worse job.
   b ☐ You needn't   2 have reminded me.

4 a ☐ I wish you would listen to me,   1 I've got something important to tell you.
   b ☐ I wish you had listened to me,   2 things might have turned out better.

Anyway, it's time I came to my conclusions.

b Choose the correct option.

1 Julie *couldn't* / *may not* have done it if I hadn't helped her.
2 If you *hadn't dropped* / *didn't drop* the ball, we would have won the game.
3 Staff *ought not to* / *needn't* complain in front of the customers.
4 I *could* / *would* prefer not to have been involved.
5 Jill *should be waiting* / *should have waited* until I got out.
6 You *might* / *should* have passed if you'd revised harder.
7 I'd much rather *hear* / *have heard* the news from you but it's too late now.
8 We *hope* / *wish* you would reconsider.
9 Oh, I wish I *can* / *could* be there with you next weekend.
10 This bedroom is a mess! It's time you *clean* / *cleaned* it up.

c Complete each gap with one word.

Michelle Hi, so how did the driving test go?
Ben It was a nightmare! I wish I ¹ *could* start all over again. If I ² _____ known it would be that bad, I would have stayed in bed.
M What went wrong?
B What went right? I'd ³ _____ not talk about it.
M Oh, go on. What did the examiner say?
B Oh, the usual stuff – 'You ⁴ _____ to have used your mirrors more, you ⁵ _____ n't have stopped so quickly. If I ⁶ _____ you, I'd slow down now …' Do you get the idea?
M Well, I suppose you ⁷ _____ have had more lessons.
B If ⁸ _____ I had had the time, and the money.
M Maybe it's ⁹ _____ you realised how important it is for you to get a driving licence.
B Oh no, now you're criticising me!

d ▶ Now go back to p.118

10B Passive reporting verbs

We use passive reporting verbs when we are generalising about what most people say or think:

*The colour white **is known** to represent purity in many cultures.*

We also use passive reporting verbs to report information from other sources. They are most common in …

- academic writing where we want to appear objective:

*It **has been shown** (Smith, 2012) that superstition influences behaviour.*

- news, either to keep the source secret or because the source is unimportant:

*It **is being reported** that the suspect escaped in a car.*

It + passive + *that* clause

We can use *it* + passive reporting verb + *that* clause with verbs like *know*, *believe*, *say*, *report*, etc.:

***It is** widely **known that** the middle of the month was unlucky for the Romans.*

*In ancient times, **it was believed that** the Sun went round the Earth.*

Subject + passive + *to* + infinitive

We can use passive + *to* + infinitive with verbs like *understand* and *think*:

*He **is understood** to be furious.*

*It **is thought to be** good luck to catch falling leaves in the autumn.*

We can follow this structure with perfect infinitives to refer to the past, or continuous infinitives for the present and future:

*She**'s said to have met** him on set.*

*He**'s reported to be working** with DeNiro again.*

It + passive + *wh-* clause

We use passive reporting verbs + clauses beginning with *wh-* words for unknown facts:

***It is not known what** was said in the meeting.*

***It was not made clear whether** or not they would be challenging the decision.*

The *wh-* clause can go first in the sentence:

***What was said** in the meeting is not known.*

▶ **4.53** **Both structures:** *acknowledge   agree   allege   assume   believe   claim   expect   know   report   reveal   suspect   rumour   say   show   think   understand*

*It **is alleged that** five men in masks carried out the attack.*
*The ship **isn't expected to be arriving** any time soon.*
*She **is reported to have made** over ten million dollars.*
*It **is said that** K2 is harder to climb than Everest.*
*The story **has been shown to be** a complete lie.*
*Latin **is thought to have been** the first international language.*

It + passive + *that* clause only: *announce   argue   imply   note   explain   suggest*

*It was **announced** that changes would be made. NOT ~~were announced to be made~~*
*It is **argued** that Cleopatra was one of the most influential women in history.*
*In the report it is **implied** that corruption was involved.*
*It should **be noted** that he gave half of his winnings to charity.*
*It was **explained** that the mysterious marks were, in fact, animal tracks.*
*It has not been **suggested** that any jobs will be affected.*

Subject + passive + *to* + infinitive only: *consider   repute*

*Brian was **considered** to be one of their best players. NOT ~~It is considered that Brian …~~*
*They are **reputed** to have made millions from the sale of their company.*

Subject + passive + *as* + adjective / noun phrase: *regarded*   seen**

*Serena Williams **is regarded as** one of the greatest ever tennis players. NOT ~~It is regarded that Serena~~*
*Sending cards on special occasions **may be seen as** old-fashioned by some.*

* regarded / seen + to be is possible but far less common.

*Walking under a ladder **is believed to be** unlucky!*

a Choose the correct option.

1 An old manuscript is said *to have / that it has* been found by a couple moving house.

2 *It / The news* is believed that it happened many years earlier.

3 In the letter it was implied *that Sam / Sam to have* released the data unknowingly.

4 Detectives *were revealed / revealed* that they still had no clues to work on.

5 Once she *was regarded / regarded* as one of the best painters of her generation.

6 It is to be expected *mistakes to be made / that mistakes will be made.*

7 Television has *been shown to / showed that* influence public opinion.

b Correct the mistakes in the sentences.

1 It ̭argued that Vancouver is the most diverse city in the world. *(is)*

2 He is said that he lived in a cave.

3 It is seen that basketball is very popular in Asia.

4 It was not reported her reply was.

5 It is suspected to the people responsible have left the country.

6 The winters are thought that they get very cold in this part of the world.

c Complete the text with the past participle of a verb in the box.

consider   expect   explain   imply   know   not understand   see   ~~think~~

There is significant cultural variation today but it is [1] ___thought___ that one of the most common, yet oldest, customs is shaking hands. From vases and other archaeological evidence, the ancient Greeks are [2] _____ to have shaken hands and the custom was [3] _____ as a sign of respect and affection. In fact, the handshake is [4] _____ to be a form of ritual because it is done in so many contexts with great attention to detail. For example, in Eastern Europe it is [5] _____ that a man's, but not a woman's, hand will be shaken every time you meet. In China, by holding on to someone's hand for a short time after a handshake it is [6] _____ that you are showing extra respect. It is [7] _____ how the custom originated but in some books it is [8] _____ that by offering your hand without a weapon you come in peace.

d ▶ Now go back to p.121

Vocabulary Focus

1A Language learning
Verb phrases

a ▶1.6 Complete the expressions in **bold** with the words in the box. Listen and check.

ear	acquire /əˈkwaɪə/	rusty	brushed
pick	struggle /ˈstrʌɡəl/	keep	
get	accustomed /əˈkʌstəmd/	hold	
practice	immersed /ɪˈmɜːst/	attain /əˈteɪn/	

1 Some learners appear to be able to _____ **language** without much formal study.
2 I really _____ **with** English idioms. I can never remember them.
3 I'm not sure if I'll ever _____ **a** native speaker **level** of competence, but I'm not sure I really need to.
4 When he went to live in Korea, he quickly **got** _____ **to** the sound of the language.
5 I have _____ **up my** Arabic because I'm going to Riyadh next week.
6 Penny's lucky – she **has an** _____ **for** languages. She learns them much more easily than me.
7 After about a year, he found he could _____ **a conversation** in Italian without too much effort.
8 Unless I **put** a new piece of language **into** _____ immediately, I find I forget it.
9 People tend to give up on second language learning too easily. You need to _____ **at it** if you want to succeed.
10 She spent six weeks in Poland and really _____ herself **in** the language and culture.
11 It's easy to _____ **up phrases** like 'hello' and 'excuse me' wherever you are in the world.
12 The sounds of Finnish are quite unique, so I found it difficult to _____ **to grips with** the pronunciation.
13 I need to practise my speaking now I'm back. I'm sure I'm _____.

b Cover **a** and match the verbs 1–6 with the phrases a–f.

1 ☐ hold   a new ideas
2 ☐ grasp   b a level/degree of competence /ˈkɒmpɪtəns/
3 ☐ get   c a conversation
4 ☐ put   d accustomed to
5 ☐ acquire   e into practice
6 ☐ attain   f a new/second language

c ▶ Now go back to p.9

Noun forms

d Complete the table with the missing noun forms. Use a dictionary to help you if necessary.

	Adjective	Noun	Verb
1	interactive /ɪntəˈræktɪv/		interact
2	distracted /dɪˈstræktɪd/ distracting /dɪˈstræktɪŋ/		distract
3	dedicated /ˈdedɪkeɪtɪd/		dedicate
4	limited /ˈlɪmɪtɪd/		limit
5	motivated /ˈməʊtɪveɪtɪd/ motivating /ˈməʊtɪveɪtɪŋ/		motivate
6	necessary /ˈnesəseri/		necessitate
7	capable /ˈkeɪpəbl/		–
8	mental /ˈmentəl/		–
9	reluctant /rɪˈlʌktənt/		–
10	interfering /ɪntəˈfɪərɪŋ/		interfere
11	competent /ˈkɒmpɪtənt/		–
12	literate /ˈlɪtərət/		–
13	exposed /ɪkˈspəʊzd/		expose
14	–		acquire
15	insightful /ˈɪnsaɪtfəl/		–
16	prestigious /presˈtɪdʒəs/		–
17	disciplined /ˈdɪsəplɪnd/		discipline

e ▶1.9 **Pronunciation** Listen to the adjectives and nouns in the table in rows 3–8.

1 Which nouns have more syllables than their adjectives?
2 Notice the stressed syllables in the adjectives. Practise saying the words and <u>underline</u> the stressed syllables in the nouns. Listen again and check.
3 Notice that the stress sometimes changes in the noun. Choose the correct option to complete the rule.

In nouns with the suffixes -tion and -ity, the stressed syllable is always *the first syllable / the syllable before the suffix*.

> **Learning Tip** Organising your records of word families by suffix can make features such as sound and spelling relationships easier to remember.

f What other nouns do you know with the suffixes -tion and -ity? Make a list and practise saying the words.

g ▶ Now go back to p.10

2B Verbs of movement

They **soared** into the air. /sɔːd/

She **hurtled** down the slope. /'hɜːtəld/

They **zoomed** /zuːmd/ / **whizzed** /wɪzd/ along the road.

It **rolled** across the floor. /rəʊld/

He **plunged** into the water. /plʌndʒd/

They **whirled** around the room. /wɜːld/

It **whooshed** through the station. /wuːʃt/

a ▶ 1.36 Match the sentences 1–10 with the pictures h–q. Listen and check.

☐ 1 He **crawled** up the stairs. /krɔːld/
☐ 2 They **marched** through the square. /mɑːtʃt/
☐ 3 She **leaped** over the rocks. /liːpt/
☐ 4 It **drifted** out to sea. /'drɪftɪd/
☐ 5 He **crept** into the house. /krept/
☐ 6 He **limped** off the pitch. /lɪmpt/
☐ 7 He **staggered** across the field. /'stægəd/
☐ 8 We **slid** down the slope. /slɪd/
☐ 9 They **rushed** to catch the train. /rʌʃt/
☐ 10 They **strolled** through the park. /strəʊld/

b Which verbs of movement in pictures a–q mean … ?

1 to move slowly
2 to move quickly
3 to move quietly
4 to move with difficulty

c Which verbs in **bold** in **a** are irregular past forms? What's the infinitive form of each?

d In pairs, take turns to test each other on prepositions of movement, using the sentences for pictures a–q. (Don't use picture h.)

> He crawled _____ the stairs.

> Up!
> He crept _____ the house.

e Change the sentence *He/She/It* + (past simple verb of movement) *down the road.* so that it matches the situations below. More than one verb may be possible.

1 He was a soldier. *He marched down the road.*
2 She was exhausted.
3 He didn't want anyone to hear him.
4 She was late for an appointment.
5 His right leg was injured.
6 She wasn't in a hurry.
7 He was on a sledge.
8 It was a bird.
9 He was on a motorbike.
10 She was a ghost.
11 It was an insect.

f Write a few sentences about an experience you've had which involved moving fast. Compare what you have written with other students.

I went on an incredibly fast ride at a theme park. The Nemesis hurtles along a track with lots of twists and turns. You whirl through the air at such high speed that you hit zero gravity. I lost both my earrings!

g ▶ Now go back to p.25

3B Landscape features

a Read the extracts from the travel stories and match them with the photographs.

1 ☐ We made slow progress through the **mosquito-infested swamp**, knee-deep in mud. We avoided the **dark** ¹_____ **of stagnant water** and eventually reached the firmer ground beyond.

2 ☐ We visited **a remote village in the foothills**. In front of the cottage was a **rich green** ²_____ where cows grazed. In the distance, beyond **wooded** ³_____, the mountains rose up into the sky.

3 ☐ To the north lies **an untouched wilderness**. The **rocky** ⁴_____ is unsuitable for farming. **Empty** ⁵_____ stretches towards the distant mountains.

4 ☐ The **rugged coastline** is famous for its beauty. From where I stood, **sheer** ⁶_____ dropped to the sea and, looking down, I saw **the mouth of a** ⁷_____ in the **cliff** ⁸_____.

5 ☐ Never before had I been to such an **arid desert**. On our third day we came to some **huge sand** ⁹_____. We knew there was no way our 4x4 would be able to cross them.

6 ☐ We were deep in **the heart of the jungle** now. Quietly we moved through the **dense** ¹⁰_____. Looking up, I saw the **forest** ¹¹_____ far above my head and heard the cries of monkeys and birds.

7 ☐ The island can only be described as **a tropical paradise**. The sight of **pristine** ¹²_____ and **calm turquoise** ¹³_____ made us forget our long journey in an instant.

> **◖) Tip**
>
> *Swamp*, *bog* and *marsh* all describe types of muddy wetlands. Many native speakers do not know the difference between these.
> • In a marsh the main plant life is types of grasses.
> • In a swamp woody plants and trees can grow.
> • In a bog the soil is poor so there is less plant life.

b ▶ 1.56 Complete the collocations in **bold** in **a** with the nouns in the box. Listen and check.

---
dunes /dʒuːnz/   moorland /ˈmɔːlənd/
meadow /ˈmedəʊ/   undergrowth /ˈʌndəɡrəʊθ/
slopes /sləʊps/   canopy /ˈkænəpi/
pools   cliffs   waters   cave
face   ground   beaches
---

c 💬 Ask and answer the questions.

1 Which of the words and phrases in **a** and **b** could describe places in your country?

2 Which other types of environment have you visited in other countries?

3 What's your favourite and least favourite type of environment to be in?

d ▶ Now go back to p.36

4A Instinct and reason

a ▶**2.11** Listen to the sentences 1–10. Match the words and phrases in bold with their meaning.

1 I'm a very **rational** thinker.
2 **On impulse**, I married someone I'd only just met.
3 I know **subconsciously** when people are lying to me.
4 If I need to decide quickly, I always go with my **gut instinct**.
5 It's important to **weigh up** the pros and cons before taking action.
6 I **had a hunch** that I should resign, and I was right.
7 I'm successful in business because I think **logically.**
8 I'd always **think twice** before trusting a stranger.
9 I'll need time to **think it over** before I decide.
10 I love taking **spontaneous** decisions. They're more fun!

a an intuitive feeling ×2
b step by step, using reasons
c think carefully ×3
d without planning ×2
e without being aware
f based on facts, not emotions

b ▶**2.12** Pronunciation

1 Listen to the pronunciation of the letters in **bold** in these words. Which sound has more than one syllable?

1 /ʃəs/	**2** /iəs/	**3** /dʒəs/
cau**tious**	spontan**eous**	gor**geous**

2 ▶**2.13** Add these words to the correct column in the table in **b1**. Listen and check. Practise saying the words.

subcon**scious**   presti**gious**   hilar**ious**   coura**geous**   ambi**tious**
simultan**eous**   pre**cious**   curi**ous**   outra**geous**   conscien**tious**

c The words in **bold** below are about the mind and feelings. What is the difference between them? Use a dictionary to help you.

1 He's a very **reasonable / rational** person.
2 She's a very **sensitive / sensible** person.
3 He's very money-**conscious / conscientious**.
4 She's very **self-conscious / self-confident**.

d 💬 Which adjective in each pair in **c** do you think describes you better?

e ▶ Now go back to p.45

4B Memory

1 I only ever **have a v_____ memory of** my journey to work. I do it on auto-pilot.

2 I **have a p_____ memory of** my cat getting run over when I was a child.

3 Once the city was rebuilt, the storm became a d_____ memory for most people.

4 Their trip to Venice **was a l_____ memory**, full of magic.

5 I **have a v_____ memory** of our team winning the World Cup when I was a kid.

6 He **has a p_____ memory** and can paint places he hasn't seen since childhood.

a ▶**2.21** Complete the sentences with the correct adjectives. Listen and check.

b ▶**2.22** Match 1–7 with a–g to make complete sentences. Check the meaning of any expressions in **bold** that you don't know. Listen and check.

1 ☐ I **vaguely remember** seeing that film years ago,
2 ☐ If I think of my time in New York,
3 ☐ I told him you were coming today,
4 ☐ The smell of freshly baked bread always **triggers a memory** of
5 ☐ Before going into class, she reads the register
6 ☐ If you **cast your mind back** to the last meeting,
7 ☐ I'll always **treasure the memory** of

a but it must have **slipped his mind.** Sorry he's not here.
b the warm welcome they gave us. It was a very special occasion.
c but I've got no idea what the story of it is.
d staying with my grandmother in the school holidays.
e the first thing that **comes to mind** is a yellow taxi.
f you'll remember we agreed to increase the fee by £10.
g to **refresh her memory** of her students' names.

c ▶ Now go back to p.49

5A Crime and justice

a ▶ 2.37 Listen to the sentences. What is the difference between the legal terms in **bold**? Discuss the meanings with a partner.

1 a Thousands of pounds in cash were found on the premises, and a 35-year-old woman was **arrested on suspicion of** money laundering.

b When the missing money was noticed, they **made an allegation of** fraud against him.

2 a She is **being held in custody** while waiting for her trial.

b He's **been convicted of** murder and sent to prison.

3 a The defence **showed evidence in court** which supported the accused's alibi.

b She **gave testimony in court** that she had seen the accused running from the scene of the crime.

4 a He was given a lighter prison sentence because he **pleaded guilty to** the crime.

b Despite a strong defence case, he **was found guilty of** the crime.

Learning Tip

When you record new words and expressions in your vocabulary notebook, it is useful to make a note of others that have a similar but slightly different meaning. This can help avoid confusion when you want to use the new language.

b 💬 Look at the phrases in **bold** in **a**. In your country, who does each thing? Who do they do it to? Use the words in the box to help you.

judge /dʒʌdʒ/
jury /ˈdʒʊəri/
policeman /pəˈliːsmən/
criminal /ˈkrɪmɪnəl/
witness /ˈwɪtnəs/
victim /ˈvɪktɪm/
defence lawyer /dɪˈfens lɔɪə/
prosecution /prɒsɪˈkjuːʃən/
someone else

c ▶ 2.38 Listen to the sentences. Which of these forms of punishment and rehabilitation are possible in your country's legal system?

a He was **sentenced to life imprisonment**.

b He had to **do community service**.

c She **served a reduced sentence for good behaviour**.

d The judge insisted that she **serve the full ten years**.

e The company was **fined** a six-figure sum.

f He was **banned from driving**.

g They suggested he be **brought face-to-face with his victim**.

h All prisoners receive either **one-to-one** or **group counselling**.

i Prisoners with mental health issues **receive psychiatric help**.

j It is necessary to hold some prisoners **in solitary confinement**.

d 💬 Order the forms of punishment and rehabilitation in **c** from 1 (= least harsh) to 10 (= most harsh), in your opinion. Compare your order with a partner.

e 💬 Discuss which crimes or types of criminals might receive each form of punishment or rehabilitation in **c**.

> Prisoners who are a danger to other inmates might be held in solitary confinement.

f ▶ Now go back to p.58

6A Adjectives: Describing images

a ▶3.2 Complete the sentences below with the adjectives in the box. Listen and check.

playful /ˈpleɪfəl/	exotic /ɪɡˈzɒtɪk/
powerful /ˈpaʊəfəl/	iconic /aɪˈkɒnɪk/
humorous /ˈhjuːmərəs/	gritty /ˈɡrɪti/
raw /rɔː/	evocative /ɪˈvɒkətɪv/
meaningful /ˈmiːnɪŋfəl/	ironic /aɪˈrɒnɪk/
well-composed /welkəmˈpəʊzd/	
nonsensical /nɒnˈsensɪkəl/	

1 The strength of emotion in this close-up of her face seemed to almost hit me. It's a truly _____ image.

2 He appears to be lifting a car with one hand. It's just not possible – it's completely _____.

3 The kittens are loving that ball of wool! It's an extremely _____ photo.

4 The photographer has captured _____ scenes of inner-city poverty. It isn't pretty.

5 It's a very _____ photo. There's a perfect balance between the foreground and the sky and the land.

6 These photos make a more _____ statement about man's impact on the environment than words could.

7 This is the most gently _____ photo in his portfolio. The expression on the man's face really makes me smile.

8 For me, the most wonderfully _____ photo in the exhibition is the frozen desert. It's another world for me.

9 It's a very _____ image. You can't look at it without feeling something.

10 This photo was taken just after he lost the match. The _____ emotion is painful to look at.

11 The picture of Neil Armstrong stepping on to the moon in 1969 is truly _____.

12 The rather _____ expression on the woman's face seems to be saying *Oh, well, life's like that.*

b Notice the suffix in these adjectives:

* play**ful**
* power**ful**
* meaning**ful**

Underline more adjective suffixes in **a**. Which adjective doesn't have a suffix? Think of two more adjectives which have each suffix you underlined.

c ▶3.3 Match sentences 1–6 with a–f. Listen and check.

1 ☐ The angle of this photo shows off the iconic architecture of the new art gallery.

4 ☐ In this photo he's wearing an exotic costume with feathers and gold buttons.

2 ☐ In this powerful photo the house stands alone against its environment.

5 ☐ All the pictures in the exhibition are virtually the same.

3 ☐ I like this photo of the room with very little furniture in it.

6 ☐ You need the perfect flower and the perfect light

a It's not too **cluttered**. /ˈklʌtəd/
b It looks **sensational**. /senˈseɪʃənəl/
c It's quite a **bleak** image. /bliːk/
d It gets a bit **repetitive**. /rɪˈpetətɪv/
e to create an absolutely **flawless** image. /ˈflɔːləs/
f It all looks very **elaborate**. /ɪˈlæbərət/

> **Tip**
> Many adverbs of degree and adjectives form very strong collocations. For example, we say *utterly miserable* and *incredibly elaborate*, but ~~utterly elaborate~~ isn't a natural collocation. It's a good idea to note adverb + adjective collocations in your vocabulary notebook.

d Underline the adverb of degree + adjective collocations in the sentences in **a**.

e Which of the adverbs of degree in the box can be used with which adjectives in **bold** in **c**?

incredibly	pretty	a little	wonderfully
extremely	utterly	rather	truly

f ▶ **Communication 6A** Now go to p.132

7A Compound adjectives: Parts of the body

> **Tip**
> Compound adjectives are formed in many ways:
> - noun + adjective: **world-famous**, **self-confident**
> - adjective + noun + *-ed*: **short-sleeved**, **cold-blooded**
> - adjective + participle: **good-looking**, **long-running**
> - adverb + participle: **hard-working**, **well-written**
> - noun + participle: **heartbreaking**, **self-made**
>
> Unless they have become one word, e.g. *heartbreaking*, the forms listed here always require a hyphen (-) between the two parts.

> **Tip**
> Compound adjectives are usually well-established collocations. Many have idiomatic meanings. For example, if a person is **tongue-tied**, it does not mean that they have a physical problem. It means they find it difficult to speak because they are shy, nervous or embarrassed.
> We can't usually invent new compound adjectives:
> *The novel is* **heartbreaking** / **mind-blowing**. NOT ~~The novel is **heart-opening** / **mind-breaking**~~ etc.

a ▶ **3.18** Look at examples 1–4 then complete 5–9. Listen and check.

- **adjective + noun + *-ed***

  1 He considers other points of view – he has an open mind. ➜ He's **open-minded**.

  2 She will always help her friends – she has a warm heart. ➜ She's **warm-hearted**.

- **noun + present participle**

  3 Carrying boxes upstairs nearly broke my back. ➜ It was **backbreaking** work.

  4 The sight of elderly people in love always warms my heart. ➜ It's a **heartwarming** sight.

  5 She always uses her left hand. ➜ She's …

  6 Don't expect any sympathy – he's got a very hard heart. ➜ He's …

  7 She made the decision with a clear head. ➜ She's …

What we should do is …

  8 Thai food makes my mouth water. ➜ It's …

  9 The sight made my jaw drop. ➜ The sight was …

b ▶ **3.19** Match the words in the boxes to make compound adjectives which can replace the definitions in italics. Use some words more than once. Listen and check.

half short hair	sighted /saɪtɪd/	headed /hedɪd/
absent narrow	raising /reɪzɪŋ/	hearted /hɑːtɪd/
light mind	boggling /bɒglɪŋ/	minded /maɪndɪd/

1 Everyone in the village disapproves of my lifestyle. They're all so *unwilling to accept different ideas*.

2 He agreed to help us move the furniture, but it was very *lacking in enthusiasm*.

3 He may forget to phone you. He's rather *likely to forget things because he's thinking about something else*.

4 Can you tell me what that sign says? I'm afraid I'm *unable to see distant things clearly*.

5 After eating nothing for ten hours, I began to feel a bit *as if I might lose my balance*.

6 I'm fed up with serious films. I'd like to see something more *happy and not too serious*.

7 The brakes on the bus weren't working properly so it was a *terrifying* journey.

8 Did you know there are 100 billion stars just in our own galaxy? It's *almost impossible to imagine*.

c ▶ **3.20** **Pronunciation**

1 Listen to the two pairs of compound adjectives. <u>Underline</u> the main stress. Is it on the first or the second word?

   mind-boggling   open-minded
   heartwarming   short-sighted

2 <u>Underline</u> the main stress in these patterns. Practise saying the compound adjectives in **a**.

   - adjective + body part + *-ed*
   - body part + present participle

d 💬 Find someone in the class who:

1 is left-handed
2 ate something mouth-watering yesterday
3 has done a back-breaking job at some time in their life
4 thinks they're open-minded
5 thinks they're absent-minded
6 has been on a hair-raising journey
7 knows a mind-boggling fact
8 has never felt tongue-tied.

e ▶ Now go back to p.81

8B Ageing and health

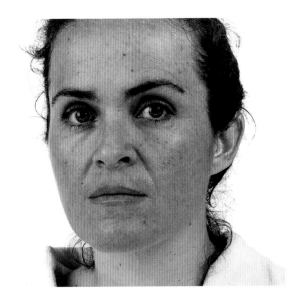

a ▶3.51 Listen to the words and phrases in the box.

| a glowing complexion   smooth skin   saggy skin |
| oily skin   dry skin   wrinkles / fine lines   freckles |
| a rash   blotches   spots/acne   firm skin   clear skin |

Which words in the box are usually associated with … ?

- youthful skin
- mature skin
- all ages

b Complete the collocations in **bold** with as many words and phrases as possible from the box in **a**. Compare your ideas with a partner. Are they the same?

1 Sunbathing can **cause** …
2 If you have an allergic reaction, your skin might **come out in** …
3 **Anti-ageing creams** are designed to **prevent** …
4 Young people are often **prone to** …
5 Most people hate it when they start **getting** …
6 A **facial** can be helpful if you **have** …
7 If you want to be a model, it helps to **have** …

c ▶3.52 Match 1–9 with a–i. Listen and check.

1 ☐ He was **showing his age**.
2 ☐ Her **eyesight is deteriorating** and
3 ☐ **Yellowing teeth**?
4 ☐ **Moisturising** daily combined with **weekly facials**
5 ☐ **Tooth loss** and **heart trouble** are
6 ☐ **Strengthening** and **toning** exercises
7 ☐ **Poor circulation** can be improved by
8 ☐ **Weight loss** can be aided by
9 ☐ There's no need to resort to painful **injections**

a Try our new **whitening** toothpaste. You'll be amazed.
b **regular cardiovascular exercise**.
c **eating a varied and balanced diet**.
d helps to **tighten** and **plump** the skin.
e His **hair was thinning** and **greying** around the temples.
f like yoga and Pilates help to give you energy.
g or **plastic surgery**.
h not inevitable parts of ageing.
i she**'s got arthritis** in her knees.

d Look at the words and phrases in **bold** in **c**. Complete the table.

Anti-ageing treatments/effects	
Superficial effects of ageing	
Health problems caused by ageing	
Healthy living	

e 💬 Answer the questions about the things in **d**.

1 What anti-ageing techniques do you think are reasonable steps to take to stop the ageing process?
2 Do you think that any of the superficial effects of ageing can be prevented/cured?
3 Which health problems caused by ageing have affected people you know? What happened?
4 Which healthy living technique is most important? Can you add any more to the table?

f ▶ Now go back to p.96

9B Describing buildings

a ▶4.19 Complete the sentences with the adjectives in the box. Listen and check.

imposing /ɪmˈpəʊzɪŋ/   nondescript /ˈnɒndɪskrɪpt/   graceful /ˈɡreɪsfəl/
innovative /ˈɪnəvətɪv/   tasteless /ˈteɪstləs/   over the top /əʊvə ðə ˈtɒp/
out of place /aʊt əv ˈpleɪs/   stunning /ˈstʌnɪŋ/   dated /ˈdeɪtɪd/

1 The council favoured an original design by a young architect because they wanted a striking and _____ town hall to bring a modern edge to their city.
2 As the town is fairly small, the large castle on the hill is really too _____ and seems _____.
3 I'm sorry, but there's nothing remarkable or new about the design of those houses – they're totally _____ and pretty _____.
4 I really like the gold leaf in the ceiling decorations, but for some people it's _____ and _____.
5 The _____, elegant lines of the building are very pleasing to the eye. It's _____.

b ▶4.20 Match the words 1–12 with the pictures below. Listen and check.

1 ☐ cabin /ˈkæbɪn/
2 ☐ skyscraper /ˈskaɪskreɪpə/
3 ☐ power station /ˈpaʊə steɪʃən/
4 ☐ housing estate /ˈhaʊzɪŋ ɪsteɪt/
5 ☐ warehouse /ˈweəhaʊs/
6 ☐ tower block /ˈtaʊə blɒk/
7 ☐ penthouse /ˈpenthaʊs/
8 ☐ studio /ˈstjuːdiəʊ/
9 ☐ bungalow /ˈbʌŋɡələʊ/
10 ☐ semi-detached /semidɪˈtætʃt/
11 ☐ mansion /ˈmænʃən/
12 ☐ retail park /ˈriːteɪl pɑːk/

c Put the words in **b** in these groups.

1 places that can be homes
2 places that are businesses
3 places that can be both

d 💬 Discuss the questions.

1 Which residential buildings are common in your country? Which are less common?
2 If you had a lot of money, would you live in a mansion, a penthouse, or neither? Why?
3 If you had to live in a small space, would you prefer a cabin or a studio? Why?

e ▶ Now go back to p.107

10A Communication verbs

a ▶ **4.39** Complete the sentences with the verbs in the box. Listen and check.

> address /əˈdres/   presented /prɪˈzentɪd/
> demonstrated /ˈdemənstreɪtɪd/   made
> go into   move on to   illustrate /ˈɪləstreɪt/

1 She _____ **her understanding** of complex social issues by explaining them in everyday language.
2 I've been invited to _____ **an audience** of business experts at a conference in London.
3 If you sense the audience is getting bored, you should _____ **a new subject** to keep their interest up.
4 Every time she got the wrong slide, she _____ **comments under her breath** that I couldn't hear.
5 She _____ **key information** in easy-to-read tables.
6 It really helps if you can _____ **the points** you want to make with specific examples.
7 Don't _____ **too much detail** during your presentation – people can only process so much new information.

b Match the phrases in **bold** in 1–8 with the definitions a–h.

1 ☐ She began by **paying tribute to** all the teachers who had inspired her throughout her school years.
2 ☐ During the speech, he **asserted** his right to express his opinion even if it wasn't a popular one.
3 ☐ He **backed up** the arguments he made by providing examples from recent research.
4 ☐ She **summarised** the key ideas in her presentation with a list of bullet points.
5 ☐ He saw his speech as an opportunity to **voice concerns about** the rise in crime in his neighbourhood.
6 ☐ The leader of the opposition **attacked** government policies in a speech that focused on the rise in unemployment.
7 ☐ In her presentation, she **sold the idea** of more flexible working hours to her managers.
8 ☐ She **concluded** by encouraging more people to try one of their free community education courses.

a to criticise a person or people strongly
b to say the most important facts in a short and clear way
c to publicly praise somebody in front of an audience
d to end a speech or presentation
e to persuade a person or people that something is a good plan
f to publicly say what you think about worrying issues
g to prove that something is true
h to make a statement strongly

c 💬 Think of people you know or in the media who do / have done the things below. Tell a partner about what happened.

1 attack government policy
2 have paid tribute to another person
3 often go into too much detail
4 sometimes make comments under their breath
5 often voice concerns about something
6 sell their ideas well

d 💬 Discuss the questions.

1 Have you ever addressed an audience of more than 100 people? If so, how did it feel? If not, how would you feel doing this?
2 If you were giving a presentation, what could you use to illustrate the finer points of a topic to other people?
3 Do you ever make throwaway remarks? If so, do other people take them seriously? If not, why don't you do this?
4 Who's an influential person from your past that you would feel comfortable paying tribute to? What would you say about them?
5 What do you think is a good way to back up your opinion on something?

e ▶ Now go back to p.116

10B Superstitions, customs and beliefs

a ▶ **4.49** Complete the sentences with the words and phrases in the box. Listen and check.

> make a wish   traditionally   customary   good fortune
> good luck charm   ward off evil

1 She wore a _____ around her neck until the day she died, at the ripe old age of 104.
2 I had the _____ to invest at exactly the right time and made millions.
3 The cautionary tales are _____ told by each generation of parents, to teach their children morality.
4 It is _____ to decorate the house with branches from pine trees at this time of year.
5 They sprinkle the beans and then sweep every room to banish demons and _____ .
6 Children _____ and try to blow out the candles. It will come true if they manage to blow them all out.

b ▶ **4.50** The words in the box are all used for talking about beliefs. Tick (✓) the ones you think you know. Try saying the words. Then listen and check.

> gullible /ˈɡʌləbəl/   convinced /kənˈvɪnst/
> plausible /ˈplɔːzəbəl/   convincing /kənˈvɪnsɪŋ/
> persuasive /pəˈsweɪsɪv/   far-fetched /fɑːˈfetʃt/
> dubious /ˈdjuːbiəs/

c Use the words in **b** to replace the definitions below in italics. Use a dictionary to help you. There may be more than one possible answer. Which words are very similar in meaning?

1 My friend says a fortune teller's advice led him to success, but I don't find this very *easy to believe*.
2 People who believe in good luck charms must be very *ready to believe anything people tell them*.
3 When she talks about magic, I'm sure what she says is true. She's very *able to make other people believe her*.
4 The idea that horseshoes bring you luck doesn't seem very *likely to be true* to me.
5 I think most things that fortune tellers say are *unlikely to be true*, to say the least.
6 My grandmother was absolutely *certain in her belief* that black cats were unlucky.
7 People's stories about seeing ghosts usually sound rather *difficult to believe* to me.

d Discuss the questions.

1 Which of the beliefs in the pictures 1–3 do you find … ?
   • convincing   • plausible   • dubious   • far-fetched
2 As a child, how gullible were you? Can you think of an example?
3 Who do you know (personally or someone well-known) who you'd describe as a persuasive person?
4 'People who are convinced they're right are usually wrong.' How true do you think this is?

e ▶ Now go back to p.119

1 There are sometimes ghosts in old houses.

2 Some people can read your fortune.

3 Some numbers are unlucky.

Writing Focus

1D Expressing opinions

Disagreement	Agreement
That's nonsense. That simply isn't true. There's no way … You're missing the point. That's easy to say, but … How can you possibly think that? That's a load of rubbish. That doesn't make sense.	You're spot on … That makes a lot of sense. You've hit the nail on the head. I would go along with that.
Uncertainty	**Partial agreement/disagreement**
I'm in two minds about this/that. I've got mixed feelings about this/that.	You've got a point, but … On the other hand, I do feel … It's true that … but … I agree up to a point …

a Cover the table. Read Eva's post and then complete the replies (1–6). Check your answers in the table.

b Which of the replies include words or phrases which soften the opinion? What words or phrases could you add to soften the other opinions?

c 💬 Which opinion do you agree with (a) most (b) least? Why?

d ▶ Now go back to p.17

EVA

The trouble with English is it's such a complicated, difficult language and it doesn't have any rules. I think they should create a simpler form of English which could be used internationally and would be easier to learn. It should definitely have simpler grammar, maybe just three tenses. And a more sensible spelling system!

Or they should choose an easier language to be the international language, like Spanish, say. Half the world speaks Spanish already. Or how about Swahili or Malaysian? They've both got nice simple grammar.

① How **can you** _____ that? You're completely **missing** _____. English is a beautiful, rich language, and that's exactly why people want to learn it.

② Well, **that's easy** _____, but you can't just 'create' a language. People speak the languages they choose to. And you say 'half the world speaks Spanish'. Well, **that simply** _____ – 400 million people isn't half the world!

③ I must say I think **you're** _____ about the difficult spelling. I had to learn English in school, so **I'd definitely** _____ **with that!** But **I've got** _____ **about** simplifying the grammar – it would make it easier to learn, but I don't think you can express complex ideas using just three tenses.

④ I'm sorry, but **that's** _____. Of course English has rules – all languages do.

⑤ What you're saying **doesn't really** _____. Why would you need to 'create' a global language? No one has to speak English, so if people speak it, obviously it means they want to and they find it useful.

⑥ Good comment – I think **you've hit the nail** _____. Spanish would make a much better world language. It's a beautiful language and it's easy to learn. I say go for it! (My mother tongue is Spanish, by the way! 😊)

2D Linking: contrast and concession

Offering alternatives	Comparing	Conceding
however *on the other hand* *alternatively*	*however* *on the other hand* *by comparison* *although* *unlike* *in contrast to* *when compared to*	*however* *nevertheless* *regardless (of)* *although* *even though* *for all that* *in spite of* *despite*
Opposing		
on the contrary		

a Complete the sentences below with the linkers in the box.

> however   when compared to   on the contrary
> regardless of   by comparison   even though

1 _____ the effort that has been put into planning the programme, attendance at activities has been disappointingly low.
2 I would recommend booking a table at a local restaurant. _____, if we are concerned about the budget, we could organise a pot luck dinner where everyone brings something to eat.
3 The social evening at the cinema was incredibly popular. _____, the turnout for the student party was extremely low.
4 _____ we used high-end caterers for the student dinner, the food was bland and overcooked.

5 Most students clearly indicated that the picnic in the park was not boring at all. _____, they said it was the activity where they had had the most fun.
6 Our social programme includes at least one activity per week. _____ programmes at other institutions, it is very full and extremely varied.

b Which other linkers from the table are possible in each gap?

c Rewrite these sentences, using the linker in brackets.

1 Even though the class was large, it was still possible to get individual attention. (despite)
2 The teacher we had was very strict. By comparison, my old teacher was very easy-going. (unlike)
3 I was very disappointed with the lunches. However, the evening meals were great. (although)
4 In spite of it raining every single day, I enjoyed everything that we did. (for all that)
5 In spite of several injuries, spirits were high among the groups. (nevertheless)

d Complete the examples with your own ideas.

1 Most students say that the social programme is an important part of their year at the university. On the other hand, …
2 Regardless of their heavy study commitments, students …
3 Feedback has generally been positive. Nevertheless, …

e ▶ Now go back to p.29

3D Writing briefly

a Read the description of a visit to Prague Castle. Where might you find this style of writing? Why?

1 an informal tourist review written for a website
2 an official review written in a travel guide
3 a travel blog diary written for yourself and your friends

> **Reviewer**
> 5 reviews
> 2 helpful votes
>
> ~~We~~ Walked up to Prague Castle in the afternoon. ~~There were~~ Lots of narrow windy streets, ~~and there was a~~ great view from the top ~~and so we~~. Took hundreds of photos! ~~Prague is a f~~Fabulous city, ~~and we're~~ definitely planning to come back next year.

b Which words have been left out?

- [ ] unimportant or repeated words that are clear from the context
- [ ] important items of information
- [ ] linking words

View from Prague Castle

4D Showing time relationships

= immediately	The moment … The instant … No sooner had … than …
= a short time later	Before long, … … was closely followed by … Subsequently, … Shortly after …
= a long time later, or longer than expected	It wasn't until … that … It was only … that … Not until … (did) … In time …

a Change these sentences, beginning with the words in brackets.

1 I saw her paintings. I immediately knew she would be a famous artist. (The moment)
2 He graduated and then he got a highly paid job in the City of London. (Shortly after)
3 As soon as I started asking questions, she got up and left the room. (No sooner)
4 We were both made redundant and then we decided to form a business partnership. (It wasn't)
5 Years later I decided to take up horse riding again. (It was only)

b Join these ideas in any suitable way, using time expressions.

1 We met – we fell in love.
2 I got home – I realised that I'd had my wallet stolen.
3 I arrived in New York – I began to feel at home there.
4 We went into business together – I discovered that he had a secret life.
5 She started training for super-marathons – she developed a pain in her knee.

c Compare your sentences in **b** with other students. Are your sentences similar or different in meaning?

d Write two or three sentences about each of these events, using expressions to show the time relationship.

1 two events in your life that happened
2 an event that happened a short time after another earlier one
3 an event that happened a long time after another earlier one

No sooner had I turned 17 than my dad bought me an old van to fix up. I didn't know how to do anything mechanical, but before long, I had treated the rust and painted the bodywork.

e Show your sentences to your partner and answer any further questions about the events.

f ▶ Now go back to p.53

---

c What words have been left out to make these reviews shorter?

1 Not much to do here in the evenings, and food in most places overpriced. Quite a disappointing place to visit.
2 Been to most resorts in Mexico but nowhere as impressive as Tulum.
3 Best time visit: late autumn, no tourists, great weather.
4 Went to Budapest last year. Much more interesting and more reasonable prices.

d How could you reduce these sentences for an online review?

1 It would be a great place for a honeymoon, because it's so romantic.
2 There was so much to take photos of. It was a good thing I had my camera with me.
3 We arrived late and we couldn't find anywhere to eat. I wasn't very impressed!
4 You should go early to beat the heat. There's a beautiful beach at the foot of the cliff which is great for cooling off.

e Write a short review (about three sentences) of a tourist attraction you visited recently. Use the same style as in the review of Prague Castle on p.170.

f Show your review to your partner and answer any questions.

g ▶ Now go back to p.41

Tulum, Mexico

5D Linking: addition and reinforcement

Adding an idea in a new sentence		Adding two ideas in the same sentence
In addition …	Furthermore …	In addition to …
What is more …	Above all …	As well as …
Besides …	… also …	Besides …
Moreover …		Beyond …

a Cover the table. Complete the sentences with one word in each gap. Check your answers in the table.

1 **As well** _____ doing online research of social media, companies usually contact previous employers for a reference.

2 Many people are careful about the information they post on social media. _____ **addition**, they often have a private profile under a different name that employers will not recognise.

3 _____ being unethical, using information from social media as a basis for discrimination against a job applicant is illegal in many countries.

4 The private life of employees should remain private. _____ **is more**, employers have no right to try and control what employees do in their own time.

5 There should be laws to restrict how much information companies can look for. _____ **all**, they should be banned from trawling for negative information.

6 Companies argue that information that is freely available online can be seen by anyone. _____ they point out that it works both ways and applicants are free to do research on a company.

b Replace the words in italics with linkers from the table. Make any other necessary changes.

It is common practice for companies to get useful information about their customers when they sign up for a free offer. Customers accept the free offer *and* they have to agree to certain terms and conditions that they don't read carefully. Companies are then entitled to bombard these customers with spam. *And* they might pass on information to other companies who will send out more spam.

It's always important to read what you sign up for and bear in mind that nothing is completely free. *And most importantly*, make sure you are aware of consumer rights in your country so you can challenge companies who use information about you in an unethical way.

c Add an extra idea to two of these sentences, using an addition linker or a reinforcement linker.

1 I always think carefully about what I write in emails.

2 A lot of companies do not allow their employees to access social media during work hours.

3 I always ask my friends not to post photographs of me on their social media pages.

d ▶ Now go back to p.65

6D Formal letters; Giving a positive impression

Formal letters
Dear Sir/Madam,
I am writing in response to …
I would like to express my (interest in / dissatisfaction with, etc.) …
Please find attached …
I look forward to hearing from you.
Yours faithfully,

Giving a positive impression
I am very much in touch with …
I enthusiastically maintain my knowledge of …
I played an active role in …
I have been able to …
I have taken a keen interest in …
I feel that, with my …, I would be very well qualified to …

a Look at these extracts from letters. Cross out one word or phrase in each group in italics that is less suitable for a formal letter.

1 I *believe / am certain / guess* that my knowledge of local sporting events will enable me to *do / write / contribute* well-informed reviews.

2 I am *writing in response to / answering / replying to* your advertisement, which *was / appeared / was published* in the March issue of your magazine.

3 I look forward to hearing from you *in due course / in a bit / soon*.

4 I'm *an enthusiastic supporter / a real fan / a keen follower* of the local football team.

5 *Here are / I am attaching / Please find attached* some sample photos which I took recently.

6 I have *considerable / loads of / extensive* experience of restaurant work.

7 I *am able to be completely flexible / am free any time / can offer a good deal of flexibility* with regard to working hours.

8 I spent some time working on a school magazine and *acquired / developed / picked up* some *relevant / priceless / valuable* editorial skills.

b Add additional formal and positive expressions from **a** to the table.

c Read the advert and Andy's application email. Rewrite it so that it is in a more formal style.

Dear Sir/Madam,
I am writing …

7D Linking: highlighting and giving examples

a Add a linking word or phrase from the table where there is a ^ in 1–7. Often more than one answer is possible.

1 The team is getting on better now. ^ they have decided to have a team dinner once a month.
2 It is already possible to perceive benefits from the training for the company, ^ the increased productivity of the team.
3 The team's productivity has gone up by 10%, ^ the increased number of completed tasks in the past month.
4 Everyone's active listening skills have improved. Masha ^ has become a good listener since doing the programme.
5 Sam and Claudio now work together more effectively. Sam makes a point of consulting Claudio about work-flow issues, ^ prioritising tasks on the schedule.
6 The team now deals with tasks in hand. ^ they focus more on getting things done and less on team politics.
7 The programme has also resulted in an improvement in the way all team members deal with people outside the team, ^ their friendlier manner with support staff.

Linkers for highlighting and giving examples	
for instance	specifically
as demonstrated by	as detailed in
as shown by	namely
such as	especially
in particular	

b You are the social programme coordinator for a staff/student social programme which is experiencing problems. Complete these sentences with your own ideas.

1 There has been little uptake of the programme of late. For instance, …
2 Overall participation in the programme in the past year has decreased, as detailed in …
3 Activities that involve … are especially …
4 Activities such as … are …

c Write sentences about the English language progress you and your classmates have made. Use linkers for highlighting and giving examples of particular achievements.

d ▶ Now go back to p.89

STAFF REQUIRED for a bookshop near the university. Flexible working hours, so ideal as a part-time job for students.

To apply, please send an email with a photo to: www.greenstreetbooks.net

job application	📎 Andy_CV

Hi there,

Saw your job ad in the student paper and I'd really like to work for you. I'm doing World Literature at university so I know quite a bit about books written by all kinds of people. I'm really into novels and travel books and that'll be useful, won't it? I've never worked in a bookshop before but I've done café work and I spent a bit of time working in a sports shop, so I know all about selling stuff to people. I'm also a nice guy and I've got loads of friends – I can chat to anybody.

So I think I'm just the kind of guy you're looking for. Here's my CV.

I could work whenever you like, mornings or evenings, all the same to me.

Hey, get in touch.

Andy

d ▶ Now go back to p.77

8D Using persuasive language

Neutral language	Persuasive language
in the city centre	in the **heart** of the city
a different experience	a **unique** experience
high standards	**exacting** standards
well-trained	**highly** trained
make a dish	**create** a dish
We promise to ...	Our **commitment** to you is ...
our basic idea	our **core values**

Writing Tip

Many of the texts you read online are for promotion, and their aim is to persuade you to buy something, do something or go somewhere. Notice how they use persuasive language, which makes things seem better, more positive or more important.

a Choose the two words or phrases in italics in each sentence which work best as persuasive language.

1 Try one of our *freshly / lovingly / well-* prepared salads.
2 All our staff work to the *most exacting / highest / required* standards.
3 We *serve / offer / sell* light meals and snacks throughout the day.
4 Café Colombia is a *nice / perfect / ideal* place to meet your friends after work.
5 You can have *complete / some / total* confidence in our specialist products.
6 Why not spend a weekend *away from it all / in the countryside / far from the bustle of the city*?

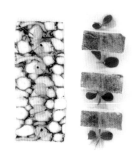

b The sentences below promote different products and places. Which are for ... ?

- a music venue
- a duty-free shop
- an airport lounge
- a bank
- a language school
- a furniture shop
- a hotel

1 *With good furniture* and each with its own individual character, our rooms offer a *really quiet* atmosphere in which to unwind after a hard day's work.
2 Our beds are *of good quality* and will *be usable for many years*.
3 We have *a lot of* perfumes and our brands are *known everywhere*.
4 The Basement is *a good place* for parties and live music events.
5 Our *well*-equipped classrooms and *good* teachers will ensure that your course is *different from the usual*.
6 *You're welcome* in our executive suite, where you can *spend* your time between flights in *comfortable* surroundings.
7 *We aim* to provide *a safe place* for your financial investments.

c Replace the words in italics in **b** 1–7 with phrases from the box to make the sentences sound more positive.

tastefully furnished   a unique learning experience
manufactured to the highest standards
an extensive range of   an ideal venue
highly qualified   truly relaxing   our mission is
globally recognised   a secure home   luxurious
stand the test of time   a warm welcome awaits you
fully   while away

d Choose a place in your town (a shop, a shopping mall, a sports facility, a hotel, a school or college). Write two sentences to promote it. Try to describe it as positively as possible.

e Read out your sentences and listen to other students. What positive features are they promoting?

f ▶ Now go back to p.101

9D Linking: reason and result

Reason	Result
One key factor is … / One of the (main) reasons is … … because of / due to / owing to (this) … … as a (direct) result / consequence of …	lead to / result in / cause / mean that … As a (direct) result / consequence … Consequently … … thus / thereby / hence / therefore …

Writing Tip

There are small differences in use between *thus / therefore* and *thereby*:

The government raised taxes, **thereby/thus/~~therefore~~** *raising a lot of money.* = direct result of action

The government raised taxes. **Therefore,/Thus,/~~Thereby,~~** *starting a business is a bad idea.* = logical conclusion

a Complete the sentences with the reason and result language in the box.

> due to   resulted in   thus   cause
> thereby   one of the main reasons

1 _____ people leave small towns is the lack of a lively cultural life.
2 Climate change has negatively affected rural environments and _____ urban migration.
3 At first, one or two family members move to the city and do well. _____, more family members join them, motivated by the hope to also do well.
4 There is sometimes disharmony in city neighbourhoods _____ the pressure urban migration puts on infrastructure and amenities.
5 Dramatic population decreases can _____ the social fabric of rural communities to disappear altogether.
6 The exodus of inhabitants from small towns leads to less demand for goods and services, and _____ the closure of many businesses.

b Correct the reason and result language in these examples.

1 The recent arrival of large numbers of people from the countryside leads to the current shortage in housing.
2 Increased pressure on city infrastructure often causes that there is a rise in taxes.
3 There are fewer jobs in small towns because the closure of so many businesses.
4 As a result the arrival of rural migrants, city schools have many more children on their roll.
5 Youth unemployment is very high in the town, thereby there's a lot of competition for jobs.

c Write four sentences about present or future changes in your neighbourhood, using reason and result language.

In my neighbourhood, a new sports centre will be built due to the fundraising efforts of the local community. As a consequence, …

d ▶ Now go back to p.113

10D Film reviews; Concise description

Ways to give information concisely	Examples
1 Add phrases between commas	Andy Newman, **a young jazz musician**, wants to become a top drummer.
2 Add phrases before nouns	**Young jazz musician** Andy Newman wants to become a top drummer.
3 Use past participle clauses	Whiplash, **directed by Damien Chazelle,** was nominated for several Oscars.
4 Use present participle clauses	Andy, **wanting to become a top drummer,** practises eight hours a day.

a Use one or more of the ways shown in the table to make these sentences more concise.

1 *Manhattan*, which is a classic Woody Allen movie, now appears a bit dated.
2 When he realises that he has only a few months to live, he decides to make as much money as possible.
3 Mike Leigh, who is a British director, is planning to make a new film.
4 Because she is determined to solve the crime, she works on the case night and day.
5 Nina, who is a promising young dancer, who is played by Natalie Portman, lives with her mother.
6 Panem, which is a totalitarian country which is set in the future, is divided into 12 districts.
7 Because they are trapped in the mountains and because they know their food is running out, they send four people off to get help.

b Write about a film you saw recently.

Write some basic information about it (name, director, outline of the story) in only *three* sentences.
Include at least two of the ways shown in the table to make the information more concise.

c Read out your sentences but don't say the name of the film. Can other students guess the film?

d Now think of a film you did not enjoy. Replace the words in italics with your own ideas and continue each sentence concisely.

Damien Chazelle's latest film, *Whiplash, is the intense and inspiring story of …*
A critical and box office *hit*, the film has …
J. K. Simmons is perfectly cast in the role of …
Miles Teller is also superb as …
The film provides a *subtle* portrayal of …
The plot focuses on …
It's an *original, thought-provoking* film and *certainly worth seeing.*

e ▶ Now go back to p.125

Audioscripts

Unit 1

▶ **1.7**

INTERVIEWER Let's hear now from Susanna Zaraysky. She speaks seven languages, and spent many years teaching English abroad and has even written a book called *Language is Music*. Um … Is this er… reluctance to learn foreign languages, um … just a feature of Britain or, do you think, all English-speaking peoples?

SUSANNA I think it's all over the English-speaking world and I think there are two main reasons: one, as I agree with your previous speaker that there's a lack of necessity. People don't see the necessity and, so, necessity breeds motivation, and for example we see that in Brazil there are English-language schools popping up everywhere because they need to learn English to be able to sell their products abroad. The other reason is, is that English speakers have little to no exposure to the sounds of foreign languages because almost all of our media is in English, so people in other countries will start to listen to music in English, watch programmes er … from the United States or from the UK or from other parts of the world in English. And so they get used to the sounds and prior er … exposure to the sounds of a language make it much easier for a student to learn a language and it's much more fun, when you have music and … and media.

I Is that what happened to you? I mean were you exposed to foreign languages from a young age?

S I was. I mean, I was born in the former Soviet Union and I came to the United States when I was three but I grew up in an area with a large Hispanic population and Vietnamese population, so I heard Spanish from a young age even though I didn't start formally studying it until I was 15 or 16. So I already knew a lot of songs in Spanish when I started learning. So, when I had to learn grammar and words, I … I had a context in which to reference to what I was learning in school. And because I already knew songs, I already knew some words and it was fun and I could pronounce things. So music is a huge aspect of language learning.

I So, you had a bit of a head start if you like, but um what would be your advice to other English speakers, perhaps averse to learning foreign languages?

S To find music that they like in the other language. Um … to find television programmes that they like in the language … To watch movies in the other language. Because your heart has to resonate with the language. You have to actually like it, because you live a language more than you study it. So you have to find something that you like about it. For example, if somebody likes watching soc … uh … football, they can watch football programmes in another language, so they're at least getting used to what it sounds like. Um … If they like a certain type of a movie, whether it's animation, they could look for those type of animation programmes in other languages.

I And er it's worth it, you reckon?

S Of course, of course. Because, you know, people … you get paid more money usually in government jobs if you speak another language. You have much more oppor … You have many more opportunities to do trade if you speak another language. And, I mean, in the United States we have 20 per cent of our population speaks another language at home, so even for domestic marketing reasons it's important.

I Susanna Zaraysky, who speaks seven languages.

▶ **1.10**

NARRATOR The word 'radio' was first used in the 1900s, although of course radios were invented long before that, in the 1820s, but they were originally called 'wirelesses'.

The word 'environmentalism' was first used in the 1910s. People began to be concerned about pollution and wildlife towards the end of the 19th century, and in 1916 a National Park Service was set up in the USA to help protect wildlife.

The word 'spacecraft', meaning any kind of spaceship or satellite, first appeared in the 1920s, at about the same time that science fiction stories became popular in films and magazines. However, the first real spacecraft, the Russian Sputnik, wasn't launched until 1957.

People started talking about 'babysitters' in the 1930s, and the word 'technophobe', meaning someone who has a fear of technology, was first used in the 1940s. This was about the time when people started using technology such as vacuum cleaners and washing machines in the home.

'Brainwashing' is making people believe an idea by constantly telling them it's true. This word was introduced in the 1950s. And an 'in-joke' – a joke that is only understood by a particular social group – was first used in the 1960s.

In the 1970s people first started talking about 'Bollywood' – the Indian film industry based in Bombay – in other words, the Bombay version of Hollywood.

The concept of 'ecotourism' came in in the 1980s when the tourism industry began to respond to the demand for tours which benefited, or at least did not harm, the local ecosystem.

The 1990s saw the invention of 'blogs' – originally called 'web logs' – as more and more people became connected by the Internet. And, in the 2000s, people all over the world started doing the Japanese puzzle, Sudoku.

The word 'selfie' was introduced in 2013, to describe photos people take of themselves with their mobiles – although the first, known selfie was taken 170 years earlier by Robert Cornelius, who took a photo of himself using a mirror in 1839.

▶ **1.11**

PAUL Language has been changing much faster since people started using the Internet. Now, people pick up words and expressions from each other and new words spread much faster. This means though, a lot of new expressions probably won't last very long. LOL, BTW, Bluetooth, CD-ROM. I mean, 20 years ago these words didn't exist – no one used them. But, in a few years' time, they will have gone out of fashion and other new words will have come into the language.

ROSA Another thing that's changed is punctuation. Emailing has had an effect on the way people write. I mean, people have stopped using strict rules for punctuation, so people use commas much less than before. Spellcheckers and predictive text mean that people don't need to know how to spell. And people's spelling seems to just be getting worse: lose/loose; where/were – they don't show up on spell checkers. It's a pity. People are getting more information, but they're getting worse at expressing themselves.

GREG I agree with the article that language often changes slowly, but I think this process has been speeding up over the last few decades. A lot of American words have come into the language, probably because of TV and films. Um … for example, people used to use 'flat' but now more people have started saying 'apartment'. Because of international communication, dialects are disappearing and people are starting to speak the same kind of English. For example the word 'movies' which is originally used mostly in … in North America has now replaced 'cinema' and 'film' all around the world. In about 50 years, most dialects of English will have died out. And I think dialects are important because they're, they're part of people's identity. It's a pity they're disappearing and everything's just becoming more uniform.

CLAIRE Some people complain about new words, but it shows that the English language is alive … um … like the world is changing and languages need to change with them. And this is nothing new. Um … Older generations have always complained about language changing. They've always felt strongly about it, but … it's a natural process. New words come into the language because they enrich the language. For example, the word 'selfie' which people started using in around 2013. People had been taking photos of themselves before 2013, but they hadn't had a single word for it, so it caught on quite quickly.

And some words also change their meaning. So for example 'wireless' these days is about Internet connections. We talk about 'wireless LAN' and 'wi-fi'. The word 'wireless' had had a completely different meaning until computers came along – it meant 'radio'.

▶ **1.15** PART 1

OSCAR Well, that's all from me today. Coming up after this short break is Katya with the *City FM* news …

ALEX Nice one, Oscar.

O Yeah, not bad. You've not broken the equipment again, have you, Alex?

A No. That's your job!

…

A Hi Sara! How are you this morning? Oh. Full of the joys of spring, I see!

SARA What? Oh, Alex, it's you …

A Well, don't sound so pleased to see me!

S Sorry, message from the boss.

A Right … ?

S She wants a meeting this morning.

A And … ?

S I've got a feeling it's not exactly good news.

A Oh, don't be so negative. Nadia probably just wants to thank you for all your hard work.

S Hm, that'd be something of a surprise. When's the last time I turned in anything decent?

A Oh come on!

S Anyway, what are you so cheerful about?

A I've just booked my holiday.

S Oh, good!

A Yeah, Italy!

S Lovely. You know, my Dad is Italian.

A No way! Hey, maybe you could teach me some bits and pieces, y'know, basic survival phrases, 'please' and 'thank you' and stuff like that?

S Survival phrases? I think I need a few of them myself!

A Hey, Sara! Ciao bella!

▶ **1.16** PART 2

NADIA Ah, Sara. Take a seat.

SARA Thanks, Nadia.

N Now, do you know why I've asked to see you?

S Um … Is it something to do with our long-running series of interviews with authors?

N Exactly. Look, Oscar has already booked six authors, give or take.

S Six?!

N He's even managed to persuade Max whatsisname to come in.

S Who?

N Max whatsisname – you know, author of *Solar Wind*? The guy who wrote the entire book sitting on a bench on the Palace Pier, here in Brighton.

S Max Redwood! Wow, that's great news!

N So, how far have you got?

S Well, um, I'm still sort of like in the research phase, y'know.

N I appreciate you're still finding your feet here at *City FM*.

S Well, I'm beginning to feel like I've got the hang of things.

N OK, but you must understand … For me to be able to offer you a permanent contract here, I need to see some evidence of your capabilities.

S I understand, Nadia. I'll get something to you soon, I promise.

N Ah Oscar, do come in. Let's touch base soon, Sara.

…

ALEX (Speaking Italian badly) Scusami, signorina, parla inglese?

S Leave it out, Alex.

A Don't tell me – she's promoted you to editor-in-chief!

S Something along those lines, yeah.

A Go on, tell me all!

S Well, basically, she said if I don't get something big, like an interview with a best-selling author, I'm out of here, or words to that effect.

A Ah!

S You don't happen to know, like, a best-selling author or something, do you, Alex?

A No, 'fraid not.

S That's not your new girlfriend, again, is it?

A Yeah, it's Emma!

S She's keen, isn't she?

A Oh! Hang on, Em!

▶ 1.21

SPEAKER Well, I'd been renting accommodation, a room in a nice cottage in a village 60 miles from London, for four or five weeks, give or take. The landlord had told me at some point I'd be getting a flatmate, but to be honest, I'd kind of got used to being there on my own. To start with, I'd had all my stuff in my room, of course, but as the weeks went by, I kind of thought, 'Hmm, I could put some bits and pieces in the spare room.' And then, 'Oh! I'll put my drum kit in there too.' And so it went on. I was really making myself at home!

I'll always remember the morning I met Michelle for the first time: I had a cold, and I was still in bed feeling sorry for myself, when suddenly I heard a key turn in the lock of the front door. I raced down the stairs with the full horror of the situation dawning on me. Just as I got to the bottom step, she opened the door to see me in my pyjamas and a blind panic. She looked at me and said, 'Have I come at a bad time?', or something along those lines. That was roughly 13 years ago now, and we've been close friends ever since – after we moved all my stuff out of her room!

▶ 1.22

MAXWELL KINGSLEY I think we're in a unique situation today with regard to language diversity and there is no precedent for it in history. The English language has become the world's dominant language, and although other languages such as Chinese and Spanish are more widespread, English is spoken by the largest number of non-native speakers. In fact, there are a vastly greater number of people who speak it as a non-native language than there are people who have English as their first language. There are probably around a billion people worldwide who speak English to some degree of proficiency as a foreign or second language – it's a huge number of people. It's been estimated for example that something like 80 per cent of all conversations in English between tourists are between non-native speakers, so a Russian talking to a Japanese, or a Spanish speaker talking to a German, but using English. The implications of this are, of course, enormous.

Naturally, this is quite unrelated to the nature of the English language itself. Some people say English is an easy language, but in fact English has the same degree of complexity or simplicity as other languages, and the reasons for its dominance are largely historical, and to some extent, accidental. It just so happened, for example, that the USA adopted English as its national language, rather than French or Spanish.

I mentioned earlier that the dominance of English is unique. It's true, of course, that Latin played a similar role as an international language for around a thousand years, starting with the Roman Empire and continuing until the 16th century. Latin was the language of science and of theology, and rather like English today, it was used in intercultural communication. But its use was limited to a few highly educated people, so it wasn't used nearly as widely as English is today. English is used by everyone, not just a small elite.

People often talk about how English is threatening other languages, but I don't personally believe that dominance of English as a world language is going to have much effect on the diversity of human languages. It's true that smaller languages have been dying out and they will continue to die out, but that's more as a result of improved communication, and not because of the spread of English. People are going to go on speaking their own language, whether it's Russian or Italian or Arabic or whatever it is. There's no sign at all that everyone is going to drop their own language or that there will be one single language spoken by everybody. It simply isn't going to happen, in my view. So the only real disadvantage of the dominance of English, as I see it, is for native speakers of English themselves, as it means that they have less need to learn other languages, so in a sense that's an impoverishment for them.

Also, of course it's quite understandable that speakers of other major languages might resent the rise of English as a global language, but the good news for them is that the dominance of English probably won't last. Before English, French was of course the international language, at least among educated people, for a couple of hundred years, and before that it was Latin and Arabic and Greek and so on. In other words, various languages have played this role and this has come and gone over time, and no doubt it will be the same with English. Take Sumerian for example, which was the main written language in most of the Middle East for centuries. The last records of Sumerian are from the third century, so it survived as an international language for over 3,000 years, but of course now most people haven't even heard of it, it's a dead language. Compare that with English – so far English as a truly global language has been going for about 50 years at the most, so who knows what's going to happen to it? One thing that's certain is that nothing lasts forever.

Unit 2

▶ 1.30

LENA A few months ago, I went to a friend's place for dinner. It was a fun night – lots of lively company – y'know, one of those nights you feel you've talked about everything and solved the world's problems! Towards the end of the evening, I was feeling a bit tired and I just kind of sat back and watched and listened – did nothing. It was interesting. It struck me how what we say sort of defines who we are. Talking is a way of fitting in – y'know, a way of showing that we belong to a social group.

The next day I couldn't stop thinking about this and began to wonder what would happen if I just stopped talking all together and was just … silent. What would happen to me? How would I come across to other people? I decided to read up on the topic of vows of silence. There were some really interesting stories online. Often a vow of silence is for spiritual purposes and people go into some kind of retreat to cut themselves off from the outside world. I guess you could say that's not about communicating at all – it's like taking time out to focus on yourself. But some of the other stories I read were about people taking what you'd call a more public vow of silence. What I mean is they continued to live in the real world and communicate with people – just they didn't speak. Some people did this as a protest – y'know, like against censorship or something like that.

I didn't have any kind of burning cause I wanted to protest against but, for my own reasons, I was still intrigued by the idea of a public vow of silence. So I decided to take one – just for a weekend. I knew I'd find it hard to last much longer than that. I looked on it as a kind of social experiment. I knew it was going to be a challenge!

▶ 1.31

LENA So … a whole weekend without speaking. The person I found hardest to deal with was … myself. When I'm alone I often talk to myself, or sing, or hum. But, no – I wasn't allowed to do any of that. I had to keep my vocal cords completely out of action. I managed OK, except for a couple of times – like when someone held a door open for me and a little 'thank you' slipped out.

Also when my phone rang, I couldn't answer. I was quite proud that I remembered, even when someone woke me up calling early on Saturday morning. But I did text back. So, you see, I still communicated – email, text – all that sort of thing. I just had to keep my mouth well and truly shut.

The first thing that amazed me was just how easy it is to communicate without words – like, buying a coffee. I just sort of pointed to what I wanted and nodded in agreement when the person in the café got it right. I even met a friend for a chat. I could react to what I had to say by means of a facial expression. Occasionally, I did have to write some things down on a notepad, but I was amazed how much information I could get across without trying too hard.

The most interesting thing was the way other people related to me. When I was queuing in the supermarket, a woman tried to have a conversation with me. She bombarded me with questions. When she eventually realised that I couldn't or wouldn't speak, she just made up her own answers to her own questions. She had a whole conversation with herself about why I couldn't speak! She thought I was unwell.

Also my landlord was interesting. I had to go and pay my rent on the Saturday. He always goes on about something when I go and see him – he usually likes to run down some politician or other. I don't always agree with him, and we often end up having a heated discussion. But this time, I just listened … And when I left he said, 'It was great to have a good chat.' This was interesting. I don't think he really noticed that I hadn't been saying anything. He was so caught up in what he was saying he wasn't very aware of me. And it made me think … well, aren't we all a bit like that? We're all so busy talking and expressing our ideas – it's like a kind of prison that doesn't allow us to communicate with each other and see what's going on around us. Most of the time people treated me kindly. I often felt that my silence brought out the best in people.

Being silent for two days really gave me a chance to see and feel things without feeling I needed to respond or react. I mean, I often wanted to, but I had to hold myself back. And this meant I just had to let things go – just let them be. And, you know, I felt more peaceful – more connected with everyone and everything. So it really was fascinating – my weekend of silence. I recommend giving it a go.

▶ 1.37

PRESENTER Millions of visitors come to the Swiss Alps every summer. There's walking, climbing, swimming, cycling, paragliding – almost no limit to what you can do here. For some people these sports aren't exciting enough. Instead, they go base jumping. This means jumping off a cliff and free falling before opening your parachute and landing safely, they hope, in the valley below. The idea of jumping off a mountain may be a nightmare for some people. Base jumpers say it's an experience like no other. To find out, I watched 24-year-old Ada Hoffman go on her first jump.

P So Ada, you're about to go base jumping and it's your first time.

ADA Yes. I'm due to jump in about 10 minutes.

P How are you feeling? Nervous?

A Yes nervous, but also excited, very excited. I'm keyed up – you know, I'm going to enjoy this. I've been parachute jumping quite a bit. I've had training in that, I jump maybe … about er … 300

jumps. Most people say, like, 200 is a minimum, other people say 5 … 500 is a minimum so … I feel ready for this base jumping, so … , yes it feels like a natural step.

P And what are you going to do exactly? You'll be jumping off the mountain, right?

A Yes. There is a platform which sticks out over the cliff. And um … yes, basically, I'm planning to jump off that one.

P And then?

A Then I'll be jumping from about 900 metres … So … I'm aiming to free fall for exactly 25 seconds. And um … then I'm going to fall for a further 30 seconds with er … the parachute completely open.

P And land safely in the valley?

A Yes – you'd hope so, yeah.

P And how will you know when it's time to open the parachute?

A I'm going to count the seconds – that's the only way of doing it. Um … when I reach 20 seconds, or count on 20, I'm going to pull this string hard and um … then the parachute will open in about 5 seconds.

P OK, well good luck. I'll talk to you again after the jump.

A Thank you.

…

A Hi.

P Hi, you made it.

A Yes.

P So how was it?

A Oh it was good, it was a good jump. Everything was fine.

P How did it feel?

A Amazing – there's nothing like it really – absolutely amazing! A bit scary at first – you know, you walk along this platform and then you just have to jump. And then, you feel really calm, completely in control. And after the parachute opens it's quite peaceful you know … it's just … you drift down, and it's … oh … it's just wonderful.

P So will you go base jumping again?

A Oh yes, definitely. I'm definitely going to do it again, maybe I'll go later today actually. I'm also thinking of trying a tandem jump some time. You know when you jump with somebody else, you jump together? I think that should be really fun, but er … you have to be very careful.

P With the number of jumps likely to hit 30,000 this year, it's clear that the sport is highly attractive. But there's no question that it is a very dangerous sport and not everyone survives. Many people say it should be better regulated, or even banned. But base jumpers disagree.

A Well it certainly is dangerous. Yes it's very dangerous and I think you need to be aware of the risks when you take a jump. So … if you don't … if you're not aware then you maybe shouldn't jump. But you know, you're not coming here thinking, 'Oh, I'm planning to have an accident.' That's … that's not what you're aiming to do. You come here with the intention of having a great experience and … and that's what you do.

▶ 1.44 PART 2

EMMA Uh-huh … yeah … uh-huh.

ALEX Right, so I'll pick you up about seven.

E Great!

A What else is going on today, then?

E Nothing much. Max is due back soon.

A Max? Who's Max?

E My brother. He's staying with me at the moment, remember?

A Oh, yeah, that's right.

E He's getting on my nerves, to be honest. There's just not enough space!

A Wait, he's not still sleeping on the sofa, is he?

E Yes! And his stuff's everywhere!

A Hmm …

E And he's just so volatile! It's like walking on eggshells half the time.

A Isn't it about time you asked him to leave?

E Well, I keep dropping hints, but he doesn't seem to notice.

A Why don't you just tell him straight, then? Don't beat around the bush. There's a lot to be said for being upfront about things.

E I can't just boot him out!

A Hang on, did you say his name is Max?

E Yeah.

A Max Redwood?

E Yes.

A The same as that guy who wrote *Solar Wind*?

E No, he is the guy who wrote *Solar Wind*.

A You mean it is him?! Your brother is *the* Max Redwood!

E It's no big deal.

A I don't believe it! Oscar is interviewing him tomorrow!

E I know. Look, I've really got to go. Max will no doubt be hungry when he gets in. See you tonight.

A Yeah, OK. Bye then….

▶ 1.48 PART 2

EMMA So, Max, I was thinking – have you thought about the possibility of finding your own place to live?

MAX Hadn't really thought about it, to be honest.

E Well, I mean, it's not as if you're short of cash any more, is it?

M True.

E It might be in your interests to invest some of it into property.

M Invest? Property? What are you talking about?

E Well, it would be lovely to have your own workspace, wouldn't it? What do you think?

M Sure. Yeah. Yeah. But I can't think about any of that right now.

E Why not?

M Well, I've got that radio interview tomorrow.

E Uh-huh?

M I don't know what to say!

E Oh, don't worry about it. You might want to have a think about what you could say tonight.

M There's nothing else to say about *Solar Wind*! The book is the book.

E Oh Max, don't get so wound up about it. It's only an interview.

M Only an interview?! You're joking.

E Hey. I'll be able to listen to you.

M Don't you dare listen!

E Alright, alright. Calm down!

M Maybe I'll just go far, far away, take a vow of silence, live on a desert island somewhere …

E Yeah, you might as well!

M Emma!

▶ 1.50

LUBA The social activity I liked most was the whitewater rafting excursion. I'd never done anything like that at all and it was a lot of fun. It was quite expensive to do, but I think it was worth it. We had to pay for the guide and hire of the wetsuits and everything like that. But the feeling of being swept along by the current of the water was a bit like being on a roller coaster – it was infinitely more exciting because everything was far less predictable. The only negative thing that happened to me was that when I got off the raft, I slipped on a wet rock, and sort of twisted my ankle. Still, it won't stop me from trying this again.

MEHMET I did both the social programme activities: whitewater rafting and the bungee jump. The rafting was nowhere near as exciting as the jump. I loved it – so much, in fact, I'm planning to do another jump before I go back home … For me, there was one thing I found a bit strange about these activities. When we went to the river, and to the jump site, we were just picked up by a minivan driver – there was no one from the social programme who came with us. I mean, we had a good enough time just with ourselves, but it was a bit odd that no one from the committee was there. Not very friendly, I thought.

PAOLO Actually, I didn't do either of the sports activities. I like sports, but I'm not so keen on these extreme sports. The more dangerous they are, the less I want to do them. So, with the whitewater

rafting – well, I'm not such a good swimmer, and I was told it'd be a bit risky. And then with the bungee jump – well, I've never really understood the thrill of throwing yourself off a bridge. I'm quite good at 'normal' sports – football, tennis, volleyball – and I like hiking. Why do sports have to be extreme all the time? Some people complained about the cost, but that didn't surprise me. These things cost money. I don't mind paying – it's just it needs to be something I really want to do.

CHANGYING For me, the highlight of the year was doing the bungee jump. To begin with, I really wasn't sure about it and I remember when we were in the minivan on the way there, the closer we got, the more nervous I became. I almost pulled out at the last minute, but everyone encouraged me to go ahead with the jump. It was truly amazing – the initial free fall is the most incredible sensation I've ever felt – just a big rush with this amazing sense of freedom. The only negative aspect of the experience was that we had to pay half the price. A hundred dollars is a lot of money. I'd been led to believe that all these activities would be paid for. I mean, I could afford it and it was worth it, but I thought these things were meant to be covered as part of the social programme.

Unit 3
▶ 1.54

DANIELA PAPI I volunteered all over the world – building homes in Papua New Guinea, doing post-tsunami work in Sri Lanka, helping paint a school in Thailand. And I used to think it was the best way to travel. In 2005, I decided to organise my own volunteer trip – a bike ride across Cambodia with five friends. We were going to teach students we met along the way and raise funds to build a school. We spent months fundraising – through book sales, and bake sales, and speaking at community groups. We named the trip 'The PEPY Ride' – with PEPY being 'Protect the Earth, Protect Yourself' – because we were going to teach about the environment and health. The thing is, it turned out, there was more than one small problem with our plan. First of all, we didn't really know that much about the environment or health, or Cambodia for that matter. And the money that we raised for other small projects that we hadn't researched very much got wasted or landed in corrupt hands. And that school we helped to build, well, when I arrived to see it, I found a half-empty building and realised something I already should have known – schools don't teach kids, people do. I was pretty disappointed, as you can imagine, that we'd spent the better part of a year fundraising and planning and things hadn't turned out to be as simple as the celebrity volunteer trips I'd seen on TV. So, I decided to stay in Cambodia a bit longer and figure out how we could put that school building, and the rest of the funds we had raised, to better use. That 'little bit longer' turned into six years living in Cambodia. During which time, I founded an education NGO and to raise money for the non-profit work we were doing, I started a volunteer travel company – where I lead hundreds of volunteers on trips to Cambodia. At first, our tours looked a lot like that first bike ride, and I took people on trips where we'd teach English or yoga or paint a building. But I slowly began to see that I was part of a growing system that I no longer believed in. After a decade of joining and leading volunteer trips, and from interviewing volunteers from all around the world as part of a book I am now co-authoring, I now firmly believe that the growing practice of sending young people abroad to volunteer is often not only failing the communities they are meant to be serving, but also setting these travellers, and by extension our whole society, up for failure in the long run. More and more young people are going abroad to volunteer each year – as part of school requirements, to build their CVs, or part of gap-year trips. Much of this demand is fuelled by the opinion that because we come from financially wealthier countries, we have the right, or obligation to bestow our benevolence on people. Never mind if we don't speak the language, don't have the skills or experience to qualify for the jobs we are doing, or don't know anything about what life is like in that, quote-unquote, "poor place". Now, as a former serial-volunteer myself, I am in no way trying to criticise the good intentions of these volunteer travellers. I know from my former experience our desire to help is sincere. But I also now know that good intentions are not enough. Yet, good intentions are usually enough to get people to support your efforts. The praise and encouragement for international volunteering is almost blind to the details, the process, or the research for how these young volunteers are actually going to help. Throughout the time we were fundraising for that first bike trip, countless numbers of people praised our generosity and bravery – yet very few people questioned us at all about our plans. Perhaps instead of handing us a cheque someone should have asked us how we planned to learn all we needed to know to be of help to anybody. The local papers wrote articles about us that made it sound like part of our heroism was the fact that we didn't know very much. I believe that our lack of critical engagement when it comes to international volunteering is creating a double standard.

▶ **1.58**

WILL What do you think to my boat Saqba?
SAQBA Oh the boat – it's nice … no problem.
W You think it's nice? No problem?
S Yeah, no problem.
W Cool … OK, I'm going to try and get inside. Ooh … This will be my home for the next few weeks. Here we go … Can you push me off, Saqba?
S Yeah, no problem.
W Thanks, buddy … OK, see you in a few days.
S Yeah. We shall see again. Safe journey.
W Thanks, mate! My first paddle strokes. Oh … First of thousands, probably. This is absolutely amazing. It's very shallow in parts. You might be able to hear the base of the boat just rubbing along the rocks, but it's so quiet out here. I've only been going about 20 minutes and already I've seen far more wildlife than I've seen in the last three days, just in the forest surrounded by jungle. There's dragonflies buzzing around, cattle egrets, large blue herons, kingfishers … There's a whole cloud of white butterflies just on the Sierra Leonean bank. I'm completely hemmed in on both sides by jungle. Ooh, a fish, a big fish swam straight past. The water is so clean here. I'm just silently drifting up to this enormous fish eagle. I can't be much more than eight feet away from it now. It's just staring straight at me. Big white-capped head, dark wings, burgundy-brown across the back. Just close enough now to see that it's got a massive catfish in its talons. I think I might leave him to it. Managed to just get my camp sorted. So this is my first night alone in the forest. Er … I've got my mosquito net up. I'm actually in my hammock, but my hammock's on the floor because … I'm in a little stone island in the middle of the river. Just at the end of the day there was quite a large cataract and I didn't really fancy taking it on till tomorrow, so I've just camped in this little island, basically, but I'm kind of worried if it rains tonight though, that the rain might just run straight through the middle of my camp or something. I don't know though, I guess I'll find out.
I'm just trying to catch my breath. I think … I think the island last night marked the start of a series of rapids, just these rock-strewn whitewater passages, maybe 100 to 150 metres long. And then you get a short break, and then another, and then another, and another. I just took on this last one here and made a terrible mess of it, ended up sideways, hit this big rock in the middle of the river, which almost flipped the raft, just managed to get control of it again, and shot out of the bottom of this kind

of small waterfall. So I'm just taking some shelter in this eddy right now and I'm going to have to unpack everything and tip out any water that I've taken on. And the thing is – just got to be so careful because if I lose the raft, I'm finished. It's got all my communication equipment on, it's got all my food on, it's got my shelter on it. Without it, I cannot survive and now I am so far from the next village.

▶ **2.2** **PART 1**

OSCAR OK! Max. So, I'll just talk for a minute to introduce you, and then we'll begin the interview, OK? Are you ready?
MAX Er, well, yeah, er, I think so …
O OK, when the light turns red, we're live. Hello, I'm Oscar Simmons from *City FM*, and I'm here to talk to Max Redwood, author of the bestseller *Solar Wind*. Thank you for coming in to talk to us, Max!
M Thanks.
O So, as many of you will already know, *Solar Wind* is a story about space travel. And basically, in a nutshell, a group of explorers are visiting a remote planet which is populated by people, that is to say, aliens! Now, these aliens look very similar to humans, but have a radically different culture. I'd like to begin by asking you where you got the basic idea for *Solar Wind*, Max?
M Well, the idea came to me when … it came to me when …
O I mean, did you get the idea from your own travels and experiences of other cultures, for example?
M I haven't really travelled much, actually. I was planning a trip across Asia once …
O Oh, right?
M But, well, to cut a long story short, I had to cancel it, so …
O Right. So in other words, it all just came from your imagination, then?
M Well, you could say that, yes.
O OK. So next I'd like to move on to your childhood. Were you interested in science fiction growing up?
M Er… … Well … Yeah.
…
O Right, so now for the question that all our listeners will be asking … What happens next? Or, to put it another way, when will *Solar Wind 2* be published?
M Um …
O Right, I see. So it's top secret information, then?
M Um, I'm sorry?
O What I meant by that was, you're not allowed to give any dates yet?
M Er …
O Right, so, to wrap things up now, I'd just like to thank Max Redwood for taking the time out of his busy writing schedule to come in and talk to us today. Thank you, Max, and looking forward to *Solar Wind 2*!
M Yeah, thanks. No problem.
ALEX Max. Hi. Alex. I'm, er, Emma's boyfriend.
M Emma's … Alex! Of course.
A Yeah, listen, um, I've read the book …
M Look, I'm really sorry. I've got to go.
A Nice to meet you too!

▶ **2.6** **PART 2**

EMMA Oh, hello Max.
MAX You didn't listen, did you?
E Er, no. How did it go?
M It was an outright disaster! I came across as a blithering idiot!
E Calm down. I'm sure it wasn't that bad!
M OK, let me try and think about this calmly, shall I? All things considered, I think my first and last radio interview, listened to by the entire city, was, how shall I put this… ? … A complete and utter embarrassment! And my career's totally ruined! And I'll never be able to show my face again! Yes, I think that just about sums it up.
E Calm down. I'll put the kettle on. You'll feel better after a cup of tea. And a biscuit? A chocolate one …

▶ **2.9**

TONY I know Prague quite well – I've been there several times, I've got friends who live there. And, of course, it's one of the most beautiful cities in Europe. There's the old centre – exceptionally well preserved, it's full of beautiful buildings, all periods of history. And not to mention the baroque buildings in the old city centre, that've been skilfully restored and look stunning. So, yeah, I'd say it's definitely a beautiful city, definitely worth visiting, no question. But, there are hordes of tourists. The last time I was there I went to the Charles IV Bridge which crosses the river. And don't get me wrong, it's a very beautiful bridge, but it was teeming with people. It was impossible to stop and look at the view or take photos. I'd recommend going outside the main tourist season, though there's not really any time when it isn't busy. I've got friends who live there and they say they don't go to the old city centre any more – it's too crowded and too expensive. They go to the other parts of the town. It is a real shame that tourism has made these historic places unaffordable to local residents.
LOLA I went to Prague last winter and I loved it. It's got such a romantic atmosphere. Beautiful old buildings, the cobbled streets, the squares with the fountains. People say that it's been spoilt by tourism and it's true in a way. The centre gets very crowded, especially in the summer. But, if you look beyond that, and appreciate the buildings and the old-fashioned atmosphere it's, it's still really a magical place. The thing I love most in Prague is going up the hill to the castle. I went up the twisty, narrow streets, and then, there's the breath-taking view across the old city. Looking down, there's a maze of steep red-tiled roofs spread out beneath you – it's like something out of a children's storybook. I took so many photos of Prague – every corner there's something to take a picture of. It was wonderful.

Unit 4

▶ **2.14**

PORTER Now, you know that little voice in your head that questions if you've locked the car properly, or turned the iron off. That uneasy feeling that you get when you think there is something you should be doing, but you just can't remember what it is. More often than not these are groundless anxieties that simply reflect that many of us are born worriers, but sometimes that voice in your head – that gut feeling – warrants your attention. And many doctors, particularly GPs, do pay it attention when faced with a patient that doesn't quite fit the description in the textbook. All may appear well on the surface, but you're left with a nagging doubt that all is not quite as it seems. So are doctors right to heed their gut instincts? Ann Van den Bruel is a GP and research fellow at the University of Oxford.
VAN DEN BRUEL A lot of GPs especially, they recognise this feeling that they get sometimes, although not everybody admits or, or acknowledges that they sometimes act upon it – it's seen as something mysterious or maybe you should not talk about it. But it is real, and when you talk to GPs about it they're really happy to be able to share that experience of having this gut feeling and using it sometimes in their medical decision-making. So it is something real, but it's not always acknowledged as a valid, or a useful tool.
P Well, do we know if it's useful?
V Well we do, because er we've been doing studies in, for example, serious infections in children – so that's meningitis or pneumonia – and we have found that gut feeling is the most powerful predictor in general practice of a serious infection in a child.
P But how do you go about measuring the effect of something like gut feeling?
V Well, we asked doctors to record whether they felt something like gut feeling or an instinct that something was wrong in 4,000 children, and then we compared those recordings with what ultimately happened to those children and we were able to

calculate the diagnostic accuracy, if you want, of gut feeling. And we found that it is very, very accurate – it's very useful. It's not a hundred per cent right, but, the chance that something serious is going on is much higher when a doctor has a gut feeling.

P Well, Margaret McCartney's been listening in from our Glasgow studio. Margaret, I suspect that none of this will come as a surprise to you.

MCCARTNEY No … And I think gut instinct is one of those real rich seams of general practice that kind of goes under-explored, and I think, unacknowledged as well. When you talk to doctors over coffee, y'know, one of the things that we're always saying to each other is, y'know, 'I'm just not quite sure about that lady.' Or, 'I'm just not quite sure about that hanging together.' But, I think there's also a little bit of shame that goes along with it, y'know, I think sometimes it's seen as being a bit unscientific – y'know, just having this kind of … gut instinct, this sort of feeling about someone and it's a kind of slightly romantic idea that kind of harks back to the kind of um old-style videos of pictures of doctors sort of just having a feeling about someone. And for me it's not unscientific at all, it's actually highly scientific, because what you're doing is you're saying actually, out of all the people that I've seen with similar symptoms, you're just a bit different from everyone else, so it's almost like recognising that this person just doesn't quite fit the pattern but you're not quite sure in what way they don't fit in with that pattern. So what you're doing is you're opening up to saying well I'm unsure, I'm uncertain and the possibilities here are potentially something quite serious and I'm not going to just let that go.

P And this isn't the only piece of evidence that suggests that it's a powerful tool …

M No … And what I find really fascinating is when you go and ask doctors around the world, as some researchers have done, 'Do you experience a similar kind of phenomena?', all doctors will say that they do. Some people will describe it as feeling something in their stomach – something just not quite right. Other doctors will say that they feel it in their bones that something's just not right. And it's just this idea that you get something that jars – something that just doesn't quite fit properly together – and you have a sense that you're not actually very certain about what's going on here at all.

V In general practice, we have to deal with a lot of uncertainty – we don't have all the tests and all the technology the hospital doctors do have … and … so, we're used to dealing with uncertainty and we're used to not having that much at our disposal, to make our decisions. So gut feeling for us is like our safety net, when we feel 'Hmm … I'm not really happy about this', then we may want to ask a second opinion, or we may want to schedule another appointment, or we may want to give the parents very detailed information on when to come back – that's how we want to deal with that uncertainty that is left at the end of the consultation.

▶ **2.16**

TOMMY We got burgled once … and believe it or not, they got the burglars. My parents were having their kitchen renovated – security wasn't very good and the burglars got in really easily. They took all the usual stuff – the TV, jewellery, but I also had all my toys stolen. That's strange! But I did have an impressive collection of Transformer toys. I felt really upset – my world had come to an end. Now the funny thing was, my toys were actually how they caught the thieves. One went to a football game and had his bag searched as part of security – the thief took the Transformer items to sell to a mate. Now, this particular security guard had a friend who was a policeman, and he'd told him about the strange theft of my toys, and he'd got in touch, and the thief got arrested as he was leaving that game! And the good thing was I got my toys back. I was happy on the day I got them back, but I lost interest in them almost immediately. I never played with them again.

MARISSA My brother got himself locked in the garden shed at school and he couldn't get out. What happened was, was my brother didn't come home from school so my mom and I, we started looking for him and … I mean, I was with my mother and she started getting more and more upset, and at first, I didn't completely understand what was going on, but I think I picked up on the general anxiety and that made me cry.
So his disappearance got everyone looking for him, in a small forest near our house. And people searched all night calling for him – I mean, I remember them shouting, 'Charlie! Charlie!' I mean, it was terrible and … there was this desperate sound in their voice – I was so afraid.
Anyway, the next day, the teacher arrives early at school and heard my brother crying in the shed. No one knows how it happened I mean, maybe the door got locked from the outside. Anyway the funny thing is, is he's always loved gardening! I'm surprised it didn't put him off.

CLARA Er, so it was my first day at nursery, and I was left by my mother. This was the first time I'd been without her. Mum told me the nursery teacher was really worried. She said she was used to tearful upset children but, apparently, I was like an ice statue! She didn't really know what to do with me. She had me sitting on my own and I think I remember her saying something like 'I'll get you set up with some paper and crayons' but … I just sat there looking at her. I'm sure I had some kind of blank look on my face. I guess it was a kind of a shock.
Er, eventually, a little boy asked me to join in a game. I'm not sure why – I went with him … and that literally broke the ice. He got me to play when no one else could. Guess who that little boy was … ? It was my husband Andrew! We ended up being best friends at nursery and, I actually didn't see him for 15 years. And then suddenly, we bumped into each other after university and the rest is history.

▶ **2.20**

MARISSA My brother got himself locked in the garden shed at school and he couldn't get out. What happened was, was my brother didn't come home from school so my mom and I, we started looking for him and … I mean, I was with my mother and she started getting more and more upset, and at first, I didn't completely understand what was going on, but I think I picked up on the general anxiety and that made me cry.
So his disappearance got everyone looking for him, in a small forest near our house. And people searched all night calling for him – I mean, I remember them shouting, 'Charlie! Charlie!' I mean, it was terrible and … there was this desperate sound in their voice – I was so afraid.
Anyway, the next day, the teacher arrives early at school and heard my brother crying in the shed. No one knows how it happened I mean, maybe the door got locked from the outside. Anyway the funny thing is, is he's always loved gardening! I'm surprised it didn't put him off.

CHARLIE So, my sister Marissa always tells this story of me getting myself locked in a garden shed. That's just … it's just not true … I mean, I wasn't locked in … I was in there with my science teacher, Mrs James. I mean, she was showing me how to grow things from seeds. Er, we were transferring seedlings from large containers to individual ones. We were like, just so concentrated on the job we forgot about the time. Marissa has a strange idea everyone searched through the night for me and Mrs James found me in the morning. That's just not true. I think my mom was just slightly concerned I wasn't home from school. Er … my mom came with Marissa to school late in the afternoon and found me and Mrs James at work. Mrs James was er … a bit embarrassed. Mo … Mom was pleased I'd, y'know, taken an interest. Marissa was right about one thing though … Thanks to Mrs James, I've always loved gardening.

▶ **2.23** **PART 1**

NADIA So, Oscar, before you go, can we have a quick word about your interview with Max Redwood?

OSCAR Grand, yes!

N How do you think it went?

O Well, if you don't mind me saying so, it was like trying to get blood out of a stone.

N Right.

SARA Yeah, he wasn't an easy guy to talk to.

O Tell me about it! If you ask me, maybe he should stick to writing.

N I see where you're coming from, but guys, I think we're forgetting something here.

O What's that?

N We're the professionals.

O OK, but I thought I was being … professional.

N It's our job to get the best from our interviewees.

O Are you saying it was my fault?

N Look, don't take this personally, Oscar. I'm trying to be constructive.

O Really?!

N I think a good interviewer can get blood out of a stone.

O OK …

N I think we all need to learn from this.

O I do take your point, but I'm not sure there's anything more I could've done.

N I beg to differ. I agree Redwood wasn't particularly forthcoming, but my feeling is that there's always a way.

S No offence intended, Oscar, but … I couldn't understand why you were asking about a sequel.

O Well, he will be writing another book, surely?

S Well, anyway, Max clearly was a very hard nut to crack.

N With all due respect, Sara, I don't think you're in a position to tell us what does and doesn't make a good interviewer. We need to bear in mind that we're trying to run a business here. It's about getting results. We could lose a lot of listeners with an interview like that.

O OK, point taken.

N Let's pick this up again tomorrow.

▶ **2.27** **PART 2**

SARA Phew, that was hard going!

ALEX What, Nadia? Yeah, she can be quite tough, can't she?

S You're telling me! It's the first time I've heard her criticise Oscar, though.

A Probably because of his interview with Max Redwood.

S You've hit the nail on the head!

A Speaking of which …

S Such a shame. I've read his book and it's fascinating. He must have loads to say about it.

A Yeah. Speaking of which, you'll never guess what I found out recently. Max Redwood is my girlfriend's brother!

S You're kidding! Emma's brother?!

A Yep.

S No way! Have you met him?

A Um, sort of. But he is staying with Emma at the moment.

S Hey, I wonder if …

A Yeah?

S Well, y'know – could you maybe, y'know … ?

A What? Get his number for you?

S Well, yeah.

A Yeah, sure, I'll call Emma.

S Brilliant! Thanks, Alex!

A I wouldn't mention that you're a journalist to start with though.

S Hm … Yeah, you're right. I'll say I'm a fan!

A Well you are a fan, aren't you?

S Well, yeah, I suppose I am!

A Hi Emma! Yeah, listen, I've got a favour to ask about your brother …

▶ **2.29**

INTERVIEWER So you've obviously got a talent for music. Where do you think that comes from? Is your family musical?

NORA Yes and no. My parents played a lot of music, but I wouldn't say they were really musical. They listened to music all the time.

I And so you did too?

N As a child yes, we had it played to us all the time – whether we wanted it or not. My parents grew up in the sixties. They had a huge record collection – mostly rock music. So, you could say I grew up with music in that way.

I But they didn't actually play a musical instrument?

N No, none of them played anything. But, my grandfather, he was very musical.

I Oh yes?

N Oh yes! He had an incredible musical ear. He was a violinist. He played the violin in an orchestra, and he also travelled all over the world – so I think I'm similar to him in many ways – like, a professional in an orchestra. They did international tours and everything like that. So, I think I probably take after him.

I Did you hear him play?

N Yes, when I was a kid – um … about five, I think. There was this day when I was at his place, with my parents, and he was rehearsing something in another room. And I remember being intrigued with this sound. I don't know – it was almost an emotional experience – I was very drawn to it. I think that's when I became aware of music and wanted to play. And it just dawned on me – I wanted to play like that … it was that feeling that got me interested in playing. It was a really formative experience.

I But you didn't start playing the violin?

N No. I started playing my brother's guitar, actually – my older brother. He had a guitar, but he couldn't really play it. So I picked it up one day and I started playing around on it. And like, the moment I started playing, I knew it was the right instrument for me. It was really weird actually, it just felt right.

I You've been very successful in a short space of time. Are you surprised by that?

N Well, I never set out to become famous or make money. Music was always something I just did for fun. It was only when someone asked me to play on the local radio station that I thought maybe I could make a living from it. That was about a year ago.

I And now you've released an album; it's called *Memory*.

N Yes.

I Is that about your grandfather, those memories of him playing the violin? I see you've had an elderly man put on the cover.

N No, it's not really, well, maybe partly. But it's really more to do with travelling.

I Travelling?

N Yes, it started in my teens, I've always travelled a lot.

I Like your grandfather.

N Yeah, that's right.

I So where did you travel?

N Oh, lots of places. All over Eastern Europe, um … Turkey, Morocco. I went for countries that had good music. And I always tried to listen to the local music and I recorded it. It's like most people take photos, well I do too, but I also recorded sounds I heard, music especially. I always come back from travelling with my head full of music, and gradually that works its way into my songs. So you could say they're my memories, I suppose.

I Musical ones.

N That's right, yeah. These are my musical memories.

Unit 5

▶ **2.39**

NEWS READER 1 When it comes to football, I'm extremely patriotic. Who isn't? If I go to see England play anywhere in the world, there's only one football shirt you'll catch me wearing – I wouldn't be seen dead in anything else, particularly a French one. Same goes for any fan – only trouble is … the shirt can get you into trouble. So here's the thing … Man goes to Cyprus. Turns up to customs and hands over his French passport. The immigration officer looks at the passport and looks at the man. What's

he wearing? An English football shirt. Just doesn't match, does it? A Frenchman wearing an English football shirt? C'mon! Turns out this guy – this not so clever guy – well, he forged the passport – it was a fake. And, by all accounts, he missed the game. The Cypriot police have locked him up.

NEWS READER 2 Stealing things – it sure makes you hungry. Here's a story of a young man who brings new meaning to the term 'serial offender'. This 16-year-old was skipping class at high school and paying regular visits to a family home – not his family. The homeowner says he doesn't have a key to his own house so leaves it unlocked every day. So our 16-year-old truant gets into the habit of dropping in for some breakfast cereal and milk – not just once, but on a number of occasions. And it was all going well until he logged himself on to Facebook with the family's iPad … and forgot to log himself out! So our young 'cereal offender' got caught and has been detained in a local facility for young criminals.

NEWS READER 3 Ever done the pocket-dial thing? It can be a bit embarrassing. It can also get you arrested! See, this couple thought they were being very smart. They allegedly went to a supermarket and stole a whole heap of video games and DVDs. They had this great plan to pawn them for cash at the local pawn shop. Trouble is, when they were making their getaway, they pocket-dialled emergency services. I mean, they thought they were pretty smart – boasting about how the operation had gone so smoothly and how much cleverer they were, compared to other thieves. They also talked about where they were going to sell their ill-gotten gains. Of course, what they didn't realise was that an emergency services operator could overhear the whole thing and noted down all the details. So when they got to the pawn shop, guess who was waiting? The police, of course, with the handcuffs ready!

NEWS READER 4 Let me tell you about John Parsons – that very rare thing, an honest fraudster. And I have to say, Mr Parsons is extremely creative – ingenious, you could say. He was stuck in a high-security facility all nice and safe. Someone manages to smuggle in a mobile phone for him. Now, Mr Parsons gets busy and creates a fake web domain, and from this domain he emails a release form to officials – for his very own release! So out of jail he walks – a free man – and the officials don't discover his clever little scheme for another three days. But this is where the fraudster turns into an honest man – he hands himself in. Or maybe life was boring on the outside. Anyway, he's back inside serving his 15 years for numerous counts of fraud. But even lawyers and judges agree, John Parsons is nobody's fool!

NEWS READER 5 Now here's a good story. You could say that it's un-bee-lievable! Police are on the hunt for a … I guess you could call him a 'would-bee burglar'. Last Thursday night he was having a go at stealing some bits and pieces from a shed in the Jesmond Dene area. So he was busy opening all these boxes, looking for some interesting items to steal. And one of the boxes contained something with a very interesting … buzz. Inside was a hive of bees! Police are pretty sure our burglar won't have got away without a whole host of bee stings. So police want to know if there are any medical professionals or chemists out there who've treated someone with bee stings. Not very common in these winter months.

CO-PRESENTER What you might call a … bumbling crook!

▶ **2.40**

MIKE Well I actually studied biology at university and er … I've always wanted to get into conservation work. Er … And I've been trying to get work on nature reserves, in order to gain practical experience. And the trouble is I can't find a job with a paid salary – there's too many people these days who are willing to work on a voluntary basis so, er … so at the moment what's happening is I'm volunteering at weekends and I'm working in a café during the week, in order to make ends meet and pay the bills.

OLIVIA I left college in June and have a degree in tourism. Since then I've been applying for many jobs in sustainable tourism, for example, y'know, ecotourism. That's what really interests me and I'm very passionate about. But unfortunately in this current climate, it's very difficult to get a job. Unfortunately, the last job I applied for had 200 applicants, and I got on a shortlist of 10 but, er … in the end I didn't get it. The only way to gain experience nowadays seems to be to do an internship – but instead of them paying us, we have to end up paying them for this privilege!

ANDREW I applied for a job in investment banking straight after I left university. Er … my background is economics and business. I was lucky because I was immediately offered jobs by three different companies and I decided that I would go for the job that I deemed to be most interesting. Um … I managed to negotiate a higher salary than they were offering and since then I've been working very hard indeed, in order to prove myself – as there have been a lot of redundancies in the financial sector recently. And I certainly want to make as much money as possible while I can.

KAREN I left school um … at 16, and I went straight to do an apprenticeship in retail. Um … unfortunately, by the time I finished my apprenticeship a lot of people were made redundant and they couldn't keep me on. So I was unemployed for probably about two years … But, er, eventually I found a job in this large store selling sports equipment, which I'm still there, I'm working shifts. I work morning shifts, afternoon, and evening shifts. Um … I get paid by the hour so I try to get as many shifts as possible – so if I'm lucky I can get a double shift and work er … around 40 hours a week, maybe. But more often it's only around 10–15 hours a week … and that's hardly enough to live on.

▶ **2.45** PART 1

SARA Hi, Mr Redwood? I'm Sara Neroni.

MAX Hello. Just call me Max. Nice to meet you!

S Nice to meet you, too. Coffee?

M Oh, yes, please.

WAITRESS Two coffees.

M Thanks.

S I am such a fan of your work! Thank you for agreeing to meet me like this.

M Well, I try to find time for my fans. I'm just sorry we couldn't meet up sooner.

S That's fine. I know how busy you must be.

M Yeah. So, er, you work with my sister's boyfriend Alex?

S Yes, that's right. You're staying with Emma at the moment, if my memory serves me correctly?

M Just on a temporary basis, till I get my own place.

S It must be a bit hard to write, stuck in her flat?

M Well, I'm not actually doing any writing at the moment.

S No?

M No. To be honest, I think I've got writer's block. But hopefully, I'll snap out of it soon enough.

S Oh no! That must be tough.

M Well, we all have our ups and downs, I guess.

S Yeah, I suppose.

▶ **2.47** PART 2

SARA It must be really difficult writing science fiction.

MAX I suppose so. I reckon I should've been a crime writer.

S Yeah?

M When your detective solves the murder, you just invent another murder, and then away you go.

S I never thought of it like that!

M Not so easy with science fiction. I think I've said everything I wanted to say in my first book.

S Oh? I was under the impression that you were writing another book?

M No. No doubt you heard that from that guy from the radio interview.

S Oscar.

M Yeah. Him. What stands out in my mind most is that that interview was a total disaster! I'd hazard a guess that he hadn't even read my book. Hadn't even opened my book. Otherwise he wouldn't have asked about a sequel!

S Hm …

▶ **2.50** **PART 3**

MAX Still, enough about me. What about you? Presumably, you're a technician, like Emma's boyfriend, right?

SARA Well, I'm not actually …

M Oh. I think I remember Emma saying that her boyfriend's a technician at *City FM*.

S Yes, he is. But I'm a journalist, myself. Sorry.

M Oh. I see. Emma didn't mention that. I thought you were just a fan. I didn't know you were a journalist.

S Suppose you'd known, would you still have agreed to meet with me?

M Well, not after that interview with Oscar whatsisname!

S So, I suppose another interview would be out of the question.

M Time to go!

S I'm sorry! It's just that I'm a really big fan, and I really need this break. I just didn't know how else to … Look, I've read your book and I absolutely love it. And I get that there simply can't be a sequel – after all, time does stand still at the end, doesn't it?

M Right.

M Look, I might consider doing another interview.

S You would?

M But I need to have a think about it. Let's meet up again soon to talk some more?

S Oh, fantastic! Thank you so much! When are you free?

▶ **2.53**

MARIO I saw this really interesting job ad online – working in marketing for an IT company. It's a bit like my current job, but there were opportunities in the new job for more travel and I thought, 'Why not give it a go and apply?' I sent in my CV and got offered an interview immediately. I thought, 'Great!' So I had this interview with an HR person. To start off with, it went really well. She told me she was impressed by my CV, and I could feel that I was giving her the answers she wanted to hear. Y'know, you just get a sense of whether a job interview is going well or not. Then, after about half an hour, this HR woman said, 'Oh, and of course we'll need log-ins for all the social media you use.' And I replied, 'Oh, you mean the professional one?' And this kind of suspicious look crept across her face and she said, 'No, I mean all social media.' I was truly shocked – I was completely lost for words. For a minute I just sat there and didn't say anything. Eventually she asked, 'Is there a problem?' At which point I said that I didn't really think it was appropriate for a company to access private social media. Then there was this stony look in her eyes and she said, 'All staff are required to provide access to the social media they use.' I'm afraid I couldn't help myself and I said that I felt they were overstepping a boundary by asking me for this, and there were really privacy concerns. But she didn't back down. She said that the company expects access to social media, particularly of marketing staff. She said that it's essential that we project a positive image at all times – both in person and online. Well, I don't want my private life to be controlled in this way. And besides, I've heard of people getting sacked for making 'inappropriate comments' about work – but of course, it's always the company that decides what's inappropriate or not. So, in the end, I politely told this woman that I wouldn't feel comfortable working for her company and quickly left. I mean, I know everyone's life is more out there and online these days, but, demanding to see my social media – that's just a bit too Big Brother-ish for my liking.

LAILA I read this article the other day about people being surprised or shocked because prospective employers expect access to applicants' social media. I was a bit surprised by this article myself – surprised, because I thought, 'What do people expect in this day and age?' We live so much of our lives online and it's such a public thing so, I don't really see a problem with employers having a look at my social media postings. In fact, this happened to me a couple of months ago. I applied for a job as an account manager at an advertising agency. During the first interview, the guy who's now my boss asked if he could friend me and I agreed immediately – in fact, we sorted this out during the interview. This meant he could read through all my personal information and postings. He called a couple of days later to say I'd got the job. And, do you know what swung it in my favour? He really liked my way of presenting myself online, and he was impressed by the sports training and charity work that I do in my free time. He also thought my pet cockatoo was very cool! So really, why wouldn't you want to give a prospective employer this kind of access? I really think it's advisable to do so. Of course, if you've posted material that puts you in a bad light, then I can see why you wouldn't. But in that case, the real issue is the way you use social media. I think that people tend to forget that just about anything you post online can be accessed in one way or another – so if you don't want people to read it, then don't post it. Social media are so much a part of my life and I feel completely relaxed about sharing information. I do think carefully about the way I present myself, but no more carefully than I would if I walked into a room full of people I don't know. It's the same thing – what's the difference?

Unit 6

▶ **3.4**

INTERVIEWER So Monika, I understand you're an amateur photographer?

MONIKA Well, I wouldn't go that far, um … , I'm definitely amateur but I'm not a photographer yet, perhaps in the future.

I But you've been studying photography?

M Um … yes that's correct. I've been doing this course about photography and it's for complete beginners.

I Why did you decide to do the course?

M Um … I think I could blame my husband for it! Um, because he got um … he got me this fantastic DSLR um … camera and er, it is a, quite a complicated um … object really. If you don't know how to use it, it can be really complicated to take some photos. So I was wondering what I could do to … to improve, and to know how to use it. And I was um … I started with those um … kind of tutorials on YouTube that you can watch, um … but it wasn't, it wasn't good enough because they were using quite a lot of jargon and I wasn't really sure what they were referring to. Um … so I decided to do a course, to learn a little bit more about it so that I can use the tutorials in my own time.

I Have they taught you anything useful?

M The tutorials um … not really, but then when I went to the course, and I started my course, I've been doing this course now for a few weeks um … and I'm learning all the time something new so it's really, really good.

I So, do you feel more confident with your camera now?

M Um, a little bit, um, it depends on the types of photo that I want to take. Um … let's say that it's more kind of um … documentary-type photos then I would still use my auto mode, um, but I would still be quite um … perhaps … I would be thinking more about the frame and, and the composition of the photo because these are the things that I would normally learn during the course. So um, our tutor would be giving us some specific tasks on for example composition or … panning effects or different techniques and, so after that I would go outside the classroom – I would go and for example take some photos and focus on either one technique and then practise it, um, or I would just take as many shots as I can, 'cause sometimes it's … um, improvisation is also very good.

I Have you discovered any bad habits since you started your course?

M Um … I think I was taking too many photos. And … potentially I was taking photos of everything and I wasn't really following any rules. But now I know that I have to be more careful with my um settings of the camera and what exactly I want to take a photo of. Um … so when I'm taking my photos now, I'm more cautious and kind of careful how I do it and what I really want to um … take photos of.

I What's your favourite photograph that you've taken?

M I think I've got um, two pictures that are my favourite pictures. Um … the first one is … it's, it's a static photo of a building um … so when I was um … doing my course, there was this project. We were meant to take photos of an object, or of a static object. So I chose this building that is meant to be demolished. Actually, it is being demolished now. So, every single day you could kind of take a different photo of a different part of the building. So one day I was standing there and I was really lucky because they were actually taking a part of the window down, and there was this massive hole in the building. So I was able to take a few interesting photos of the whole process as well as the, just, just the hole in the building, but there was this chair just in front of the hole and it made the whole picture quite realistic like there was still life in it, but actually the building is being demolished, so that's one of my favourites. And then the second one was a completely different project when I was trying to take photos of moving objects and er, my subject was um … a three-year-old girl, and she was playing in a garden, and she had this yoga mat that her mum was using, and she was just rolling into this er … yoga mat and um, luckily for me, um, I was able to take a few interesting photos of her playing in the garden.

▶ **3.10**

READER I could see her defeat and helplessness. The attendant seemed unaware, as if his perception had grown a reptilian covering. What did she care for the campaign for the preservation and welfare of copperheads and rattlers and common grass snakes? What did she care about someday walking through the woods or the desert and deciding between killing a snake or setting it free, as if there would be time to decide, when her journey to and from school in Philadelphia held enough danger to occupy her? In two years or so, she'd retire and be in that apartment by herself with no doorman, and everyone knew what happened then, and how she'd be afraid to answer the door and to walk after dark and carry her pocketbook in the street. There was enough to think about without learning to handle and love the snakes, harmless and otherwise, by having them draped around her neck for everyone, including the children – most of all the children – to witness the outbreak of her fear.

'See, Miss Aitcheson's touching the snake. She's not afraid of it at all.'

As everyone watched, she touched the snake. Her fingers recoiled. She touched it again.

'See, she's not afraid. Miss Aitcheson can stand there with a beautiful snake around her neck and touch it and stroke it and not be afraid.'

The faces of the children were full of admiration for the teacher's bravery, and yet there was a cruelly persistent tension; they were waiting, waiting.

'We have to learn to love snakes,' the attendant said. 'Would someone like to come out and stroke teacher's snake?'

Silence.

One shamefaced boy came forward. He stood petrified in front of the teacher.

'Touch it,' the attendant urged. 'It's a friendly snake. Teacher's wearing it around her neck and she's not afraid.'

The boy darted his hand forward, rested it lightly on the snake, and immediately withdrew his hand. Then he ran back to his seat. The children shrieked with glee.

'He's afraid.' someone said. 'He's afraid of the snake.'

The attendant soothed. 'We have to get used to them, you know. Grownups are not afraid of them, but we can understand that when you're small you might be afraid, and that's why we want you to learn to love them. Isn't that right, Miss Aitcheson? Isn't that right? Now who else is going to be brave enough to touch teacher's snake?'

Two girls came out. They stood hand in hand side by side and stared at the snake and then at Miss Aitcheson.

I wondered when the torture would end. The two little girls did not touch the snake, but they smiled at it and spoke to it and Miss Aitcheson smiled and whispered how brave they were.

'Just a minute,' the attendant said. 'There's really no need to be brave. It's not a question of bravery. The snake is harmless, absolutely harmless. Where's the bravery when the snake is harmless?'

Suddenly the snake moved round to face Miss Aitcheson and thrust its flat head towards her cheek. She gave a scream, flung up her hands, and tore the snake from her throat and threw it on the floor, and, rushing across the room, she collapsed into a small canvas chair beside the Bear Cabinet and started to cry.

I didn't feel I should watch any longer. Some of the children began to laugh, some to cry. The attendant picked up the snake and nursed it. Miss Aitcheson, recovering, sat helplessly exposed by the small piece of useless torture. It was not her fault that she was city-bred, her eyes tried to tell us. She looked at the children, trying in some way to force their admiration and respect; they were shut against her. She was evicted from them and from herself and even from her own fear-infested tomorrow, because she could not promise to love and preserve what she feared. She had nowhere, at that moment, but the small canvas chair by the Bear Cabinet of the Natural Science Museum.

I looked at my watch. If I hurried, I would catch the train from Thirtieth Street. There would be no time to make the journey through the human heart. I hurried out of the museum. It was freezing cold. The icebreakers would be at work on the Delaware and the Susquehanna; the mist would have risen by the time I arrived home. Yes, I would just catch the train from Thirtieth Street. The journey through the human heart would have to wait until some other time.

▶ 3.11 PART 1

SARA Er, Nadia?

NADIA Yes?

S I've got some great news! I met up with Max Redwood the other day, and he says he's going to consider doing another interview with us!

N What?

S Max Redwood? He says he'll think about doing another interview with us.

N Oh, I don't know about that, Sara. You know, after last time.

S I know, but he's really hot stuff at the moment!

N That's true, but would he actually have something to say?

S Well, if I do the proper preparation …

N To be honest, it won't even be my decision, Sara. I'd need to get Paul to sign off on this.

S Paul?

N It would need someone more senior than me to give the go-ahead for this. There's a lot of risk involved. It was a disaster last time. We need some really compelling reasons to go down this route again.

S I see. Well, I could come up with those! Look, I really think this is worth a shot.

N Well look, why don't I invite Paul to our next team meeting and we can raise it then?

S OK, great!

…

N OK, the next item on the agenda is the author interview series. And, as I mentioned earlier, I've invited Paul today to get his take on it. OK, so over to you, Sara.

S Thank you.

P That's not a picture of Max Redwood, is it?

S Yes, that's right – an up-and-coming author, but not a forthcoming one, as poor Oscar discovered!

O You can say that again!

N Oscar!

S … And there were many questions left unanswered. Now, as luck would have it, I bumped into Max the other day and I've got him to consider doing another interview.

My focus today is on this second interview. Let me talk you through why our listeners want to hear more from Max Redwood. Well, first and foremost – he wrote his book from a bench on the Palace Pier right here in Brighton. However, he's not just a local celebrity – he's becoming famous on a national level. Let me take you through some facts and figures.

O This is a bit over the top, is it not, Sara?!

S I think these facts speak for themselves: sales of nearly half a million; rumours of a huge advance offered for a second novel; translations into eight languages; 300,000 Twitter followers … I don't want to labour the point, but one thing is clear – Max Redwood is on the road to becoming an international best-selling author.

Turning now to the focus of the interview itself, I've decided to talk about the creative process behind his work.

More specifically, I propose to find out how science fiction writers like Redwood can imagine in such detail places and events that they can't possibly have experienced in real life.

So to recap on what I've been saying, I'm proposing to re-interview Max Redwood, due to his imminent stardom, and focus on what inspired him to write Solar Wind. Now, if you'd like me to elaborate on anything I've just said, go right ahead.

O What will you do if Max won't reveal any interesting information?

S Well, I'll just have to cross that bridge when I come to it. But, I'm planning to work quite closely with him in the run-up to the interview, so there shouldn't be any nasty surprises on the day.

P That's absolutely the way to go. And you've clearly put a lot of effort into this, Sara. Thank you. But I'm going to have to give it some thought.

S OK.

P Nadia, can we touch base again on this later?

N Sure. That's fine. OK, moving on to the next item …

▶ 3.14 PART 2

ALEX Atishoo! Sorry …

SARA Oh, you're back!

ALEX Yeah.

S How are you feeling?

A Well, not a hundred per cent to be honest, but, y'know …

S Well, anyway … I've been dying to tell you about my meeting with Max the other day!

A Of course! How was it?

S Pretty good, on the whole. But he thought I was a technician like you, and he was a bit angry when he found out I was a journalist.

A Oh sorry. I told you not to mention that you were a journalist.

S Not to worry. He didn't seem to mind too much in the end.

A Well, that's good.

S Anyway, more to the point, he's agreed to think about doing another interview!

A Great!

S Yeah, I've just been presenting some ideas on it to the team.

A Hm. Have you got any further with the famous sequel that Oscar was talking about?

S Actually, no.

A No?

S No, there can't be a sequel because his first book was the end of the story.

A Oh?

S Because at the end time …

S AND A … stands still!

A Oh, I see what you mean …

S Yeah, it's a bit of a sore point with him, actually …

A Hmm. So he's reached the end of his story, but has he done the beginning?

S What?

A Well, if he can't do a sequel, he could do a prequel, y'know, what happens before the events in Solar Wind.

S Hmm, I wonder. You might be on to something there, Alex …

▶ 3.17

1 SPEAKER 1 Well I thought she sang wonderfully. What an amazing voice! I don't know how she does it.

SPEAKER 2 Yes, she really is great.

S1 I think it's one of the best productions I've seen here.

S2 So it should be for that price!

S1 Well, she is quite a big name.

S2 Mm.

2 SPEAKER 3 Hmm, interesting. But, why all those gloomy colours?

SPEAKER 4 Yeah, a bit depressing, weren't they? I thought the early landscapes were the best. They were more colourful.

S3 Yeah, I liked those – they were quite lively.

3 SPEAKER 5 Mm, nice here, isn't it.

SPEAKER 6 Yeah, it's one of my favourite places. I often come here after work. It's so relaxing.

S5 Yes, I hate those places where all the tables are crammed together, and you can't hear yourself speak.

S6 Yeah, me too. So … um, what shall we order?

4 SPEAKER 7 Wow, amazing!

SPEAKER 8 Yeah! Great special effects … Pity it wasn't 3D though.

S7 Yeah, it was cool, that bit where he jumped out of the helicopter.

S8 Yeah, and landed safely! Don't know how he did that.

5 S1 Ooh, I really needed that. I haven't worked out for over a week. I've just been sitting in front of the computer every day – I've been getting so unfit … Nice place …

SPEAKER 9 Yeah, they've got a good range of equipment. Good trainers, too.

S1 Have you been a member long?

S9 Yeah, let me see, next month, I will have been coming here for exactly a year, I think. So about a year, yes. I come here most afternoons. It's not so full then.

S1 Oh well, maybe I'll join.

Unit 7

▶ 3.28

SPEAKER 1 Politicians, media pundits, writers and students get away with claims that are not based on fact.

If I was ruler of the world for a day, I would install fact-checker apps into our smartphones, into our computers, so that when facts were broken, when people told lies, or told mistruths, our phones went 'Brrrrrrrr!', or the lines on our computer screen popped up in red. That way, we'd know what was fact and what was fiction.

Of course, I wouldn't apply it to everyone. I wouldn't apply it to poets, to novelists and others who specialise in imaginary ideas. My aim would be to ensure that we benefit from the age of the Internet of things to have an Internet of facts and ideas, and through this we would hopefully get away from the infuriating falsehoods that are being widely disseminated.

Over time, good ideas would be spread far and wide, and bad ideas would be seen as a joke, rather than being the source of misinformation and perpetuating ignorance.

SPEAKER 2 The invention I would like to propose is a remote control that can modulate the amount of sensory information you get – the amount of sound, or smell, visual information, etc.

I came up with this idea because I cycle around London quite a lot, and every day I notice how much I am bombarded with the sounds of traffic and the smells of the city and visual advertising and media. I think this is something that in general people deal with in a number of different ways. Often it relies on putting more information or stimulus into your body, like wearing headphones or looking in your phone. A remote control would allow you to tone down what's there. I imagine it would work like a force field you can set at your ideal level, because everyone is different, and everyone has different ideal levels, and it just filters everything that comes in and out.

SPEAKER 3 Well, my idea for changing the world is quite simple, and it can be justified on the grounds of justice and fairness. It is simply that when someone is interviewed, for a job, for example, that they should have to conceal their appearance. They would have to wear a mask. They would not be able to exploit their, let's say, personal or their social, visual capital. They would have to be judged according to their merit. It would create a level playing field. It would ensure that the best person was recruited to a company – irrespective of whether that person was good-looking or ugly, as conventionally determined.

It would serve the interest both of fairness in respect of that person's rights, and it would ensure a level playing field therefore for that reason. But it would also ensure the most meritocratic outcome – the best person would be chosen for the job.

▶ **3.29**

SPEAKER 1 It's hard to argue with the idea that we want truth over falsehood. I think the trickiest part of this is actually knowing what the truth is and what facts are and aren't correct. And so, my biggest concern would be that the fact app might itself be full of falsehoods that we haven't found out yet, or could be used to deceive us.

SPEAKER 2 I was intrigued though by the idea that you want to filter out these noises or smells or whatever it is when you're cycling. Isn't there a danger you could miss out something that's rather important for your safety? For example, you might just miss that taxi that was coming round the corner that you didn't know about. So turned down, you go straight into it. So I think you'd need a smart filter which would be able to recognise what was essential for you to see and hear, red traffic lights, for example, and what could safely be filtered out, like advertisements or noise from building sites.

SPEAKER 3 It's a fascinating idea, and it's very close to home for me because I've hired hundreds of people and done hundreds of job interviews, many of which have been over Skype or telephone. And I think I like the values and the spirit behind the suggestion. My hesitation about it is that you know they say 80 per cent of communication is non-verbal, and I think a lot comes across in expressions and bearing. Some of it is unfortunate and shouldn't influence your decision. Some of it is actually essential, I think – to assess someone's characteristics for a job. So I'm not sure what I think.

▶ **3.31**

PRESENTER Welcome to *From My Bookshelf* – the weekly programme where guests talk about a book that they think everyone should read. This week's guest is media expert and commentator Zelda Freeman. Welcome Zelda, thank you very much for being here today. Tell us about your book.

ZELDA Well um … the most intriguing book I've read in the past few years – *Rewire* by Ethan Zuckerman – er, he's an academic, um, and he thinks deeply about the role of media in our society.

P Zuckerman. The main thing about his book, I hear, is that he's challenging the myth about the Internet, is that true?

Z Yes, er … the myth. And what's interesting is that we only think we're more connected … But, the point he's making is, that we're actually wrong. Er, in some ways, the Net manages to isolate us.

P So we're all connected together but we're isolating ourselves? That sounds like a contradiction – how is that possible?

Z Well, use myself as an example. I use the Internet to find out news. I read a lot of newspapers online, but it's only British ones that I read. There's nothing stopping me from reading an English language newspaper in China – it's just a click away. But, I don't. What Zuckerman is saying is that the Internet is a very powerful tool, but very few of us exploit it to its full potential.

P I have to ask – does it matter?

Z Well, yes … The reason why it matters is that we're living in an age of economic and physical connection. Um, our economies are connected. So, if the share market in the US sneezes, then we all feel the effects. Um, a dangerous virus breaks out somewhere in the world and it can travel around the globe very quickly. And more people are moving around. What we really need to understand is how other countries and cultures work. We're more linked into each other than we used to be so, we need to be a lot more cosmopolitan.

P But in the 21st century, I'm sure a lot of people already know this. Does it actually matter if we don't do anything about it?

Z Well, good point … I mean, Zuckerman makes a very good point about that. We tend to think we know more than we actually do. It's a kind of false cosmopolitanism. And he uses this example because we know we could in theory read *The Times of India* online, but we almost begin to imagine that we actually do that, although in reality we don't. It's the possibility of connection that means we begin to think of ourselves as being cosmopolitan.

P So we begin to think that a possibility is a reality?

Z Exactly, I mean that's fine for many things, but as far as the Internet is concerned, I really think we need to think about it a bit more.

P So why do you think that we don't connect more?

Z Well Zuckerman suggests that our online behaviour is not that different from our offline behaviour. Um, so for example we form social groups according to the people we meet as we grow up, and we get together with people with similar attitudes and interests.

P So like we do in social media, we only friend people we want to actually be friends with?

Z Yes, that's right. What we don't do is explore much beyond that. But the thing is, we can – we actually have the potential to do that.

P So does Zuckerman himself, does he have any suggestions?

Z Well, he says that all we need to do is 'disconnect' from our current way of thinking and 'rewire'. We all have to learn to behave in a very different way.

P How?

Z That's the problem. It's a challenge. You need to identify what he calls 'bridge figures'. These are people who are able to translate ideas from one culture to another. They can explain it, give it context, and they help us to understand it.

P So like in some kind of magazine or journal?

Z No not really. He means being much freer than that. So, for instance, bloggers. These are people who have a passion for this kind of thing. Um … their information needs to be open and accessible and therefore it's free for everyone.

P Won't this just be more information online that people don't read?

Z So, as I mentioned before, business and politics are more and more connected. Um, um, business and political leaders need to be genuinely cosmopolitan in this day and age. So people who are 'bridge figures' are likely to assume more and more important roles in business, and also in politics. They've rewired already. So, if we want to do well in the world, we need to rewire as well.

▶ **3.37 PART 1**

MAX Excuse me a moment, I'll have to take this … Hi Wendy … Yes, I agree, we do need to talk this through. I'm with someone right now though. Can I call you back? Yes. OK. Speak later. Bye. Sorry about that.

SARA No worries. Sometimes it can't be avoided.

M It was my publisher asking about another book.

S Oh? Most writers would be over the moon to get the opportunity to write a second novel.

M Yeah, but I'm not sure I could, even if I wanted to.

S I'm sure that's not true, Max. I'm sure you'll come up with something soon. Hey, y'know, Alex had a good idea yesterday, for more to the *Solar Wind* story.

M Alex?

S Yeah. You know how we said a sequel is impossible … Well, he said you ought to write a prequel. Y'know … Tell the story of what happens before *Solar Wind*.

M So, you've been talking this through with my sister's boyfriend?

S Well, yes, I thought it might be a good idea …

M I think it's a bit out of order!

S Sorry?

M First, you hide the fact that you're a journalist. Then, you go gossiping about me to the whole world! It's not on!

S Well, I wouldn't say Alex is the whole world, exactly …

M To be perfectly honest, I'm not sure I can go through with another interview.

S You're right. I was out of line.

M People poking their noses in! I've had it up to here with it!

S Max, please, it's not like that! I'm sorry, it was inexcusable of me to pretend I was a fan, but … I think you're overreacting here.

M Maybe so, but I think we had better call it a day. Please don't bother me again.

▶ **3.41 PART 2**

EMMA Oh, hello Max! Take a look at this house. Isn't it gorgeous?

MAX Yeah, nice.

E Look, it's dead cool. This website allows you to take a virtual tour around the house.

M Right. But surely that price is way out of your league.

E Yeah, but I thought … for you.

M Me? Why?

E Well, you need somewhere to live.

M Why don't you just come out with it? You're throwing me out!

E No, no, no, of course not. Look, there's no need to get so worked up about it!

M Why is everyone trying to organise my life for me today? First Sara, now you!

E Max!

M Why doesn't everyone just get off my back?!

E Look, calm down, Max. I'm sorry. That wasn't very tactful of me, was it? But, y'know, you do need a place of your own. We both do, to be honest.

M You're right. As always.

E Max.

M I'm sorry I overreacted. I don't know what came over me. I've just been really stressed recently. But I had no right to take it out on you like that.

E It's OK. We all lose it from time to time.

M Me more than most!

E Hmm. What were you saying about Sara?

M Oh. Apparently, she and Alex have been discussing my next book. Alex's got a brilliant idea, I'm told.

E Oh, I see. And what's that?

M Well, that I should write a prequel.

E Not a bad idea.

M Do you honestly think that that idea hasn't crossed my mind?!

E Oh, Max! Don't get all angry again, please!

M Well, for goodness' sake! I'm fed up of being completely misunderstood all the time!

E Well, if you've had that idea, why haven't you done anything about it?

M Well … you wouldn't understand.

E Try me! Y'know this is just typical you! Constantly whining about how nobody understands you, but given half the chance, you can't be bothered to explain what's going on in that big head of yours.

M Emma! All right then, fine. I'll tell you. I'm scared that I'll ruin *Solar Wind* by writing something rubbish that everyone hates.

E What?

M I'm scared, Em.

E Do you remember that time you wrote that short story for the school newspaper?

M Not really.

E Oh, come on, you do so. What was it called … ? Um …

M *Solar Breeze.*

E It wasn't, was it? Anyway, you write that story, the whole school loves it, Mum and Dad are beside themselves with pride, as are you, and Miss Hall suggests you enter the National Short Story competition. Do you remember?

M Yes.

E And what a hoo-ha that was! You were entering the competition, you weren't entering the competition, you were, you weren't. Mum, Dad and I had to endure listening to at least 30 versions of it – sometimes even in the middle of the night. We all went without sleep for about three weeks.

M Emma, look, I know where you're going with this, OK.

E Good! And in the end, you won first prize! And I was so proud of you, Max.

M You were?

E Yeah! Because the thing about my big brother is … he always pulls it off. Am I right, or am I right?

M You're right.

E And tell me, how did you leave it with Sara?

M Sara? I guess I overreacted there too, if I'm honest. Well, I had a bit of a go at her, actually. Stormed off … I know what you're thinking. Right again. I'd better ring and apologise.

E Yeah, I think you'd better do that, Max.

▶ **3.43**

CLAUDIO Deep down, Masha is a nice person. I mean, if we go and have a coffee together and just talk about everyday things we get on just fine. But in meetings she really winds me up. She's the most stubborn person I know. What annoys me is that once she gets hold of an idea she won't let it go. She'll defend her idea and get quite aggressive about it. And sometimes she just won't stop talking and I'm sitting in a meeting and inside myself I'm saying 'Stop talking now, please!' Admittedly, she does have really good ideas sometimes. In fact, she's very creative, but she doesn't seem to understand that there can be other ways of looking at things. What she needs to do is lighten up – get a sense of humour. In this job, what you need more than anything else is the ability to laugh at yourself.

MASHA There's something a bit old-fashioned about Sam that I find very sweet. It's the thing I like about him the most. He has lots of funny little habits, like every morning he has coffee and a chocolate biscuit at exactly 9.45am. It's always the same kind of biscuit, and only ever one. The trouble is that this kind of precision affects the way he works. His attention to detail is incredible, but it's a bit of a handicap. What frustrates me is the way he absolutely refuses to start work on a project until he understands absolutely everything about it. And then when a project is underway, if there's something that he thinks doesn't make sense, he'll call everything to a halt until he thinks it's sorted out. Sometimes it's just so unnecessary, and it really slows things down. But sometimes the question he is asking is the right one to ask. And I have to admit, he's really good at predicting where problems might come up. But I just wish he was a bit more flexible.

SAM I sit next to Claudio in the office. The one thing I really appreciate about him is he's quiet. I don't like working next to someone who talks all the time. However, I know for a fact that when it looks like Claudio is really concentrating on something, he's reading a newspaper online. I can see his screen. I don't really think he should be doing that. And in team meetings I find him a bit strange. What unsettles me is the fact he doesn't say a lot. He spends a lot of time sitting there looking bored or with a cynical smile on his face. I sometimes get the feeling that he's … well, that he's laughing at the rest of us. Still, when he does say something, it's

usually worth listening to. Sometimes, when I notice a problem in a project, it'll be Claudio who comes up with the solution. Vicki, our team leader, she likes that. I always get the feeling that Claudio's her pet. He is clever, but I think he's a bit lazy and I'm not altogether sure he's sincere.

VICKI I'm really going to have to do something about the team I manage. We're supposed to be working on projects that improve business processes, but I feel like we spend more time managing each other than the project. We're not pulling together as a team. Team meetings have become really … painful – there's no other word for it. The main reason why this is happening is that they just can't seem to communicate well with each other. Masha talks all the time and wants everything done her way. Sam interrupts and goes off on tangents, and Claudio just sits there looking as though everything were beneath him. I mean they all have their strengths. Masha's great ideas person, and Sam is brilliant at anticipating problems. And Claudio is the ultimate fixer – and he has a good sense of humour. But each individual is caught up in their own agenda. What we need to do is some kind of team-building course or something.

Unit 8

▶ **3.45**

PRESENTER We all sleep at night, but it's surprising how little most people know about sleep. We talked to sleep researcher Jonathan Wilson, to find out what science has to tell us about sleep. Jonathan, first of all, all animals including humans need sleep – but … why do we need it?

JONATHAN Well that's a surprisingly difficult question to answer. The simple answer is, we don't really know. But there are several theories about it. One is that it helps us to conserve our energy during the period when it's least useful to search for food, and another is that sleep provides a time when the body can repair and restore itself, and it seems this is especially important for the brain. One thing we know for sure is that we do need to sleep. Most people sleep for about 8 hours, which means we sleep for one third of our lives – so on average that's 25 years spent asleep. The other thing we know is you can't go for too long without sleep – it simply isn't possible. The longest recorded time that anyone has stayed awake continuously is 11 days.

P So what's the ideal length of time to sleep? Is it eight hours?

J Not necessarily. Again we don't know for sure, but research suggests that people who sleep six-and-a-half to seven-and-a-half hours live the longest. So it seems the popular idea that we need eight hours' sleep isn't really true and many people can easily get by on only six hours a night. Babies need most sleep, of course – about 16 to 20 hours a day for new-born babies, and that gradually decreases as they get older.

▶ **3.48**

PRESENTER Good afternoon. Well, some of you saw the article on our website last week. It explained how an eight-hour sleep may not be good for your health after all. And how people used to have what scientists call 'segmented sleep', which means they had two sleeps every night, not one. Well, we've had lots of people calling in to tell us that they do, in fact, sleep in two separate chunks and they've been filling us in on what they get up to at night. First of all, we've got Matt from Brighton on the line. Hi Matt … so, tell us what you do at night.

MATT Yeah I usually go to sleep around ten or eleven. I naturally wake up at about one in the morning or two in the morning. I feel quite wide awake and restless. Then I get tired again at around three am, I drop off to sleep until about seven o'clock or so. My friends have always made fun of my sleep patterns. My wife used to force me to get out of bed 'cause I would lie there tossing and turning all night and I couldn't sleep a wink and it would disturb her.

P Right, of course! So what did you do about that?

M Well, I actually decided to use the time creatively. Now, I walk around Brighton taking pictures in the night. Some people might be a bit nervous walking around at er, y'know, two in the morning, but it is actually a really beautiful time to be out, you have the whole city to yourself and it is really, really great for taking photos. There was a wild storm last night and a full moon, so I was itching to get out there with my camera.

P Right, well thanks Matt. So that's one idea if you're suffering from insomnia – get out there and take some photos. Now, we have Saba on the line from Amsterdam, in the Netherlands. Saba?

SABA Yes, hi, how are you?

P You also get up at night?

S Yes. I've always been a light sleeper, I don't really sleep much um … I wake up at about four am every night to practise er yoga. I, I love yoga. Most of the time I do it at home but er once a week, I drive to this really great yoga studio in Amsterdam, and I practise there with about 20 other people, and we've all really become friends now.

P So they all get up, every night?

S Yes, er, we all have er the same pattern now. Sometimes I even get my husband to join us, if he's having trouble sleeping. But most of the time he's fast asleep and doesn't even notice when I get up. He sleeps like a log.

P OK, so you just slip away and go to your yoga class.

S Well I try to, yes. Depending on how busy the day is.

P And now we have Bernie from Manchester.

BERNIE Hi.

P Tell us about your sleep pattern.

B Well um … I'm an artist, er if that's not too bold a claim. I also work as an art teacher. And the way it works for me is most nights I tend to wake up in the middle of the night, feeling great, wide awake, full of beans, feeling very creative. Er … and usually I have a very strong image in my head that I've usually got from a, a dream. And what I do is I get up, er, get my paints out and I paint a picture.

P A picture? From your dream?

B Yes, that's right. Yeah, most of my work comes from dreams. Quite literally I'm a surrealist, I suppose. Yeah, it helps me to deal with issues and um … work through things. I find the whole process of dreaming very therapeutic.

P Interesting. And then you go to sleep again.

B Yeah, I mean what tends to happen is I go back to bed, and then I'll drift off to sleep for a couple of hours. But I'm, I'm always up at seven o'clock. After all, I've got to teach at art college.

P You never oversleep?

B No, no, I'm always fine. Er sometimes I will have a nap later in the day – I'm not as young as I was – y'know, after lunch.

P Thank you, Bernie. So Bernie has three sleeps, two at night and one in the afternoon. I think I'll try that one myself. And lastly we have Iain, who grew up in Indonesia.

IAIN Hi there, yes.

P Iain, tell us about it.

I Ah yes, um … well it's quite interesting. I grew up among the Yali people in Papua, which is er, part of Indonesia. My parents lived in a very remote area. My mum was a medical worker and Dad was an anthropologist, and we all lived in a remote village. I lived there until I was 16, and er, as a child I used to camp and go hunting with my, my friends in the Yali tribe. We would go to bed more or less after sunset and we always woke up during the night.

P The whole village?

I Yes. Um … we'd, we'd hear people talking, y'know, someone would start a fire. Sometimes we would eat er sweet potato before going back to sleep until about five thirty or six. At home with my parents, y'know, I would get the regular eight-hour sleep, but with my friends, I slept like they did – it just seemed more natural.

P OK, thanks Iain, very interesting. And now we're going to listen to …

PETER BOWES And are you that meticulous about what you eat?

MARTIN KNIGHT I am – I weigh and measure everything I eat and almost never eat out. I eat about, maybe, instead of like two or three big meals throughout the day, I eat maybe, like ten smaller meals – it kind of staves off hunger that way. This is what I actually usually eat – first meal of the day – only about 170 calories. So the first thing I'm going to do is this kale and er chard mixture I kind of made myself, it's put in the food blender and I weigh out 55 grams – that'll be 30 calories.

P And you do this every morning?

M I do. Right first thing and then every time I eat – which sounds pretty onerous, but actually isn't so bad.

P And you're getting, I assume, mostly carbohydrates from this?

M I'm going to add olive oil here, so in fact, it's going to be about 50 per cent fats.

P So what else do you have with this?

M OK, well … Let me finish measuring out the kale here first. I have to measure it to the … to the gram, there we have it – that's about 30 calories. Then I have sprouted oats, 16 grams, so that's er that's about 70. Then this tomato paste here, and … 33 grams of that, and … almost done now. There we go. And then finally, add some olive oil, that's 9.2. Now oils you have to measure to a tenth of a gram, and be that accurate. And we're there!

P Can I taste it?

M Ah … if you'd like to, yes!

P I have to say it doesn't look hugely tasty to me, or appetising.

M No, no I can understand that perfectly, yeah. Um, here's a spoon.

P Here goes.

M It's very colourful anyway.

P It's actually not that bad.

M No, with the oil, so, so the pepper in it er gives it more of a flavour … more of a flavour than you might think.

P The oil helps. Not so sure about so much tomato in my breakfast like this.

M Oh, OK! That's one of my favourite things …

P But, y'know, really not as dreadful as I had expected.

M Oh, OK! Surprised you, huh? I try and actually have a kind of window of eating – from about eight till five in the afternoon, so maybe like eight or nine hours, and then I don't eat outside of that.

P Ever go to a restaurant for lunch?

M Ah … not very often. Maybe a few times a year.

P How do you cope with that?

M Er, like socially? Well, um, either take um some nuts, which I weigh beforehand – um maybe 200 calories of that. Or, um, I drink some water or tea round there. There's always some fluid there you can drink. It's … it's not as bad as it might sound.

P As well as his extreme diet, Martin Knight lives a Zen-like, stress-free existence in California. He practises yoga, goes jogging and lifts weights in his garden. And he says extending his life isn't his primary concern.

M For me, it's more about quality of life, right here and now, the daily. I don't really think about the abstractions of living longer, although that … that might happen.

P You're 49 now. How do you feel?

M Um I feel really good. I feel as good as I did ten, twenty years ago – I don't really feel any different.

P Do you feel better in a sense since your diet has changed?

M In some ways actually I do – I have a steadier energy level throughout the day, when before I maybe kind of dipped in the afternoon – y'know, it's more of a steadier level. And … I think um you more kind of have a higher alertness too. When you have a little bit of hunger in the background, then you're more aware, more alive.

NADIA You're here late, Sara.

SARA Oh, hi Nadia. Yeah, I've got a lot on.

N How is the preparation coming along?

S Good, yeah. I'm just so grateful for this opportunity.

N Well, it could have gone either way with Paul, really. But he said he could see how much it meant to you, and the work you'd put into the presentation. He feels confident you can make the interview a success – we both do.

S Oh, thanks Nadia.

N So, what kind of stuff are you getting from Max?

S There's a couple of interesting angles we could take in terms of revealing his inspirations.

N Oh?

S Yeah, I asked him how he got into science fiction and he said he started getting ideas on life on other planets when he was a kid. He broke his leg, and to cheer him up his dad bought him a telescope. He said he couldn't sleep at night and he used to spend hours looking up at the night sky.

N Hmm …

S So maybe we could explore the idea that insomnia breeds creativity …

N Well, I'm not sure about the insomnia bit – it's a bit of a tenuous link … but overall I think you've got some really good material here.

S But you haven't heard the best bit yet!

N What's that?

S He has an idea for his next book, and, he's giving us the title of it first!

N Wow! What is it?

S It's … wait for it … *Gravity Zero.*

N Hmm. Interesting … Are you OK there, Oscar? I didn't hear you come in.

OSCAR Yeah, yeah, I'm fine. Just forgot my car keys … again!

N Anyway, Sara, I can't believe you've got us an exclusive on that! Well done! Good night, Oscar.

O Night.

MIRANDA *Breaking News Online.* Can I help you?

OSCAR Hello, is that Miranda Hall?

M Yes, speaking.

O Oh, hello. This is Oscar Simmons. We met at a few press conferences. I don't know if you remember?

M Oh yes, Oscar Simmons, from *City FM.* Yes, I remember.

O Great, well, I'm calling because I've been doing a little, um, what you might call freelance work? Anyway, I've got some information you may be interested in – straight from the horse's mouth, I think it's fair to say.

M What kind of information?

O Exclusive information about our very own Max Redwood. Y'know, author of *Solar Wind?*

M Oh right, the guy who famously wrote the whole book staring out to sea from the end of the Palace Pier.

O Exactly. I can give you an article about him, including a sneak preview of his next book.

M I didn't know he was writing a second novel?

O He is! And I'm offering you the chance to be the first to announce it – with the title.

M The title? Well, yes, that would certainly be of interest. There's just the issue of how much you would like for it.

O Well, how much would you be willing to pay?

M Oh, I think we'd be prepared to offer, say, two fifty? Would that be a fair suggestion?

O Two fifty! Could you see your way to increasing that a little? I was kind of hoping for something more in the region of five hundred.

M No, out of the question. What would you say to three fifty? In principle, of course. I'd need to see the article first.

O Three fifty – is that your best offer?

M Fair's fair. Remember we haven't even seen what you're offering yet.

O OK, three fifty. We've got a deal.

M And I need it by one o'clock! I want it on the website by today.

O What? Today? Er, how flexible can you be on that?

M Well, if I don't get it by two and it's not the kind of thing I'm looking for, the deal's off.

O OK, fair enough. One last thing …

M What's that?

O Would you mind keeping my name off the article?

M Freelance and anonymous, eh?

O Yeah.

M No problem.

O Great. Thanks.

M Thank you.

INTERVIEWER Next on *Healthy Living*, we talk to a chef whose style of cooking is based on ingredients our ancestors would have eaten in the Old Stone Age or the Palaeolithic era, around say 100,000 years ago. Julia Dean is head chef at the newly opened restaurant *Ancestors*. Julia! 100,000 years – that's going back a very long way.

JULIA Yes, it is, and you can go back much further than that. The Palaeolithic was a major period in our development as humans. It was the era where we truly became human – we started using tools, we learned to cook, and so on. It was also a period that lasted for a very long time – well over a million years, and that's very significant, because it means that during this time our bodies adapted to a certain lifestyle and to a certain diet. After that, we settled and planted crops and our diet changed – the so-called Agricultural Revolution. But that was only 10,000 years ago – it's not a very long time at all relatively speaking.

I OK, so your idea is that our bodies are still adapted to life in the Stone Age – we've changed but our bodies haven't.

J Yes, that's exactly right. We've got different technology, but we're the same people as we were then, physically. So all the foods we ate then are what our bodies are accustomed to – they're what's good for us.

I So you mean meat?

J Yes, wild meat. Also fish of course, and we dug up roots and found edible plants. So we ate fish and meat and lots of vegetables and seeds and nuts and … and also fruit, but of course only in season when we found it.

I But no milk.

J No, what we didn't eat was dairy products, and we didn't eat refined grains like wheat or rice – these came much later. And of course that explains why many people find these foods difficult to digest, and it's a diet that makes you gain weight and is essentially not very healthy – much less healthy than what was eaten earlier.

I OK, I see why you chose the name, *Ancestors*, for your restaurant. So, if I go to your restaurant, I'll get the kind of food my ancestors ate in the Stone Age? It sounds a bit primitive.

J Well, don't worry. We won't just give you hunks of meat and a few nuts! The idea of our cooking is to use these ingredients, but, of course, to create sophisticated, modern and very tasty dishes using them. So people come to our restaurant because they love the food, of course. But at the same time, they know they're eating healthily – they're eating what's good for them.

I Well, put like that it sounds very tempting. I wish you the best of luck.

J Thank you.

I That was Julia Dean, explaining *the Stone Age Diet*. And now …

Unit 9

🔊 4.15

PRESENTER Cities around the world are growing more crowded by the day. All us city dwellers experience the frustration of ever-increasing traffic on our roads, and wear and tear on our amenities. Keeping transport moving, and public amenities functional, is an ongoing problem the folks who run our cities have to deal with. With an estimated five billion inhabitants of the world's cities by 2030, the challenge has never been greater … So, today … many major cities around the world are looking to mobile technology for their solutions. And there are a handful of products out there already that are aimed at helping to optimise the way we live in cities. One example is an app called 'click-and-fix'. It's in use in a number of cities and what it does is to let you communicate with your city maintenance services. People use their mobiles to let the city know where there's a problem – something's broken or out of service – and then the idea is it'll get fixed straight away. Or at least they get updated on what's being done about it. Michelle Thornton in Boston, USA shows us how it works.

MICHELLE Well, look I'm just going along the street and if I see something that needs fixing I can report it. It could be anything, like a pothole, or graffiti on a wall, or if something's been vandalised, or even a place where you're repeatedly having to risk your neck to get across the road – anything like that. So, right now, we're going past a park and there's a railing that's been smashed in here – it's all bent. So I'll go on the app and then I just take a snap of it – and I'll choose the most appropriate issue category, so I'll choose 'park issue' – the app knows where I am of course, and then … just send it off. And you can see it comes up here, it's saying it's received. Then I can look it up later and it will tell me if it's 'in process' or hopefully 'fixed'. I think it's a great idea. It means that I, as a citizen, can be more involved. So it's a kind of democracy in action if you like, and it also saves the city money.

4.16

FRANK I've got an app here, on my phone, called *Trainspotting*. I use this all the time – in fact I couldn't manage without it. I commute into town and it actually shows me, not just when the train's due, but exactly where it is – which is great because sometimes the station announcements are basically all over the place. You can't really trust them. So, I can get the map here, blow it up a bit like that and, yeah, there's my train! It's just left the last station and it's due in … two minutes.

RITA OK, this isn't an app, but it's an information screen. And they've got these screens all around the city – they're all over the place. And it can tell you whether your health is OK, which is really useful – especially for elderly people. So you press this panel here and it reads your blood pressure, and your body mass index, blood sugar level, pulse – all those things. And it also tells you how stressed you are. It reads the whole thing just from contact with your finger – it's a touch screen. It's amazing! So let's give it a whirl … I put my finger on it … Press OK … Print … OK, it's printing it out now … There we go. Let's see if I'm OK or whether I'm about to keel over. No, it says everything's normal, that's a relief – but 'stress level high', it says. Ah well … what can you do?

NICK Yes, well this isn't an app, but it's a cool idea. It's called *Strawberry Tree*, and these are artificial trees and they're dotted around the city. They're basically solar-powered phone charging points. They're shaped like trees, so they blend in. And the canopy consists of solar panels, which feed into batteries for charging your mobile or your laptop. It's all free, of course. So you can go to the park, sit and chat to people, or you can drink coffee, and they charge up your phone for you. It suits me because I've got a mind like a sieve – I'm always going out without charging my phone, so it's a real life-saver for me.

4.27

NEWS READER As Chinese tower blocks get higher and stranger, the debate is getting fiercer. The architects of this building in the city of Suzhou say it's a mix of western form and Chinese subtlety. Local residents see it differently.

LOCAL MAN [Speaking in Chinese]

NR 'We call it the giant pair of pants,' this man says. 'The giant pair of pants' isn't the only iconic modern building to have come in for a barrage of barbed criticism from Chinese Internet users – complaining about what they see as increasingly outlandish foreign designs, completely out of keeping with Chinese culture and architectural heritage.

DR ZHENG SHILING The danger is er for some cities – they don't have this need and they just construct so many high-rise buildings as a symbol. Er … one city constructed a, a 300 high-rise building … Another city would like to construct a 400 metres, and another 600, and so on. This competition is nonsense.

NR But the Chinese skyscraper is sprouting fast and might soon get even faster. This took little more than a week and now the company behind it says it will build the world's tallest skyscraper in just three months. Heritage is important, some experts say, but so too is solving the problem of China's overcrowded cities.

TIMOTHY JOHNSON A city like Shanghai – 20 million people already, could easily go to 30 to 40 million people, and I, I would subscribe that spreading that out further and further away from a kind of central core is more detrimental, it's less sustainable, than keeping things more dense, and going vertical.

NR But with more than 300 skyscrapers currently under construction in China, the debate is only going to intensify. Is the country laying the foundations for a well-planned urban future, or flying by the seat of its architectural pants?

4.28 PART 1

EMMA You're cheerful today!

MAX Yeah, well, I am. It seems like everything's falling into place, at last.

E Oh?

M Yeah! My new book's coming together well and I really think it's going to work. And, guess what? I think I've found a place to live.

E Wow, that's brilliant!

M Yeah, it's in a renovated warehouse, down by the marina.

E Sounds very avant-garde! Hey, Max … there's an article about you on *Breaking News Online*. Look!

M But … I've never even spoken to anyone at *Breaking News Online*! This is outrageous! Listen: 'Night owl Max Redwood spent his childhood gazing up at the night skies …' This is beyond belief!

E But it's true. I remember when Dad gave you that telescope.

M They've got no right to publish this! Where on earth did they get this from?! Who wrote it?

E There's no name.

M I don't believe it! They've even got the title of my next book in here!

E Let's see … '*Gravity Zero* …' So they do!

M But I haven't told … Sara! It's disgraceful! How dare she?! …

E Sara? But she doesn't work for *Breaking News*!

M No, but she's the only person I've told.

E Hmm, let's not jump to conclusions. There's something fishy about this. Why would Sara give the exclusive information that she needs for her big break to someone else?

M I don't know … I'm lost for words!

E I smell a rat.

M What do you mean?

E Someone else at *City FM* must have leaked the information.

M Maybe … Anyway, whoever it was, they've got no right! I'm ringing them right now!

E Hold your horses, Max! Think about what you want to say first.

4.30 PART 2

MAX This is Max Redwood, and I'm calling to express my dissatisfaction … No … no … This is Max Redwood and words cannot express my anger … Oh, for goodness' sake. Hello, is that the editor-in-chief at *City FM*?

NADIA Yes, speaking.

M This is Max Redwood. I really feel you owe me an explanation for the article which appeared on *Breaking News*.

N Yes, I've just seen that. I can assure you that we are just as upset as you are.

M Really? Well … I spoke in confidence to Sara Neroni. The next thing I know, I'm in an anonymous story online, and the title of my next book has been announced! It's totally unacceptable! Don't you think you should take full responsibility for this?

N There's no need to raise your voice, Mr Redwood. I do understand, and I have every intention of investigating the matter. Should I discover that any of the team have been involved, I can assure you, there will be consequences.

M How would you feel about someone you trusted revealing your confidential information in the press?! You've failed to fulfil your responsibility to protect my privacy!

N I really don't know what else I can say … Once I get the lie of the land, I'd like to invite you in and we can discuss it face-to-face.

M Absolutely not. And I'd appreciate it if you didn't try to contact me again. It's over. Finished. Finito. The end.

4.33 PART 3

NADIA Oscar.

OSCAR You wanted to see me?

N Take a seat. Have you got something to tell me, Oscar?

O Er, no, should I?

N There's an article on *Breaking News Online* about Max Redwood.

O Oh?

N Yes. It gave me a strong sense of déjà vu actually … it's full of Sara's information – including the title of the book.

O Really?

N Yes.

O So, are you thinking someone leaked it?

N Yes, I am, Oscar. You were the only other person in the office last night. I know you overheard our conversation.

O What are you saying?

N What's more, I happened to find this business card on your desk – 'Miranda Hall, Editor-in-Chief, *Breaking News Online*'… Had a little rendezvous with Miranda, have we?

O I don't know what you're talking about.

N Oscar, by selling information to other organisations, you are in breach of your contract.

O You can't sack me. I'll take you to court!

N I'm not going to sack you, you're right. You're going to resign. If you take us to court, you'll lose, and you'll never work in journalism again. I'll expect your letter of resignation in the morning.

4.36

CAFÉ WORKER So … a flat white and a long black. That's $7.50.

LIZZIE Here you are.

RON But isn't it my turn?

CW Thanks.

L The coffee's on me, Ron.

R You sure, Lizzie?

L Well, look on it as a kind of celebration.

R Really?

L Yeah.

R Shall we sit here?

L Yep.

R So … What's up?

L What do you mean?

R Well, you don't exactly look like you're jumping for joy. In fact, I'd say you almost look a bit miserable.

L Thoughtful – not miserable.

R OK. But you still haven't told me – what are we celebrating?

L It's Josh – he's won a scholarship – University of Auckland Academic Excellence.

R Lizzie, that's great! Pass on my congratulations to him. Oh, that's wonderful – proud mum, eh?!

L Yeah, yeah – I do feel proud. He's studied hard and done really well.

R So why the long face?

L Well, it just hit me, y'know, this whole thing of Josh leaving home – off to the big smoke …

R Yeah nah, it's hard when they leave the nest. When Jessica went off to uni last year it took me a while to get used to her … not being there.

L Yeah, I remember.

R It did mean I was able to reclaim the bathroom for myself!

L A lot to be said for that!

R But I still miss her.

L Yeah, Josh is my first to go.

R Well, they'll probably all go and live elsewhere in the long run – all our kids.

L Yeah – they've got to really, though, don't they?

R Well, they can't stay in this town and hope to get a decent education!

L Problem is – and this is what I've been thinking about – nor are they likely to return. I mean, even if Josh did want to come back and live here, there wouldn't be any jobs for someone with an engineering degree.

R Yeah, Jessica reckons she wants to get into marketing or something like that. Don't see much chance of her coming back here to do that.

L But that's the thing – see, everyone just goes off to Auckland or Wellington and they never come back. And then small towns like these – they just get smaller and smaller.

R But it's not just the kids going off to study, is it? What about when they shut down the timber mill – that meant a big exodus.

L Yeah, we've lost just over a thousand people in the last five years. Makes me feel like packing up myself and moving on.

R Yeah, I have to say the thought has crossed my mind.

L But imagine – the price you'd get for your house here and then the price of houses in a place like Auckland. I just couldn't afford to do it.

R Nope, we're better off sitting tight.

L Yeah nah, you're probably right.

R And the truth is, I'm not unhappy – life's a whole lot less stressful here.

L That's certainly true.

R And I've got some good friends – like yourself. We can keep each other sane.

L Yeah, but this scholarship thing – it just made me think. Like, I could see we might end up being the last generation that lives in a town like this. I mean, will the population just keep getting smaller and smaller – and then what?

R To the point that we don't exist any more?

L Yeah, something like that.

R But, hey, enough of these pessimistic thoughts – let's just celebrate Josh doing well for himself.

L Yeah. I must have done something right bringing him up.

R Maybe, but any kid's only as smart as their mother! Or their father!

L Absolutely!

Unit 10

▶ 4.40

ROB I agreed to be best man at my friend Dan's wedding. I mean, I was really thrilled that I was asked – it was a great honour. I was fine with the whole thing – you know, organising the pre-wedding party, the ring – everything. I just threw myself into it. But the one task that really unnerved me was having to give a speech at the reception. I'm just hopeless at giving speeches – they make me feel right out of my depth. I should never have agreed to be best man, but, it's Dan, Dan's best mate. Anyway, I decided to get organised and I planned the whole thing out. Y'know, I thought of some funny stories about Dan and all that sort of thing. And I worked out who I

needed to acknowledge and say thanks and all that stuff. I put it all on little cards, so by the time the big day came around, I was feeling reasonably on top of things. Just before going to the church, I started feeling really jittery, and while I put all the cards in the pocket of my jacket, I forgot to check they were all there. I really regret not doing that. Anyway, we got to the reception and I somehow managed to get through the speech … Got a few laughs at my jokes. I thought I'd made a good job of it. But Dan was giving me these funny looks. The card I forgot was the one where I thanked the bride's parents and all that sort of thing. And the bride, Jessica, was not impressed. So now there's this strange tension between Dan and me, and Jessica is very cool with me. It's all a bit awkward. I mean, it was a genuine mistake. If only I'd checked those cards. And I have to say that part of me wishes that Dan hadn't asked me to be best man. Oh well, I guess they'll get over it. Eventually.

CHANTAL Ever since I started my present job, I've had this really strange relationship with this colleague of mine, Martin. Back then, we were both at the same level in the company and it's like he somehow resented that – like I should have started out on a lower level or something. Who knows? We had to do this joint presentation to managers on a project to upgrade the IT systems in the company. We worked out the content together – well, actually, a lot of the ideas were my ideas. And then, Martin agreed to make our PowerPoint slides look good – he's good at that kind of thing. So anyway, everything was on a memory stick and Martin said he'd take it home and work on it and make it look really professional. I really wish I'd copied the presentation on to my hard drive. You know the golden rule – always make a copy, otherwise it's a recipe for disaster. So, the next day, we go upstairs to this meeting room to give our presentation. Martin plugs the memory stick into the laptop and … it's just not there. He's incredibly apologetic and says he can't understand what went wrong and all that sort of thing, but … I have my suspicions … For a minute I was in a state of absolute panic and then I thought 'I can do this.' So when all the managers came in I just told them the truth – that we'd had a problem with IT, but that I would give the presentation anyway. You see, the one thing Martin didn't know about me is that I'm very good at improvising. And I just explained the whole project and it went like clockwork. The managers were all impressed and I really made my mark. In fact, I'm pretty sure my presentation led to my promotion and I became manager of the project we were presenting. If it was Martin who sabotaged the presentation, I've no doubt he now regrets deleting all that data. Not me! Had he been less underhand, I might not have the job I've got now.

MILOS I'm a volunteer paramedic on an air ambulance service. It's very costly to run a service like this, so we need to do quite a bit of fundraising. One of the ways we can do this is by going around to different community groups and talking about our work. It's not something I'd say that I enjoy, but I can do it well enough. This friend of mine, Teresa, has given me a few tips. She told me to look at a point towards the back of the room, and avoid looking at people's faces – it can put you off. Anyway, I was giving a speech to a parent–teacher association at the local primary school, and about half-way through, for some reason, I looked down at people in the front row. And there she was – Ivana – looking up and giving me a gorgeous big smile. Ivana was the most beautiful girl in our class at school. She wasn't my girlfriend, but I used to wish she were. So in the middle of the speech, my heart melted, I turned to jelly … I couldn't go on – I was completely lost for words. I just sort of stood there like an idiot and grinned back at her. I grinned and she grinned and … well, what a romantic fool! I was sort of saying to myself, 'C'mon, get a grip on yourself!' But, no way. You know, if I had listened to Teresa's advice, I might have been

OK. In the end, I think I … sort of apologised and told people to look at the website, and then I made a pretty quick exit. Needless to say, we didn't get many donations from the Parent–Teacher Association. If it wasn't for my stupidity, we could have raised more money that day. They haven't asked me to give any more speeches – a good thing – I'm just sticking to being a paramedic these days.

▶ 4.48

SPEAKER All these objects are lucky charms from different parts of the world. They're all supposed to bring luck or protect you in some way.
This is a horseshoe, and these were traditionally nailed above doorways in Britain and also in the USA, and they bring good luck to the household. Because they're over the door, they stop bad luck entering the house and they protect it against magic spells. Some people say it's important that the open side should be upwards, so the luck doesn't 'run out'. In other words the horseshoe collects the luck for you.
Now this one is a special kind of mirror, which are traditionally used in China, and they're an important part of feng shui. It's customary to hang them above the front door of a house, and they always face outwards so they can ward off evil and protect the house. The idea is that the mirror deflects any bad energy coming towards the house, so it's very important that you should hang them outside the house, not inside.
And this figure of a cat is called *maneki-neko*, which literally means 'beckoning cat'. You may see these if you go to a Chinese or Japanese shop or a restaurant – they're often just by the door. They come from Japan originally, and they're supposed to bring good fortune to the owner. You see the cat's paw is raised – sometimes it's the left paw and sometimes it's the right paw. If it's the left paw, this attracts customers. And if the right paw is raised, it invites good fortune and brings wealth to the owner – so it's a good idea to have both kinds!
And these are wish bracelets, which are worn as a good-luck charm in Brazil. And they're also worn just as a fashion accessory because they look good. The idea of these is, you tie the ribbon three times round your wrist and you make a wish with every knot you tie. If the ribbon wears out naturally and falls off your wrist, your wishes will come true. So it's really important not to cut the ribbon off.

▶ 4.54

PRESENTER Even if you don't go to the theatre or know much about Shakespeare, you've probably heard of Shakespeare's character, Macbeth, who murders the king of Scotland and then becomes king himself, only to be destroyed by his enemies and by his own guilt. What is not so well known is that *Macbeth* is also considered an unlucky play by actors. Actor Naomi Atkins is about to play the role of Lady Macbeth in a new production at the Cavendish Theatre. Naomi, tell us about the superstition – the play is supposed to be cursed, isn't it?

NAOMI Yes, that's right. And especially it brings bad luck if you mention the play by name when you're in the theatre. So, we always refer to it indirectly – we always call it 'the Scottish play' or 'that play'. Some actors even avoid quoting lines from it before a performance. As you know, the play opens with a scene with three witches cooking a magic potion, and people say it's especially unlucky to quote the witches' lines at the opening of the play.

P And what happens if you say the word, *Macbeth*. Are you cursed?

N Yes, or the production is – something's bound to go wrong. But, there's a kind of penalty you can pay, to make it all OK again. This actually happened to me. I said the name of the play by mistake during rehearsals.

P What happened?

N Well, to stop the curse, I had to leave the theatre building straight away, then when I was out in the street, I had to spin round three times, spit, curse and then knock on the door to be allowed back in.

P And that neutralised the curse?

N That neutralised it, yes. We had a good laugh about it. It was a bit of a joke, but you'd be surprised how seriously some people take it.

P Do we know where this comes from? Why is the play cursed?

N Well no one knows for certain, but as I said the play does start off with a scene where witches are casting spells, and Shakespeare is believed to have got the words from real witches. And then the witches saw the play, and they put a curse on it because, of course, the play revealed their spells.

P Another explanation I heard was there's a lot of sword-fighting in the play, so people think there's more chance for someone to get injured. So it's unlucky in that way.

N Yes, there are lots of different ideas. Another explanation is that the play was very popular, so it was often put on by theatres that were in debt as a way to increase their audience numbers. But then of course, the theatres normally went bankrupt anyway, so they put the blame on the play and they said it was cursed.

P That's a nice idea.

N Yes, I like that one. As I say, nobody really knows.

▶ 4.55 PART 1

MAX I asked you not to contact me again, didn't I?

NADIA I know that, Mr Redwood, but I just wanted to –

M You've got a nerve!

N Sorry, if I could just finish what I was saying, Max!

M Oh, go on then!

N I've managed to track down the source of the leaked story about you …

M Don't tell me! Sara was gossiping about me again –

N Sorry to interrupt, but Sara wasn't idly gossiping. She was updating me on her research and was overheard by another journalist, who showed some very poor judgement. He's no longer a member of our team, I hasten to add.

M I see.

N I'd like you to at least consider coming in for your interview with Sara tomorrow. I know how much she was looking forward to it. And I think it would be refreshing for all of us, after our experiences with Oscar Simmons!

M Hmm …

▶ 4.56 PART 2

SARA Thanks for this, Max.

MAX No worries.

S Hello. My name is Sara Neroni, and I'm going to be talking to Max Redwood, author of the best-selling science fiction novel *Solar Wind*, and who is in the process of writing his second novel, *Gravity Zero*. Good to see you, Max!

M Thanks. And good to see you too, Sara.

S Now, as anybody who's read your first book will know, you're an incredibly imaginative, creative person, Max, but where do you get your inspiration from? Could you tell us a little bit about that, please?

M Before we get started, can I just make a point about creativity? I just wanted to say that … it doesn't come easily all the time. I was in a bad place up until recently. I thought all of my ideas had dried up … but, my fans got me through that and encouraged me to keep at it.

S Oh, really? I'm glad to hear that.

M But anyway, to answer your question about inspiration, I think I first got interested in space travel when I was growing up.

S Speaking of which, you grew up here in Brighton, didn't you?

M Yeah, that's right. It was really my dad who got me into space – I mean, first got me interested in space! He bought me this telescope and we would look up at the stars at night together. I'd imagine all sorts of weird and wonderful worlds up there.

S AND M And did you say / And I never …

S Please, after you.

M Yeah, as I was saying, I never forgot those worlds.

S Now if you don't mind me coming in here, you had trouble sleeping as a child, didn't you?

M Yeah, that's right. So I spent more time than most kids that age in my own little world …

▶ 4.58 PART 3

SARA Thanks, Max. I think that went really well.

MAX Yeah – seemed to go OK. I quite enjoyed it actually!

A Hats off to you both!

S Well, credit where credit's due – Max made it so easy.

M Well …

S You were so different this time, weren't you? Y'know, from that interview with Oscar?

A Well, that's because you're a better interviewer than Oscar.

M That's right, you are.

A And I'll tell you what, I overheard Nadia singing your praises this morning.

S Really?

A Gushing, she was. Thinks you're the best thing since sliced bread!

S Do you think my job is safe then?

A Definitely.

M Listen, Sara … Alex and Emma are coming over to my new place tonight. You'd be very welcome.

S Thanks very much, Max. I'd love to.

M Great.

A Oh, wait till you see the place, Sara. It's a converted warehouse. It's massive, isn't it, Max?

M I suppose so.

S Oh, plenty of room for dancing then!

M Well, it's not going to be that kind of thing, really.

A No?

M Well, I thought we could all sit down together and watch *Moon Station X*.

S AND A Oh … Great …

▶ 4.62

SASHA I'm a review addict. I'd never dream of going to see a film without checking the reviews online first. I think it's worth seeing whether a film has good reviews or bad reviews. Even if someone has recommended it to me, I like to read the review first before I … see it myself. And I find that online reviews are good because I get a very wide range of different opinions. I like this because it's more reliable than the newspaper reviews that are written by the so-called experts. Y'know, the online reviews are written by ordinary people like me. I also like reviews um, for accommodation and travel destinations, products, electronic equipment. It's one of the incredible things about the Internet – everything's been reviewed by someone, somewhere in the world.

MARIE I read a lot of film reviews, mainly in newspapers and magazines. I trust a professional opinion and there are actually some reviewers that, er I can really rely on to recommend some good films. But I don't read the reviews to help me decide whether I should watch a film or not – I read it afterwards so it doesn't spoil it. I think, also it's interesting to compare the review with what I initially thought of the film. And er, it can usually help me understand the film better, especially if it's a, a more obscure or complex film. And also reading the review can sometimes help me in case I missed something in the original film. I, I don't like the er … kind of Internet, amateur reviewers because I mean you don't even know who these people are – and er, they may not even have the same taste in cinema that I might have.

KIM I can never be bothered with reviews. I mean I usually download films and watch them at home. I hardly ever go to the cinema any more. I choose something that I like the look of – it doesn't have to be great – it's just a way for me to switch off completely after work and wind down, y'know – it's just relaxation. I really don't understand why some people take films so seriously. I do look at reviews for some things. I mean if I'm going to buy a laptop or a TV and I'm spending that much money on something then, yes, there's a difference between the products. But, not for films.

ISSER I avoid reading reviews of films or TV series, especially TV series, because I just don't trust them because I think it's just one person's opinion and I'd rather go and see a film with an open mind – without any preconceived ideas about what it might be like. Reviews nearly always contain spoilers of some kind. They mention something about a character or something that is about to happen. I don't like that. I'd rather start watching a film without knowing anything about it. And … sometimes, if I really like the film, I would like to go and read the review after I've seen it, er, but definitely not before.

Verb patterns

When followed by another verb (and object) (and indirect object), individual verbs follow different patterns:

verb + sb/sth + infinitive without *to*
She *makes me wash* the dishes.
I *saw the bus arrive*.

verb + *to* + infinitive
She *agreed to give* a presentation next week.
He *tends not to be* comfortable with new people.

verb + sb/sth + *to* + infinitive
I *asked the guests to wait* outside.
They *want him to come* to the party.

verb (+ sb/sth) + verb + *-ing*
He *admitted cheating* on the test.
He *hates us visiting* unannounced.

verb + preposition (+ sb/sth) + verb + *-ing*
I'm *concentrating on revising* this weekend.
She *insisted on him leaving* at three.

Some verbs have different meanings in different patterns.

admit	verb + verb + *-ing*
admit to	verb + preposition (+ sb/sth) + verb + *-ing*
advise	verb + sb/sth + *to* + infinitive verb + verb + *-ing*
agree	verb + *to* + infinitive
aim	verb + *to* + infinitive
allow	verb + sb/sth + *to* + infinitive verb + verb + *-ing*
anticipate	verb + verb + *-ing*
appear	verb + *to* + infinitive
appreciate	verb (+ sb/sth) + verb + *-ing*
approve of	verb + preposition (+ sb/sth) + verb + *-ing*
argue about	verb + preposition (+ sb/sth) + verb + *-ing*
arrange	verb + *to* + infinitive
ask	verb + (sb/sth) + *to* + infinitive
attempt	verb + *to* + infinitive
avoid	verb (+ sb/sth) + verb + *-ing*
beg	verb + (sb/sth) + *to* + infinitive
begin	verb + *to* + infinitive
believe in	verb + preposition + verb + *-ing*
can afford	verb + *to* + infinitive
can't help	verb + verb + *-ing*
can't stand	verb (+ sb/sth) + verb + *-ing*
care about	verb + preposition + sb/sth + verb + *-ing*
challenge	verb + sb/sth + *to* + infinitive
choose	verb + (sb/sth) + *to* + infinitive
claim	verb + *to* + infinitive
consider	verb + verb + *-ing*
continue	verb + *to* + infinitive verb + verb + *-ing*
*dare	verb + *to* + infinitive (be brave enough) verb + (sb/sth) + *to* + infinitive (challenge sb)
decide	verb + *to* + infinitive

demand	verb + *to* + infinitive
deny	verb + verb + *-ing*
demand	verb + *to* + infinitive
deserve	verb + *to* + infinitive
discuss	verb (+ sb/sth) + verb + *-ing*
dislike	verb (+ sb/sth) + verb + *-ing*
encourage	verb + sb/sth + *to* + infinitive
enjoy	verb (+ sb/sth) + verb + *-ing*
expect	verb (+ sb/sth) + *to* + infinitive
fail	verb + *to* + infinitive
fancy	verb + verb + *-ing*
feel (sense)	verb + sb/sth + infinitive without *to*
feel like	verb + preposition + verb + *-ing*
finish	verb + verb + *-ing*
*forget	verb + *to* + infinitive (an obligation) verb + verb + *-ing* (an event)
forget about	verb + preposition (+ sb/sth) + verb + *-ing*
forbid	verb + sb/sth + *to* + infinitive verb + verb + *-ing*
force	verb + sb/sth + *to* + infinitive
get (opportunity)	verb + *to* + infinitive
*go on	verb + *to* + infinitive (do a new activity) verb + verb + *-ing* (continue same activity)
happen	verb + *to* + infinitive
hate	verb (+ sb/sth) + *to* + infinitive verb (+ sb/sth) + verb + *-ing*
hear (noise)	verb + sb/sth + infinitive without *to*
help	verb (+ sb/sth) (+ *to*) + infinitive
hope	verb + *to* + infinitive
imagine	verb (+ sb/sth) + verb + *-ing*
insist on	verb + preposition (+ sb/sth) + verb + *-ing*
instruct	verb + sb/sth + *to* + infinitive
intend	verb (+ sb/sth) + *to* + infinitive
invite	verb + sb/sth + *to* + infinitive
involve	verb (+ sb/sth) + verb + *-ing*
keep	verb + verb + *-ing*
learn	verb + *to* + infinitive
let	verb + sb/sth + infinitive without *to*
like	verb (+ sb/sth) + *to* + infinitive verb (+ sb/sth) + verb + *-ing*
long	verb + *to* + infinitive
love	verb (+ sb/sth) + *to* + infinitive verb (+ sb/sth) + verb + *-ing*
make	verb + sb/sth + infinitive without *to*
manage	verb + *to* + infinitive
mention	verb (+ sb/sth) + verb + *-ing*
mind	verb (+ sb/sth) + verb + *-ing*
miss	verb (+ sb/sth) + verb + *-ing*
motivate	verb + sb/sth + *to* + infinitive

need	verb (+ sb/sth) + *to* + infinitive
notice	verb + sb/sth + infinitive without *to*
object to	verb + preposition (+ sb/sth) + verb + *-ing*
offer	verb + *to* + infinitive
order	verb + sb/sth + *to* + infinitive
pay	verb + sb/sth + *to* + infinitive
permit	verb + sb/sth + *to* + infinitive verb + verb + *-ing*
persuade	verb + sb/sth + *to* + infinitive
plan	verb + *to* + infinitive
plan on	verb + preposition + sb/sth + verb + *-ing*
postpone	verb + verb + *-ing*
practise	verb + verb + *-ing*
prefer	verb (+ sb/sth) + *to* + infinitive
prepare	verb (+ sb/sth) + *to* + infinitive
pretend	verb + *to* + infinitive
proceed	verb + *to* + infinitive
propose	verb + *to* + infinitive
recall	verb + verb + *-ing*
recommend	verb + verb + *-ing*
refuse	verb + *to* + infinitive
regret	verb + verb + *-ing*
*remember	verb + *to* + infinitive (an obligation) verb (+ sb/sth) + verb + *-ing* (an event)
remind	verb + sb/sth + *to* + infinitive
require	verb + sb/sth + *to* + infinitive
resent	verb (+ sb/sth) + verb + *-ing*
resist	verb (+ sb/sth) + verb + *-ing*
resume	verb + verb + *-ing*
risk	verb (+ sb/sth) + verb + *-ing*
say	verb + *to* + infinitive (instructions)
see	verb + sb/sth + infinitive without *to*
seem	verb + *to* + infinitive
start	verb + *to* + infinitive
*stop	verb (+ sb/sth) + *to* + infinitive (purpose of stopping) verb (+ sb/sth) + verb + *-ing* (activity)
succeed in	verb + preposition + verb + *-ing*
suggest	verb + sb + infinitive without *to* verb + verb + *-ing*
swear	verb + *to* + infinitive
talk about	verb + preposition (+ sb/sth) + verb + *-ing*
teach	verb + sb/sth + *to* + infinitive
tell	verb + sb/sth + *to* + infinitive (instruction)
tend	verb + *to* + infinitive
think about	verb + preposition (+ sb/sth) + verb + *-ing*
threaten	verb + *to* + infinitive
tolerate	verb (+ sb/sth) + verb + *-ing*

*try	verb + verb + -ing (a new activity) verb + to + infinitive (unsure of success)		want	verb + sb/sth + to + infinitive		would like / love / hate / prefer, etc.	verb (+ sb/sth) + to + infinitive
understand	verb (+ sb/sth) + verb + -ing		warn	verb + sb/sth + to + infinitive			
urge	verb + sb/sth + to + infinitive		watch	verb + sb/sth + infinitive without to			
			worry about	verb + preposition (+ sb/sth) + verb + -ing			

Phonemic Symbols

Vowel sounds

Short

/ə/	/æ/	/ʊ/	/ɒ/
teacher	man	put	got
/ɪ/	/i/	/e/	/ʌ/
chip	happy	men	but

Long

/ɜː/	/ɑː/	/uː/	/ɔː/	/iː/
shirt	part	who	walk	cheap

Diphthongs (two vowel sounds)

/eə/	/ɪə/	/ʊə/	/ɔɪ/	/aɪ/	/eɪ/	/əʊ/	/aʊ/
hair	near	tour	boy	fine	late	coat	now

Consonants

/p/	/b/	/f/	/v/	/t/	/d/	/k/	/g/	/θ/	/ð/	/tʃ/	/dʒ/
pill	book	face	van	time	dog	cold	go	thirty	they	choose	jeans
/s/	/z/	/ʃ/	/ʒ/	/m/	/n/	/ŋ/	/h/	/l/	/r/	/w/	/j/
say	zero	shop	usually	me	now	sing	hot	late	red	went	yes

Irregular verbs

Infinitive	Past simple	Past participle	Infinitive	Past simple	Past participle
arise /ə'raɪz/	arose /ə'rəʊz/	arisen /ə'rɪzən/	overtake /ˌəʊvə'teɪk/	overtook /ˌəʊvə'tʊk/	overtaken /ˌəʊvə'teɪkən/
bear /beə/	bore /bɔː/	born /bɔːn/	rebuild /riː'bɪld/	rebuilt /riː'bɪlt/	rebuilt /riː'bɪlt/
beat /biːt/	beat /biːt/	beaten /'biːtən/	rethink /riː'θɪŋk/	rethought /riː'θɔːt/	rethought /riː'θɔːt/
bend /bend/	bent /bent/	bent /bent/	rise /raɪz/	rose /rəʊz/	risen /'rɪzən/
bet /bet/	bet /bet/	bet /bet/	seek /siːk/	sought /sɔːt/	sought /sɔːt/
bid /bɪd/	bid /bɪd/	bid /bɪd/	set /set/	set /set/	set /set/
bind /baɪnd/	bound /baʊnd/	bound /baʊnd/	shake /ʃeɪk/	shook /ʃʊk/	shaken /'ʃeɪkən/
blow /bləʊ/	blew /bluː/	blown /bləʊn/	shine /ʃaɪn/	shone /ʃɒn/	shone /ʃɒn/
burn /bɜːn/	burnt /bɜːnt/	burnt /bɜːnt/	shoot /ʃuːt/	shot /ʃɒt/	shot /ʃɒt/
burst /bɜːst/	burst /bɜːst/	burst /bɜːst/	shrink /ʃrɪŋk/	shrank /ʃræŋk/	shrunk /ʃrʌŋk/
cling /klɪŋ/	clung /klʌŋ/	clung /klʌŋ/	shut /ʃʌt/	shut /ʃʌt/	shut /ʃʌt/
deal /dɪəl/	dealt /delt/	dealt /delt/	sink /sɪŋk/	sank /sæŋk/	sunk /sʌŋk/
dwell /dwel/	dwelt /dwelt/	dwelt /dwelt/	smell /smel/	smelt /smelt/	smelt /smelt/
feed /fiːd/	fed /fed/	fed /fed/	sow /səʊ/	sowed /səʊd/	sown /səʊn/
flee /fliː/	fled /fled/	fled /fled/	spin /spɪn/	spun /spʌn/	spun /spʌn/
forbid /fə'bɪd/	forbade /fə'bæd/	forbidden /fə'bɪdən/	split /splɪt/	split /splɪt/	split /splɪt/
foresee /fə'siː/	foresaw /fɔː'sɔː/	foreseen /fɔː'siːn/	spread /spred/	spread /spred/	spread /spred/
hang /hæŋ/	hung /hʌŋ/	hung /hʌŋ/	swear /sweə/	swore /swɔː/	sworn /swɔːn/
lay /leɪ/	laid /leɪd/	laid /leɪd/	sweep /swiːp/	swept /swept/	swept /swept/
lead /liːd/	led /led/	led /led/	swing /swɪŋ/	swung /swʌŋ/	swung /swʌŋ/
leap /liːp/	leapt /lept/	leapt /lept/	tear /teər/	tore /tɔː/	torn /tɔːn/
lie /laɪ/	lay /leɪ/	lain /leɪn/	undo /ʌn'duː/	undid /ʌn'dɪd/	undone /ʌn'dʌn/
light /laɪt/	lit /lɪt/	lit /lɪt/	upset /ʌp'set/	upset /ʌp'set/	upset /ʌp'set/
offset /ɒf'set/	offset /ɒf'set/	offset /ɒf'set/	wind /waɪnd/	wound /waʊnd/	wound /waʊnd/
overdo /əʊvə'duː/	overdid /əʊvə'dɪd/	overdone /əʊvə'dʌn/			
overhear /əʊvə'hɪə/	overheard /əʊvə'hɜːd/	overheard /əʊvə'hɜːd/			

Acknowledgements

The publishers would like to thank the following teachers and ELT professionals for the invaluable feedback they have provided during the development of the C1 Student's book:

Peggy Alptekin, Turkey and the Gulf; Daniel Hernández, Mexico; Hugo Gustavo Fabila Patiño, Mexico; Hilary Plass, Spain; Wayne Rimmer, Russia; Rodrigo Rosa, Brazil.

The publishers are grateful to the following contributors:

Graham Hart: Audio recordings
Matt Devitt, Peter Durgerian and Nick Coombs, Headfirst Productions: Video recordings
Matt Devitt: Video music composition and performance
Charlotte Macpherson Photography: Commissioned photography
Hilary Luckcock: Picture research

The authors and publishers acknowledge the following sources of copyright material and are grateful for the permissions granted. While every effort has been made, it has not always been possible to identify the sources of all the material used, or to trace all copyright holders. If any omissions are brought to our notice, we will be happy to include the appropriate acknowledgements on reprinting.

The publisher has used its best endeavours to ensure that the URLs for external websites referred to in this book are correct and active at the time of going to press. However, the publisher has no responsibility for the websites and can make no guarantee that a site will remain live or that the content is or will remain appropriate.

Text on p. 8 adapted from 'Ellen MacArthur: my career in languages' by Louise Tickle, The Guardian, 29.08.2013 © Guardian News and Media Limited 2013; Text on p. 8 adapted from 'Why languages matter to me: Eddie Izzard, Alastair Campbell and more' by Louise Tickle, The Guardian, 28.08.2013 © Guardian News and Media Limited 2013; Text on p. 8 adapted from 'Thomasina Miers: learning Spanish on a Mexican food odyssey' - video, The Guardian, 02.04.2015 © Guardian News and Media Limited 2015; Text on p.10 and Listening (Audio Script) from 'BBC: polyglot explains how to learn languages, foreign languages = $, £, € and jobs' interview with Nick Chambers and Susanna Zaraysky, 30.01.2012 BBC, Newshour, © BBC Worldwide Learning; Quote on p. 20 from 'We all crave it, but can you stand the silence? The longest anyone can bear Earth's quietest place is 45 minutes' by Ted Thornhill, 05.04.2012, © Mail Online 2012; Text on p. 20 adapted from 'Experience: I've been to the quietest place on Earth' by George Michelson Foy, The Guardian, 18.05.2012 © Guardian News and Media Limited 2012; Text on pp. 23,24 adapted from 'Why Some of Us Are Thrill-Seekers' by Angela Haupt US News and World Report, 6.08.2012 pp.1-2. Copyrighted 2015. U.S. News & World Report. 116781:0615BC; Text on p. 32 adapted from 'Pod Caribbean Children's Home - Belize - Volunteer Reviews': Linda and Malcolm – 2013 and 'Pod Community Projects - Ghana - Volunteer Reviews': Debbie – Child care, baby weighing and building, 2014, © Personal Overseas Development Ltd 2013/2014. All Rights Reserved; Text on p. 34 and Listening (Audio Script) from 'The Problem with Volunteering' by Daniela Papi, 01.05.2013 BBC Radio 4: Four Thought, © BBC Worldwide Learning; Text on p. 36 simplified from ' 'Surviving malaria on the Mano River' by Will Millard BBC News Magazine, 13.09.13 BBC News Magazine: Four Thought, © BBC News 2013; Text on pp. 36,37 and Listening (Audio Script) from 'Journey of a lifetime, Mum Says 'You're a Long Time Dead' by Will Millard, BBC Radio 4 Journey of a lifetime, The River Wild (Episode 1) 2013, © BBC Worldwide Learning; Text on p. 46 and Listening (Audio Script) from 'Glucosamine for osteoarthritis; Alcohol addiction; Gut instinct', Dr Mark Porter, BBC Radio 4: Inside Health, 12.02.2014 © BBC Worldwide Learning; Text on p. 48 simplified from ''Witness For the Defense: The Accused, the Eyewitness, and the Expert Who Puts Memory On Trial'' by Dr. Elizabeth Loftus and Katherine Ketcha St. Martins Press, 01.09.1992, © St. Martins Press 1992, permission granted by the author Dr. Elizabeth Loftus; Text on p. 56 adapted from 'Inside Halden, the most humane prison in the world' by Amelia Gentleman, The Guardian, 18.05.2012, © Guardian News and Media Limited 2012; Text on p. 60-61 adapted from 'Six surprisingly well-paid jobs' by Donna Ferguson, The Guardian, 07.08.2014, © Guardian News and Media Limited 2014; Text on p. 68-69 adapted from '14 Lessons Elliott Erwitt Has Taught Me About Street Photography' by Eric Kim, Eric Kim Street Photography Blog, 23.09.2013, Eric Kim with permission; Text on p. 71 and Listening (Audio Script) from 'You are Now Entering the Human Heart' by Janet Frame in Selected Short Stories 01.12.2009, Pages 246- 251, © Janet Frame Trust with permission from the Wylie Agency; Text on pp. 80-81 from Rise of the Machines: Meet Bina48, the robot who can tell jokes, recite poetry and mimic humans with startling ease by Emily Anne Epstein, 19.07.2012, Mail Online; Text on p. 82 and Listening (Audio Script) from 'A lie detector on your phone' by Ian Goldin, Future 60 second idea, 16 .06.2014, BBC World Service, © BBC Worldwide Learning; Text on p. 82 and Listening (Audio Script) adapted from 'A remote that can reduce street noises' by Anja Kanngiese, Future 60 second idea, 26.09.2013, BBC World Service, © BBC Worldwide Learning; Text on p. 82 and Listening (Audio Script) adapted from 'Job candidates must wear masks' by Maurice Fraser, Future 60 second idea, 25.02.2012, BBC World Service, © BBC Worldwide Learning; Text on p. 83 from REWIRE:DIGITAL COSMOPOLITANS IN THE AGE OF CONNECTION by Ethan Zuckerman. Copyright © 2013 by Ethan Zuckerman. Used by permission of WW.Norton & Company,Inc.; Text on p. 84 adapted from 'This column will change your life: loneliness and temperature' by Oliver Burkeman, The Guardian, 01.06.2013, © Guardian News and Media Limited 2013; Text on p. 92 simplified from 'Segmented sleep: Ten strange things people do at night' by Stephanie Hegarty, BBC News Magazine, 22..02.2012, BBC News Magazine, © BBC News 2012; Text on p. 93 adapted from 'The myth of the eight-hour sleep' by Stephanie Hegarty, BBC News Magazine, 22..02.2012, BBC News Magazine, © BBC News 2012; Text on p. 96 adapted from 'Aubrey de Grey: We don't have to get sick as we get older' by Caspar Llewellyn Smith, The Guardian, 01.08.2010, © Guardian News and Media Limited 2010; Text on p. 97 and Listening (Audio Script) adapted from 'Can extreme calorie counting make you live longer?' by Peter Bowes, 24.03.2013, BBC World Service,

© BBC Worldwide Learning; Text on pp. 104-105 from 'No kerbs, pavements or nanny-state signs: Britain's longest clutter-free street is unveiled to make things SAFER By Ray Massey, 02.02.2012, Mail Online; Text on p. 108 adapted from 'Zaha Hadid: 'I don't make nice little buildings' by Xan Brooks, The Guardian, 22.09.2013, © Guardian News and Media Limited 2013; Text on p. 109 and Listening (Audio Script) adapted from 'Pants' skyscraper? China reacts against latest tall building' by John Sudworth, 08.12.2012, BBC News World © BBC Worldwide Learning; Quote on p. 116 from Ashley Ormon with permission; Quote on p. 116 from Emma Watson's UN Speech on Gender & Equality, Emma Watson with permission; Quote on p. 116 from 'The Scaffolding of Rhetoric' by Winston S. Churchill (1897). Reproduced with permission of Curtis Brown, London on behalf of the Estate of Winston S. Churchill Copyright © The Estate of Winston S. Churchill; Quote on p. 116 and text on p. 117 adapted from 'How to give a killer presentation' by Chris Anderson, Harvard Business Review, June 2013. Copyright © 2013 Harvard Business School Publishing. All rights reserved. Harvard Business Publishing is an affiliate of Harvard Business School. One-time permission to reproduce granted by Harvard Business Publishing.

The publishers are grateful to the following for permission to reproduce copyright photographs and material:

Key: L = left, C = centre, R = right, T = top, B = bottom, b/g = background
p7: Corbis/Frans Lanting; p8(T): Rex/Steve Meddle; p8(L): Getty/Chris Jackson; p8(R): BBC/Jeff Overs; p9: Rex/David Crump/Daily Mail; p10(T): Susanna Zaraysky; p10(BL): Getty/Image Source; p10(BR): Alamy/PhotoAlto; p11(L):Alamy/World History Archive; p11(R): Alamy/Picture Press; p16(1): Corbis/Hero Images; p16(2): Alamy/D J Clark; p16(3): Shutterstock/Olga Nayashkova; p16(4): Corbis/didi/amanaimages; p16(5): Corbis/Mondelo/epa; p16(6): Alamy/Itani; p16(7): Corbis/Dinodia; p16(B): Corbis/Juice Images; p19: Getty/David Trood; p20: Getty/alacatr; p21: Ellary Eddy; p22: Corbis/Michael Haegele; p23(TL): Alamy/M ShieldsPhotos; p23(TR): Alamy/Jack Sullivan; p23(C): Alamy/Jorchen Tack; p23(B): Corbis/Christian Heeb/JAI; p24: Corbis/2/ Peter Cade/Ocean; p25(L): Alamy/Aurora Photos; p25(R): Shutterstock/r.classen; p28(paintballing): Alamy/digitalknight; p28(pony trekking): Getty/Hemis.fr RM; p28(bungee jumping): Getty/Multi-bits; p28(tree-top adventuring): Shutterstock/ Dmitry Naumov; p28(karting): Getty/Galina Barskaya; p28(whitewater rafting): Getty/Matthew Micah Wright; p28(BL): Shutterstock/Grisha Bruev; p28(BCL): Getty/Juanmonino; p28(BCR): Shutterstock/Gelpi JM; p28(BR): Getty/ Photo Talk; p31: Phil Clarke Hill/In Pictures; p32(Debbie): Corbis/Emma Tunbridge; p32(C)(Ghana): www.podvolunteer.org; p32(T): www.podvolunteer. org; p32(Linda & Malcolm): Corbis/C12; p32/33(b/g): www.podvolunteer.org; p33: www.podvolunteer.org; p34(T)): Clore Social Leadership Programme; p34(BL): Corbis/Paul Souders; p34(BR): Corbis/Destinations; p35(T): Will Millard; p35(B): Will Millard; p36(1): Alamy/John King; p36(2)(dragonfly): Shutterstock/Kletr; p36(2)(fish eagle): Shutterstock/Kobus Tollig; p36(3): www.mosquitohammock.com; p36(4): Corbis/2/David Freund/ocean; p37: Will Millard; p40(main): Corbis/Dmitry Rukhlenko; p40(inset L): Alamy/Radomir Rezny; p40(inset R): Corbis/Heather Elton/Design Pics; p43: Corbis/Edgar Su/ Reuters; p46: Alamy/Glow Asia RF; p47(T): Getty/Betsie van der Meer; p47(BL): Corbis/noonland/Westend61; p47(BR): Alamy/M J Perris; p49(B): Shutterstock/ AGCuesta; p52: Shutterstock/Michael Plachy; p53: Getty/Tim Gerard Baker; p55: Corbis/Minden Pictures; p57a): Rex/Trond Isaksen; p57(b): Corbis/Heiko Junge/epa; p57(c): Corbis/Alex Masi; p57(d): Rex/Trond Isaksen; p59(TL): Getty/Mint Images - Bill Miles; p59(TR): Corbis/Jose Luiz Pelaez, Inc/Blend Images; p59(BL): Alamy/MBI; p59(BR): Getty/Thomas Northcut; p60: Corbis/ Georges Antoni/Hemis; p61: Alamy/Cultura Creative; p64(L): Shutterstock/ El Nariz; p64(C): Alamy/Itani; p64(BR): Corbis/Graham Oliver/Juice Images; p65: Getty/Westend61; p67: Corbis/Ilya Naymushin; p68: Magnum/Elliot Erwitt; p69(T)(b/g): Getty/Andrew Bainbridge/EyeEm; p69(C): Corbis/Horst Ossinger/dpa; p70(T): Agnieszka Kurzeja; p70(B): Monika Schmitt; p71: Alamy/H Mark Weidman Photography; p72: Corbis/Michael Gunther/Biosphoto; p74(headshot on screen): Callum Patrick Hughes/Ben Hare; p76(inset L): Alamy/Lebrecht Music & Arts Photo Library; p76(inset R): Getty/rilueda; pp76/77(b/g): Alamy/Arcaid Images; p79: Corbis/BSIP; p80(L): Corbis/Yuya Shino/Reuters; p80(C): Getty/Fort worth Star – Telegram; p80(R): Alamy/Frank Rumpenhorst/EPA; p81: Alamy/Frank Rumpenhorst/EPA; p82(TL): Shutterstock/ Syda Productions; p82(TR): Superstock/Blue Jean Images; p82(C): Alamy/ Robert Harding Picture Library Ltd; p83(TR): Corbis/Matthias Kulka; p83(BL): Corbis/Zero Creatives; p84: Oliver Burkeman/Jeff Mikkelson; pp84/85: Getty/ Thomas Juul; p88(1): Shutterstock/Monkey Business Images; p88(2): Corbis/ Hill Street Studios/Blend Images; p88(3): Corbis/Buero Monaco; p88(4): Corbis/ Erik Isakson/Blend Images; p88(Claudio): Getty/Erik Isakson; p88(Marsha): Getty/Juanmonino; p88(Sam): Corbis/John Lund/Drew Kelly/Blend Images; p88(Vicki): Corbis/William Casey; p91: Alamy/dpa picture alliance archive; p92(T): Alamy/PhotoAlto; p94(Matt): Shutterstock/wavebreakmedia; p94(Lise): Shutterstock/Steve Photography; p94(Bernie): Corbis/B.Boissonnet/ BSIP; p94(Iain): Shutterstock/pkchai; p95(L): Corbis/Adam Gault/Science Photo Library; p95(C): Corbis/Klaus Tiedge; p95(snail): Shutterstock/Elena Schweitzer; p95(emu): Shutterstock/a_v_d; p95(bee): Shutterstock/Peter Waters; p95(lips): Rex/Steve Meddle; p95(platza): Alamy/Anton Starikov; p96: Rex/Roland Kemp; p97(T): Getty/T Popova; p97(chard): Shutterstock/Anna Sedneva; p97(sprouted oats): Shutterstock/Sergey Chayko; p97(kale): Shutterstock/Joseph S.L. Tan Matt; p100(chef): Corbis/Peter M Fisher; p100(T): Corbis/Ed Reeve/VIEW; p100(BL): Corbis/Kent Lacin LLC/the food passionates; p100(BC): Alamy/Bon Appetit; 100(BR)/101(BL): Alamy/Victor Fisher; p101(BC): Alamy/dpa picture alliance archive; p103: Alamy/ChinaFotoPress; p104: Courtesy Royal Borough Kensington & Chelsea, photographer Olivia Woodhouse; p105(TL): Alamy/James Brunker; p105(TR): Lyke de Wit; p105(BL): Airport Corridor Transportation Corporation, Pittsburgh; p105(BR): Friends of Congress Square Park; p106: Utah Department of Transportation; p107(L): Corbis/Serguei Fomine/Global Look; p107(TC): Alamy/James Freeman; p107(TR): Corbis/Rolf Hicker/All Canada Photos; p107(C): Corbis/Nathan Willock/VIEW; p107(BC): Shutterstock/ BasPhoto; p107(BR): Getty/Gale Beery; p108(T): Steve Double; p108(B): Alamy/LOOK Die Bildagentur der Fotografen GmbH; p109(T): Getty/STR/ Stringer; p109(C): Getty/Gregory Warren; p109(BL): Shutterstock/Elnur;